PAKISTAN AT THE CROSSROADS

RELIGION, CULTURE, AND PUBLIC LIFE

RELIGION, CULTURE, AND PUBLIC LIFE

Series Editor: Karen Barkey

The resurgence of religion calls for careful analysis and constructive criticism of new forms of intolerance, as well as new approaches to tolerance, respect, mutual understanding, and accommodation. In order to promote serious scholarship and informed debate, the Institute for Religion, Culture, and Public Life and Columbia University Press are sponsoring a book series devoted to the investigation of the role of religion in society and culture today. This series includes works by scholars in religious studies, political science, history, cultural anthropology, economics, social psychology, and other allied fields whose work sustains multidisciplinary and comparative as well as transnational analyses of historical and contemporary issues. The series focuses on issues related to questions of difference, identity, and practice within local, national, and international contexts. Special attention is paid to the ways in which religious traditions encourage conflict, violence, and intolerance and also support human rights, ecumenical values, and mutual understanding. By mediating alternative methodologies and different religious, social, and cultural traditions, books published in this series will open channels of communication that facilitate critical analysis.

For a complete list of the books in this series, see page 347–348.

PAKISTAN
AT THE
CROSSROADS

DOMESTIC DYNAMICS
AND EXTERNAL PRESSURES

CHRISTOPHE JAFFRELOT
EDITOR

COLUMBIA UNIVERSITY PRESS ■ NEW YORK

Columbia University Press
Publishers Since 1893
New York   Chichester, West Sussex
cup.columbia.edu
Copyright © 2016 Columbia University Press
All rights reserved

Library of Congress Cataloging-in-Publication Data

Pakistan at the crossroads : domestic dynamics and external pressures /
Christophe Jaffrelot, (ed.).
pages ; cm.—(Religion, culture, and public life)
Includes bibliographical references and index.
ISBN 978-0-231-17306-3 (cloth : alk. paper)
ISBN 978-0-231-54025-4 (e-book)
1. Pakistan—Politics and government.   2. Pakistan—Foreign relations.
I. Jaffrelot, Christophe, editor.   II. Series: Religion, culture, and public life.
DS389.P34264 2016
954.9105'3—dc23
2015024699

Columbia University Press books are printed on permanent and durable acid-free paper.
This book is printed on paper with recycled content.
Printed in the United States of America
c 10 9 8 7 6 5 4 3 2 1
Cover design: Martin Hinze

CONTENTS

PART II: THE INTERNATIONAL DIMENSIONS

ACKNOWLEDGMENTS

This collection of essays draws from two conferences that were organized at Columbia University thanks to the support of the Alliance Program (Columbia University, Sciences Po, Polytechnique, and Paris 1—Sorbonne). These meetings were hosted by the Center for Democracy, Toleration, and Religion, now a part of the Institute for Religion, Culture, and Public Life (IRCPL).

These meetings would not have been possible without the personal involvement of Alfred Stepan, who engaged with the participants in the most stimulating way on both occasions. Melissa Van, assistant director of IRCPL, played a key role in the organization of these conferences and in the finalization of the book. Karen Barkey, the successor of Al Stepan at the helm of the IRCPL, and Walid Hammam, her assistant director, subsequently made the publication of this book possible.

Last but not least, the formatting of this volume owes much to Maryam Mastoor, whose dedication to the cause of scholarship impressed me when she worked at the Centre de Recherches Internationales (CERI), at Sciences Po, my alma mater in Paris, as an intern.

PAKISTAN AT THE CROSSROADS

INTRODUCTION

PAKISTAN, THE INTERFACE STATE

Christophe Jaffrelot

Pakistan has been characterized by scholars as, among other things, an "ideological state" (like Israel), because of the political reinterpretation of Islam by its founding fathers, including Muhammad Ali Jinnah; a "garrison state," because of the key role of the military; and as a "terror state," because of the rise of radical Islamic movements in its midst. But its trajectory may be best captured by another, encompassing, feature not contradictory with the qualifications mentioned above: its ability to navigate at the interface of domestic and external dynamics, which makes relevant two other formulas—those of "client state" and "pivotal state."

Every country strategizes at the crossroads of the national and the international—to say nothing of the transnational—to maximize its resources. But in the case of Pakistan, this interaction has reached uncommon proportions, given its geographic size, its population (almost 200 million people), and its nuclear status. Countries of the same league are generally less dependent on outside support and less porous to foreign influences—be they religious, cultural, or economic.

The root cause of this extraversion lays in the Pakistani feeling of vulnerability that crystallized vis-à-vis India as early as 1947—a sentiment that was reinforced by the then hostile attitude of Afghanistan. Subjected to encirclement, Pakistan looked immediately for external support. The United States was the first country Pakistan turned to, but it also made overtures to China and Middle Eastern countries, especially when Washington distanced itself from Islamabad.

Although this policy was associated primarily with the army, whose quest for foreign, sophisticated military equipment knew almost no limit, civilian politicians rallied around the same strategy, and not only for security reasons. Among other things, the political personnel—which drew mostly from a tiny elite group—found that financial support from the outside was a convenient way to obviate a modern taxation policy, one which their milieu and key supporters would have resented. The political economy rationale of the army's extraversion cannot be ignored either, as the Pakistani military does not pay taxes either and has developed business activities. The Pakistani army, therefore, enjoys a much better lifestyle than most of the rest of society.

Civilians and military officers also converged in the use of (sometimes foreign) mujahideen in the waging of jihad in Afghanistan and Kashmir— the favorite tactic of the army over the last three decades. Z. A. Bhutto supported Hekmatyar and Rabbani against the Kabul regime as early as the 1970s. This strategy gained momentum under Zia during the war against the Soviets. But Benazir Bhutto was prime minister of Pakistan when the army supported the Taliban and when Islamabad recognized the Taliban regime in 1996. And neither Benazir nor Nawaz Sharif had objections toward the support of foreign mujahideen in Kashmir.

The promotion of external ties by the military and civilians for security and socioeconomic reasons reflects the growing commonality of their worldview and (more or less illicit) interests. Their elite groups form a closely knit establishment comprising a few hundreds of families. Indeed, the difference between the most authoritarian phases of civilian rules and the most moderate forms of military dictatorship has tended to differ in degrees more than in nature over the last forty years.

As a result, Pakistanis may look for alternatives to their rulers of the day not among the usual suspects any more (the dominant opposition party or a new Chief of Army Staff) but out of this circle entirely. They may turn more to the judiciary, parties that have not been tried yet, and the Islamist forces that do not articulate a discourse of social justice inadvertently. Are these developments the indications of even more domestic tensions in a country already on the verge of civil war in regions like Baluchistan and Karachi? And what part can external variables play in this context? These are some of the questions this volume tries to explore.

PAKISTAN: A CLIENT STATE OR A PIVOTAL STATE?

FEAR OF ENCIRCLEMENT

The complex of Pakistani leaders vis-à-vis India emerged as early as 1947, partly because they were convinced that those who ruled in New Delhi had not resigned themselves to Partition and craved for what the Hindu nationalists called *Akhand Bharat*—a (re)unified India.[1] Jinnah, in a hand written note, expressed these views in 1947–1948:

1. The Congress has accepted the present Settlements with mental reservations.
2. They now proclaim their determination to restore the unity of India as soon as possible.
3. With that determination they will naturally be regarded as avowed Enemies of Pakistan State working for its overthrow.[2]

The need to defend Pakistan was particularly acute among the security apparatus. Ayub Khan, who was to be appointed chief of the army in 1951, considered in 1948 that "India's attitude continued to be one of unmitigated hostility. Her aim was to cripple us at birth."[3] As a result, as Khalid Bin Sayeed wrote in 1965, so far as foreign policy was concerned, "Almost every action of Pakistan can be interpreted as being motivated by fear of India."[4] Indeed, as late as 1963, an editorial of the newspaper founded by Jinnah, *Dawn*, emphasized that "If the main concern of the Christian West is the containment of Chinese Communism, the main concern of Muslim Pakistan is the containment of militarist and militant Hinduism."[5]

The fear of India was reinforced by the Afghan attitude. In the 1940s, Kabul had asked the British to let "their" (Kabul's) Pashtun tribes decide whether they wanted to accede to Afghanistan or to become independent. Pakistan was not even an option. After the creation of Pakistan, Afghanistan refused to recognize the Durand Line as an international border. As a result, Pakistan was doubly unachieved, with Kashmir partly under the control of India and its western frontier still unofficial. To make things worse, some Afghan leaders supported the irredentist idea of Pashtunistan, which would have amalgamated the western districts of Pakistan to those of South Afghanistan to form a new, ill-defined, administrative unit. In September 1947, Afghanistan was the only country in the United Nations not to support the entry of Pakistan. At the same time, like the Pashtun nationalist leader Abdul Ghaffar Khan, who had supported the Congress against the British, the Kabul government was close to India.

U.S.–PAKISTAN RELATIONS: A PATRON AND ITS CLIENT STATE

Pakistani leaders turned first to the United States for support. Jinnah tried primarily to sell his country's strategic location. In September 1947, he declared: "The safety of the North West Frontier is of world concern and not merely an internal matter for Pakistan alone."[6] The United States concurred when the Cold War unleashed itself in Korea. It then recognized Pakistan as one of its regional brokers in charge of containing communism in Asia. This security-based rapprochement was made easier by the rise to power of two ex–army men, Dwight D. Eisenhower and Ayub Khan, the former having no real problem with the latter's coup in 1958. Pakistan joined the Southeast Asia Treaty Organization (SEATO) and the Central Treaty Organization (CENTO) and, in exchange, got access to increasingly sophisticated American arms and substantial financial aid. After ups and downs, this relationship culminated during the anti-Soviet war in Afghanistan, when the Pakistani army was offered billions of dollars, plus F-16 fighter jets, to support the mujahideen. The post-9/11 war in Afghanistan resulted in even more arms and money. In thirteen years, from 2002 to 2015, Pakistan, a partner of the United States in the war against Al Qaeda and Islamic terrorism at large, has received about $30 billion, as well as arms (including F-16s, more useful against India than against the Taliban). As more than half of this amount was security related, the U.S. government financed about one-fifth of the regular military budget of Pakistan.

These developments may suggest that Pakistan is, in fact, a kind of rentier state. But the countries that are usually described that way owe this quality to their natural resources (typically, oil and/or gas). In the case of Pakistan, the rent comes from the strategic location of the country—it is a frontline state facing global threats like communism or Islamic terrorism. The difference does not end here. Rentier states are usually more passive than Pakistan. In contrast to the oil-producing countries, which did mostly one thing only—built the Organization of Petroleum Exporting Countries (OPEC)—Pakistan advocated its case vis-à-vis the United States to become a client state. It obliged its patron by acting according to its wishes in order to deserve the billions of dollars it got. Certainly Pakistan retained some autonomy, but it also took risks because of American demands—as evident from the Soviet reactions when Moscow discovered that the U2s that were flying over its territory came from Pakistan.

A clientelistic relationship is often unstable. Based on mutual interests more than on affinities, cultural or ideological, it is subject to constant renegotiations. Today Pakistan is keen to renegotiate the terms of its relations to the United States for several reasons, as I show in chapter 8: Islamabad and Washington do not share a common enemy any more in Afghanistan, the U.S.–India rapprochement has transformed the old regional equation, and the Obama administration is seen as damaging the country's sovereignty.

In fact, Pakistan would very much like to pivot to other patrons—including China and Saudi Arabia, as it did partly in the past.

WHAT "ALL-WEATHER FRIEND"?

In 1950, Pakistan recognized China when the latter country was rather isolated, as if Karachi (the then capital) was preparing the future, understanding before everyone else that Beijing was bound to have complicated relations with India—in spite of the then warm relations between Nehru and Chou-En Lai. China, appreciative of the Pakistanis' move, decided to exchange its coal against their cotton, which had no place to go after the Indian mills were cut off from the places where this textile plant was produced. Diplomatically, the Pakistani–Chinese rapprochement found expression in the way Karachi spared Beijing at the United Nations during the Korean War. In 1963, Pakistan and China granted each other the status of the most favored nation, and the airlines of both nations were allowed to operate in the other's territory and sky—something Chinese leaders appreciated as they could now go west through Pakistan.

But the real turning point came about when China attacked India in 1962. Not only did this war reconfirm that Beijing and Islamabad had a common enemy, but afterward both countries, in December 1962, swapped some territory in Kashmir—something India resented a lot.

The following war, between India and Pakistan in 1965, gave an opportunity for China to show its benevolence to its partner in South Asia. China displayed signs of solidarity, while the United States was imposing sanctions against Pakistan as well as India—which, being bigger and closer to the USSR, was bound to be less affected. In 1967, both countries signed a maritime agreement to provide port facilities to each other's ships.

Diplomatically, China supported Pakistan as one of the permanent members of the UN Security Council on the Kashmir issue, and Pakistan helped China to relate to the United States after Nixon decided to make overtures to Beijing. When Kissinger secretly traveled to China to prepare the ground for Nixon's visit, he left from Pakistan, accompanied by high-ranking Pakistani officers.

In the domain of defense, China helped Pakistan to balance its dependence vis-à-vis the United States by selling arms. As early as 1967, China committed itself to deliver one hundred tanks and eighty MIGs to Pakistan. In 1982, Chinese weapons systems made up 75 percent of Pakistan's tanks and 65 percent of its air force. In 2005, China provided Pakistan with four naval frigates, and today China and Pakistan are jointly producing the J-17 Thunder fighter. In the same vein, China helped Pakistan to develop its nuclear bomb. In 1986, China and Pakistan concluded a comprehensive nuclear cooperation agreement. In fact, both countries were already cooperating clandestinely in this field. By the early or mid-1980s, Pakistan had acquired sensitive technologies from China to build its bomb. During the following decade, Beijing helped Islamabad to build a 40 megawatt reactor, which could be used to provide plutonium for its weapons program.[7]

For China, arming Pakistan was clearly a good way to force India to look west instead of east, as the two largest Asian powers are potentially rivals in Southeast Asia. Besides, Pakistan has given China access to the Indian Ocean. In 1967, the ancient Silk Route between Xinjiang and Gilgit was "reopened." Then, in 1971, the Karakorum Highway was inaugurated. Culminating at 15,397 feet above sea level, it is still the highest paved international road in the world. Ultimately, this route is supposed to lead to Gwadar, a Baluch deep-sea port in which the Chinese have invested $200 million and 450 personnel for its construction since 2006. But constructing the planned 1,864-mile-long railway line between Kashgar and Gwadar will cost up to $30 million per mile in the highest mountains, and to make things even more complicated, the highway will go through parts of one of the most unstable provinces of Pakistan, Baluchistan. Guerillas have already kidnapped and killed several Chinese engineers in Gwadar.

Whether Pakistan will be in a position to pivot to China in order to emancipate itself from the American influence is not easy to predict, as Serge Granger and Farah Jan emphasize in this volume. China may be cautious not to alienate India, an emerging power and an important trade partner. Additionally, the Chinese may worry about the connection between Uyghurs and Pakistani jihadis. Finally—and most important—China is not prepared to help Pakistan financially as much as the United States is. When Islamabad turned to Beijing in 2008, while it was coping with a severe economic crisis, Beijing had only small loans to offer. But if China is not prepared to give aid to Pakistan, it has announced a massive investment of $46 billion in the framework of the "One route, one belt" project connecting China to central and west Asia.

The other partner to which Pakistan could turn is Saudi Arabia. In fact, the Middle East was the region of the world where Pakistan found its first allies, preceding even its alliance with the United States. In the early 1950s, it signed treaties of friendship with Iran (1950), Iraq (1950), Syria (1950), Turkey (1951), Egypt (1951), Yemen (1952), and Lebanon (1952). But, considering the American support of Israel, many Arab countries objected to Pakistan joining CENTO in 1954. The Saudi ambassador to Karachi described this move as "a stab in the heart of the Arab and Muslim states." Many Arab countries also strongly objected to the Pakistani support of the West during the Suez crisis (1956); this included Saudi Arabia and Egypt, which felt closer to India at that time.

By the 1960s, Pakistan, in the Middle East, was left with few non-Arab, pro-West allies, most importantly, Iran and Turkey, with whom Pakistan created the Regional Co-operation Development in 1964. In 1962, Saudi Arabia did not support Pakistan when a resolution on Kashmir came up for discussion in the United Nations, so as to not alienate India.

Things changed after the 1971 war. Pakistan probably considered itself as being more part of the Middle East after its Bengali wing—bordering Southeast Asia—was gone. More important, the country felt very vulnerable and let down by the United States, which, again, had not done much to support Pakistan against India except to send the aircraft carrier USS *Enterprise* to the Bay of Bengal. In spite of what official history textbooks say, China did not fully come to the rescue of Pakistan either. Z. A. Bhutto, who had always had reservations about Pakistan's American allies, made a "journey of resistance" to Iran, Turkey, Morocco, Tunisia, Libya, Algeria, Egypt, and Syria. His tour continued in May and June later that year, as he visited Saudi Arabia, Kuwait, the United Arab Emirates, Iraq, Lebanon, Jordan, Ethiopia, Mauritania, Guinea, Nigeria, Sudan, and Somalia. He was looking mainly for money for the Pakistani economy and to build the "Islamic bomb." According to Zahid Hussain, Libya "supplied Pakistan with uranium from 1978 to 1980."[8] In 1998, it seems that Saudi officials attended the Pakistani nuclear test, and the Saudi defense minister visited the laboratory of the father of the Pakistani bomb, A. Q. Khan, in 1999.

What did Pakistan have to give in return? Soldiers have been one of its most significant export products. Between 1972 and 1977, Islamabad concluded military protocols with Saudi Arabia, Libya, Jordan (where General Zia ul Haq himself had served in 1970, leading the Pakistani mission which took part in the operation against the Black September insurgency of the

Palestine Liberation Organization), Iraq, Oman, the United Arab Emirates, and Kuwait. By the late 1970s, Pakistan had sent almost 2,000 military advisors and trainers to the Middle East. That was the beginning of a long-lasting relationship. Approximately 50,000 Pakistani soldiers served in the Middle East in the 1980s, including 20,000 in Saudi Arabia, a country that was becoming a close partner of Pakistan. In 1981, Riyadh financed the $800 million purchase of forty F-16s, and in the 1980s, Saudi Arabia also paid for the Pakistani bomb in a context that was now dominated by the post–Iranian Revolution rivalry between Tehran and Riyadh and the anti-Soviet jihad in Afghanistan.

The Iranian Revolution resulted in a competition between Saudi Arabia and Iran—between Sunnis and Shias—and the Afghan war fostered the Saudi mobilization in favor of the anti-Soviet mujahideen. Riyadh promised to spend as much as the United States to fight this jihad. At least $3 billion more (the amount Washington gave) therefore transited through Pakistan. In both cases, Pakistan was involved—as an ally or as the battlefield of a proxy war whose stake was the Shia–Sunni conflict, which was to be known as "sectarianism."

The Saudi influence over Pakistan is not only (geo)political and financial. It is also cultural and religious. First, the Saudis have been in a position to fund a large number of *dini madaris* (Koranic schools) in Pakistan in the context of Zia's Islamization policy and, more important, during the anti-Soviet jihad, which gave the Saudis a great opportunity to expand. Second, Pakistani migrants in the Gulf countries and in Saudi Arabia (about five million people sending $20 billion of remittances annually) brought back to their country a different version of Islam—and sometimes prejudices against Shias.

In spite of the formidable rapprochement (and even osmosis) that has developed between Pakistan and Saudi Arabia since the 1970s, Riyadh is not likely to be a patron to the same extent as Washington for Pakistan, as Sana Haroon demonstrates in chapter 10. First, the Saudis are not prepared to alienate India, a traditional partner that imports 11 percent of its oil from the kingdom. They have wanted India to join the Organization of Islamic Conference as an observer since 1969—a move Pakistan has always vetoed. Second, Pakistan is not willing to alienate Iran, a neighbor that could sell gas to a country badly affected by an energy crunch today. Third, Riyadh may not be in a position to give Pakistan as much money as the United States.

Washington, therefore, will probably remain a key partner by default for the Pakistani establishment, so long as the United States is prepared to help

Islamabad. The American administration will probably reduce its support to Pakistan because of the financial crunch and because it will have fewer and fewer troops to supply in Afghanistan. But the United States will probably continue to be an important player in Pakistan and remain in a position to watch the Islamist and nuclear activities in the country.

WHAT DOMESTIC DYNAMIC?

The Pakistani establishment needs support from outside for financial reasons as much as it does for security—two dimensions that are sometimes difficult to disentangle. Without American money, Pakistan would not have been able to make ends meet during some phases of its history. But its recurrent (chronic?) state of financial crisis, as I suggested above, has fiscal roots.

Pakistan is one of the countries with the lowest tax burden in the world, as Shahid Javed Burki and Adnan Naseemullah show in chapter 6. The tax-to-gross domestic product (GDP) ratio rose from 9 percent in 1964–1965 to 14 percent in 1990 before returning to 8.9 percent in 2013.[9] It further diminished to 7 percent in 2014,[10] because, among other things, of the doubling of tax exemptions—Rs 477.1 billion (including Rs 96.2 billion on income tax)—which shows that the government continued with its pro-rich policy.[11] These figures are also due to fraud (one specialist estimated in the 1990s that less than 1 percent of the people who are supposed to pay income tax do so).[12] Things have not improved considerably since then. In 2013, the income tax-to-GDP ratio has fallen to 3.5 percent, with taxpayers numbering about 1.5 million people.[13] This state of things is the reflection of a robust convergence of interests of the establishment elite groups—including the politicians and the army chiefs. But the convergence does not stop there.

CONVERGENCE OF CIVILIAN AND MILITARY RULERS—OR THE MAKING OF AN ESTABLISHMENT

The political economy of Pakistan harks back to the early years of the Muslim League. Indeed, the separatism advocated by Jinnah's party proceeded to a large extent from power-hungry elites who combined clerical competence and an aristocratic lineage but who were about to suffer a drop in status because of the rise of their Hindu rivals. Their aspiration to perpetuate a dominant status played a structuring role in the crystallization of the "two-nation theory." After Partition, elites' quest for domination (and their sense of entitlement) found expression in the monopolization of power by Mohajir politicians. Soon after, the latter were gradually replaced by "feudals" and, after the 1958 coup, by army men. Since then, politicians and the army have been locked in a conflict for decades in Pakistan, as evident from their alternation in power every 10 years or so. But a form of modus vivendi, even of convergence, has emerged. There is a natural tendency of occasional observers of Pakistan to point out an opposition between the forces of freedom, associated with civilians, and those of oppression, identified with the military. These two camps do indeed exist, but to present the former as relying on the body of civilians hostile to the military would be an oversimplification, simply because equating civilians with democrats is highly questionable in Pakistan. The limits of democratization stem from a web of complex factors, including the political culture of the civilians. Since the country's inception, Jinnah, its founding father, a product of the viceregal system,[14] favored the construction of a centralized state over a parliamentary system. His successor, Liaquat Ali Khan, continued in the same vein, reining in political parties that he saw as divisive forces and even neglecting his own Muslim League, which would never become a national cornerstone similar to the Congress Party in India. The disappearance of these two Mohajir leaders left the democratically inclined Bengalis in a face-off with the Punjabis, who were averse to democracy, because of opposite demographic reasons (Bengalis were in a majority) as well as their dominant role in the bureaucracy and the army that democracy would have affected. The Punjabi bureaucrats and the military were not, however, the only ones to reject the democracy ideal backed mainly by the Bengalis: politicians in Punjab—and in West Pakistan in general—displayed the same attitude. Z. A. Bhutto himself rejected the results of the 1970 elections won by Mujibur Rahman. Not only did the West Pakistani politicians not wish to fall under Bengali rule, but they also embodied a political culture stamped with "feudalism," made up more of clientelism and factionalism.

Certainly, however, the phase of democratization under Bhutto was without a doubt the most convincing of all in that the military was brought back under the authority of a civilian government, which gave the country a parliamentary constitution in 1973 and undertook large-scale social reforms. But the momentum did not last long, primarily because of Bhutto's own contradictions. Less a democrat than a populist, more an authoritarian than a parliamentarian, more a centralizer than a federalist, and as much a socialist as a product of his social background, he turned his back on parts of his platform—and thus on the middle and working classes that supplied much of the Pakistan Peoples Party (PPP) leadership[15]—to co-opt the landowning elite.[16] Most of all, having little respect for basic freedoms, including that of the press, he denied Pakistan free elections in 1977, giving the army, already reinvigorated by military operations in Baluchistan, the arguments it was waiting for.

The period from 1988 to 1999 contrasts with the Bhutto era due to the control the military continued to exercise over civilians who were supposedly back in command. Neither Benazir Bhutto nor Nawaz Sharif would even manage to complete their terms. But if the army has become so powerful, it is also because of the weakness of the political class, some elements of which prefer to collaborate with the military rather than join forces with their democratic adversaries. This was true of Nawaz Sharif, who in a sense was the army's creature and who would play into its hands against Benazir Bhutto, who herself accepted the little bit of power the military allowed her instead of playing the regime opposition card, as her brother Murtaza had advised. Yet, there is a point in common between the Bhutto years and the 1990s: when Prime Minister Nawaz Sharif was finally at the helm with an absolute majority, he abused his power just like his rival's father had, an additional sign of the weakness of democratic culture among civilians.

But the political culture of none other than Benazir Bhutto, presented as the most liberal of all, especially in the United States, had just as many flaws as that of her predecessors. One of her close associates, Tariq Ali, summed up the situation that prevailed with the formation of her second cabinet in 1993:

> The high command of the Pakistan Peoples Party now became a machine for making money, but without any trickle-down mechanism. This period marked the complete degeneration of the party. The single tradition that had been passed down since the foundation of the party was autocratic centralism. The leader's word was final. Like her father in this respect, Benazir never understood that debate is not only the best medium of confutation, of turning the ideological tables. It is also the most effective form of persuasion.[17]

The current phase of democratization is probably at the midpoint on a scale of civil–military relations. The Eighteenth Amendment (2010) has given the government greater power than what it had in the 1988–1999 period but less than during the Bhutto era, as the army retains supreme control over key policies regarding nuclear power, Afghanistan, Kashmir, and so forth. Once again, civilian power suffered from its divisions.

Although Nawaz Sharif, after being forced into exile by his former Chief of Army Staff (COAS) in 1999, struck an alliance with Benazir Bhutto to oust the military from power, she was once again to strike a deal with Pervez Musharraf in 2007, and he (Nawaz) was once again tempted to play into the military's hands to oust the PPP during the "Memogate" episode in 2011.

Even if today's political parties have greater influence on the course of public affairs than in the 1988–1999 period, they are not necessarily more democratic. Aside from ongoing practices of patronage among the "feudals"—who are also urban business people, such as the Sharif family—having copied the clientelistic and factional ways of their rural predecessors (in that sense, "feudalism" is a mind-set more than a socioeconomic phenomenon), almost all the political parties have become family enterprises over time, in financial terms as well. As Maleeha Lodhi writes, "The personalized nature of politics is closely related to the dominant position enjoyed throughout Pakistan's history by a narrowly-based political elite that was feudal and tribal in origin and has remained so in outlook even as it gradually came to share power with well-to-do urban groups. . . . The urban rich functions much like their rural counterparts with their efforts at political mobilisation resting more on working lineage and biradari connections and alliances than representing wider urban interests."[18]

The disconnect of this political milieu from the public good is patent in its refusal to levy taxes—so as not to pay any themselves—while there can be no public good without tax revenue (not to mention tax fairness). But the disconnect is aggravated by the transformation of political parties into (unofficially) lucrative family enterprises, as is evident in the personal enrichment of the political elite. In 2007, the list of the richest Pakistanis showed that Asif Ali Zardari—who was not even president at that time—came second with an estimated fortune of $1.8 billion; the Sharif brothers came in number four with $1.4 billion.[19] Six years later, Nawaz, who had become prime minister for the third time, turned out to be the richest parliamentarian, with declared assets of Rs 1.824 billion. One of his ministers, Shahid Khaban Abbassi, was also a billionaire.[20] In 2010, a report of the Pakistan Institute of Legislative Development and Transparency showed that the sitting members of Parliament were three times richer than those who had been elected previously—and in many cases they were the same people.[21] In June 2014, the minister for planning and development, Ahsan Iqbal, declared that he had started negotiations with Switzerland "to bring back around $200 billion stashed by Pakistani politicians in Swiss bank accounts."[22] Around the same time, the Lahore High Court issued a notice to sixty-four politicians "on a petition seeking directions for the politicians to bring their foreign assets back to Pakistan."[23]

In the 1990s, the politicians' corruption and Nawaz Sharif's authoritarianism alienated many citizens who took refuge in abstention or placed their faith in the army, as evident from Musharraf's popularity in 1999. But although the military has appeared as a savior every now and again, it has tended to emulate similar ways and means.

As Aqil Shah shows in this volume, military coups have followed almost the same pattern for more than four decades in Pakistan, as can be seen in their choreography since 1958. Each time, the army takes control peacefully, hands power over to its chief—wherefore the notion of consensual coup d'état—and replaces the "politicians" presented as harmful to the nation, with the more or less clear approval of the judicial apparatus, thereby reinforcing the impression of a consensus, a notion that does not exclude authoritarianism, even if variants appear here and there. The Zia years thus contrasted with the Ayub Khan/Yahya Khan era by their harshness and the Islamization policy for which they were the framework. But Musharraf revamped the initial "model" to some extent.

Each episode of dictatorship results in the violent crushing of political, union, and ethnonationalist leaders (hundreds of Baluch nationalists "disappeared" under Musharraf); more or less strict control of the media; greater rapprochement with the United States; militarization of the state apparatus (former or active officers appointed to posts usually reserved for civilians); and the development of what Ayesha Siddiqa calls Milbus ("military business," the economic activities of the army), an ongoing process that reached its height under Musharraf, placing the army at the head of an empire.[24]

Not only do the phases of state militarization always begin (and more or less unfold) the same way, but they also generally end in the same fashion. After a number of years, civilians mobilize and manifest their desire for regime change. At the vanguard of such protest movements are students and trade union activists (as in the 1968–1969 agitation, with Z. A. Bhutto's rise to power and his political appropriation of the unrest), bona fide political parties (such as the Movement for the Restoration of Democracy of 1981–1983), or legal professionals (as in the anti-Musharraf movement of 2007). But agitation itself never explains the fall of dictators. Each time external events also play a role, such as the war of 1965 in the case of Ayub Khan, the loss of East Bengal under Yahya Khan, the plane crash in the case of Zia, and the second war in Afghanistan, which exacerbated opposition to Musharraf, seen as a lackey to the United States.

But even if street protest alone cannot bring down dictatorships, it largely explains their trajectory and especially the way in which all the military autocrats have been induced to make the same concessions each time. All have had to seek new sources of legitimacy in constitutive elements of the democratic process: the people, a facade of constitutional legality, and political parties. None have been able to dispense with a referendum—however rigged. Beyond that, all have given the country a constitutional framework, leading them if not systematically to give up their uniform, at least to don the title and sometimes the attire of president. All have carried the process of "civilianization" to the point of appointing a prime minister and legalizing political parties.

The trajectory of Pakistani military regimes is without a doubt the sign of the resilience of a democratic culture based as much on its attachment to the law (the liberal–legal aspect of democracy) as on the strong foothold of political parties, especially the PPP (the pluralist aspect of democracy). Consequently, politics in Pakistan moves within much better defined limits than what its chronic instability might suggest: the ground could not be better mapped out. Dictators all have had to liberalize their regime after some time and civilians never asked for all the power. Even its tempo seems regulated: just about every ten years, power changes hands between politicians and the military and vice versa.

That said, the opposition between democratic politicians and dictatorial military men should be placed in perspective. Many parties have ended up making compromises with the military. The Pakistan Muslim League (Quaid-e-Azam) (PML-Q) is the very prototype of these "khaki parties" that cropped up as soon as Ayub Khan founded his party—which the father of PML-Q president Chaudry Shujaat Hussain moreover already led. In the 1980s, Nawaz Sharif placed his sense of political maneuvering in the service of Zia and then played into the hands of the Inter-Services Intelligence (ISI) to undermine Benazir Bhutto. She returned the compliment to the very end, as attested by the "deal" she made in 2007 with Musharraf at the expense of the Pakistan Muslim League (Nawaz) (PML-N). In the end, is there really such structural antagonism between civilians and the military? Many observers have come to consider political and army leaders as belonging to the same world. Ayesha Siddiqa thus speaks of an "elite partnership."[25] Steven Cohen, like Mushahid Hussain, refers to the domination of an "establishment."[26] Hussain, himself a member of it—he was information minister under Nawaz Sharif before joining the PML-Q and becoming its secretary general—describes this establishment as made up of only some 500 people belonging to various circles, as much civilian as military.[27]

The border between these two worlds has been shown to be porous on the right side of the political chessboard, Muslim League leaders having gone over to Zia (cf. Nawaz Sharif and Chaudhry Nisar Ali Khan, home minister since 2013) and later Musharraf (cf. the PML-Q). But this process ended up affecting PPP leaders as well.

Generals' sons moreover have very naturally gone into politics after the death of their fathers. Ijaz ul Haq, the son of Zia ul Haq, and Humayun Akhtar Khan, the son of General Akhtar Abdur Rahman, joined the PML-Q, whereas the son of Ayub Khan joined the anti-Bhutto Pakistan National Alliance (PNA) in 1977 and then the PML-N—he was minister of foreign affairs in Nawaz Sharif's government. These three persons show that the dynastic syndrome has not only affected civilians. Other figures epitomize the convergence of civilian and military circles. The most significant is probably Syed Sharifuddin Pirzada, a lawyer who was Jinnah's personal secretary before going on to work with all the perpetrators of coups d'état from Ayub Khan to Musharraf, in particular to counsel them in legal matters. But S. S. Pirzada also performed services for Z. A. Bhutto and Nawaz Sharif. He is the quintessential establishment man, with his share of corruption—moreover admitted, as he confessed his wrongs to journalist Ardeshir Cowasjee in these words: "Accept me as I am with warts, blemishes, briefcases and all. If it were not for all the weak and corrupt governments of Pakistan, I would not be where I am today."[28]

What binds together the Pakistani establishment is a sense of class interest. The quest for personal enrichment it not restricted to "feudals" or businesspeople turned politicians; it has spread to the army, which as we have seen has become a lucrative enterprise that is not exempt from corruption. Even if Pakistan has no real "democrats" or real "autocrats" that have survived over time like the Burmese junta, it has a wealth of authoritarian "plutocrats" that can be labeled an establishment. This blend of authoritarianism and patrimonialism is reminiscent of what Max Weber called sultanism, a type of regime that the German sociologist first detected in the Ottoman Empire.

The convergence of political and military grandees in this version of sultanism explains why no regime, be it civilian or military, after more or less timid attempts by Ayub Khan and Bhutto, has tackled social inequality—hence the lack of fair taxation.

In 2007, the president of the Supreme Court Bar Association arraigned the Pakistani army in a very telling way:

The Pakistan Army was once renowned for its discipline, its fighting skills and its unflinching fortitude in the face of adversity. It is now notorious for its commercial avarice and its skill in making political deals. When its generals spend their time establishing real estate projects, farming, constructing roads, managing utilities, manufacturing cornflakes, running aviation companies, operating banks, administrating educational institutes and playing politics, it is unsurprising that both national and international observers question their ability and willingness to fight and win the war against militants in Waziristan.[29]

In fact, the communion of political and military elites in a sultanic model tended to erect the judiciary as the only institutional alternative.

IN QUEST OF ALTERNATIVES

In 2007, for the first time in Pakistan's history, it was not unionists or political agitators but lawyers and judges who, as much in the street as in the courts, brought down a military regime with the support of the media, which, despite its tendency to make compromises, can be to a large degree highly determined and even courageous.

The 2007 movement needs to be seen in a larger perspective because what is known as a phase of "judicial activism" in Pakistan started in 2005 with the appointment of Chief Justice Iftikhar Muhammad Chaudhry. Justice Chaudhry has fought not only against Musharraf's authoritarianism rule but also against the disappearance of Baluch nationalists and Islamist militants. Lately, he mobilized against Zardari's corruption, to such an extent that he forced Prime Minister Yusuf Raza Gilani to resign in 2012 because Gilani did not want to initiate a proper investigation. The Chief Justice has not spared the former military rulers either. In October 2012, he chaired a three-member bench of the apex court, which gave an unprecedented judgment against former COAS general Aslam Beg and former Director General of the ISI (DGISI) Asad Durrani. In 1996, Air Marshal (retired) Asghar Khan had filed a petition in the court accusing them both—among others—to have distributed money (Rs 60 million) to opponents of Benazir Bhutto to ensure her defeat in the 1990 elections. The court ordered the government to investigate the matter because it ruled that Beg and Durrani had violated the Constitution while rigging the elections and that legal proceedings had also to be initiated against those who had received money.

As Philip Oldenburg argues in chapter 3, the growing influence of the judiciary may contribute to make political competition more clean and therefore restore the confidence of the public in the state institutions. This may result in the return of the voters in the electoral process. The main beneficiary of this changing landscape may be Imran Khan, the only national politician who has never been associated with power at the center. The anti-American protest that he has articulated in his campaign against the drone attacks in the Federally Administered Tribal Areas (FATA) has attracted a lot of support. This popularity translated somewhat into votes in 2013, but the resilience of the PTI remains to be seen, as Mohammed Waseem shows in chapter 2, on political parties in Pakistan.

However, the prestige of Iftikhar Chaudhry did not only come from his fight against discredited (ex-)rulers. It also reflected the hunger for justice that is probably today one of the most powerful driving forces of Pakistani society—partly because of the rise of inequalities and the way the establishment is amassing fortunes. This is one of the factors that explains the attractiveness of the Islamist discourse.

Certainly, the Islamist groups have benefited over the last three decades of Zia's Islamization policy, the multiplication of *dini madaris*, the successful anti-Soviet jihad in Afghanistan, and—in the case of the Sunni groups—the rise of sectarianism. But today they cash in on anti-American feelings (fostered by the "occupation" of Afghanistan and the attacks against Pakistani sovereignty) and a craze for (social) justice. Indeed, the expansion of some of the most militant groups is due not only to the support of Al Qaeda but also to the social agenda of rather plebeian movements. Their revolutionary potential is obvious in the FATA—where they rule in large territories, sometimes dispense a form of justice, and are replacing the old elite groups. In fact, the old tribal leaders, Maliks and Khans, have been executed in large numbers by young fighting Mollahs.

The social dimension of this jihad explains that traditional parties (including the Jama'at-e-Islami, a former ally of Zia) have lost most of their relevance. In fact, they are looked at as part of the establishment by the most radical group, not only because some of them (including the Jamiat-e Ulama-e Islam (JUI) are regular occupiers of ministerial positions, but also because they are cut off from the plebeians. Therefore, there is a societal element in the battle that is taking place in the FATA—but also in Punjab—as Mariam Abou Zahab shows in chapter 4. Deeply entrenched social hierarchies are at stake. This component can only make the—already intense—military conflict even more devastating.

The unleashing of terrorist violence in response to the military interventions of the Americans (via the drones) and the Pakistani army (on the ground) in the Pashtun area has reached unprecedented levels in the last few years. In four years (2008–2013), 12,107 terrorist attacks (including those by suicide bombers) have killed 16,030 people—including a large number of police and soldiers.[30] As Hassan Abbas shows in chapter 5, Pakistan is facing a major security challenge domestically, and the growing awareness among the military that the main challenge may not come from India but comes from the inside could explain the North Waziristan operation that started in June 2014.

This critical situation shows that Pakistan is paying the price for the support it gave to jihadists for decades—since the 1970s—in order to "bleed India" in Kashmir and to acquire some "strategic depth" in Afghanistan, the country on which Avinash Paliwal focuses in chapter 7, in relation to Pakistan. Indeed, as evident from the basic assumption of this volume, the return to normalcy of Pakistan domestically implies a normalization of its relations with both its neighbors, India and Afghanistan.

* * *

In contrast to this introduction, the chapters of the present volume begin not with the external factors but with the domestic issues. If the book, therefore, ends with the international context, it is not only because it is more logical to the human mind to think about particular problems before turning toward larger ones. Whatever the order in which the arguments are presented, this book analyzes the internal and external dimensions of the Pakistani trajectory, as well as their interaction.

NOTES

1. Aparna Pande, *Explaining Pakistan's Foreign Policy* (London: Routledge, 2011), 29.
2. This note is reproduced in Gohar Ayub Khan, *Testing Times as Foreign Minister* (Islamabad: Dost, 2009), 309.
3. Mohammad Ayub Khan, *Friends Not Masters: A Political Autobiography* (1967; Islamabad: Mr. Book, 2006), 65.
4. Khalid Bin Sayeed, "Pakistan's Foreign Policy: An Analysis of Pakistan's Fears and Interests," *Asian Survey* 4 (1965): 747.
5. Cited in Pande, *Explaining Pakistan's Foreign Policy*, 24.
6. Cited in Dennis Kux, *The United States and Pakistan, 1947–2000: Disenchanted Allies* (Baltimore: Johns Hopkins University Press, 2001), 20.
7. Today the nuclear status of Pakistan is a major asset vis-à-vis the United States. In fact, Washington is probably prepared to support Pakistan beyond its natural

inclination because of the need it feels to maintain a channel of communication with a nuclear—and proliferating—country.

8. Zahid Hussain, *Frontline Pakistan: The Struggle with Militant Islam* (New York: Columbia University Press, 2007), 168.

9. Shahbaz Rana, "Breaks for the Elite: Tax Exemptions Cost Exchequer Rs 239.5 Bn in FY13," *Express Tribune*, June 12, 2013.

10. Zeenia Shaukat, "What's in It for the Poor?" *Newsline*, July 2014, 63. Another source gives a higher tax-to-GDP ratio at 10.5 percent: Khaleeq Kiani, "Tax-to-GDP Ratio down," *Dawn*, May 17, 2005, http://www.dawn.com/news/1106847.

11. Mubarak Zeb Khan, "Economic Survey 2013–14: Tax Exemptions Double to Rs 477 Bn," *Dawn*, June 3, 2014, http://www.dawn.com/news/1110220.

12. Hafiz Pasha, "Political Economy of Tax Reforms: The Pakistan Experience," *Pakistan Journal of Applied Economics* 10, no. 1–2 (1994): 50.

13. Sakib Sherani, "Fixing the Tax System," *Dawn*, June 14, 2013, http://beta.dawn.com/news/1018130/fixing-the-tax-system.

14. On the impact of this legacy on Jinnah, see Khalid bin Sayeed, "Continuation of the Viceregal System in Pakistan," in *Pakistan: The Formative Phase* (London: Oxford University Press, 1968), 221–300.

15. On this "betrayal," see Lal Khan, *Pakistan's Other Story: The 1968–69 Revolution* (Lahore: Struggle Publications, 2008).

16. Shahid Javed Burki, *Pakistan Under Bhutto, 1971–1977* (London: Macmillan, 1980).

17. Tariq Ali, *The Duel: Pakistan and the Flight Path of American Power* (London: Pocket Books, 2008), 173.

18. M. Lodhi, "Beyond the Crisis State," in *Pakistan: Beyond the "Crisis State,"* ed. M. Lodhi (London: Hurst, 2011), 54–55.

19. "Pakistan Rich List 2008," http://teeth.com.pk/blog/2007/12/08/pakistans-rich-list-of-2008.

20. Meena Menon, "Nawaz, the Richest of Them All," *The Hindu*, December 27, 2013, 22.

21. "How Rich Are Pakistani MNAs? MNA Tops List with Rs3.288bn," *Pakistan Defence*, September 14, 2010, http://www.defence.pk/forums/national-political-issues/72754-how-rich-pakistani-mnas-pppp-mna-tops-list-rs3-288bn.html.

22. Shahbaz Rana, "$200b Stashed Abroad," *Express Tribune*, June 10, 2014, http://tribune.com.pk/story/719722/200b-stashed-abroad-talks-with-swiss-authorities-will-begin-in-august-says-ahsan/.

23. "64 Politicians Issued Notices over Foreign Assets," *Dawn*, May 11, 2014, http://www.dawn.com/news/1105340.

24. Ayesha Siddiqa, *Military Inc.: Inside Pakistan's Military Economy* (London: Pluto, 2007).

25. Ibid.

26. S. Cohen, *The Idea of Pakistan* (Lahore: Vanguard Books, 2005), 69.

27. See his articles in the *Nation*, November 3, 1996, and June 18, 2002, as cited in S. Cohen, *The Idea of Pakistan* (Lahore: Vanguard Books, 2005), 69.

28. Jane Perlez, "On Retainer in Pakistan, to Ease Military Rulers' Path," *New York Times*, December 7, 2007, http://www.nytimes.com/2007/12/15/world/asia/15pirzada.html?pagewanted=all.

29. Muneer A. Malik, "The Rocky Road Ahead," *Dawn*, August 7, 2007, reprinted in Muneer A. Malik, *The Pakistan's Lawyers' Movement: An Unfinished Agenda* (Karachi: Pakistan Law House, 2008), 312.
30. Pakistan Security Report for 2008, 2009, 2010, and 2011, Islamabad, Pak Institute for Peace Studies. See www.san-pips.com.

PART I

THE DOMESTIC SCENE

CHAPTER 1

THE MILITARY AND DEMOCRACY

Aqil Shah

The Pakistan military has repeatedly intervened to arrest the development of democracy in the country, ruling Pakistan directly for almost half the country's existence. Between 1947 and 2012, not even once did an elected government complete its tenure and peacefully transfer power to another elected government. All of Pakistan's previous transitions to democracy were aborted by military coups. Even when the armed forces were not in power, they maintained a firm grip on national politics. Pakistan made its latest transition to democracy in 2008 when the military extricated itself from government, once again, after eight years of authoritarian rule under General Pervez Musharraf (1999–2007). In 2013, Pakistan finally broke its curse of zero democratic turnovers when the Pakistan Peoples Party (PPP) completed its full constitutional term of five years and surrendered power, and its main challenger, Nawaz Sharif's PML-N, emerged victorious in the parliamentary elections held in 2013, both at the center and in Punjab Province.

In order to understand the trajectory of civil–military relations since 2007, this chapter examines the mode of military disengagement from politics while locating military interventions and dominance in historical perspective. Faced with a mobilized opposition led by the "lawyers' movement," seeking to reinstate the sacked Supreme Court Chief Justice Iftikhar Muhammad Chaudhry, the military government reached out to the largest opposition party, the PPP, to negotiate its exit. But despite blows to its public standing and without extracting any formal legal safeguards to preserve its interests once it had left power—conditions associated with the diminution of military entitlements in other contexts[1]—the Pakistan military was able to retain its core institutional privileges, concerning control over its internal structure, national security missions, budgetary allocations, intelligence gathering, and so on.

What explains why the military remained strong enough to maintain its political and strategic influence in the post-authoritarian context despite a weakened military-led authoritarian regime?[2] How and to what extent have the military's entitlements impeded the consolidation of democratic government,[3] including the procedural minima of civilian control over the military?

In order to answer these questions, this chapter makes a twofold argument. First, it contends that the paradox of weak military government–strong military institution was the result of structural differentiation between these two components of the state that allowed the institutional military to disassociate itself from the authoritarian regime and withdraw on its own terms.[4] While the government and the military were connected at the top by the president and army chief of staff, General Musharraf, the institution was not directly involved in government. Many military officers were appointed to the civilian bureaucracy, but the military institution did not hierarchically take over direct command of the state. There were no military councils of ministers and no reserved seats for members of the military in the Parliament, as in Suharto's Indonesia or Pinochet's Chile. In fact, the large majority of the military was focused on combat readiness against its archrival India and, to a lesser degree, on counterinsurgency missions against Taliban militants in the country's Federally Administered Tribal Areas (FATA) bordering Afghanistan.

Therein lies the crux of the matter: the almost permanent perceived threat from India makes the government-institution distinction imperative for the maintenance of military cohesion and integrity and accords the armed forces a preeminent strategic position within the state that is unaffected by the political or economic performance of a particular military government. Thus, while the antiregime mobilization attacked the legitimacy of the military government, the military institution qua institution generally managed to remain above the political fray. No less important, the uniformed military did not directly participate in repressing the antigovernment protests, which enabled it to leave power without incriminating itself in the unsavory deeds of the despot. In fact, the high command compensated for the military institution's association with the military government by withdrawing support from Musharraf during the opposition movement, thus depriving him of his core power base and ultimately convincing him to resign.

Second, the chapter argues that the degree to which the military can impose constraints on democratic governance after it leaves power is better explained by focusing on two interrelated dimensions of civil–military relations in a new regime: military prerogatives and military contestation.[5] Military prerogatives are policy areas where "whether challenged or not, the military as institution assumes they have an acquired right or privilege, formal or informal, to exercise effective control."[6] Contestation is the military's "articulated disagreement" or protest against the policies of civilian governments that challenge its prerogatives.[7]

The chapter proceeds in the following manner. The next section traces the formative historical conditions that helped foster the military's institutional prerogatives. It then illuminates the context of the military's latest institutional extrication, paying special attention to the interacting processes of authoritarian liberalization, opposition mobilization, regime weakening, transitional bargaining, and the actual transition to civilian rule in 2007–2008. Finally, it examines post-authoritarian civil–military relations in Pakistan from the perspective of military prerogatives and military contestation of civilian authority to assess their impact on the consolidation of democratic rule.

THE HEAVY HAND OF HISTORY: "NATION-STATE" BUILDING UNDER CONDITIONS OF WARFARE

Given a bitter rivalry in the decade preceding independence, Pakistan's founding Muslim League leadership, led by Mohammad Ali Jinnah, suspected that the Congress government of India viewed the creation of Pakistan as a "temporary recession of certain territories from India which would soon be reabsorbed."[8] The onset of the territorial conflict between the two countries over the princely state of Kashmir, which sparked military hostilities in 1947–1948, turned this suspicion into deep insecurity, further complicated by irredentist Afghan claims on Pakistan's northwestern territories.[9] It also spurred the "militarization" of the Pakistani state in the early years,[10] thus providing the context in which the generals could increase their influence in domestic politics and national security policy while at the same time observing constitutional procedures. As state building and survival became synonymous with the "war effort," the civilian leadership diverted scarce resources from development to defense[11] and abdicated its responsibility of oversight over the military, thereby allowing the generals a virtual free hand over internal organizational affairs and national security management.

Reinforcing the emergence of this warrior state was an equally crucial political handicap: Pakistan lacked the primary background condition that makes democracy (and, by implication, civilian democratic control of the military) possible: national unity.[12] In the words of Christophe Jaffrelot, Pakistan's was a "nationalism without a nation."[13] Pakistan emerged from British colonial rule with a deep ethnic diversity that overlapped with its geographical division into two wings, West Pakistan and East Pakistan, separated by Indian territory. While West Pakistan (or, more precisely, the migrants or Mohajirs from northern and western India and the Punjabis) dominated the central government and its institutions, East Pakistan had a territorially concentrated and politically conscious Bengali majority, which was excluded from the armed forces and the civil bureaucracy.[14] Independence provided a "brief moment of political unity."[15] However, the West Pakistani elites' desire to forcefully integrate the Bengalis and other smaller West Pakistani ethnic groups (Pashtuns, Sindhis, and the Baluch) into the "nation-state," while denying the legitimacy of all claims for political representation, participation, and regional autonomy based on subnational identities, led to the centralization of power, which decreased provincial autonomy and further strained the internal cohesion that can greatly facilitate the crafting of democratic institutions.

Strong political parties can be crucial to political stability and democratic consolidation. In particular, parties with "stable roots in society" have the capability to peacefully moderate and mediate social conflict. The Muslim League had weak social and organizational roots in Pakistan.[16] Hence, the League leadership's ability to "govern with consent" was complicated by the existential political threat stemming from the numerical logic of electoral democracy. Rather that pursuing "state-nation" policies that could help the development of "multiple and complementary identities" and accommodate distinct ethnic and cultural groups within a democratic federal framework, Pakistan's founding elites followed "nation-state policies" designed to create a single nation congruent with the political boundaries of the state, albeit for "reasons of state" or political expediency.[17] However, this national unification project only exacerbated "the chasm between the ideology and sociology" of Pakistan, especially by politicizing Bengali identity.[18] For instance, even though 98 percent of the majority Bengalis (54 percent of the total population) spoke Bangla, the central government denied that language the national status it deserved and imposed Urdu (the first language of only 7 percent of the total population) as the sole state language immediately after independence, which sparked a "language movement" in East Pakistan as early as 1948.

Seeking to consolidate state authority, Jinnah and his successors found a ready-made governing formula in the iron fist of viceregalism. Backed by the military, the viceregal executive sacked noncompliant civilian cabinets (1953), delayed constitution making, disbanded Parliament when it crafted a federal democratic constitution (1954), removed an elected government in East Pakistan (1954), and ultimately amalgamated the provinces of West Pakistan into "One Unit" to create parity with East Pakistan (1955–1956). As governmental legitimacy was eviscerated under the heavy burden of authoritarian centralization, especially in East Pakistan, the emerging guardians of national security in the military developed serious doubts about the appropriateness and feasibility of parliamentary democracy in a fragile polity threatened by external threat and internal dissension. By the mid-1950s, the military under its first Pakistani commander-in-chief, General Ayub Khan, had dropped its pretensions of political neutrality and was no longer concerned merely with protecting its autonomy or budgets. Instead, the generals (and influential civilian bureaucrats) began to envisage a new form of "controlled" democracy "suited to the genius" of the Pakistani people.[19]

Here, institutional developments within the military had important consequences for civilian politics because they reinforced the officer corps' emerging guardian mentality. Starting in the early 1950s, the military underwent a formative process of institutional transformation from an "ex-colonial" army into a "national" army with a corporate identity and ethos of its own. This process of institutional development was further spurred by military training, expertise, and armaments Pakistan received for allying with the United States to contain the threat of Soviet expansionism. This increased the capabilities of Pakistan's small army, including its firepower, mobility, multiterrain operations, and command and control, thereby boosting the military's "already high confidence in itself."[20] This rapid military professionalization also conflicted sharply with the perceived failure and instability of civilian politics, especially the inability of politicians to craft an appropriate political system that would ensure national harmony and economic development. The high command believed that only a united and prosperous Pakistan could stand up to India and blunt the chances of the external (Indian) abetment of internal strife.[21] Thus, American Cold War security assistance contributed to fanning the army's praetorian ambitions by rapidly modernizing it, which reinforced the soldiers' belief in the superiority of their skills over civilian politicians and was crucial to the high command's decision to expand into an array of civilian roles and functions. Initially, the military called the shots under the cover of a Janowitzian "civil–military coalition" figuratively headed by the governor general.[22]

After Pakistan's first constitution came into force in March 1956, it was only a matter of time before national elections installed a government of autonomist Bengalis and their West Pakistani allies.[23] In October 1958, the military demolished the constitutional order and established a "preventive autocracy"[24] to preempt the "chaos" it thought would be unleashed by the country's first universally franchised elections, which would likely have brought the "India-friendly" and presumably "communist" Bengali nationalists to power. Within a decade of Pakistan's independence, the military effectively interrupted the process of democratic evolution (however tenuous and flawed it was), and Pakistan has yet to recover from that fateful setback.

This outcome contradicts the conventional wisdom in the political science literature. Drawing on the work of Stanislav Andreski,[25] several scholars argue that external security threats result in civilian supremacy over the military. As Samuel Huntington described it, "from the standpoint of civilian control, happy is the country with a traditional enemy."[26] The logic is that when a mortal enemy is knocking on the gates, civilians and the military unite to fight it.[27] As a result, the military becomes focused exclusively on external defense, as long as civilians supply it with the resources necessary to carry out its mission.[28] As I have argued elsewhere, Pakistan's experience suggests that this prevalent interpretation of the relationship between the soldier and the state ignores a crucial intervening variable: national unity.[29] External threats can be unifying or divisive depending on the degree of antecedent domestic cohesion,[30] especially during the early stages of state formation. Put simply, the greater the shared sense of political community, the more likely that security threats will unify civilian and military elites across the board and focus the military outward and away from society. Otherwise, military danger and crises can "subdue civilians and pass all powers to the generals."[31] Ethnic divisions between West and East Pakistan (as well as within West Pakistan) limited the prospects of a unified response to external danger, which ostensibly raised fears among civilian and military governing elites that external enemies could exploit internal disunity, which spurred the imposition of authoritarian emergency measures to maintain what they perceived to be national security, which in turn alienated the Bengalis and ultimately led to state breakup in 1971.

Over time, repeated military coup d'états and military or military-led governments (e.g., 1958–1969 under General Ayub, 1969–1971 under General Yahya Khan, 1977–1988 under General Zia ul Haq, and 1999–2008 under General Musharraf) that have followed each coup have led the military to entrench its prerogatives. For instance, the military claims a large chunk of the national budget (for example, 4.5 percent of gross domestic product on average between 1995 and 2009)[32] without any meaningful civilian oversight. It has also used its privileged position in the state to appropriate public resources (e.g., in the form of concessionary land grants for officers' housing societies and subsidies for its "welfare foundations") that has expanded its commercial and business interests into vitals sectors of the economy. Though not the original motivation for military intervention in politics, "Military Inc." acts as an added incentive for maintaining its political influence.[33]

The military's "clientalistic" ties to the United States have repeatedly reinforced the military's praetorian propensity. This relationship "reached its culmination" during the Central Intelligence Agency's covert anti-Soviet war in Afghanistan when Washington supplied the Pakistani military with F-16s, and the Inter-Services Intelligence (ISI) "received billions of dollars to support the Mujahideen."[34] The post-9/11 U.S. occupation of Afghanistan made Pakistan a "frontline" ally once again, leading the Bush administration to back the Musharraf government as a key ally in fighting Al Qaeda, thus lending military rule a degree of external legitimacy and even more aid.[35]

ENTER AND EXIT MILITARY GOVERNMENT: CONTEXT, CHOICE, AND CONTENTION (1999–2007)

The proximate roots of the current state of civil–military relations can be traced to the military government of General Zia. The 1977 coup, which brought him to power, ended the elected PPP government of Prime Minister Zulfiqar Ali Bhutto (1971–1977). Having co-opted and/or divided opposition to his rule and ruthlessly contained antiregime mobilization by the PPP-led Movement for the Restoration of Democracy (MRD), Zia transformed the country's first democratically crafted parliamentary constitution of 1973 into a semi-presidential hybrid, with a powerful president and a weakened prime minister (PM) to guarantee the military's continuing tutelage of elected government after he gradually civilianized his regime in the early 1980s. One of the key prerogatives acquired by the military president was the power to appoint military service chiefs previously reserved for the PM. An even more politically far-reaching prerogative concerned presidential decree powers under Article 58(2)B of the constitution, which empowered the president to arbitrarily sack civilian governments. After Zia's death in a plane crash in 1988, the military institution decided to extricate ostensibly due to the high institutional cost to the military of holding on to government after a decade of military rule.[36] But facing a divided and weakened opposition, the military was able to preserve Article 58(2)B and presidential control over top military appointments.

In the decade that followed the transition from authoritarian rule, the military used presidential decrees to prematurely unseat three elected governments—two belonging to the PPP led by Benazir Bhutto (1988–1990, 1993–1996) and the third to Nawaz Sharif's right-of-center Pakistan Muslim League government (PML-N, 1990–1993)—mainly when they challenged military prerogatives. Upon assuming power with a two-thirds majority in 1997, the Parliament led by Sharif's PML-N abolished the presidential coup prerogative and reappropriated the power to appoint military service chiefs to the PM. In October 1999, the military under General Pervez Musharraf seized power when Sharif tried to fire the general in the wake of civil–military tensions over the military-initiated Kargil war with India.

After overthrowing the civilian government, Musharraf appointed himself as "chief executive" of the country, created a military-dominated National Security Council (NSC), and initiated a politically motivated "accountability" drive to target the regime's opponents, especially the PML-N. Like his military predecessors, Musharraf had his coup legitimized by the Supreme Court under the "doctrine of state necessity," albeit subject to a three-year grace period for holding parliamentary elections.[37]

Facing legitimacy problems inherent to authoritarian regimes, Musharraf initiated a process of gradual political liberalization: relaxing curbs on civil liberties, opening up private broadcast media, and allowing limited political pluralism. In April 2002, he organized a fraudulent referendum to appoint himself as president for five years. In the meantime, the military ISI created a new right-wing political party, the Pakistan Muslim League (Quaid-e-Azam; PML-Q), to act as the civilian face of the military government. The PML-Q mainly comprised disaffected, coerced, or bribed defectors from the PML-N. It also facilitated the creation of the Muttahida Majlis-e Amal (MMA, or United Action Front), an alliance of six Islamist parties of different theological and sectarian persuasions, to further squeeze the PML-N's right-of-center vote. No less important, the regime decreed electoral rules to marginalize the opposition leadership, such as the Sharif and Bhutto-specific clause barring anyone from holding the office of prime minister more than twice. It finally held a manipulated parliamentary election in October 2002, which brought the PML-Q to power at the center, and in the largest Punjab Province, thereby allowing the military government to cloak itself in the universally respectable veneer of democracy.[38] With the help of the PML-Q and its Islamists allies in Parliament, Musharraf amended the constitution in 2003 to revive presidential coup powers, as well as presidential authority to appoint high state officials, including military service chiefs.

But liberalization turned out, as it often does, to be a dangerous gamble. Once an authoritarian regime permits even limited contestation, it sends out the signal to society that the "costs of collective action" are no longer high.[39] As a result, previously barricaded arenas of opposition become available for contestation, especially if "exemplary individuals" were willing to probe the boundaries of the regime's tolerance. And here the strategic choices and symbolic leadership provided by the Chief Justice of the Supreme Court, Iftikhar Muhammad Chaudhry, helped unite and galvanize opposition in both civil and political society.[40]

Pakistan's courts have typically condoned military interventions in the past, thereby endowing legitimacy on successive authoritarian regimes and indirectly aiding the endurance of military prerogatives. Chaudhry himself was part of the twelve-member bench of the Supreme Court that legalized Musharraf's coup in May 2000 and was a member of several others that validated Musharraf's extraconstitutional actions, including his presidential referendum and his retention of the post of army chief during his first presidential term. However, this judicial appeasement began to unravel when Justice Chaudhry was appointed to the country's top judicial post in 2005. Buoyed by support from the newly independent media, the Chaudhry court began to challenge the military government through public interest litigation, intervening to regulate commodity prices, canceling corrupt public sector privatization contracts, and pursuing the cases of hundreds of "disappeared" persons, mostly terror suspects illegally detained by military intelligence agencies since Pakistan joined the U.S.-led war on terrorism in 2001.

In 2007, Musharraf's five-year presidential term was set to expire.[41] No longer certain that the Supreme Court would endorse him as president in uniform, the general and his intelligence chiefs made an ill-fated attempt in March 2007 to fire Justice Chaudhry for alleged misuse of authority.[42] The move sparked countrywide contentious mobilization led by the Supreme Court Bar against what it termed the government's assault on judicial independence. The protests were focused on the narrow goal of restoring the Chief Justice, but they also tapped into latent political resentment against the military-led government, mobilizing broader opposition from the media, rights organizations, and political parties.[43] To the distress of General Musharraf, the Supreme Court rejected the charges against Chaudhry and restored him to office in June 2007.

Because he could not easily mend fences with Sharif, whom he had exiled to Saudi Arabia in 2000, Musharraf had made efforts to reach out to the self-exiled former premiere and PPP leader, Benazir Bhutto. But facing judicial activism and pressure from civil society added urgency to his need for striking a power-sharing pact with her party. As the most popular and "moderate" politician of the country, Bhutto was also the choice of the United States (and the United Kingdom) for a civilian partner in Pakistan who could salvage Musharraf by broadening the popular base of his regime.[44] Bhutto's main motivation for engaging the regime was to end her decade-long political exile and return to power. She placed several key preconditions on the table: Musharraf's retirement as army chief, free and fair elections, the lifting of the Bhutto (and, by default, Nawaz Sharif) specific ban on seeking a third prime ministerial term, and, most important, the removal of "politically motivated" corruption charges against her and her spouse, Asif Ali Zardari.

Direct meetings between Bhutto and Musharraf, followed by several rounds of talks between their trusted aides—including then Director General of the ISI (DG-ISI) General Ashfaq Pervez Kayani on behalf of the military government—reportedly resulted in a "deal" in October 2007, under which the PPP agreed to support Musharraf's reelection as president in return for a retraction of the corruption cases and the removal of the third-term ban on her election as prime minister.[45] Although he did not remove the bar on her reelection, Musharraf agreed to rescind the corruption charges and enacted an amnesty law, the National Reconciliation Ordinance (NRO), in the same month, which paved the way for Bhutto's return. He then moved to secure a second presidential term by a controversial parliamentary vote with the PPP's help.[46]

However, acting on petitions, the court suspended the NRO and stayed the presidential election results until it could make a final decision about Musharraf's eligibility for reelection as a president-in-uniform. Expecting an adverse ruling on his reelection bid, Musharraf suspended the constitution, declared a state of emergency on November 3, 2007, and put Chaudhry and other defiant judges under house arrest. Backed by the military high command, the general armed himself with a new authoritarian constitution, the Provisional Constitutional Order (PCO), to purge the courts.[47] He then packed the Supreme Court with loyalist judges and had them legalize his reelection.

Musharraf's "second coup" hastened the military government's demise by galvanizing a broader civilian opposition in both political and civil society, comprising lawyers, students, academics, journalists, activists, opposition parties, and ordinary citizens. In response, the government cracked down, arresting thousands of protesters and gagging the media. The regime's actions made it politically difficult for Bhutto to continue her cooperation with Musharraf, and she was obliged to demand his resignation, a step that temporarily coalesced the opposition by bringing the PPP and the PML-N closer together.[48]

Although the general staff had formally supported the emergency,[49] another five years of Musharraf's "military" presidency did not have a strong constituency among members of the officer corps, already demoralized by fighting "Washington's" war on terror on their own soil. Jealously protective of its institutional prestige and status, now sullied by its close association with a detested and degraded military ruler, the military institution withheld its active support from Musharraf. Responding to pressure from the middle ranking and junior officers, the corps commanders reportedly decided that they could "no longer stand by Musharraf and provide him institutional cover," when he had become the main target of collective rage in political and civil society.[50] Although the antiregime protest movement did not constitute a "people's power" insurrection that could have forced the military's hand, the uniformed military generally avoided direct involvement in repression because of the potentially adverse effects on its reputation.

The Bush administration also insisted that Musharraf relinquish his uniform and hold elections.[51] Having lost the crucial backing of his commanders and reeling under domestic and external pressure, the general finally resigned his army post in November 2007, ended the emergency in December of the same year, and ultimately organized parliamentary elections in February 2008. Although Bhutto was murdered during the election campaign, the PPP, under her widower, Asif Ali Zardari, won a plurality of seats in the National Assembly (the lower house of Parliament) and formed a short-lived coalition government with the PML-N, both at the center and in the largest and politically most important Punjab Province. The two parties also cooperated in Parliament to start impeachment proceedings against the civilian President Musharraf for "high treason," which finally pushed him out of office in August 2008.

It is important to discuss the nature and structure of the Musharraf-led authoritarian regime to understand how the institutional military was able to extricate without having to compromise on its expansive prerogatives. The 1999 coup, which brought the military to power, was an institutional act, carried out by the military institution in response to perceived threats to military integrity posed by the then prime minister Sharif's actions. Thus, the authoritarian government was clearly military in its origins. But its nature and structure were relatively less militarized than those of the well-known military governments in the Southern Cone of Latin America and even the previous military government of General Zia. Although as army chief of staff Musharraf was the indisputable head of both the military government and the military institution, he did not declare martial law like Zia (or even Ayub) in part because of the reduced acceptability and increased diplomatic and financial costs of military rule in the post–Cold War international environment.

In his capacity as chief martial law administrator, Zia had formally established an advisory council comprising both members of the top brass and civilians. Some army corps commanders held cabinet-level appointments while others acted simultaneously as provincial governors.[52] The military was also hierarchically involved in executive and judicial functions through special military courts and geographically organized martial law administrations. In contrast, the military had no direct role in the cabinet or any other top public office in the Musharraf period. This structural separation between the two was also evident in the level of military involvement at the lower levels of government. For instance, even though over a thousand individual military officers were seconded to different agencies and levels in the civil bureaucracy,[53] the hierarchical military did not assume any direct role in day-to-day governing, with the exception of the "army monitoring teams" tasked with a brief watchdog role over civilian agencies after the coup.[54] However, much like the previous military governments of Ayub and Zia, the bulk of the officer corps was engaged in performing purely military duties and thus out of the public gaze, even during the height of the antigovernment mobilization in 2007.

There was also a historical factor at play. To a considerable degree, the military's widely accepted (mainly in the Punjab, the center of both political and military power) external mission against India has insulated it from any potential challenges to its control over organizational structure and functions once it has left power. The clear and present external threat has long provided the Pakistan army with an important source of the institutional cohesion needed to avoid the factionalism that typically engulfs politicized militaries during transitions.[55]

CIVIL–MILITARY POLITICS AFTER THE EXTRICATION

Keen to wipe off the stain of the military government from the military institution, Chief of Staff General Kayani, who replaced Musharraf in that post in November 2007, pledged to keep the military away from politics.

Toward this end, he made several "democratic" overtures. He reportedly banned officers from keeping contact with politicians and announced the recall of active-duty personnel from the bureaucracy. The relative success of the two main opposition parties, the PPP and the PML-N, in the 2008 parliamentary elections shows that the military institution, especially the ISI, generally did not rig the ballot in favor of the PML-Q as it had done in 2002. Press reports also indicated that the high command closed down the ISI's notorious "political" wing implicated in rigging elections and blackmailing and/or bribing politicians in the past.[56] All these steps led some observers to contrast Musharraf's political behavior to General Kayani's apolitical professionalism.[57]

Somewhat unexpectedly, the military also did not contest changes in the constitution that were designed to erode its tutelage of government. For instance, the PPP-led government decided to formally abolish the defunct NSC in 2009,[58] which sought to "bring the military [in the government] to keep them out," as Musharraf described it.[59] The most significant democratic reform was the eighteenth constitutional amendment. Signed into law in April 2010 with a unanimous parliamentary vote, the amendment restored the constitution to its parliamentary essence by diminishing the powers of the president, including the reassignment of presidential authority to appoint military service chiefs, to the elected chief executive. Most crucially, it abolished the president's "coup" powers under Article 58(2)B, thereby depriving the military of an important constitutional tool for securing its interests. Similarly, the government and the opposition have collaborated in reforming electoral institutions and processes to make the ballot more credible and transparent. In particular, a bipartisan parliamentary committee will appoint the chief election commissioner and the four members of the Election Commission from a list provided by the prime minister and the leader of the opposition in the national assembly (the appointments were previously a presidential prerogative). A similar procedure will govern the appointment of the caretaker prime minster.[60]

The military's studied silence over these far-reaching reforms masked a cold cost-benefit calculation. Musharraf-era rules and structures like the NSC were secondary to such first-order organizational priorities as preserving corporate autonomy and de facto influence over national security decision making. The generals tolerated their abolition in part because of the institutional imperative to delink the military from the structures and rules that symbolized the perpetuation of the ancien régime. No less important, the mobilized opposition in political and civil society had demanded an end to military government and a return to competitive elections, with a restoration of the 1973 constitution to its pre-1999 form as a key rallying point. Hence, even if the military had wished to retain a formal seat at the table, it was either too soon or risky after a prolonged period of military government to resist a reform that enjoyed broad political support.

However, the military's "professional" pose masks deeper institutionally held assumptions about the desirability of high military prerogatives and military tutelage of government. The high command continues to consider drastic military solutions to political crises as legitimate, albeit as "temporary" measures. Even as he projected himself as a democrat, Kayani believed that "military interventions are sometimes necessary to maintain Pakistan's stability." In fact, he compared coups to "temporary bypasses that are created when a bridge collapses on democracy's highway. After the bridge is repaired, then there's no longer any need for the detour."[61] The military's belief in the appropriateness of interventions is particularly revealed during crises, such as the political deadlock over the deposed judges in February–March 2009. Although the PPP government had released the judges from house arrest immediately after assuming power, it was reluctant to reinstate Chief Justice Iftikhar Chaudhry because of his known opposition to the NRO. Still, President Zardari had assured his main coalition partner, the PML-N, that his government would restore the judges, which was a key plank of that party's 2008 election campaign. However, Zardari reneged (first in May and again in August 2008), fearing that the Chaudhry-led court would repeal the corruption amnesty.

In August 2008, the PML-N formally left the coalition government.[62] With the government stalling on the judges' issue, the leadership of the lawyers' movement decided to march on Islamabad and hold a *dharna* (sit-in) before Parliament on the second anniversary of the sacking of Justice Chaudhry (March 9, 2007). The PML-N joined hands with the lawyers, as did other parties, including the Jama'at-e-Islami (JI) and the Pakistan Tehreeke Insaaf (PTI, or the Pakistan Movement for Justice).[63] In a preemptive strike, Zardari used a court ruling disqualifying the Punjab chief minister and Sharif's brother, Shehbaz Sharif, from holding electoral office to dismiss his government and impose governor's rule in the province.[64] To repair what was seemingly a breaking of the "bridge of democracy,"[65] General Kayani intervened and reportedly threatened to implement the "minus-one formula," that is, the ouster of President Zardari while keeping the rest of the government intact.[66] Under army and opposition pressure, the PPP government finally relented and reinstated the Chaudhry court on March 16, 2009.

Such "near coups" introduced enough uncertainty about the military's intentions to keep the PPP government looking over its shoulders. Ultimately, governing in the shadows of a military having high prerogatives and a demonstrated ability to contest civilian authority, the elected leadership has chosen not to exercise certain prerogatives either due to a lack of capacity or because it has simply abdicated responsibility in anticipation of military noncompliance. For example, in 2008, the government placed all the "law enforcement agencies" under the operational command of the Chief of Army Staff (COAS) or fighting militancy, designating him as the "principal" for deciding "the quantum, composition and positioning of military efforts."[67]

Critics have rightly questioned the government's ostensibly poor governance performance.[68] But it is important to acknowledge that the democratically elected leadership's ability to provide sound government was impaired by pernicious authoritarian legacies. In addition to high military prerogatives, it also had to contend with Musharraf's continuation as president until August 2008; economic crises (including severe energy and food shortages), the ethnic conflict in Baluchistan, and the Taliban insurgency in the FATA; as well as more deeply seated structural problems, including high military spending, low levels of taxation, high indebtedness, weak civilian administrative capacity, and pervasive poverty. Additionally, the PPP government won only a thin parliamentary majority, making it dependent on fickle coalition politics.

In fact, unlike the civil–military "troika" model of the 1990s (i.e., when the prime minister was usually pitched against the president and the army), executive–military interaction quickly resolved into a "dyarchy" between the army led by General Kayani and the PPP-led coalition governments led by Prime Ministers Yusuf Raza Gilani (2008–2012) and Raja Pervez Ashraf (2012–2013), de facto controlled by President Zardari in his capacity as party cochair.

However, the Supreme Court led by Justice Chaudhry emerged as a third institutional power, deriving its claims to authority and legitimacy from the lawyers' movement. For instance, the Chaudhry court struck down the NRO as unconstitutional in December 2009 and ordered Prime Minister Gilani to petition Swiss authorities to resume inquiry into a corruption case involving the president.[69] In July 2012, the judges convicted Gilani for contempt of court, thereby disqualifying him from public office and consequently unseating him as prime minister.[70]

Insofar as democratic consolidation rests on the acceptance of democracy as the only game in town by all politically significant actors, political parties have a key role. In general, political parties appear united on the need for unfettered parliamentary democracy, as reflected in the Eighteenth

Amendment. For the most part, they have behaved in a democratically loyal fashion, keeping their opposition within the bounds of constitutional procedure. But the utopia of a democracy properly "guided" by the military continues to have currency among some politicians (as well as members of the media and civil society). For instance, in 2011, top leaders of the then opposition PML-N proposed the integration of the military into national decision making.[71] The ethnic Karachi-based Muttahida Qaumi Movement (MQM) went a step further, inviting the generals to seize power and salvage Pakistan from corruption.[72] In August 2013, its leader, Altaf Hussain, demanded that the army take control of Karachi's administration.[73] However, in a positive development, most other parties in Sindh, including the PML-N, PTI, and JI, rejected the proposal on the grounds that only civilians should handle civilian matters.[74]

The real test of politicians' loyalty to the democratic process was the May 11, 2013, elections, which marked the first transition from one democratically elected government that had completed its tenure to another. It is true that an orchestrated campaign of violence by the Taliban in the run-up to the elections against "pro-American," secular parties like the Awami National Party (ANP), the MQM, and the PPP tilted the playing field in favor of more conservative parties, like the PML-N. Allegations of localized voter fraud on polling day also marred the balloting process. Despite these problems, the Election Commission was able to hold an election generally considered free and fair by international observers.[75]

The PML-N won a simple majority of seats in the National Assembly and a two-thirds majority in the Punjab assembly, thereby forming governments in the center and the Punjab. Notably, almost all political parties accepted the election results. And unlike the past, when parties in control of the federal government would typically try to prevent the opposition from forming provincial governments, the PML-N allowed the PTI and Baluch nationalist parties to form their own governments in Khyber Pakhtunkhwa and Baluchistan. The dyarchical civil–military arrangement also continues under the Sharif government, although the new president, Mamnoon Hussain, who replaced Zardari in September 2013, is a PML-N loyalist.

As discussed in the following section, military prerogatives have curtailed the autonomy of the PPP government since 2008, and they act as an independent source of democratic weakness by virtue of the undue power they endow on the military. Similarly, military contestation—often amplified through the mobilization of influential actors in the media and the judiciary—generates policy conflict and undermines the authority and credibility of the government because it indicates the lack of regime autonomy.[76]

In sum, the two dimensions combine to limit the government's ability to exercise sovereign power and erode the prospects of the institutional consolidation of democracy.

INSTITUTIONAL AUTONOMY

As a corporate organization, the military seeks to enhance internal control and limit external interference. However, the military's prerogatives over its internal structure and functions limit the scope for the establishment of civilian supremacy over the armed forces. After the transition, the military has sought to maintain and, in some cases, even increase control over military promotions and appointments. For instance, General Kayani has unilaterally awarded service extensions to several general officers beyond the age of retirement, including the last Director General of the ISI, Lieutenant General Shuja Pasha (2007–2012). In 2010, he also secured an unparalleled three-year extension of his tenure as army chief of staff, clearly eroding the government's prerogative to appoint an army chief of its own choice.[77]

In July 2008, the military vetoed the government's decision to extend civilian control over the ISI by placing it under the "operational, financial and administrative control" of the interior ministry. But the military virtually forced it to backtrack within hours of the official notification, revealing the limits it can impose on civilian authority.[78]

AUTONOMY FROM EXECUTIVE CONTROL AND
PARLIAMENTARY OVERSIGHT

Although the PM is the country's chief executive, de facto control over the three armed services (army, air force, and navy) rests with their respective service chiefs and senior commanders. The authority to appoint military service chiefs is the constitutional prerogative of the PM, but its de facto exercise is also curtailed because the military decides the "pool" of candidates to be considered for the job. Given that choosing the COAS is one of the few levers of civilian authority over the army, past prime ministers have sought to appoint army chiefs based on their perceived loyalty. Sharif was faced with the decision to appoint Kayani's successor upon the latter's retirement in November 2013. Although Sharif had declared his intent to choose a new COAS on the basis of seniority and merit,[79] it would not be surprising if he settled for a general on the basis of his perceived political leanings.[80]

Parliamentary oversight is an established principle for exercising democratic civilian control over the military. In Pakistan, Parliamentary Standing Committees on Defense (the National Assembly and the Senate has one each) are technically empowered to examine defense budgets, administration, and policies. However, given the history of military dominance and a strictly enforced tradition of secrecy, these committees have focused mainly on politically nonsensitive issues, such as irregularities in the civil aviation authority and military housing. Besides, senior military officers typically avoid appearing before these committees. Instead, the army invites (and expects) members of Parliament to come to the general headquarters for briefings.[81]

In contrast to the ineffective standing committees, Pakistani legislators have tried to reduce military prerogatives over the country's defense policy by creating a special Parliamentary Committee on National Security (PCNS) to provide them with "guidelines" and "periodic reviews" on important security policies, especially counterterrorism.[82] The committee set a good precedent when it refused to attend a military briefing on foreign policy at army headquarters and publicly reminded the army that it is subservient to Parliament, not vice versa.[83] After a U.S. helicopter attack on Salala, Mohmand Agency, killed twenty-four Pakistani soldiers in November 2011 and prompted Pakistan to halt North Atlantic Treaty Organization (NATO) supply lines, the PCNS took a proactive stance in drafting the new rules of engagement with the United States and NATO, recommending greater transparency in military dealings between the two states, the parliamentary approval of all foreign military agreements, an end to U.S. drone strikes against Al Qaeda and Taliban militants because of civilian casualties, and the denial of Pakistani territory to such militants. With minor changes, a joint sitting of the Parliament approved these policy guidelines, but their implementation remains dependent on military consent.

The undetected May 2, 2011, U.S. Special Forces raid in Abbottabad that killed Osama bin Laden badly tarnished the military institution's public reputation. In fact, the military's humiliation offered a rare opportunity for the affirmation of civilian control, for instance, by firing the top military leadership. However, the military deftly deflected responsibility by taking its case to Parliament. Senior military officials, including the DG-ISI Lieutenant General Pasha and deputy chief of the air force, appeared before a special joint parliamentary session. Pasha admitted that the agency's failure to detect bin Laden's presence in Pakistan was an "intelligence lapse." Nevertheless, he also used the occasion to stir anti-American sentiments by blaming the United States for carrying out a "sting operation" on an ally.[84] The strategy worked. Instead of calling the military to account, the joint session strongly condemned U.S. unilateral actions on Pakistani territory and reposed "full confidence in the defense forces . . . in safeguarding Pakistan's sovereignty, independence and territorial integrity and in overcoming any challenge to security."[85]

INDIA POLICY

The military has a low threshold of tolerance for what it considers civilian interference in its foreign policy prerogatives, such as Pakistan's India policy. In the past, democratic governments of both the PPP and the PML-N have sought to ease tensions and normalize trade with India if only to reduce the military's domestic power and monopoly over national security. In November 2011, the PPP-led cabinet decided, in principle, to grant India the status of most favored nation after a series of talks between the commerce ministers of each country. However, the military reportedly pressured the government to "slow track" the process on the grounds that its trade policy was out of sync with security policy. [86]

Like the PPP, the Sharif government has sought to normalize bilateral relations with India, including trade liberalization, much to the chagrin of the military, which continues to pursue a "Kashmir first" approach in dealing with its archenemy. For instance, despite increased tensions along the Line of Control in Kashmir in July and August 2013, Sharif, who has long been committed to regional conflict reduction, called for a bold foreign policy review in August 2013 focused on Pakistan's eastern neighbor, as a way of freeing up resources for economic development.[87] However, the government backtracked in the face of military resistance.[88]

Initially, Sharif also sought to exercise greater control over national security policymaking in general. However, his rhetoric of civilian supremacy is matched only by his government's pragmatic accommodation of military demands and interests. For instance, it has reconstituted the Defense Committee of the Cabinet (DCC)[89] into a broader Cabinet Committee on National Security (CCNS) with a broader ambit to facilitate civil–military coordination in light of Pakistan's complex internal and external security environment. Chaired by the prime minister, the CCNS will include the ministers of foreign affairs, defense, interior, and finance, as well as the Chairman Joint Chiefs of Staff Committee (CJCSC) and the three service chiefs. The committee "will formulate a national security policy that will become the guiding framework for its subsidiary policies—defence policy, foreign policy, internal security policy, and other policies affecting national security."[90] Unlike the DCC, to which the military chiefs were invited when needed, the CCNS will have them as permanent members.[91] Sharif's advisor on national security and foreign affairs, Sartaj Aziz, the principal civilian architect of the new committee, suggests that this formal integration of the military into national defense policymaking will help enhance coordination and reduce misperceptions between civilians and the military.[92] In reality, though, Sharif's government seems to have fulfilled the military's long-standing preference for institutionalizing its de facto dominance over defense policy by making the military service chiefs members of a committee of the cabinet.

DEFENSE ADMINISTRATION AND BUDGETS

The Ministry of Defense (MoD), headed by a civilian minister, is formally responsible for the policy and administrative matters related to the three armed forces.[93] As in other government ministries, a secretary acts as the chief administrative and accounting officer. In addition, a special division of the Finance Ministry performs monitoring of military expenditures to ensure compliance with budgetary rules and regulations. In reality, civilian oversight is more nominal than real.[94] No policy that affects the military can be implemented without its consent. Moreover, active-duty (and retired) military officials typically occupy strategic policy positions in the MoD, thus facilitating the military's formal control over defense management. For example, the current defense secretary is a former lieutenant general, as was his predecessor. An additional secretary heads each of the three main wings of the ministry that deal with policy matters related to the army, air force, and navy, as well as important interservices organizations, such as the ISI and the Inter-Services Public Relations (ISPR). At present, all three secretaries are serving military officers of the rank of major general or equivalent.[95] The military occupation of the MoD goes beyond the question of civilian capacity and reflects the assumption that civilians cannot be trusted with "sensitive" matters and that only uniformed men have the expertise to manage military affairs.[96]

In terms of budgetary allocations, the military has made nominal concessions, since 2008, by allowing the disclosure of an itemized annual budget before Parliament.[97] Yet it has evaded any real accountability on the grounds that the disclosure of "sensitive" budgetary matters will undermine national security by exposing critical information to "enemy agents." It has also advised the government to "streamline" wasteful civilian expenditures rather than questioning the military budget.[98]

ROLE IN INTELLIGENCE

The generals exercise exclusive control over intelligence and counterintelligence, mainly through the ISI. Although the ISI de jure reports to the PM, it is essentially a military intelligence organization officered by active-duty armed forces officers and headed by a three-star army lieutenant general (designated as director general) whose de facto boss is the army chief. In other words, the ISI operates under the army's chain of command.

Since the 1980s, when it acted as a conduit for Central Intelligence Agency (CIA) and Saudi money and weaponry to the Afghan mujahideen fighting the Soviets, the agency has evolved into a formidable and feared military organization with deep involvement in politics and policy, which has "eroded the rule of law" and "distorted civil-military relations."[99] Besides meddling in politics on behalf of the army high command, the agency has encroached on civilian law enforcement and investigation functions. For instance, the ISI conducted its own parallel inquiry into the assassination of Benazir Bhutto and kept crucial evidence hidden from civilian investigators. Even more seriously, it undermined the investigation by publicly releasing an allegedly intercepted communication implicating the then head of the Pakistani faction of the Taliban (known as the Tehrik-e Taliban Pakistan or TTP), Baitullah Mehsud.[100]

The ISI also spearheads the military's pursuit of "strategic depth" against India by waging asymmetric warfare through militant proxies. Even as the military fights some TTP factions in South Waziristan and other tribal agencies, the ISI continues to provide the "good" Afghan Taliban with sanctuary and logistical support for fighting coalition troops in Afghanistan. According to official figures, suicide bombings and other terrorist attacks have claimed the lives of more than 40,000 Pakistanis, not including the deaths of an estimated 2,000 security forces personnel.[101] In 2009, militants successfully attacked and infiltrated the heavily guarded army general headquarters, killing eleven military officials and taking over three dozen hostages.[102] Despite the clear negative feedback effects of its selective counterterrorism policies, as well as international pressure and isolation, the military's internal discourse[103] and actions reveal that it continues to believe in the utility of using militancy as a tool of foreign policy. The ISI-backed Haqqani network's attack on the U.S. embassy in Kabul in September 2011 heightened tensions between the two countries as the Obama administration stepped up pressure on Pakistan to eliminate the group's sanctuaries in North Waziristan.[104] And even as then President Zardari pledged to take action against the Haqqanis,[105] the army demurred on the grounds that its troops were stretched thin by existing deployments in the FATA.

After years of stalling to protect its strategic assets, the Pakistan military finally launched an offensive, code-named Zarbe Azb (or the strike of the Azb, the Prophet Mohammad's sword) in June 2014. The immediate trigger for the operation was the daring June 8 terrorist raid on Pakistan's main international airport in Karachi reportedly carried out by the Islamic Movement of Uzbekistan on behalf of the TTP. It is still not entirely clear what Pakistan hopes to achieve from this latest assault, said to involve some 25,000–30,000 ground troops, artillery, tanks, and fighter aircraft. The military's main target appears to be the Pakistani Taliban and Uzbek and other foreign militants, even though it has vowed to "eliminate" all terrorist groups holed up in the area "regardless of hue and color along with their sanctuaries."[106] Aside from reports that the Haqqanis were relocated to the adjoining Kurram Agency,[107] the army's local commander tellingly admitted that the militant leadership had already escaped the area in anticipation of the military assault.[108]

HARNESSING THE MEDIA AND THE JUDICIARY

Beyond contesting civilian policy initiatives or simply "shirking," the military remonstrates through the "creative management" of public opinion.[109] The military has long been concerned with maintaining its public image and with the role the media can play in national security management.[110] Adapting to the growing power of the media in a globalizing world and wary of domestic and external concerns about the restriction of civil liberties under authoritarianism, the Musharraf military government had extensively liberalized the broadcast news media. At the same time, the military expanded the ISPR, its media branch, to increase its institutional capacity to more effectively police both electronic and print media.[111] The ISPR vigilantly controls journalists' access to "sensitive" defense information, such as the military's counterinsurgency operations in the FATA. In addition, the ISI runs its own powerful "Information Management Wing," which metes out both punishments and rewards. In recent years, the agency has been widely accused of intimidating and blackmailing journalists, while cajoling others through both monetary incentives and "exclusive" stories to sway public opinion against designated internal and external foes. For instance, after the CIA operative Raymond Davis was arrested in Lahore for killing two Pakistanis in January 2011, the ISI leaked the names of fifty-five American "spies" to show how the PPP government's lax visa policy had made it possible for the CIA to expand its network within Pakistan.[112] It also deliberately leaked the name of the CIA station chief in Pakistan to settle scores with the Americans for the humiliation they had caused it with the raid that killed bin Laden.[113]

That highly embarrassing aerial intrusion and an audacious May 22 militant attack on a heavily fortified naval base in the port city of Karachi temporarily strained the patron–client relationship between the military and prominent pro-military sections of the media. Some "friendly" journalists launched unexpected criticism of the military for its disastrous policies of nurturing militants and its transparent incompetence despite receiving a large share of the national budget.[114] In turn, the military publicly warned its critics to stop "trying to deliberately run down the Armed Forces and the Army in particular" and threatened "to put an end" to "any effort to create divisions between important institutions of the country."[115] At least in one case, the generals seem to have lived up to their words. On May 29, 2011, the ISI allegedly abducted, tortured, and brutally murdered the Pakistani journalist Saleem Shehzad, just a day after he exposed links between Al Qaeda and navy personnel.[116] Similarly, on April 19, 2014, unknown gunmen shot Hamid Mir, a well-known journalist and news anchor at the popular Geo TV, in the port city of Karachi. Before the attack, Mir had informed his family and close associates that the ISI was plotting to assassinate him and that the agency should be held responsible if he was harmed. After Geo TV hurriedly broadcast the allegations, splashing a picture of the DG-ISI Lieutenant General Zaheerul Islam Abbassi across TV screens in Pakistan for hours, the ISI had Pakistan's Defense Ministry petition the Pakistan Electronic Media Regulatory Authority (PEMRA), the country's electronic media regulator, to revoke Geo TV's transmission license and initiate criminal charges against its management for defaming the state. In addition, ISI-backed militant organizations, such as the Jamaat-ut-Dawa, staged angry protests, which competitor pro-military media organizations then broadcast along with talk shows segments questioning the patriotism of Mir and Geo TV. Ultimately, Geo and its affiliated newspapers were banned from military bases and units,[117] and the ISI reportedly pressured cable TV operators around the country to block the channel's transmission.

Another notable example of the military's media manipulation was its handling of the public debate surrounding the Kerry-Lugar-Berman Bill, signed into law by President Barack Obama as the Enhanced Partnership Act of 2009, which offers Pakistan $1.5 billion annually in nonmilitary, developmental U.S. aid for five years. While the civilian government welcomed the aid, the military joined right-wing opposition parties and publicly expressed its outrage[118] over "critical provisions [that] were almost entirely directed against the Army," particularly the conditioning of American military assistance on certification by the U.S. secretary of state that the military was operating under civilian control and keeping out of political and judicial processes.[119] The military also reportedly encouraged TV talk show anchors to mobilize public opinion against the law by presenting it as a blatant example of U.S. interference in Pakistan's internal matters, which it could then use to pressure the Americans into modifying the legislation.[120] Thus, cable news channels concocted conspiracy theories, painting the bill as part of America's sinister design to weaken the country's security institutions as a way of depriving it of nuclear weapons. While openly praising the military for its principled stand against the Americans, many in the media targeted the PPP government, portraying it as an American stooge out to sell the country's honor.[121]

Beyond trying to control the popular media, the military has used judicial activism to preserve or enhance its institutional prerogatives over national security. General Kayani hurriedly called an "emergency" corps commanders' meeting and publicized the appointment of a new head of the 111 Brigade, the army unit that executes military coups, to signal that a coup might be in the offing. Before the two sides could reach the brink, the civilian government reportedly backed down.

The main goal of the contentious antiregime mobilization that facilitated Musharraf's demise was the restoration of the sacked judges of the superior judiciary. The Chaudhry-led court's triumphant return has endowed it with the moral and legal authority to assert its autonomy and power. In addition to media manipulation, the military has sought to harness judicial activism to protect "national security" from threats posed by the political leadership. This strategy was exemplified by the so-called Memogate affair, in which Mansoor Ijaz, a U.S. businessman of Pakistani origin, alleged in a *Financial Times* op-ed that the PPP government had sought his assistance in seeking U.S. help to avert a military coup in the wake of the bin Laden killing.[122] The alleged memorandum, requesting American intervention, was ostensibly written by Pakistan's then ambassador to the United States and Zardari confidante Hussain Haqqani, who had played an instrumental role in the Kerry-Lugar aid. In return, the government pledged to appoint a new "U.S.-friendly" national security team, abolish the ISI's external operations or "S" wing to stop the agency's support to Islamist militants, and place Pakistan's nuclear program under international safeguards. After establishing the "authenticity" of the memo, the military pressured the government to investigate the matter and hold the ambassador to account.[123]

Denying involvement, the government recalled and fired Haqqani and tasked the PCNS with determining the truth behind the allegations. But the parliamentary inquiry was prematurely undermined when, sensing an opportunity for political gain, the opposition PML-N filed a petition in the Supreme Court seeking a judicial investigation. Heeding the advice of the army and ISI chiefs who defiantly broke ranks with the civilian government by declaring the memo a "national security" threat,[124] the court readily agreed to constitute a judicial inquiry commission.[125] Deeply embarrassed by the army's "unconstitutional" and "illegal" court statements, Prime Minister Gilani responded with a firm warning to the generals that his government would not tolerate a "state within a state."[126] He then fired the MoD secretary, a former general loyal to Kayani, and appointed a trusted civil servant to the post. The army retaliated by reminding the PM that his accusations could have "potentially grievous consequences for the country."[127] As coup rumors began circulating in the media, General Kayani signaled the army's intent to instigate a coup by calling an "emergency" corps commanders' meeting and replacing the commander of the 111 Brigade.[128] Before the two sides could reach the brink, the civilian government reportedly backed down.

"Memogate" serves as a potent recent exemplar of the military's ability to achieve its objectives by adapting its methods to changed political conditions. In the past, the "memo" might have been sufficient to persuade the military to destabilize the government or launch a coup. But with its public reputation badly tarnished by both a long decade of military rule and its more recent professional failures in a context defined by new centers of power, the military has learned to exercise its influence by other means. Despite the military's apparent political weaknesses, however, the civilian government was either unable or unwilling to press its advantage in part because of the very real fear of a coup,[129] as well as judicial challenges to its authority. Amidst media reports that the government was planning to sack the army and ISI chiefs for their illegal actions, the Supreme Court admitted a petition seeking to restrain the civilian government from using its constitutional prerogative to remove the two.[130]

But the judiciary's relationship with the military is not clear-cut. Although it has aligned itself with the military on national security, the judges have also questioned the military's human rights violations. The Chaudhry court's aggressive pursuit of the so-called missing persons was one of the reasons why Musharraf tried to sack Chaudhry in 2007. However, since its restoration in 2009, the court has continued to investigate these cases. In at least one harrowing case, involving eleven illegally detained terror suspects, four of whom died in ISI custody, the court ordered the agency to produce the remaining seven in court, allow them proper medical care, and explain the legal basis of their detention.[131] The judges have also reprimanded the military for its alleged human rights violations in Baluchistan, even specifically demanding an end to all military operations (including the paramilitary Frontier Corps' "kill and dump" operations) and abolishment of the "death squads" run by the ISI and Military Intelligence (MI).[132] However, ISI and MI officials continue to impede judicial inquiries by denying involvement, blaming the disappearances on foreign intelligence agencies, and delaying action on court directives by claiming immunity under the cloak of national security.[133] In May 2012, the military openly defied the court's orders to produce two missing Baluch activists by allegedly dumping their dead bodies on the roadside.[134] Yet the courts have yet to indict or convict even a single military official. Hence, these toothless inquiries have done little to puncture military presumption of impunity. In fact, the military has paid little heed, and senior military officers, including the inspector general of the Frontier Corps, continue to defy judicial authorities.[135]

Under mounting public criticism for selectively targeting civilians, the Supreme Court dug up the 16-year-old Mehran Bank scandal that embarrassed the military. Ultimately, it held the former army chief, General Aslam Beg (retired), and former DG-ISI, Lieutenant General Asad Durrani (retired), responsible for violating the Constitution. However, rather than risk antagonizing the generals, it vaguely instructed the government to take "necessary legal action" against them, while issuing specific instructions that the politicians who took bribes should be interrogated by the Federal Investigation Agency.

SUPRALEGALITY

In a democracy, the military (or other state institutions) cannot be above the rule of law. One important mechanism for reducing the military's power and prerogatives is its integration into the civilian judicial system.[136] The Pakistani military operates outside the purview of civilian law with virtual impunity. It protects its supralegal status through several means.

On the one hand, the military habitually evades accountability to the law where its own members are concerned on the grounds that it has stringent internal mechanisms that obviate the need for external scrutiny.[137] For instance, even though Musharraf had retired from the army, the generals obtained for him a "safe passage" to avoid his possible impeachment by Parliament, which would have further besmirched the military's carefully protected public image as the impeccable guardian of the national interest. The military also initially stonewalled the efforts of the 2010 UN Commission of Inquiry formed to investigate Benazir Bhutto's murder because of the alleged involvement of senior army officers in the Musharraf regime's cover-up of the incident. The commission's final report claims that Major General Nadeem Ijaz Ahmed, the then head of MI, had ordered local police officials to "hose down" the crime scene within two hours of the suicide attack that killed Ms. Bhutto, resulting in the loss of crucial forensic evidence.[138] While Kayani and Pasha eventually met with the head of the commission, the COAS turned down the commission's request that Ahmed appear before it to clear his name. Similarly, in the infamous National Logistics Cell scam that surfaced in 2009, two generals, one major general, and two civilians stood accused of causing a loss of almost Rs 2 billion ($200 million) by investing public moneys in the stock market in violation of government rules.[139] However, Kayani stonewalled civilian investigations by reportedly initiating an internal inquiry. In July 2011, the National Assembly's Public Accounts Committee ultimately referred the case to the National Accountability Bureau, the government's primary anticorruption agency. But Kayani protected the three ex-army officers from civilian scrutiny by taking them "back on the strength" of the army so that they could be tried under the Army Act of 1952.[140]

On the other hand, the military has expanded its own legal prerogatives over civilians, albeit with the government's acquiescence. For instance, through amendments to the Army Act, the military has empowered itself to try civilians in military courts for offenses considered prejudicial to the security of Pakistan.[141] Similarly, the Action in Aid of Civil Power Act (2011) authorizes the military to detain terror suspects indefinitely during its operations in the northwestern border areas (FATA and Provincially Administered Tribal Areas). While the ISI and the MI have no legal powers of arrest, they have allegedly detained, tortured, and even killed suspected Islamic militants[142] with American and British complicity.[143] In Baluchistan, they have resorted to classic "dirty war" tactics against nationalist leaders and rights activists.[144] As one military intelligence official reportedly told an illegally detained Baluch politician, "even if the president or chief justice tells us to release you, we won't. We can torture you, or kill you, or keep you for years at our will. It is only the Army chief and the intelligence chief that we obey."[145]

Growing media focus on military corruption in the wake of scandals involving army officers and the Supreme Court's occasionally aggressive stance toward the military intelligence services have predictably prompted a pushback. Apparently sensing a "sinister campaign" designed to undermine the military leadership and drive a wedge between the soldiers and the officers that would erode institutional cohesion, Kayani issued a sermon-cum-gag order to "all systems" civilians. In it, he obliquely reminded the media that they should desist from maligning the institution of the army for individual lapses that have yet to be proven. Indirectly criticizing the Supreme Court for asserting its supremacy, he went on to question the notion that any one individual or institution has a monopoly on defining the national interest. Ultimately, Kayani warned against "acting in haste," which would weaken the "institutions."[146] The judges took heed. In at least one case, where an ISI brigadier was charged with kidnapping a civilian, the Supreme Court itself restrained the police from executing his arrest orders because "it was a matter of respect of an institution."[147]

However, the Court did challenge the military's presumptions of impunity by ordering the PML-N government to prosecute Musharraf (who returned to Pakistan to contest the May 2013 elections) for suspending the Constitution and imposing emergency rule in November 2007. The government initiated treason charges against the former general president in November 2013, and the three-judge Special Court established for the purpose indicted him in April 2014. Not surprisingly, the military interpreted the trial as an affront to the "dignity" of the institution,[148] openly articulating its opposition when the government did not heed the "advice" of Army Chief General Raheel Sharif (who replaced Kayani in that position in November 2013) to "move on" by letting Musharraf travel abroad for medical treatment.[149] It then sought to destabilize the government by backing and orchestrating public protests led by Imran Khan and the Canada-based pro-military cleric Tahirul Qadri against alleged electoral rigging in the 2013 parliamentary elections.[150]

CONCLUSION

Since yielding power in 2007–2008, the military has seen its broader governmental prerogatives shrink (like the NSC, which was effectively disbanded in 2009), because of the lack of any legitimacy for such a role in the immediate post-authoritarian context. At the same time, it has successfully resisted periodic civilian challenges to its core institutional prerogatives through both active and passive noncompliance, thereby undermining the authority of elected government led by the PPP and, on occasions, threatening its survival. In most conflicts with the PPP government, the military prevailed. The government accepted the military's preferred outcomes to avoid losing power. The military's relationship with the current PML-N government, too, has been fraught with tensions over Sharif's decision to prosecute Musharraf as well as his attempts to seek peace with India.

Brute coercion is less effective for protecting its interests in a post-transitional context defined by a broad-based rejection of military rule as an alternative governing formula and the empowerment of new institutional centers of power and persuasion, such as the higher judiciary and the broadcast media, as a result of both authoritarian liberalization under Musharraf and the contentious politics that facilitated his government's demise. Hence, the military has adapted itself to this new setting by steering the course of change and trying to obstruct unfavorable governmental initiatives by mobilizing the support of judges, journalists, and pro-military politicians like Imran Khan. Overall, the exercise of military prerogatives, especially in the management of national security policy, acted as a major source of civil–military friction between 2008 and 2014.

Military prerogatives are obviously not the only impediment to democracy. In fact, the prospects of continued democratization are complicated by myriad political, economic, and security challenges. Rampant political corruption, poor governance, growing inflation, chronic energy shortages, and almost dwindling essential public services reduce public trust in government and encourage the politics of "system blame." Terrorist violence and Islamist militancy, which afflict both the northwestern border areas and the Punjabi heartland, fuel political instability and weaken the writ of the government. Democracy might have a better chance of consolidation if elected governments can deliver on public expectations, solidly move toward resolving Pakistan's urgent problems, and, together with their oppositions, respect democratic and constitutional norms in both rhetoric and practice. The prospects of sustained democratization will depend to a considerable degree on the extent to which civilian political leaders can demonstrate unity, thereby denying the military the opportunity to exploit political divisions and assume responsibility for the direct or indirect conduct of national affairs. In fact, the military-sponsored political crisis of 2014 exerted a "rally around democracy" effect on opposition parties in Parliament, and they backed Sharif in his government's tussle with the PTI.

However, as I have argued in this chapter, a continuing major source of democratic vulnerability is a military that is only conditionally loyal to democratic rule and continues to exercise nondemocratic prerogatives that restrict the autonomy and authority of democratically elected leaders. In the past, the military has dealt major blows to the process of democratization in Pakistan. It has either directly intervened to overthrow governments or limited the authority and autonomy of elected governments. Military coups and rule have deepened the country's structural problems by providing shortcuts that prevent solutions through the political process. In this context, the transfer of power from one elected government to another in May–June 2013 carried considerable symbolic significance simply because it has never happened before. The real question is whether democratic turnovers will become a norm. For the foreseeable future, it seems likely that Pakistan might be heading toward an unstable equilibrium of its civil–military arrangement in which formal civilian supremacy becomes a euphemism for the military's formal and active participation in politics and national security. In other words, this would constitute a situation in which the military does not seize direct power but formally insinuates its nondemocratic privileges into the functioning of democracy.

NOTES

1. See Samuel J. Valenzuela, "Democratic Consolidation in Post-Transitional Settings: Notion, Process, and Facilitating Conditions," Working Paper No. 150 (University of Notre Dame: Kellogg Institute, December 1990). See also Scott Mainwaring, "Transitions to Democracy and Democratic Consolidation: Theoretical and Comparative Issues," in *Issues in Democratic Consolidation: The New South American Democracies in Comparative Perspective*, ed. Scott Mainwaring, Samuel J. Valenzuela, and Guillermo O' Donnell (Notre Dame: University of Notre Dame Press, 1992), 294–341; Terry L Karl, "Dilemmas of Democratization in Latin America, *Comparative Politics* 23, no. 1 (1991): 1–21.

2. An anonymous reviewer objected to the term "post-authoritarian" because of the "authoritarian behavior and attitudes" permeating the Pakistani state and society. This chapter uses "post-authoritarian" merely to describe the period after the end of military government to distinguish it from the democratically elected government, which does not imply that either the state or society is free of nondemocratic structures or beliefs. But it is important to acknowledge that even the most advanced or established democracies can contain some authoritarian elements in their governments or political culture.

3. The anonymous reviewer also had a problem with the use of terms like "democracy" and "democratic government" as a substitute for civilian rule in Pakistan because of the "authoritarian tendencies" of civilian leaders. Jaffrelot makes a similar point in the introduction to this volume that the difference between elected and nonelected governments is typically a matter of degree because both exhibit authoritarian features. However, for normative and analytical reasons, we would be remiss to lump elected governments with military-authoritarian ones because the former originates in, and is sustained by, a collective "voted" decision, whereas the latter is a product of the application of organized coercion and is defined by the imposition of the will of the generals. Insofar as democracy is a system of government in which universally enfranchised, competitive elections determine "who governs," and elected officials are not de jure accountable to, nor have to share their power with, the administrative institutions of the state (including the military), this chapter uses the terms "democracy," "democratic government," and "civilian rule" interchangeably for governments that meet these procedural minima. Hence, the PPP government (2008–2013) was democratic, but Musharraf's government was authoritarian despite its civilianization between 2002 and 2007.
4. Alfred Stepan, *Rethinking Military Politics: Brazil and the Southern Cone* (Princeton, N.J.: Princeton University Press, 1988), 30–31.
5. Ibid., 93–102.
6. Ibid., 93.
7. Ibid., 68.
8. Chaudhry Mohammad Ali, *The Emergence of Pakistan* (Lahore: Research Society of Pakistan [first impression], 1975), 175.
9. Pakistan's Pashtun-majority North West Frontier Province (presently known as Khyber Pakhtunkhwa) was part of Afghanistan until the British annexed it in the nineteenth century.
10. "Militarization" is used here in the Andreskian sense of the "subservience of the whole society to the needs of the army." See Stanislav Andreski, *Military Organization and Society* (Berkeley: University of California Press, 1968), 184–185.
11. Ayesha Jalal, *The State of Martial Rule: Pakistan's Political Economy of Defense* (Lahore: Sange Meel, 1995), 49–51.
12. Dankwart Rustow, "Transitions to Democracy: Towards a Dynamic Model," *Comparative Politics* 2, no. 3 (April 1970): 350.
13. Christophe Jaffrelot, ed., *Pakistan: Nationalism Without a Nation* (New Delhi: Manohar, 2002).
14. For instance, only one of the 133 Indian Civil Service (ICS)/Indian Political Service (IPS) officers who opted for Pakistan was a Bengali. Moreover, Bengalis were less than 3 percent of the strength of the military, a legacy of the institutionalized colonial policy of military recruitment from among the martial races of North India, such as the Punjabis and the Pashtuns. This colonial policy was left untouched in Pakistan. See Rounaq Jahan, *Pakistan: Failure in National Integration* (New York: Columbia University Press, 1972), 20; Stephen P. Cohen, *The Pakistan Army*, 2nd ed. (Karachi: Oxford University Press, 1998), 44.
15. Yunas Samad, *A Nation in Turmoil: Nationalism and Ethnicity in Pakistan, 1937–1958* (New Delhi: Sage, 1995), 90–125.

16. The demand for Pakistan was articulated primarily by elites from Muslim-minority areas who feared the economic, political, and cultural domination of the Hindus in a united India. The League was formed primarily to preserve the interests of this privileged minority. See D. A. Low, "Provincial Histories," in *The Political Inheritance of Pakistan*, ed. D. A. Low (New York: Macmillan, 1991), 7–8. On the social origins and composition of the Muslim League, see Maya Tudor, *The Promise of Power: The Origins of Democracy in India and Autocracy in Pakistan* (New York: Cambridge University Press, 2013), esp. 56–64, 123–149.

17. For an excellent discussion of the conflicting logics of the "nation-state" and politically salient sociocultural differences and how to reconcile them by crafting "state nations," see Juan Linz, Alfred Stepan, and Yogendra Yadav, *Crafting State Nations: India and Other Multinational Democracies* (Baltimore: Johns Hopkins University Press, 2011), 1–38.

18. Jaffrelot, *Nationalism Without a Nation*, 18.

19. Mohammad Ayub Khan, *Friends, Not Masters: A Political Autobiography* (Karachi: Oxford University Press, 1967), 217. See also Ayub's biography by his chief of staff, Colonel Mohammad Ahmed, *My Chief* (Lahore: Longman's, Green, 1960); Major General Sher Ali Pataudi (retired), *The Story of Soldiering and Politics in India and Pakistan* (Lahore: Lahore Publishers, 1976), esp. 146–161.

20. Major General Fazle Muqeem Khan, *The Story of the Pakistan Army* (Karachi: Oxford University Press, 1963), 159.

21. Ayub Khan, *Friends, Not Masters*, 36.

22. The preeminent American military sociologist Morris Janowitz defined a "civil-military" coalition as one in which the military "expands its political activity and becomes an active political bloc," and civilian executives or parties can "remain in power only because of the passive assent or active assistance" of the armed forces. See his *Military Institutions and Coercion in Developing Countries* (Chicago: University of Chicago Press, 1977), 83.

23. Jahan, *Pakistan: Failure in National Integration*, 53.

24. K. J. Newman, "Pakistan's Preventive Autocracy and Its Causes," *Pacific Affairs* 32, no. 1 (March 1959): 18–33.

25. In Andreski's words, "the devil finds work for the idle hands: the soldiers who have no war to fight or prepare for will be tempted to intervene in politics." *Military Organization and Society*, 202.

26. Samuel Huntington, *The Third Wave: Democratization in the Late Twentieth Century* (Norman: University of Oklahoma Press, 1993), 234; Michael C. Desch, *Civilian Control of the Military: The Changing Security Environment* (Baltimore: Johns Hopkins University Press, 1997), 11–17.

27. This argument is derived from the German social theorist George Simmel, who argued that conflict can be an "integrative force" because it strengthens group consciousness and the awareness of separateness. See his *Conflict*, trans. Kurt H. Wolf (Glencoe, Ill.: Free Press, 1955), 17–18.

28. Desch, *Civilian Control of the Military*.

29. Aqil Shah, *The Army and Democracy: Military Politics in Pakistan* (Cambridge, Mass.: Harvard University Press, 2014).

30. As Lewis Coser pointed out, the unifying effect of conflict with "out groups" may be dependent on some degree of prior internal cohesion and integration. Otherwise, it can result in repression and tyranny. See his *The Functions of Social Conflict* (Glencoe, Ill.: Free Press, 1956), 87–89.

31. Harold D. Lasswell, "The Sino-Japanese Crisis: The Garrison State Versus the Civilian State," *China Quarterly* 11 (1937): 649. See also "The Garrison State," *American Journal of Sociology* 46, no. 4 (January 1941): 455–468.

32. Muhammad Azfar Anwar, Zain Rafique, and Salman Azam Joiya, "Defense Spending–Economic Growth Nexus: A Case Study of Pakistan," *Pakistan Economic and Social Review* 50, no. 2 (Winter 2012): 164.

33. Ayesha Siddiqa, *Military Inc.: Inside Pakistan's Military Economy* (London: Pluto, 2007).

34. Christophe Jaffrelot, "Introduction" in this volume.

35. The United States has provided over $25.9 billion in aid to Pakistan since 2001. Of this, $15.8 billion has been security assistance, including reimbursements for the military's operations in support of the U.S.-led "war on terror." See Susan B. Epstein and K. Alan Kronstadt, "Pakistan: U.S. Foreign Assistance," Congressional Research Service, July 1, 2013, 10, https://www.fas.org/sgp/crs/row/R41856.pdf.

36. Hasan Askari Rizvi, "The Legacy of Military Rule in Pakistan," *Survival* 31, no. 3 (May–June 1989): 256. See also Michael Hoffman, "Military Extrication and Temporary Democracy: The Case of Pakistan," *Democratization* 18, no. 1 (January 2011): 75–99.

37. *Syed Zafar Ali Shah and Others vs. General Pervez Musharraf, Chief Executive of Pakistan* (PLD 2000 S.C. 869).

38. Aqil Shah, "Pakistan's 'Armored' Democracy," *Journal of Democracy* 14, no. 4 (October 2003): 26–40.

39. Guillermo O'Donnell and Phillipe Schmitter, *Transitions from Authoritarian Rule: Tentative Conclusions about Uncertain Democracies* (Baltimore: Johns Hopkins University Press, 1996), 49.

40. The following discussion of government–judiciary conflict is based on Shoaib A. Ghias, "Miscarriage of Chief Justice: Judicial Power and the Legal Complex in Pakistan Under Musharraf," *Law and Social Inquiry* 35, no. 4 (Fall 2010): 985–1022.

41. Under the 1973 constitution, an electoral college comprising both houses of the Parliament and the four provincial assemblies indirectly elects the president.

42. The 1973 constitution bars active-duty civilian or military officials from holding any other public office. Musharraf had secured a one-time waiver from the Supreme Court in 2002.

43. See "Daylong Running Battles Across Capital" and "Opposition Flexes Muscles on Protest Day," *Dawn*, March 17, 2007.

44. Helene Cooper and Mark Mazzetti, "Backstage, U.S. Nurtured Pakistan Rivals' Deal," *New York Times*, October 20, 2007.

45. Benazir Bhutto, *Reconciliation: Islam, Democracy and the West* (New York: HarperCollins, 2008), 225–230. See also "Benazir Defends Deal with Musharraf," *The News*, April 26, 2007.

46. Opposition parties boycotted Musharraf's reelection by the same Parliament that had elected him in 2002, except for the PPP, which abstained from the vote.

47. The PCO mandated that all superior court justices take a new oath pledging unconditional obedience to the regime or lose their office. The almost two-thirds who refused to comply were sacked.

48. During the 1990s, each of the two parties had alternated in government twice. When out of power, each typically connived with or encouraged the military against the other. Realizing that their zero-sum rivalry had played into the hands of the military, Sharif and Bhutto had signed a "Charter of Democracy" in May 2006, in which they had pledged not to "join a military regime or any military sponsored government [or] solicit the support of military to come into power or to dislodge a democratic government." The parties fell out once again over the PPP's rapprochement with General Musharraf, which the PML-N saw as a betrayal of the Charter. See "Text of the Charter of Democracy," *Dawn*, May 16, 2006.

49. See "Proclamation of Emergency," *Dawn*, November 4, 2007.

50. Author's interview with a retired army major general, Rawalpindi, August 2012. See also Jay Soloman and Zahid Hussain, "Army Grows Cooler to Musharraf," *Wall Street Journal*, February 13, 2008.

51. Delcan Walsh, "Bush Tells Musharraf to Choose Ballot Box or Uniform," *Guardian*, November 7, 2007.

52. Rodney W. Jones, "The Military and Security in Pakistan," in *Zia's Pakistan: Politics and Stability in a Frontline State*, ed. Craig Baxter (Boulder, Colo.: Westview, 1985), 76.

53. Massoud Ansari, "The Militarization of Pakistan," *Newsline*, October 15, 2004.

54. Human Rights Watch, "Reform or Repression? Post-Coup Abuses in Pakistan" (New York: October 2000), http://www.hrw.org/reports/2000/pakistan.

55. Collective threats can unite and cohere members of a group. See Lewis Coser, *The Functions of Social Conflict* (Glencoe, Ill.: Free Press, 1956).

56. Umar Cheema, "The Man Who Rigged the 2002 Polls Spills the Beans," *The News*, February 24, 2008.

57. See, for instance, Mark Sappenfield, "Musharraf Successor Kayani Boosts Pakistan Army's Image," *Christian Science Monitor*, February 5, 2008. See also Jay Soloman and Zahid Hussain, "Army Grows Cooler to Musharraf," *Wall Street Journal*, February 13, 2008.

58. "Bill to Abolish NSC Soon," *Nation*, February 25, 2009.

59. Quoted in Ian Talbot, *Pakistan: A Modern History* (London: Hurst, 2006), 401.

60. The caretaker prime minister is appointed by the president in consultation with the incumbent PM and leader of the opposition in the National Assembly (NA) within three days of its dissolution. In case of a deadlock, each forwards two names to an eight-member parliamentary committee comprising four members each from the treasury and opposition benches. If the committee is unable to reach a decision in three days, the Election Commission has the authority to appoint the caretaker PM from the committee's shortlist within two days. See the Constitution of the Islamic Republic of Pakistan, Article 224 and 224 A.

61. "50 Most Powerful People of the World," *Newsweek*, http://www.thedailybeast .com/newsweek/2008/12/19/20-gen-ashfaq-parvez-kayani.html.

62. PML-N cabinet ministers had resigned from the cabinet in May 2008 after the first mutually agreed deadline to restore the judges passed.

63. The PTI is a right-of-center party led by the charismatic former Pakistani cricket team captain Imran Khan. The party projects itself as an alternative to the two major parties, the PPP and the PML-N, based on its nondynastic and presumably honest leadership. It has combined an anticorruption message with a virulent anti-Americanism popular with Pakistan's urban middle classes. In the 2008 elections, Khan won the sole NA seat for the party. However, the party emerged as the third largest in the NA in the May 2013 elections and formed a coalition provincial government with the JI in the Khyber Pakhtunkhwa.

64. "Governor Rule in Punjab," *Nation*, February 26, 2009.

65. "50 Most Powerful People of the World."

66. Rauf Klasra, "Political Deal Worked Out," *The News*, March 13, 2009.

67. Iftikhar A. Khan, "Carrot and Stick Plan to Tackle Militancy: COAS Gets Vast Powers," *Dawn*, June 26, 2008.

68. See, for instance, Sakib Shirani, "A Governance Framework," *Dawn,* January 13, 2012. See also Sabir Shah, "A Review of the PPP Government's 53 Month Performance," *The News*, August 27, 2012.

69. The charges pertain to Zardari and his spouse accepting illicit "commissions" through offshore agents for the award of a pre-shipment inspection contract to SGS/Cotecna in 1994.

70. The PPP government eventually backed down and drafted the letter in accordance with the court's wishes, although executive–judiciary friction has far from subsided. In January 2013, the Supreme Court ordered the arrest of PM Ashraf for allegedly taking bribes in 2010 when he was minister for water and power.

71. Observers saw party president and Punjab chief minister Shahbaz Sharif's call for including the military and the judiciary in a proposed all-parties conference to tackle Pakistan's many multiple crises as an indication of the party's permissive attitude to a temporary military intervention. See, for instance, "Call for Intervention," *Dawn*, March 9, 2011.

72. "Altaf Again Invokes 'Patriotic' Generals," *Dawn*, February 12, 2011.

73. "Altaf Demands Army for Karachi," *Nation*, August 27, 2013.

74. "Political Parties Reject MQM's Call for Army," *Pakistan Today*, August 28, 2013.

75. EU Election Observation Mission, Preliminary Statement, May 13, 2013, http://www.eueom.eu/files/dmfile/eom-pakistan-preliminary-statement-13052013-en.pdf.

76. Ibid., 100.

77. "General Kayani Gets Three Year Extension," *Nation*, July 23, 2010.

78. Omar Warraich, "Pakistan's Spies Eludes Its Government," *Time*, July 31, 2008, http://www.time.com/time/world/article/0,8599,1828207,00.html.

79. On the eve of the elections, Sharif told an Indian journalist, "I will go by the book; I will go by the merit. Whosoever is senior most, will have to occupy . . . the next one, the next in line." See "Sharif Not to Play Second Fiddle to Army," *Hindu*, May 6, 2013.

80. Lieutenant Colonel Muhammad Ali Ehsan, "Appointing a New Army Chief," *Express Tribune*, July 29, 2013.

81. See, for instance, "ISI, Army to Brief NA, Senate Committees," *Dawn*, October 11, 2011.

82. National Assembly of Pakistan, "Consensus Resolution of the In-Camera Joint Sitting of Parliament," October 22, 2008, http://www.na.gov.pk/en/resolution _detail.php?id=39.

83. See "Parliamentary National Security Committee Refuses to Attend GHQ Briefing," *Dawn*, October 11, 2011, http://Dawn.com/2011/10/11/national-security -committee-refuses-to-attend-ghq-briefing/.

84. "Denying Links to Militants, Pakistan Spy Chief Denounces U.S. Before Parliament," *New York Times*, May 13, 2011.

85. National Assembly of Pakistan, "Resolution on Unilateral U.S. Forces Action in Abbotabad," May 14, 2011, http://www.na.gov.pk/en/resolution_detail.php?id=52.

86. "Civilians, Military Consulted on Trade with India," *Dawn*, November 5, 2011.

87. See "PM's Address to the Nation: Nawaz Sharif Dreams of Making Pakistan an Asian Tiger," *Express Tribune*, August 19, 2013.

88. "Military Blocking Pakistan–India Trade Deal, Says Shahbaz," *Guardian*, February 13, 2014.

89. The DCC was the highest governmental forum for defense policymaking.

90. "DCC Reconstituted as CCNS," Associated Press of Pakistan, August 22, 2013, http://www.app.com.pk/en_/index.php?option=com_content&task=view&id =247202&Itemid=1.

91. This is the logic provided by the ostensible architect of the CCNS, Sharif's advisor on national security and foreign affairs, Sartaj Aziz. See his *Between Dream and Realities: Some Milestones in Pakistan's History* (Karachi: Oxford University Press, 2009), 242–245.

92. Ibid.

93. Defense Division, Ministry of Defense, Government of Pakistan, www.mod.gov .pk (accessed April 4, 2012).

94. See "No Control Over Operations of Army, ISI," *Dawn*, November 22, 2011.

95. Ministry of Defense, Government of Pakistan, www.mod.gov.pk (accessed December 8, 2014).

96. See *Pakistan Army Green Book: Nation-Building* (Rawalpindi: General Headquarters, 2000), 15.

97. In prior years, the military's budget was just a lump sum figure.

98. "ISPR Chief Decries Criticism of Defense Budget," *The News*, March 14, 2011.

99. "Report of the United Nations Commission of Inquiry Into the Facts and Circumstances of the Assassination of Former Pakistani Prime Minister Mohtarma Benazir Bhutto" (New York: United Nations, 2010), 59, http://www.un.org/News /dh/infocus/Pakistan/UN_Bhutto_Report_15April2010.pdf (accessed September 2, 2011).

100. Ibid., 62.

101. "War on Terror Toll Put at 49,000," *Express Tribune*, March 27, 2013; "Terrorists Killed 40,000 Civilians, 2,250 Security Personnel," *Nation*, January 19, 2010, http://costsofwar.org/article/pakistani-civilians.

102. "Timeline of Pakistan's Defense Sites Attacked by Militants," *Dawn*, August 16, 2012.

103. See, for example, Major General Shaukat Iqbal, "Security Politics of the Region: Indo-U.S. Nexus and Security Challenges of Pakistan, in *Pakistan Army Green Book* (Rawalpindi: General Headquarters, 2011), 107–113; Major General Shafqaat Ahmed, "Multi-Dimensional Threat to the Security of Pakistan," in *Pakistan Army Green Book: The Future Conflict Environment* (Rawalpindi: General Headquarters, 2008), 1–10; Major General Muhammad Ahsan Mahmood, "Future Conflict Environment: Challenges and Responses," in *Pakistan Army Green Book: The Future Conflict Environment* (Rawalpindi: General Headquarters, 2008), 17–24; Brigadier Shaukat Iqbal, "Future Conflict Environment: Challenges for Pakistan Army and the Way Forward," in *Pakistan Army Green Book: The Future Conflict Environment* (Rawalpindi: General Headquarters, 2008), 43–50.

104. Elizabeth Bumiller and Jane Perlez, "Pakistan's Spy Agency Is Tied to Attack on U.S. Embassy," *New York Times*, September 22, 2011.

105. "Zardari Vows Operation Against Haqqanis," *Dawn*, November 9, 2011.

106. "Zarbe Azb Operation: 120 Suspected Militants Killed in North Waziristan" *Dawn*, June 16, 2014.

107. "The Battle for Kurram," *News on Sunday*, August 24, 2014, http://tns.thenews .com.pk/battle-for-kurram-agency/#.VIczp4c81ow.

108. "Taliban Fled Pakistani Offensive Before It Began," *BBC News*, July 10, 2014, http://www.bbc.com/news/world-asia-28241352.

109. Author's interview with a former military intelligence official, Islamabad, January 2012.

110. See, for instance, the book by former head of military public relations Brigadier A. R. Siddiqui, *The Military in Pakistan: Image and Reality* (Lahore: Vanguard, 1996). Military officers writing in professional publications continually stress the need to "guide" and manage the media for the projection of national interest and consensus building on important issues to prevent exploitation by hostile foreign and domestic forces. See also "Defense and Media," ISPR (Rawalpindi, 1991), esp. 15–22; Brigadier Jehanzeb Raja, "Role of Media and Its Importance in Future Conflict Environment," in *Pakistan Army Green Book: Low Intensity Conflict* (Rawalpindi: General Headquarters, 2008), 83–92; Major General Shafqaat Ahmed, "Multi-Dimensional Threat to the Security of Pakistan," in *Pakistan Army Green Book: Low Intensity Conflict* (Rawalpindi: General Headquarters, 2008), 1–10; Commodore Asaf Hamayun, "Media as an Instrument of Strategy," *NDC Journal*, 2002, 196–209.

111. Huma Yusuf, "Conspiracy Fever: The U.S., Pakistan and Its Media," *Survival* 53, no. 4 (2011): 106.

112. Ansar Abbassi, "Names of 55 U.S. Suspects on the Loose," *The News*, March 12, 2011.

113. "Leak of CIA Officer Name Is Sign of Rift with Pakistan," *New York Times*, May 9, 2011.

114. See Aaj Kamran Khan Key Saath (Tonight with Kamran Khan), Geo TV, May 4, 2011, http://www.youtube.com/watch?v=C_88jfndamw (accessed February 9, 2012). See also Talat Hussain, "The Problem Within," *Dawn*, June 13, 2011.

115. ISPR, "139th Corps Commanders Conference," press release, June 9, 2011.

116. See Saleem Shehzad, "Al-Qaeda Had Warned of Pakistan Strike," *Asia Times Online*, May 27, 2011, http://www.atimes.com/atimes/South_Asia/ME27Df06.html.

117. Aqil Shah, "The Generals Strike Back," *Foreign Affairs*, December 9, 2014, http://www.foreignaffairs.com/articles/141379/aqil-shah/the-generals-strike-back.

118. See ISPR press release, October 7, 2009.

119. Embassy of the United States, Islamabad, "Ambassador Meets with Kayani and Pasha about Kerry-Lugar," October 7, 2009, http://www.cablegatesearch.net/cable.php?id=09ISLAMABAD2427.

120. Yusuf, "Conspiracy Fever," 106.

121. Ibid., 97.

122. Ijaz, "Time to Take on Pakistan's Jihadist Spies," *Financial Times*, October 10, 2011, http://www.ft.com/intl/cms/s/0/5ea9b804-f351-11e0-b11b-00144feab49a.html#axzz3q83vQzSf

123. Then ISI Director General, Lieutenant General Shuja Pasha secretly visited Mr. Ijaz in London, and reportedly collected incriminating transcripts of text messages exchanged between Haqqani and Ijaz. See Ahmed, "When Mansoor Ijaz Met General Pasha," *Newsweek* (Pakistan), November 20, 2011.

124. "Memogate: COAS Submits Rejoinder to SC," *The News*, December 21, 2011.

125. The commission was ordered to investigate the "authenticity" of the memo and to determine whether sending the memo to senior American officials "is tantamount to compromising the sovereignty, security and independence of Pakistan. See "Memogate Probe: Full Text of the SC Decision to Form Commission," *Express Tribune* (Karachi), December 3, 2011.

126. "State Within a State Not Acceptable," *Pakistan Today*, December 22, 2011.

127. ISPR, press release, January 11, 2012.

128. "Commander 111 Brigade Changed," *The News*, January 11, 2012.

129. The last time a civilian government tried to prematurely retire an army chief, in October 1999, the army executed a coup.

130. "Government Does Not Want to Sack Army, ISI Chiefs," *Nation*, January 20, 2012; "Court Admits Petition on Saving Army and ISI Chiefs," *Express Tribune*, February 28, 2012.

131. "Adiala Missing Inmates: ISI and MI Not Superior to Civilians, Says SC," *Express Tribune*, March 1, 2012.

132. "Disband Agencies' Death Squads," *The News*, September 28, 2012.

133. See "SC Seeks Progress Report on Missing Persons," *Daily Times* (Lahore), February 9, 2012; "Missing Persons: ISI, MI Counsel Says RAW and Mossad Involved," *Express Tribune*, March 16, 2012; "SC Seeks Report in Missing Person's Case," *Frontier Post*, July 23, 2013.

134. "Two Bodies of Missing Persons Found in Baluchistan," *Express Tribune*, May 1, 2012.

135. "Security Agencies Not Cooperating with Top Court," *Express Tribune*, August 27, 2013.

136. See Narcis Serra, *The Military Transition: Democratic Reform of the Armed Forces* (New York: Cambridge University Press, 2010), 83.

137. "Investigating Generals: Army Refuses to Assist NAB in NLC Scam," *Express Tribune*, March 11, 2012.

138. "Report of the United Nations," 33.

139. The NLC is a monopolistic army-run logistics and transportation agency, even though it falls under the administrative purview of the National Logistics Board, an attached department of the federal Planning and Development Division.

140. The fate of that inquiry remains unknown.

141. Pakistan Army (Amendment) Ordinance, 2007, http://www.na.gov.pk/uploads /documents/1302673360 974.pdf (March 1, 2012).

142. "Peshawar High Court Judge Says Missing Persons Killed After Courts Pressure Agencies," *The News*, July 24, 2013; "ISI Denies Torturing Man to Death in Custody," *Express Tribune*, September 28, 2011.

143. See "Globalizing Torture: CIA Secret Detention and Extraordinary Rendition," Open Society Foundations, New York, 2013, https://www.opensocietyfoundations .org/sites/default/files/globalizing-torture-20120205.pdf.

144. "Enforced Disappearances by Pakistan Security Forces in Baluchistan," Human Rights Watch, July 28, 2011, https://www.hrw.org/news/2011/07/28/pakistan-security -forces-disappear-opponents-balochistan.

145. Pakistani intelligence official to Bashir Azeem, the 76-year-old secretary-general of the Baluch Republican Party, during his unacknowledged detention, April 2010. Ibid.

146. "Kayani Hits Back: Apparent Reaction to the Bashing of Generals," *Dawn*, November 6, 2012.

147. "Supreme Court Takes U-Turn on Arrest of ISI Brigadier," *Daily Times*, July 24, 2013.

148. See "Army Will Preserve Its Honor at All Costs," *Express Tribune*, April 7, 2014.

149. "A Day After the Indictment: Government Advised to Let Musharraf See His Mother," *Express Tribune*, April 2, 2014.

150. The most damning revelations about the PTI's collaboration with the ISI came from the party's former president, Javed Hashmi, whom Imran Khan summarily removed from that position after he opposed storming the Parliament. He claimed that Khan was receiving direct instructions from the intelligence agency to coordinate his protests with those of Tahirul Qadri to put maximum pressure on the government. See "Imran Khan Said Can't Move Forward Without Army: Hashmi," *The News*, September 1, 2014.

CHAPTER 2

THE OPERATIONAL DYNAMICS OF POLITICAL PARTIES IN PAKISTAN

Mohammad Waseem

This chapter seeks to understand the role of political parties as an expression of the current patterns of conflict in Pakistan. Political parties operate in the field according to the established as well as unfolding rules of the game and thus provide road signs on the way to understanding the inner dynamics of the system. The first section of this chapter outlines the profile of political parties encompassing issues and policies and their modes of expression, from legislative debates to aggressive political participation, such as mob violence or target killings. The second section deals with five parties that matter in the perpetual power game on top—the Pakistan Peoples Party (PPP), the Pakistan Muslim League—Nawaz (PML-N), the Pakistan Tehreeke Insaaf (PTI), the Muttahida Qaumi Movement (MQM), and the Awami National Party (ANP). The third section focuses on smaller parties, including the two Islamic parties—as well as miniscule parties operating on the margins of the system. Their importance lies essentially in the way they lay out the turf and thus give expression to the ambitions, aspirations, grievances, and frustrations of groups and communities that are not fully represented in the system. These observations bring out the specific features of political parties in the way they are poised to shape the contours of state power and to contribute to the national discourse.

This chapter deals with political parties as they operate out in the field, raising contentious issues, mobilizing the public in pursuit of their disparate agendas, and taking positions on matters of domestic and foreign policy. Political parties typically function both within and outside the Parliament as well as in the electoral and nonelectoral contexts. The historical research on political parties of Pakistan generally deals with them as parliamentary and electoral entities.[1] There are few studies of individual parties in terms of their mass appeal, patterns of recruitment, organizational structure, and changing ideological positions.[2] However, the task of understanding the political crisis in the country in 2012–2013 becomes easier if we look at political parties in terms of their day-to-day activity or "normal" politics, distinct from the "extraordinary" politics in and around elections that compresses issues, policies, and the group dynamics in a mode of hyperactivity during the campaign.[3]

BEYOND ORGANIZATIONAL DIMENSION

Although the organizational route to analysis of political parties has the potential for explaining their resilience, there is a need for understanding their political behavior in terms of their patterns of leadership, public discourse, and relevance for the political system. The organizational approach to political parties such as the MQM, the Jama'at-e-Islami (JI), and the ANP is now part of the conventional wisdom.[4] However, the high organizational potential of these parties has a differential impact on their public standing, their electoral support, and their capacity to shape politics. For example, the JI was never an electoral party of any significance in terms of government formation at the federal or provincial level, except during the untypical and arguably maneuvered elections in the North West Frontier Province (NWFP)—today Khyber Pakhtunkhwa (KP)—in 2002. The JI boycotted the 2008 elections in protest against Musharraf's maneuvered election as president in October 2007, followed by an emergency on November 3 when he sacked scores of judges and packed higher courts with his hand-picked judges. The party's political significance has plummeted since. Similarly, the MQM's acknowledged institutional potential notwithstanding, it has become the most controversial party in the country. In 2011, Zulfikar Mirza, the ex-interior minister of the PPP government in Sindh, broke ranks with his party and declared the MQM a terrorist organization and its leader Altaf Hussain a killer. As opposed to the JI and MQM, the three mainstream parties PPP, PML-N, and PTI have a lax organizational structure characterized by a gap of communication between leaders and workers, absence of meaningful party elections, and a low level of party discipline. However, the PPP and PML-N along with their breakaway factions managed to get 70 percent of the total vote on average for the 1980s, 1990s, and 2000s and form governments at the federal level, often in coalition with smaller parties. There seems to be a poor fix between the organizational input and the electoral output of political parties in Pakistan.

In this chapter, I propose to look into party politics in Pakistan beyond an organizational matrix and focus on their day-to-day operational dynamics at and around the point of intersection between the party on the one hand and its perception and projection of issues and policies and modes of expression and mobilization on the other. What is important is the way the party leadership feels obliged to opt for public action through a public statement, a press release, a TV interview, a press conference, a public rally, or a "long march" to the Parliament house in Islamabad, the Punjab Assembly, or a Sufi shrine, such as Data Darbar in Lahore. This requires an analysis of the policy behind selection of the issue in question, the strategy behind the timing of action, and the decision about a joint action sponsored by an alliance of parties or a solo flight. The action can pursue a longer-term ideological goal, such as establishment of sharia in the country, or a medium-term objective, such as stopping the war against terror. Also, one finds a series of rallies sparked by immediate causes, like the murder of two Pakistanis by American spy Raymond Davis and his subsequent release from jail in early 2011 or the U.S. drone attacks on targets in the Federally Administered Tribal Areas (FATA).

On the one hand, party leadership decides on political action or nonaction in the perspective of the space provided by the political system. On the other hand, the agenda and the course of action of a political party are underscored by the ideological, factional, and personal input into the decision-making channels on top. The former reflects civic liberties and political freedoms available to parties and groups for expression of their opinions and pursuit of their strategies. The latter focuses on the specific ways of understanding, and responding to, the public issues adopted by various political parties that lead to internal debate, cleavages between leaders and workers, and successive periods of readiness and restraint for coming out in the open and taking a public position. In this sense, this inquiry deals mainly but not exclusively with politics on the street.

A WEAK PARLIAMENT

We need to look at political parties beyond mere parliamentary entities. Parliament took a back seat during the process of democratization in Pakistan after the 2008 elections. It operated as a subordinate house vis-à-vis the executive, as opposed to, for example, the House of Commons, which operated as a coordinate house.[5] Parliament took a delayed action, if at all, in the form of resolutions. In 2009, it passed a resolution for conducting peace negotiations with the Taliban in KP. However, it was followed by the military action in Swat and South Waziristan against the express wishes of public representatives. The decision of political parties in favor of making peace with the Taliban was prompted by factors other than ideological or policy preferences. For example, only a minority, the core Islamic elements on the floor, such as Jamiat-e Ulama-e Islam (JUI), wanted "peace" with the Taliban as a matter of policy. The relatively secular ANP government in Peshawar felt helpless in the face of the advancing march of the Taliban into large areas of Malakand Division and the killing of scores of its party men, with no indication of support from the general headquarters (GHQ) of the army in Rawalpindi for launching a counterterrorist operation. Thus, it opted for the "peace" resolution to avoid confrontation with the militants. That meant that it virtually ceded territory to a proto-Taliban group Tanzeem Nifaz Shariat Mohammadi (TNSM) as a "no-go area" for the provincial government and ultimately for the state.

The PPP government in Islamabad (2008–2013) voted for "peace" to avoid the opposition propaganda for not wanting "peace" with the Muslim brethren against the "infidel" Americans. Also, it wanted to restore the writ of the state in the face of terrorist operations. It wanted the Parliament to endorse its perceived policy of nonaction against the Taliban and its ally TNSM. Only the MQM abstained, mainly because it wanted to attract the attention of the diplomatic community by creating a profile of a secular party for itself. Others, especially the PML-N and PML-Q (Quaid-e-Azam), similarly tried to save their skin from criticism of Islamic and anti-American groups. It can be argued that the resolution expressed not the political will to go for peace with the Taliban but the fear of being labeled as anti-Islamic. That explains why the subsequent military operation did not elicit any negative response from the leading parliamentary parties PPP, PML-N, PML-Q, ANP, and MQM. In 2011, the Parliament voted for stopping the U.S. drone attacks on the militants' hideouts in the FATA and thus provided a platform for expressing an increasingly popular demand among the articulate sections of the public. Neither the government nor the opposition believed that the resolution would make any difference as long as the security apparatus approved these attacks in the framework of the strategic alliance between Pakistan and the United States. No serious negotiations between the two allies took place on this issue at any time.

On a different note, the passage of the Eighteenth Amendment brought about significant changes in the Constitution by amending eighty-nine articles and transferring forty out of forty-seven subjects from the Concurrent List to the residual category controlled by provinces.[6] The amendment was rooted in the deliberations of the Parliamentary Committee for Constitutional Reform steered by Senator Raza Rabbani. It arrived at a consensus after a painstaking process of agreement, disagreement, and compromise between the party representatives in the Committee. When Nawaz Sharif publicly aired his reservations about the change of name of NWFP to Pakhtunkhwa, the media criticized his move as backstabbing. Nawaz Sharif was obliged to step back and agree to a compromise formula by adding Khyber to the name. The Parliament eventually and quietly passed the amendment without any fireworks, in view of the prior understanding between political parties off the floor. The behavior of political parties in Pakistan is typically more representative of their policy preferences on political and constitutional issues as expressed and crystalized outside the Parliament rather than inside it.

In March 2012, the Parliament again picked up the initiative to redefine the U.S.–Pakistan strategic alliance. A series of setbacks in relations between the two countries forced a reconsideration of commitment to the partnership in the war against terror. It started with the Central Intelligence Agency's Abbottabad operation on May 2, 2012, which located and killed Osama bin Laden, and came to a head with the North Atlantic Treaty Organization (NATO) attack on Salala check post inside Pakistan territory, killing twenty-four soldiers. Islamabad retaliated by putting a halt to the NATO supplies that passed through Pakistan and got the Shamsie air base—that was used for flying drones—vacated by the United States. The parliamentary committee for national strategy recommended to the National Assembly that the drone attacks and NATO supplies, among other things, be stopped. The mainstream current of anti-Americanism was led by Islamic parties—some of them banned as terrorist organizations—and political leadership on the right led by Imran Khan, leader of the PTI. The media and the opposition claimed that the decision in this regard had already been taken and that the parliamentary debate was just an exercise in churning out an expression of the national will in a formal sense. In June 2012, the Supreme Court disqualified Prime Minister Gilani for contempt of court, in the midst of a perceived clash of the two institutions of judiciary and Parliament. The PPP was obliged to elect Raja Pervez Ashraf as a lame duck chief executive up to the elections.

BEYOND ELECTIONS: DYNAMICS OF A POLITICAL SOCIETY

A study of party politics in an electoral framework dwells on the analysis of the election system, the campaign, the manifestos, and the content and style of mobilization of people in pursuit of victory at the polls. While an election carries immense explanatory potential, it compresses the group dynamics into the mold of patron–client relations in countries such as Pakistan. The leadership seeks to maximize its gains in the number of votes and seats as a short-term objective, irrespective of its relevance for the longer-term issues of policy. Thus, after the 2008 elections in Pakistan, the two historically competitive political entities, the PPP and the PML(N), with more or less defined—though increasingly blurred—ideological positions on the left and right of the center, settled down along their traditional standpoints on policy matters. It is the expression, projection, and manipulation of profile and policy in a nonelectoral context that brings out the internal and lasting dynamics of political parties. Rather than formal party positions, it is the informal but sustained political attitudes that define politics in Pakistan, as elsewhere.

Accordingly, this chapter deals with political attitudes as expressed through party action or nonaction in the period between the two elections. It covers the PPP-led government after the 2008 elections and the PML-N government after the 2013 elections. The political situation in Pakistan has been conducive to a relatively unshackled and unconstrained expression of opinion and mobilization of people through the media.[7] This phenomenon can be ascribed to two major factors, one structural and the other operational. Structurally speaking, the country has been in a postmilitary democratization phase that was underscored by tense relations between the civilian and military wings of the state. Ironically, this phenomenon indirectly opened up space for a "free" media that has been increasingly critical of the both the PPP and PML-N governments but that spared the army and, to a large extent, judiciary. In the period under consideration, the media, especially television, often lambasted political parties and their leaders. The military and Inter-Services Intelligence (ISI), together known as the "establishment," have been understood to be in favor of a media that was critical of the civilian wing of the state. The political opposition thrived on freedom of action and expression—ranging from tabling motions against the government's actions and policies on the floor of elected assemblies to arranging rallies, demonstrations, and strikes. The phenomenon of a weak civilian government operating under the vigilance of the army characterized the post-Musharraf period of civilianization after 2008, largely following the Brazilian model.[8] The media generally deferred to the military establishment in terms of operating within the broad contours of foreign policy and defense strategy. This pattern came to a peak during the media war between India and Pakistan after the 2008 Mumbai attacks. At home, the media took on the elected government forcefully, given the latter's insecure position in the power structure.

The fact that political parties of various shades have been able to operate relatively freely in recent years provides a rationale to dwell on their policy opinions, internal squabbles, competition for public vote and attention, and ideological orientations as covered by the media. The establishment has been generally perceived to be vigilant about a civilian government from behind the scenes. That has kept the latter under constant pressure and constrained its space in the domain of public policy. The gap between the civilian and military wings of the state provided space for social and political movements, sit-ins, shutter-down strikes (closing shop), and other forms of political agitation. In this way, the political dynamics of the society found a coherent expression through legislative activity, street demonstrations, and aggressive political participation in the form of militant activities including extortion, murder, and arson. Pakistan under the PPP and PML-N governments presented a scene of relatively unconstrained mass mobilization by political parties and its expression through the media.

MAJOR PARTIES AS CONTENDERS FOR POWER

Pakistan is a multiparty democracy of some standing. There were forty-nine political parties registered with the Election Commission of Pakistan in 2008 and 216 in 2013.[9] The discussion in this section focuses on the mode of action and public profile of the PPP, PML-N, PTI, MQM, and ANP, that is, the parties that made a serious bid for power. Other political parties either did not have the credentials or did not rear reasonable ambitions for government formation at the federal or provincial level.

PPP

The PPP is the most widely researched party in Pakistan.[10] Its organizational issues in the beginning of its present stint in office revolved around the question of whether the Central Executive Committee (CEC) or the informal core committee—President Asif Ali Zardari's version of a kitchen cabinet—should make crucial decisions about party matters.[11] The CEC formally approved the official move to sponsor a UN probe into Benazir Bhutto's assassination and showed concern about the unwieldy cabinet size. It adopted the strategy for nonconfrontation with the judiciary even as it claimed that the latter had been politicized and that (intelligence) agencies controlled its deliberations. The party high command conveyed messages to party activists through the CEC, for example, to forbid them from commenting on conspiracy theories that the army or ISI—specifically their chiefs, Generals Kayani and Pasha, respectively—sought to destabilize the PPP government.[12] One member, Qayum Jatoi, was sacked for criticism of the army and judiciary. The CEC functioned as the nerve center of the party in terms of acknowledgment of the privilege and loyalty of its members. Aitzaz Ahsan's membership in the CEC was suspended during the lawyers' movement against the PPP government in 2008–2009 and then restored in a move to co-opt him in the face of street agitation led by Nawaz Sharif. Aitzaz staged a comeback in 2012 as lawyer for a beleaguered prime minister who was embroiled in a contempt-of-court case for not writing a letter to the Swiss banks for investigation into President Zardari's accounts. In this way, the CEC remained a convenient platform for public recognition of party stalwarts as well as for projection of the message from the party leadership.

The PPP has a long tradition of overlap between party faithfuls and personal faithfuls, representing the ideological wing and the power elite, respectively.[13] The former often harked back to the "true message" of Z. A. Bhutto and Benazir Bhutto and thus functioned as a de facto conscience keeper of the party that represented party cadres and workers. They started a Bhutto Legacy Movement in Peshawar in pursuit of a demand to implement the party manifesto that promised to serve the poor and the destitute. They planned a province-wide tour, demanded a party convention to solve the workers' problems, and expressed apprehensions about the decline of the popularity graph of the party. Workers asked the leadership to hold party elections and regularly meet them instead of appeasing the non-PPP coalition partners. They showed a measure of disappointment after first participating in the movement for restoration of judges in 2007–2008 and then facing the dilemma of supporting Zardari, who similarly resisted the return of Chief Justice Chaudhry and others to the Supreme Court.[14] For its part, the party leadership was apprehensive about playing the workers' card. President Zardari first approved a rally of the PPP Youth Organization to protest against the high-handedness of the judiciary but then stopped it for fear that it might run wild and direct anger against the judges or even assault the premises of the Supreme Court.[15] Dissidents claimed that the perceived communication gap between the leaders and workers was a deliberate strategy to keep workers on their toes.

As the tension between the judiciary and the executive took a turn for the worse, the cochair of the PPP, President Zardari, demanded resignation from all the party legislators at the federal and provincial levels. The party leadership feared a "conspiracy" and sought resignations as a contingency plan to put its own house in order and slap its authority over the parliamentary wing. The idea was that if an in-house arrangement leads to a new coalition-based government, the PPP legislators should not be part of it. In the event, 106 members of the Punjab Assembly belonging to the PPP submitted their "loyalty affidavits," if not proper resignations, to President Zardari.[16] The PPP feared a loss of majority on the floor of the Parliament. It occupied 128 seats in the National Assembly, along with coalition partners at thirteen for the ANP, twenty-five MQM, eight JUI, five Pakistan Muslim League—Functional (PML-F), and seventeen independents, bringing the total to 193. But the JUI left the coalition after its minister Azam Swati implicated the PPP minister Syed Hamid Raza Kazmi in the hajj scam and both were sacked. The MQM resigned thrice from the treasury benches in protest against the alleged nonacceptance of its demands that kept the incumbent government insecure in the game of numbers. The PPP felt obliged to co-opt the PML-Q—the erstwhile "king's party" in the government. The old party cadres and workers had long identified the late patriarch of the present leadership of the PML-Q—Choudhry Zahooor Ilahi—with President Zia, especially as he had publicly endorsed the execution of Z. A. Bhutto in 1979. Later, he was killed allegedly by the militant wing of the PPP, Al-Zulfikar, led by Bhutto's son Murtaza. Zardari himself called it the Qatil (murderer) League immediately after Benazir's assassination in December 2007. Not surprisingly, Zardari's move elicited a negative reaction in the party ranks.

The classical description of the PPP as a populist party holds ground even four decades after its inception in 1967.[17] In the cynical version of this approach, the party is understood to be unwilling to go by any rules or regulations and norms or traditions. Critics pointed to its lack of substance and vision and consistent play on the theme of victimhood because of the unnatural deaths of Z. A. Bhutto and Benazir Bhutto, along with her two brothers. The idiom of the party's spokespersons continued to be laced with hyperboles and projection of fatality as immortality.[18] The party maintained that Benazir, through her assassination, signed the social contract with her blood.[19] Benazir's husband, Asif Zardari, as the new party leader, managed to keep the party united, led its triumphant march to government formation after the 2008 elections through a coalitional arrangement, and successfully mobilized support for his own election as president. He was considered a trusted ally by Washington and somebody that GHQ was willing to work with. He championed the process of transformation of the political infrastructure by establishing provincial autonomy and canceling the presidential powers to dissolve the National Assembly through the Eighteenth Amendment. In a series of political moves—the Ninth National Finance Commission Award, the Gilgit-Baltistan Order, and the Baluchistan initiative—Zardari changed the political landscape in a longer-term perspective. Under him, the Constitution regained some of its original character by shedding various provisions periodically inserted by military rulers and indeed moved considerably further in the direction of provincial autonomy.[20]

Despite all this, Zardari became the most controversial elected president in Pakistan's history. Soon after the honeymoon period, he was subjected to severe criticism from various actors on the political stage. The Supreme Court declared Musharraf's National Reconciliation Ordinance (NRO) null and void and asked the PPP government to open up corruption cases against the president in the Swiss courts.[21] As the judiciary asserted its power, the pro-democracy elements acutely feared the crumbling of the civilian edifice of authority. The media projected the message of the president's alleged corruption all around and charged that Zardari had sold out to the United States by pursuing the war against terror in the American interest, thus compromising national sovereignty. Public anger was reserved for the unsatisfactory performance of the PPP government relating to an all-embracing price hike, periodic shortages of foodstuffs, electricity, petrol, and natural gas, and deterioration of the security situation because of terrorist attacks. A Pew Research Center poll found that Zardari's approval ratings were 20 percent in 2010, comparable to a 17 percent approval rating for the United States; in contrast, 61 percent of those polled approved of General Kayani, and 71 percent approved of Nawaz Sharif.[22] The leaders of the PML-N, PTI, JI, and other opposition parties accused Zardari of manipulation, jugglery, duplicity, and Machiavellian foul play. A columnist in the *News* found the PPP flotilla leaky, shaky, and rickety, led by "Admiral Asif Ali, through his masterly trims, timely turnings of the tiller, frequent adjustments in the rudder and the keel," and charged that the PPP government was in survival mode, constantly fighting fires rather than governing.[23]

PML-N

The PML-N that formed the government after the 2013 elections is a legatee of the All India Muslim League in British India. That party was divided into a dozen factions bearing various suffixes indicating the names of factional leaders. After Zia died in an air crash in August 1988, there emerged two rival factions of the ruling Muslim League—the "king's party"—led by the ex-prime minister Muhammad Khan Junejo and Punjab's chief minister Nawaz Sharif. The latter faction emerged as a separate party in 1992. The PML-N is a mirror image of the PPP in terms of dynastic leadership, its vast baggage of corruption charges, a history of dismissal of its previous governments at the hands of both the army (1999) and the civilian president (1993), a weak organizational structure, and vulnerability to factionalism induced by extraparliamentary forces. The party has retained its ideological position on the right of the center, its power base in Punjab, and its appeal in the urban centers for the last two decades. In 2011, Nawaz Sharif took a public position against the political role of the army. His new stance drew on his unceremonial exit from power at the hands of Musharraf a decade ago, followed by imprisonment—including solitary confinement for three months—and long years of exile to Saudi Arabia. He returned in 2007 with a commitment to never encourage, accept, or abet the army's role in politics. Nawaz Sharif kept himself distant from any move to topple the PPP government because he saw in it a return to the army's role as king maker and his own subservient role as an elected prime minister in a future scenario. This realization shaped the PML-N's attitude toward the PPP government in an essentially noncombative framework, characterized by reluctance to engineer a move to destabilize the civilian setup that would lead to surrender of initiative back to the army. Some argued that the PML-N's commitment not to upset the cart let the PPP-led coalition off the hook despite its bad governance.

Nawaz Sharif was exposed to the Islamization program of Zia as part of the government in Punjab from 1981 to 1988. In 1988, he contested elections from the platform of an alliance with JI called Islami Jamhoori Ittehad put together by ISI against the PPP. As prime minister (1990–1993), he got the Shariat Bill passed by the National Assembly. His government was dissolved before he could steer the bill through the Senate. His ideological grooming under the Saudi government for nearly a decade further pushed him to a mission-mantled approach to politics. Disparate conservative elements who opposed Musharraf's self-serving secular posturing and partnership with the United States in the war against terror found in Nawaz Sharif—Musharraf's nemesis—an Islamic and putatively anti-American alternative. Nawaz Sharif remained somewhat noncommittal about the role of the Taliban in the wake of a series of terrorist attacks. His brother, Punjab's chief minister, Shahbaz Sharif, made a public appeal to the Taliban to spare the province in view of their shared struggle in the past. The media lambasted him for showing empathy with terrorists. The banned jihadi parties claimed to have contributed to the victory of the PML-N candidates in the 2008 elections. According to WikiLeaks, Shahbaz Sharif tipped a banned jihadi party, Jamaat-ut-Dawa, about the impending move of the United Nations to freeze its account. Musharraf claimed that Nawaz Sharif was a closet Taliban. President Zardari referred to him as Maulvi (cleric) Nawaz Sharif during his address in Nodero in July 2011. Conversely, Nawaz Sharif has shown sensitivity to the need for a modern, not orthodox, Islamic system, a tolerant and plural society, as well as regional peace. When Nawaz Sharif referred to Ahmedis, the followers of a heretical sect, as brothers during the campaign for a by-election in Chakwal, Islamic groups boycotted him. He was also criticized by a certain anti-India lobby called the "Pakistan movement" group for speaking in favor of friendship and opening of trade with India.

The PML-N brought back several members from its huge breakaway faction, PML-Q, whom Musharraf had co-opted. In the Punjab Assembly, these PML-Q co-optees helped the PML-N keep its minority government in place after it eased the PPP members out of the coalition in 2008. Under Zardari, the PML-N's political stance toward him remained unclear. Sometimes it declared that it would not support the replacement of the PPP government by a "national government"—a euphemism for a military-sponsored political arrangement. At other times, it hinted at supporting change. Sometimes it demanded midterm elections but later feared that these would be mediated through the army. The party demanded that Musharraf should be brought back from abroad for trial through Interpol. Its charge sheet against Musharraf included his misadventure in Kargil in 1999; illegal takeover on October 12, 1999; war against his own people (meaning the war against terror); use of the National Accountability Bureau to blackmail politicians into submission; murder of the Baluch leader Akbar Bugti; atrocities perpetrated on the Baluch activists, including abducting and killing them; and operation against the Red Mosque in Islamabad on the occasion of the "Israeli-Zionist Bush Cheney Junta of War Criminals."[24] Chief Minister Shahbaz Sharif was reported to have had a secret meeting with Chief of Army Staff (COAS) General Kayani that was subsequently disapproved of by Nawaz Sharif. Shahbaz's statement that the army and judiciary should play their role as stakeholders in the stability of the political system created a backlash in the media and political circles.

The conflict between the PPP government and the Supreme Court provided the PML-N an opportunity to keep pressure on the former by upholding the cause of independence of the judiciary. In 2009, the PML-N put its full weight in favor of reinstatement of Chief Justice Chaudhry after Shahbaz's government collapsed as a result of a court ruling. The party questioned Zardari's eligibility for the presidential election in 2008 in the light of the NRO, presidential immunity, and appointment of judges. Nawaz Sharif faced opposition within the party for compromising parliamentary sovereignty by encouraging a rally in favor of the Supreme Court. All along, the fear of passing the initiative back to the army kept Nawaz Sharif from burning his bridges in conflict with the PPP. The PTI leader Imran Khan accused him of making a secret deal with Zardari to keep the status quo.

Nawaz Sharif filed a case in the Supreme Court in November 2011 after the "Memogate" scandal put President Zardari in the dock for "conspiring" with the United States to save his government from the army, allegedly in exchange for strategic cooperation that covered access to nuclear installations. Nawaz Sharif pleaded with the Supreme Court to investigate the matter. Meanwhile, Zardari was able to sort out matters with the top brass that was itself under pressure due to allegations about the ISI chief's maneuverings in certain Middle Eastern countries, including Saudi Arabia and Kuwait, launching a military coup straight after the Abbottabad operation in May 2011. As the court case lingered on into May 2012, Nawaz Sharif settled for a compromise with the PPP government in the impending Senate elections. Meanwhile, Imran Khan denigrated the two leaders as plunderers, cheats, and wheelers and dealers.

The PML-Q faction got fifty seats in the 2008 elections. It was divided into three factions—one joining Zardari, another Musharraf in his reincarnation as a leader in exile, and the third (Like-minded Group) Nawaz Sharif. In June 2012, the PML-Q—led by Choudhary Shujaat Husain and Pervez Illahi—enjoyed a crucial role as king maker because it carried sufficient numbers for the PPP to put together a majority in the National Assembly to elect the new prime minister after Gilani was disqualified by the Supreme Court. They even vetoed the two PPP candidates for that position, Ahmed Mukhtar and Qamar Zaman Kaira, and instead supported Raja Pervez Ashraf. The PML-Q virtually collapsed in the 2013 elections.

PTI

Imran Khan's PTI was virtually a one-man party for fifteen years, until 2011. None of the mainstream political leaders acknowledged its role as a significant political actor nor sought alliance with it. Imran was generally dismissed as a product of intelligence agencies and as a creation of the media. But all this did not render him irrelevant for party politics in Pakistan because he gave public expression to the deep concerns of a large number of people from the educated middle class. They found in him a janitor who would cleanse the Augean stables of politics in the country. He upheld the Mosaic myth of leading his nation to the Promised Land. Under the post-2008 democratic dispensation, he was able to regroup quite a few like-minded people around him. He carried out a blitzkrieg on television, condemning the leading politicians of corruption, bad governance, and total neglect of the downtrodden masses. Although Imran's party has its own CEC that meets periodically, a published manifesto, and a youth wing called Insaf Students Federation, it lacks the trappings of a typical political party in terms of a viable and stable hierarchical structure, ideological and policy orientation of cadres and workers, and network of influential locals as potential winners in an electoral contest.

Imran's main profile is one of a rebel, an angry person who challenges authority in social, economic, and political domains of public policy. He finds the system at a dead end, representing a rotten status quo that would eventually pave the way to revolution.[25] A recurrent theme of his speeches is the need for change in the system. Critics found in it change for change's sake because of Imran's lack of clear thinking about his policy objectives. Imran saw a civil disobedience movement against bad governance round the corner, corruption as cancer of the society, and revolution through ballot as the way out. He had campaigned for Musharraf for his controversial presidential referendum in 2002 but fell out with him when he was not given a leading role in the subsequent civilian setup. In 2007, he reemerged as a firebrand orator on the TV screen attacking Musharraf. He was part of the All Pakistan Democratic Alliance that boycotted the 2008 elections. While the PML-N and the JUI later opted to take part in elections, Imran and others were left in the lurch. Imran incessantly accused the Zardari government of selling Pakistan's sovereignty to the United States by joining the war against terror and demanded "liberation from American slavery."[26] He promised to tackle the problem of terrorism in ninety days. He took a tough stand on the American spy Raymond Davis during his trial in court in 2011. After Davis's release, he castigated the government for complicity with the United States. The PTI filed a petition in court against the U.S. drone attacks and threatened to launch a march on Islamabad if these attacks did not stop. Imran demanded the release of Pakistani expatriate Dr. Afia Siddiqui, who was awarded a sentence of 86 years by a U.S. court for attacking American troops in Kabul.

Imran constantly admonished Nawaz Sharif for paying only Rs 5,000 as income tax and sixty-one Members of the National Assembly (MNAs) for paying no income tax at all.[27] Imran heaped invectives against Zardari as a corrupt person, criticized Musharraf's NRO for exonerating the former from legal action for corruption, and demanded to reopen cases against Musharraf. Imran persistently demanded midterm elections to get rid of the incumbent ruling setup based on a bogus National Assembly.[28] Ideologically, Imran continued to be close to Islamic parties. He publicly rallied with them against the United States. The PTI manifesto did not criticize Islamic extremism and suicide bombing. He wanted no change in the controversial Blasphemy Law. He appealed to "jeaned jihadis," that is, the conservative educated and professional youth with a modern veneer.[29] On October 30, 2011, he organized a public rally in the famous Minar Pakistan Park in Lahore, which upgraded his profile as a national leader and left a mark on the youth in particular and the articulate sections of the public in general. Dozens of high-profile disgruntled members of the PPP, PML-N, PML-Q, JUI-Fazl ur Rehman (JUI-F), ANP, and PML-F joined the PTI in a wave that was incessantly termed by Imran as a "tsunami." He claimed that he would form the next government, that he would start a civil war if he was denied victory through a rigged election, and that he had now a credible number of heavyweights within the party for winning the election. However, various political leaders and commentators alleged that he was the new horse fielded by ISI. The media termed him "Taliban Khan." The traditional leadership of all shades woke up to Imran's emergence on the national scene. As a leader, Imran evoked two contradictory responses. At one end, he was accorded a pivotal role in starting a process of revolution as Mr. Clean. He was accredited with "personal and political credibility, integrity, compassion, dedication, fairness and justice," with credentials as a "managerial guru" and as a "compassionate visionary."[30] He was admired for introducing transformational politics as an expression of his doctrine of political change. At the other end, he was seen as a Taliban apologist kowtowing Islamic parties, of duplicity in his personal life, of sponsoring a cult of personality, and of being a revolutionary with "fundamental contradictions, u-turns and half-baked theories."[31] Imran thought of himself in the same vein as Z. A. Bhutto and his meteoric rise in 1970. While political pundits estimated that he would get fifteen to twenty-five seats in the National Assembly in the 2013 elections, the PTI's own estimates put the party's fortune at a hundred seats from Punjab alone. However, the elections produced a major surprise: the ascendancy of the PTI as the second largest party by vote and the third by seats in the National Assembly.

The MQM shares a culture of sacrifice with the PPP. While the PPP focuses on its martyred leaders, the Bhuttos, the MQM constantly refers to its "martyred" party workers in the context of the military operations of 1992–1994 and 1995 as well as targeted killings before and after. Unlike the Sindhi, Pakhtun, and Baluch nationalist parties that identify with their respective provinces and claimed historical roots, the MQM and its Mohajir constituency miss out on both geography and history. This community suffered a gradual decline in its superordinate position in jobs and services over two generations after independence.[32] The MQM has developed a sense of persecution all around.[33] It alone among ethnic parties faced conspiracy theories about its sponsorship by the army. It was speculated that the 1983 Movement for Restoration of Democracy agitation led by the Sindhis as a belated reaction to the execution of Z. A. Bhutto in 1979 pushed Zia to create a Mohajir party in Sindh.[34] Later the MQM joined Musharraf and put together a ruling coalition in Karachi along with the PML-Q in 2003. After the 2008 and 2013 elections, it formed a coalition with the PPP that was aborted soon after, in the earlier elections more than once.

In 2010, its leader, Altaf Hussain, publicly asked the "patriotic generals" to act against the corrupt government in martial law–like operations and referred to Charles de Gaulle's model to cleanse society.[35] He also asked the Supreme Court to order the army to move against the corrupt politicians and "feudals" under Article 190 of the Constitution. The MQM faced numerous imponderables from the beginning. At a quarter of the population of Sindh, Mohajirs could never capture power in the province through elections without provincial reorganization. The idea of carving out a separate province of Karachi lingered on for half a century and again surfaced in May 2012. Nearly half of the Mohajir population of Sindh lived outside Karachi, while half of Karachi's population was non-Mohajir. The project of a Karachi Province was expected to lead to a bloody partition process involving the cross-migration of Mohajirs and non-Mohajirs, as a mirror image of the cross-migration of Hindus, Sikhs, and Muslims in 1947.

The MQM's opponents accuse the party of indulging in militant activities against its political adversaries from rival parties, non-Mohajir ethnic communities—Pakhtuns and Sindhis—and its own breakaway faction, MQM-Hakiki.[36] The party has been subjected to allegations of social violence by way of extortion from shopkeepers, traders, and industrialists. The electoral behavior of the MQM has been criticized for coercion, registration of bogus votes, and rigging the elections. The party continues to look for a larger role at the national level beyond its ethnic heartland. In 2010, it held conventions in Lahore, Multan, and Rawalpindi in an aborted move to demonstrate its nationwide appeal. The MQM wanted to revive Musharraf's local bodies system. Because it could not control the provincial administration in Sindh, it wanted to secure the administration of the Mohajir-dominated urban centers of Karachi and Hyderabad.[37] Musharraf had merged the five districts of Karachi into one urban district that remained the MQM stronghold for five years under its energetic mayor. In the face of the PPP government's abrupt move to revive the old pattern after the MQM left the coalition for the third time in a row, the latter was obliged to bargain for the withdrawal of that initiative as a precondition for rejoining the coalition. In October 2012, the party was able to push for legislation for local government through the Sindh Assembly, which elicited a severe backlash from Sindhi nationalists.

The MQM often played the role of opposition within the ruling coalition on such issues as price hikes, the provisions of the annual budget relating to imposition of new taxes, increases in the general sales tax, wheat subsidies, the alleged rigging of elections in Gilgit-Baltistan, and not being allowed to contest and "win" two seats for the Azad Kashmir Assembly in 2011. The Sindhi dissident voices, led by the PPP's interior minister Zulfikar Mirza, were overly fatigued by the perceived intransigence of the MQM, even as the federal government struggled to keep the party on board. In a TV address in September 2011, Altaf Hussain threatened to raise an army—Haq Prast Lashkar—to fight terrorism. The MQM's pitched battles with the ANP—the party of Pakhtuns in Karachi—and the Sindhi–Baluch conundrum from Lyari continued to make headlines. During the 1990s and 2000s, the MQM's street power set the pattern for other parties, especially the ANP and later the PPP, to develop their own activist groups. In 2014–2015, these parties were engaged in a war of attrition in the background of a police operation against militants and Altaf Hussain's call for division of Sindh.

ANP

The ANP, as a Pakhtun nationalist party, fought to carve out a space for itself in Karachi, which is considered to be the biggest Pakhtun city, even surpassing Peshawar, the heartland and capital of KP. The ANP's dynastic leadership goes back to the 1930s, when Abdul Ghaffar Khan took up the cause of Pakhtun nationalism.[38] In Pakistan, both Ghaffar Khan and his son Wali Khan spent years in jail for their alleged anti-Pakistan stance and separatist ambitions. For its part, the party has been reduced from the leading provincial party called Khudai Khidmatgars, or Red Shirts, after the color of the party dress, in the decade before independence to one of the five contenders for power in KP. Talking with the ANP leadership is termed an "interview with history."[39] The ANP is a self-confessed secular party among the most religious community of Pakistan. The party became a target of the Taliban and proto-Taliban groups after they fled Afghanistan and landed in KP post-9/11. By July 2010, these groups had killed 485 leaders, cadres, and workers of that party, including the son of the information minister and two members of the KP Assembly. The party has been caught between its ideological heritage of nonviolence, a cultivated social conscience, and a commitment to renaissance of the Pakhtun language and literature on the one hand and Talibanization of the Pakhtun society in the 1990s and 2000s on the other.

President Zardari (2008–2013) delivered on his promise to change the name of the NWFP to Pakhtunkhwa through the Eighteenth Amendment and earned the lasting gratitude of the ANP. However, the PPP's role in the three-way battle for street power in Karachi somewhat alienated the ANP's leadership. The latter found the PPP overly committed to saving its coalition with the MQM. It wanted the army to control target killings in Karachi even as, traditionally, the ANP and the army have been poles apart. The latter considered the ANP's predecessor, the National Awami Party (NAP), a traitor to the cause of national integration and fought with the Baluch guerillas from 1973 to 1977 after the dismissal of the NAP government in Quetta by Z. A. Bhutto. The Supreme Court declared the NAP to be against Pakistan's integrity in 1975 and banned it. During the 1990s, the party reasserted itself on the political stage and entered into successive ruling coalitions led by the PPP and PML-N. The new generation of ANP cadres and workers carry autonomist ambitions for KP and look for security of life, jobs, and business in Karachi. Party politics in KP was not smooth under the ANP government (2008–2013), accompanying a downward trend of its popularity. In Karachi, the party's constituency faced the usual dilemmas of the third generation of a migrant community, looking for space in the land of migration. The party was routed in the 2013 elections, winning a mere handful of seats in the Khyber Pakhtunkhwa Assembly and one seat in the National Assembly.

SMALLER PARTIES: LAYING OUT THE TURF

Various "rightist" parties belonging to the Islamic and conservative political spectrum continue to operate on the margins of the system, largely carrying a message of transformation of the state and society. Several jihadi organizations proliferated in the society in the first decade of the twenty-first century, ironically under Musharraf, some allegedly sponsored by ISI. Shah Ahmad Noorani's Jamiat Ulema Pakistan declined from the 1980s onward in the face of the rising MQM. Among the Muttahida Majlis-e Amal (MMA) parties, a Wahhabi outfit, Jamiat Ahl Hadith, enjoyed a limited appeal. The banned Tehrik-e Nifaz-e Fiqha Jafria, a Shia party, along with its breakaway faction, Tehrik-e-Jafria, and its new incarnation, Majlis Wahdatul Muslimeen, had no electoral prospects. The JUI-Samiul Haq, based on a madrasah that trained mujahideen in Akora Khatak from the 1980s on, has stagnated. Its leader emerged on top of the Defense of Pakistan Council in 2011, an alliance of Islamic parties including extremist and banned militant outfits. Only JI and JUI-F remained mainstream Islamic parties.

JI

The current politics of the two Islamic parties JI and JUI reflects two different Islamic cultures. The JI represents Islamic ideology, national and international networking, vigilante culture, and anti-Indian, anti-American, and anti-Zionist political attitudes. The JUI represents tribal Islam of the Pakhtun variety, a mosque-and-madrasah network, and a sectarian identity based on the Deobandi school of thought. The JI supported Gulbuddin Hikmatyar and Ahmed Shah Masood against the Taliban in Afghanistan in 1996 and interpreted the Taliban's ascendency as a U.S. conspiracy. Later, the JI appropriated the Taliban's cause. When a JI rally in Peshawar was attacked by the Taliban in 2010, its leadership accused the U.S. intelligence agency Blackwater for it, since Blackwater was made up of CIA contractors. After video showing the Taliban publicly lashing a 17-year-old girl from Swat was released in 2009, the JI claimed that the story and the video were fake and fabricated. The JI has a study circle mind-set. Its 6,213 registered members undergo periodic training workshops for ideological indoctrination that leads to self-righteousness, missionary zeal, and a commitment to changing morals and manners, politics and economics, and the region and the world.[40] It has an all-embracing agenda pertaining to personal piety, interest-free banking, Islamic education through textbooks, and passing and safeguarding Islamic laws, such as the Hudood Ordinances and the Blasphemy Law. Its indoctrinated workers disapprove of New Year's, Valentine's Day, and birthday parties as Western imposition, Basant as a Hindu festival,[41] and Nouroze as a Zoroastrian practice—all un-Islamic.[42] It has resorted to intimidation tactics to stop the showing of *Burqavaganza*, a play critical of the use of the hijab and veil staged by the Ajoka theater in Lahore, on the basis that the play ridicules Islamic mores. The party has launched several anti-America rallies. It has been in step with such groups as Hizbut-Tahrir, which operates mainly among expatriate Muslims in the West to establish Khilafat. The JI has popularized a dichotomy between Islam and the West and condemned the ruling elite as stooges of American imperialism. Amir Munawwar Hasan (2011) represented the first generation of leadership from the JI's student wing, Islami Jamiat Talaba, and was followed by a veteran of MMA activist politics, Sirajul Haq, in 2014.

The JI is a vanguard party of virtuosos committed to heralding the movement toward an Islamic revolution from the top, presuming that it would have a trickle-down effect. That explains its failure to connect with the people and mobilize them along the mundane issues of daily life. The JI has been criticized for spreading bigotry, anti-Westernism, hatred against non-Muslim minorities, and support for the Taliban. It has several subsidiary organizations, such as the Islamic Lawyers Movement. While its youth organizations, Pasban and Shabaab Milli, are no longer active, the party has operated more through schools, colleges, and universities than through madrasahs and thus influenced a large number of students who got subsequently recruited into official and professional positions.[43] The party has failed at the polls but succeeded in spreading its message that religion and politics are one in Islam, that Islam is a complete code of life, that the Christian West has been inherently inimical to the Islamic world since the Crusades, and that America is committed to destroying Pakistan. It has upheld the cause of safeguarding national sovereignty in terms of security of Pakistan's nuclear assets against the perceived Indo-Israeli conspiracy to destroy them, endorsed by the United States. It considered the MQM a terrorist organization and threatened to stage a long march to Islamabad for establishing peace in Karachi. The JI lost its Mohajir constituency in Sindh, its partners in the MMA, its relatively populist and articulate leader Qazi Hussain Ahmed, and some electoral ground in its stronghold in KP in 2008 and 2013—even though it could form a coalition government with PTI in this state after the 2013 elections.

The JUI-Fazl ur Rehman has been a strident Deobandi sectarian party close to the Taliban in terms of ideological moorings and organizational links. Under Musharraf, it was the mainstay of the MMA government in Peshawar and a coalition partner of the PML-Q in Baluchistan. Its chief, Fazl ur Rehman, was appointed leader of the opposition in the National Assembly by Musharraf in 2003, even though he was not supported by the majority of the opposition. The JUI focused on keeping a high public profile. It got its clerics and party stalwarts appointed on key positions in the PPP-led ruling setup after 2008. Whereas the JI has never been a coalition partner of "secular" parties such as the PPP or ANP, the JUI has partnered with both of them. In 2009–2010, it continued to give an impression of leaving the PPP-led government in protest against its pro-U.S. policies, ostensibly to placate its constituency among the Taliban.[44] It also wanted to include Ahle-Sunnat-wal-Jamat, the political wing of the banned militant anti-Shia party Sipah-e-Sahaba Pakistan in the "revived" MMA. The JUI mediated between the Taliban and the government for signing peace deals in the FATA in 2009. The JUI's oppositional politics within the government related to, for example, the budgetary cuts for the ministries under its control and criticism of the budget for following the instructions of the International Monetary Fund and the World Bank.[45] It continued to talk about unfulfilled promises such as changing policy vis-à-vis the United States. The JUI left the coalition in protest against the sacking of its minister Azam Swati, the main financier of the party who had a huge business concern in the United States and who later joined the PTI. Fazl ur Rehman fielded himself as a candidate for prime minister in June 2012 even as his party had only eight members in the Assembly. In the 2013 elections, it emerged as the second largest party in Khyber Pakhtunkhwa Assembly as the leading opponent of the PTI.

At the other end, the Baluch nationalist parties were reduced to small groups of people belonging to their respective tribes. The (Baluch) National Party (NP) and the Pakhtunkhwa Milli Awami Party (PKMAP) dominated the political scene in Baluchistan in 2014. The NP upholds the Baluch nationalist cause through democratic means under its new leader, Chief Minister Abdul Malik Baloch. The PKMAP is a major coalition partner of the NP and the PML-N in Quetta and Islamabad. The NP and PKMAP demonstrate a liberal and progressive perspective on issues of de-conflation between religion and politics, devolution of power to federating units, and adoption of democratic means to achieve political goals. Baluch nationalism remained without an authentic and inclusive representation in the political system. The Jamhoori Watan Party and Baluch National Party (BNP), based on Bugti and Mengal tribes, respectively, remained relatively less visible outfits.

THE 2013 ELECTIONS

The 2013 elections displayed an enhanced level of political participation with a voter turnout of 55 percent as compared with 44 percent in 2008, an upgraded list of registered voters (thanks to the work of the election commission, which eliminated many bogus voters), and a clear mandate.[46] The military establishment generally played a role in election campaigns either up front, as in 1964–1965, 1985, and 2002, or as a backstage player, as in 1970, 1988, 1990, and 2008. This role was selectively characterized by manipulation of selection of party candidates, creation of party factions, deployment of partisan election officers, control over the media coverage of political parties, and even outright changes of election results.[47] In 2013, the army projected its "neutral" profile. An "independent" Election Commission and a "neutral" caretaker government were put in place on the basis of understanding between the treasury and opposition benches in the National Assembly. However, political parties faced a new menace from outside the parliamentary system in the form of the Taliban. This group threatened and later attacked the three "liberal" and "secular" parties—the PPP, ANP, and MQM—and virtually drove them out of the field in terms of reaching out to their voters. Nearly 300 persons were killed and 900 injured in 148 attacks from January to May 2013.[48] The PPP was also rendered "leaderless" as the Lahore High Court barred President Zardari from participating in politics. The party leadership took the threat seriously after Benazir's assassination in 2007. The ANP's leader, Asfandyar Wali Khan, was unable to address a single public meeting. Hundreds of his party members had already been killed by the Taliban. The Taliban "sanctioned" only the PML-N, PTI, JI, and JUI-F to run election campaigns. This meant that only Punjab, where the PML-N and PTI campaigned, had a real election, while Khyber Pakhtunkhwa and Sindh lacked party activity out in the open. Baluchistan was the target of both the proto-Taliban groups and the militant section of the Baluch nationalists.

A lot of rhetoric about change in the system came from the PTI and others without a clear set of policies or an attractive ideological framework. The election soon emerged as a battle of titans who claimed they could deliver the nation from misery. Anti-Americanism, an anti-corruption agenda, and support for negotiations with the Taliban in search of peace moved to the center stage of the election discourse. Politics took a turn to the right, as the liberal parties succumbed to the Taliban attacks as well as to the anti-incumbency factor in both Islamabad and Peshawar.[49] Under these circumstances, the media emerged as a new arena for political contest by way of providing a forum for public debate among contestants and as a medium for the paid party advertisement.

The election results brought several surprises. Instead of a hung Parliament as predicted by analysts, there was a clear lead for the PML-N, which formed the government in Islamabad and Lahore. The extent of the collapse of the ANP in Khyber Pakhtunkhwa and the PPP in Punjab was beyond all expectations. The PTI's rise was phenomenal, as it bagged thirty-one seats in the National Assembly and formed a coalition government in Khyber Pakhtunkhwa. The party ate into the vote banks of the MQM, PPP, and ANP, where Imran Khan emerged as the viable alternative for disgruntled activists and voters, especially from the urban middle class. However, this pattern of voting did not change the political landscape of Punjab, where Nawaz Sharif continued to have a stable support base after winning back electoral heavyweights from the PML-Q that collapsed during the campaign. At the other end, Islamic parties nosedived in the election, with the sole exception of the JUI-F, partly because the Islamic agenda was hijacked by the Taliban operating militantly from outside the system. Still, the JI joined the ruling coalition in Peshawar, and the JUI-F did so in Islamabad. This kept both of them visible on top.

Finally, the election results led to regionalization of politics whereby political parties clung to their core areas of support in an election marred by uncertainty, not the least due to militancy.[50] This applied to the PML-N in Punjab, the PPP and MQM in rural and urban Sindh, respectively, the JUI-F in Khyber Pakhtunkhwa, and a plethora of miniscule tribal-based parties in Baluchistan. Only the PTI covered new ground partly as a result of its accommodation by the Taliban and possibly the tacit support of the "establishment," as alleged by many analysts. Overall, the 2013 elections testified to the primacy of political parties as leading actors on the political stage of Pakistan, along with their leaders as icons for party identification. The period between the 2013 and the next elections was expected to stabilize the emergent pattern of party politics at a new pedestal characterized by the emergence of a new party PTI in the Parliament, reincorporation of Islamic parties back in the mainstream, and possible revival of "liberal" parties, such as the PPP and ANP. However, within a year, Prime Minister Nawaz Sharif faced the greatest challenge to his government as the PTI launched its sit-in in Islamabad on August 14, 2014, as a protest against the alleged rigging in the 2013 elections. A minor religio-political group, Minhajul Quran, led by cleric Tahirul Qadri, joined hands with Imran Khan. Together they were able to shake the democratic dispensation. However, all the parliamentary parties got together in the face of the grim prospect of a military takeover, especially after a PTI renegade, Javed Hashmi, "revealed" the links of the two mavericks with the establishment.

CONCLUSION

This chapter sought to analyze internal cleavages, organizational problems, and personal and ideological conflicts within political parties and their modes of expression and mobilization. Some broad features of political parties in the country have been visible. For example, they are leader parties par excellence. Nawaz Sharif, Asif Zardari, Imran Khan, Altaf Hussain, Asfandyar Wali Khan, and Fazl ur Rehman are inseparable from their respective parties. As icons, they appeal to the party's followers in the public and symbolize a one-window operation in the context of negotiations and bargaining with other players on the political stage. The key to the dynastic leadership lay with the followers' need for party identification. Zardari's leadership provided the grand symbol of identification with a political party in the absence of an elaborate hierarchical structure, an ideology, a set of policies, and a clear class-based constituency. The ability of Zardari to keep the leading factions of the PPP united and to crystallize an appropriate projection of the PPP legacy played a crucial role in keeping the party as a serious contender of power in the field. At the other end, Nawaz Sharif is responsible for reinventing the Muslim League for the past quarter of a century, in the process establishing a pattern of patrimonial leadership that survived his absence from the political scene for eight long years. The 2008 and 2013 elections show that the PML-N's appeal is now confined to Punjab. Inaction for a decade when Nawaz Sharif was in exile cost the party in terms of organizational work. Asfandyar Wali Khan represents Ghaffar Khan's charisma, which has diluted over a span of three generations. However, it is still morally appealing in the framework of Pakhtun nationalism. Fazl ur Rehman is a legatee more of the Deobandi network of mosques and madrasahs than of intrafamily transition of leadership. Imran Khan represents an option for middle-class citizens of Pakistan as a messiah. Outside KP, he lacks a rural constituency that has been the backbone of the electorate in terms of voter turnout. The PTI's core moved from a team of ideologues and reformers to electoral contestants prior to the 2013 elections. In the JI's case, the new leadership elected in 2014 is bland and uninspiring and carries few prospects of a credible showing at the polls. At the other end, Altaf Hussain's remote-control leadership draws on fossilized positions, couched in a rhetoric projecting the party's middle- and lower-middle-class demands and aspirations.

One can argue that the leader rather than a set of policies provides the framework for resilience of public support for political parties. While the liberal intelligentsia and civil society in general and the PTI in particular sharply criticize what they consider a cult of leader, the family-based leadership represents continuity in terms of a broad spectrum of policies and ideologies. Political parties have kept the modicum of democracy in place in Pakistan as a source of legitimacy through the Parliament. They structure the political conflict by rationalizing the message of contending forces and providing a sense of order to a fluid situation. They keep the public in the picture during the period between elections. They have mobilized the public on all issues through all means for almost all the time during the post-Musharraf period. The demand for change in the system has yet to acquire a transformative character, in the absence of a class-based idiom and a realistic set of policies. At least partly due to the strident role of the electronic media, people now identify political parties with corruption, dynastic politics, bad governance, and pursuit of the foreign agenda, such as war against terror. At the same time, political parties in Pakistan are the makers and shapers of a massive—though amorphous—system of institutional representation of electoral contestants who have scant economic and political resources to get things done for their constituents on their own. This fact promises to keep parties at the heart of the political system of Pakistan almost as a structural requirement.

NOTES

1. Rafiq Afzal, *Political Parties in Pakistan*, 3 vols. (Islamabad: National Institute of Historical and Cultural Research), 1998.
2. Philip Jones, *The Pakistan Peoples Party: Rise to Power* (Oxford: Oxford University Press, 2003).
3. David M. Farrell and Webb Paul, "Political Parties as Campaign Organizations," in *Parties Without Partisans*, ed. Russell J. Dalton and Martin P. Wattenberg, 102–128 (Oxford: Oxford University Press, 2006).
4. Imran Farooq, *Imperatives of Discipline and Organization* (Urdu), MQM official document, Karachi, n.d., 6–7.

5. Mohammad Waseem, *Democratization in Pakistan: A Study of the 2002 Elections* (Karachi: Oxford University Press), 31.

6. Shahid Javed Burki, "The 18th Amendment: Pakistan Constitution Redesigned," ISAS Report No. 112, National University of Singapore, September 3, 2010, 10–14.

7. Philip Oldenberg, *India, Pakistan and Democracy: Solving the Puzzle of Divergent Paths* (Abingdon: Routledge, 2010), 84.

8. Edward Viola and Scot Mainwaring, "Transitions to Democracy: Brazil and Argentina in the 1980s," *Journal of International Studies* 38, no. 2 (1985): 194–196.

9. Anwer Abbas, "ECP Registers 216 Political Parties for Upcoming Polls," *Pakistan Today*, January 14, 2013, http://www.pakistantoday.com.pk/2013/01/14/national /ecp-registers-216-political-parties-for-upcoming-polls/.

10. Jones, *Pakistan Peoples Party*; Shahid Javed Burki, *Pakistan Under Bhutto* (London: Palgrave Macmillan, 1980); Anwar Hussain Syed, *The Discourse and Politics of Zulfikar Ali Bhutto* (London: Palgrave Macmillan, 1972); and Stanley Wolpert, *Zulfi Bhutto of Pakistan: His Life and Times* (New York: Oxford University Press, 1993).

11. *Dawn*, May 10, 2010.

12. *Express Tribune*, September 24, 2010; *The News*, December 7, 2010.

13. Mohammad Waseem, *Politics and the State in Pakistan* (Islamabad: National Institute of Historical and Cultural Research, 2007), 311–312.

14. *The News*, May 16, 2010.

15. *The News*, July 5 and 6, 2010.

16. *The News*, June 17–18, 2010.

17. Khalid bin Sayeed, *Politics in Pakistan: The Nature and Direction of Change* (New York: Praeger, 1980); Waseem, *Politics and the State in Pakistan*; and Saadia Toor, *The State of Islam: Culture and Cold War Politics in Pakistan* (London: Pluto, 2011).

18. Benedict Anderson, *Imagined Communities* (London: Verso, 1985), 10–11.

19. Qamar Zaman Kaira, "Founding Day of PPP-III," *The News*, December 2, 2010.

20. Mohammad Waseem, "Pakistan, a Majority-Constraining Federalism," *India Quarterly* 67, no. 3 (2011): 222–224.

21. Sohail Khan, "Next Week Crucial as SC Takes up Constitutional Matters," *The News*, May 22, 2010.

22. Pew Research Center poll, www.daily.Pak/p19394.

23. Farrukh Saleem, "So, Let It Be," *The News*, December 26, 2010.

24. Mohammad Anis, "PML-N Issues 14-Point Charge Sheet Against Musharraf," *The News*, October 12, 2010.

25. *The News*, September 20, 2010.

26. *Nation*, November 12, 2010.

27. *The News*, September 20, 2010.

28. Mumtaz Alvi, "Imran Wants Third Umpire Action on Closure," *The News*, April 8, 2011.

29. Saleem H. Ali, "The Imran Khan Factor," *Express Tribune*, February 22, 2011.

30. Haider Mehdi, "A Meaning Behind Everything," *Nation*, October 9, 2011.

31. Mahreen Khan, "Imran's Revolutionary Road," *Express Tribune*, October 30, 2010.

32. Yunas Samad, "In and Out of Power but Not Down and Out: Mohajir Identity Politics," in *Pakistan: Nationalism Without a Nation*, ed. Christophe Jaffrelot (New Delhi: Manohar, 2002), 66–68.

33. Mohammad Waseem, "Ethnic Conflict in Pakistan: Case of Mohajir National-ism," in *Millennial Perspectives: Essays in Honour of Kingsley de Silva*, ed. G. Peiris and S. W. R. de A. Samarasinghe (Colombo: Law and Society Trust, 1999), 458.

34. Brigadier A. R Siddiqi, *Partition and the Making of the Mohajir Mindset* (Karachi: Oxford University Press, 2008).

35. Shaheen Sehbai, "Monumental Disaster, Monumental Mismanagement," *The News*, August 23, 2010.

36. Waseem, "Ethnic Conflict in Pakistan," 464–465.

37. *Nation*, August 23, 2010.

38. Waqar Ail Shah, *Ethnicity, Islam and Nationalism: Muslim Politics in the North-West Frontier Province, 1937–47* (New York: Oxford University Press, 1999), 167–175.

39. Suhail Warraich, "Interview with History: Recalling Some Rare Moments with Legendary and Prophetic Wali Khan?" *The News*, May 16, 2010.

40. Amer Mateen, "Special Report on the JI," *The News*, May 31–June 1 and 2, 2010.

41. Kite flying is an expression of welcoming the spring season.

42. Amer Mateen, "Special Report on the JI," *The News*, May 31–June 2, 2010.

43. Mateen, "Special Report on the JI."

44. *Daily Times*, May 28, 2010.

45. *Nation*, June 6, 2010.

46. See Imtiaz Alam, "Pakistan's Tenth Elections," *South Asia Journal*, April–June 2013, 11–16.

47. See Waseem, *Politics and the State*, 246–249, 396–399, 430–435.

48. Pakistan Institute for Peace Studies, "Election 2013: Violence Against Political Parties, Candidates and Voters," Islamabad, May 2013, https://www.google.fr /?gws_rd=ssl#q=Pakistan+Institute+for+Peace+Studies%2C+"Election+2013: +Violence+Against+Political+Parties%2C+Candidates+and+Voters.

49. Umar Farooq, "In the 'Right' Direction," *The Herald*, April 2013, 42–48.

50. See Mohammad Waseem and Mariam Mufti, *Political Parties in Pakistan: Organization and Power Structure* (Lahore: Lahore University of Management Sciences, 2012), xxiii.

CHAPTER 3

THE JUDICIARY AS A POLITICAL ACTOR

Philip Oldenburg

The political landscape of Pakistan has always had a prominent place for its judiciary, and particularly the Supreme Court.[1] The emergence of a judicially active court led by Chief Justice Iftikhar Muhammad Chaudhry and then the exhilarating 2007–2009 Lawyers' Movement seemed to mark a watershed in the Supreme Court's role, from junior partner to the military and bureaucracy in times of crisis, to an institution autonomously exercising power. Indeed, it can be argued that "had it not been for the revival of the rule of law and for a mechanism to enforce constitutional limits on power abuse by elected officials [in 2008–2013], democracy would not have survived in Pakistan."[2] These developments conjured up the image of a rule of law directed by a judiciary of integrity and vision, supported by a large and vigorous segment of civil society, the lawyers. The lawyers have since lost their heroic image, and the Supreme Court, after the retirement of Chief Justice Chaudhry in December 2013, has not asserted itself in the way it had. It has continued to claim the political high ground, but it is unclear whether it would favor a "juristocratic" democracy.[3]

Pakistan has what some label a "partial" democracy, or a "hybrid" regime, that oscillates between an autocracy, when the military is openly in power, and a flawed democracy, when relatively free and fair elections occur, forcible suppression of dissent declines, but the military retains control over significant parts of the state. On the whole, in the country's history, the judiciary has played the role of a rubber-stamp institution legitimizing military-bureaucratic rule.

Institutions of that hybrid regime such as Parliament and political parties are weak. Policies and programs and laws are not conceived and written in Parliament and provincial legislative assemblies; rather, that has been done mainly by a handful of insiders in the offices of the ruling political party's leader. A major exception, though, and perhaps a sign of the changing times, was the bargaining that produced a unanimous vote in favor of the Eighteenth Amendment in 2010, which was conducted across party lines, in committees. Most political parties have organizations that are hardly active between elections or episodic street mobilizations; none have a leadership selection process that avoids personalistic choices. In recent decades, none of the major political leaders have demonstrated a taste or capacity for statesmanship, as opposed to skills of jockeying for power.

Civil society also seems bereft of either great leaders or organized social movements capable of changing the regime's character. The media—first print and now television and the Internet—have been allowed to develop significant independence and influence in the last thirty years. Some parts of the media have been able to put a small dent in the government's general unaccountability, and a succession of flawed elections in the 1990s also did a bit.

In this context, the Lawyers' Movement, which Sattar calls the "rule-of-law" movement,[4] has brought a new possibility to the fore: that the initiative for establishing the rule of law in a revived democracy in Pakistan would come from the judiciary. Some members of the judiciary, and particularly Chief Justice Chaudhry, seemed to think that the judiciary—essentially the Supreme Court, with occasional help from High Courts—could do this from its constitutionally established position of independence and power. But to establish that position will probably require the acceptance of the higher judiciary as a more purely political force.

THE JUDICIARY AND THE EXECUTIVE BEFORE 2007—AND THE LAWYERS' MOVEMENT

The judiciary has not had much success in preserving democratic government. As Mahmud summarizes his very detailed argument, "the successive constitutional crises that confronted the Pakistani courts were not of their own making. But the doctrinally inconsistent, judicially inappropriate, and politically timid responses fashioned by these courts ultimately undermined constitutional governance."[5] The details of the judiciary's willingness to bend to the will of the de jure or de facto executive head of the government—starting with Governor-General Ghulam Muhammad in 1954—are enshrined in a series of major court decisions that have been carefully analyzed by scholars and lawyers.[6] Mostly these conflicts have been conducted with due decorum, but in 1997, perhaps as a reflection of the general trend of declining respect for all institutions of government, the Supreme Court became a literal battleground, when political workers of Nawaz Sharif's ruling party stormed the building to prevent the hearing of a contempt case against the prime minister. Hamid Khan says, "it was indeed one of the most despicable assaults on the courts in judicial history."[7] Finally, "the Supreme Court committed collective suicide."[8] The judiciary's willingness to bend to political change continued. After the 1999 coup, Justice Chaudhry, whose removal eight years later became the focus of the Lawyers' Movement, was one of the 85 percent of superior court justices who swore an oath to uphold General Musharraf's Provisional Constitution Order (PCO) of 1999.[9] In 2000, the Supreme Court followed tradition in legitimizing Musharraf's coup.

In March 2007, there was a dramatic departure from this pattern: the Chief Justice refused to resign even when President General Musharraf, presiding publicly over a group of the most powerful men in the Pakistan government, put him under pressure to do so. After his refusal and the first wave of the Lawyers' Movement, the Chief Justice was restored to his office by the Supreme Court in July 2007. In November 2007, when Musharraf declared a state of emergency and issued a new PCO, in a reversal of the earlier ratio, roughly two-thirds of the justices of the Supreme Court and High Courts refused to take an oath under the PCO, after which the Chief Justice was put effectively under house arrest and the lawyers' leaders jailed.[10] It was not until more than a year after the February 2008 election that the winning parties' commitment to restore the Chief Justice to his office was fulfilled.

The crisis of the judiciary and the Lawyers' Movement has been well described in a number of popular and scholarly writings.[11] General Musharraf's desperate attempt to retain full powers, in the quasi-coup of November 2007, and Benazir Bhutto's assassination in December 2007, paradoxically produced a reasonably free and fair election in February 2008,[12] in which the military's decision not to interfere was crucial. After the election of May 2013, "free and fair" with some major blemishes, there was a peaceful handover of government from one party coalition to its opposition, the first in Pakistan's history. The military has, however, retained its accustomed sphere of control over virtually all national security matters and has not relinquished its economic enterprises and positions in civilian administrative institutions.

There were five phases in this crisis, linked to each other by the figure of Chief Justice Chaudhry. The first, in which the Supreme Court under his leadership demonstrated an unusual activist bent, ended when Musharraf attempted to force Chaudhry's resignation and then suspended him, in March 2007. In the second phase, the lawyers mobilized around the effort to get the Supreme Court to restore him, which succeeded in July. The third phase began with the political bargains struck by Musharraf with the Pakistan Peoples Party (PPP) that brought Benazir Bhutto back to Pakistan; the Supreme Court's rulings that allowed Nawaz Sharif to return as head of the Pakistan Muslim League—Nawaz (PML-N); and the election of Musharraf to the presidency (and his final relinquishing of the office of Chief of Army Staff).

Then, apparently feeling threatened with loss of office by a possible decision of the Supreme Court, Musharraf declared a state of emergency, on November 3, 2007. This time he put all the lawyers' leaders firmly into jail for three weeks, after which they were put under house arrest (and released by the newly elected government, only in March 2008). A PCO was promulgated, and the Chief Justice and others were replaced. But the December 27 assassination of Benazir Bhutto shifted the political landscape, and Musharraf's allies lost the elections of February 2008.

The fourth phase began with the election of 2008, which brought the PPP to power. However, reneging on its campaign promise and agreement with the opposition PML-N to restore the "PCO judges," the PPP broke the solidarity of the sixty-four Supreme Court and High Court judges who had stood by Chaudhry and who had refused to take the oath under the PCO; fifty-eight judges accepted reappointment without insisting on Chaudhry's reinstatement. In the end, the issue of the restoration of judges was reduced to Chaudhry and a few other judges.[13] The Lawyers' Movement reemerged, threatening a "long march" to Islamabad to force the PPP government to fulfill its agreement. The restoration finally happened on March 16, 2009, with the decisive pressure to get it done apparently coming from Chief of Army Staff General Ashfaq Pervez Kayani.[14]

In the fifth phase (which ended with the retirement of Chief Justice Chaudhry in December 2013), the Supreme Court resumed the judicial activism that had apparently provoked General Musharraf in the first place.[15] Major issues revolved around the National Reconciliation Ordinance (NRO), declared unconstitutional on December 19, 2009;[16] a threatened confrontation with Parliament on the power to appoint judges in the Eighteenth Amendment to the Constitution some months later;[17] and the revival of the NRO case in January 2012. The court forced the ouster of Prime Minister Gilani in June 2012, having held him in contempt for refusing to write a letter to the Swiss authorities asking to reinstate corruption charges against President Zardari; in November, the new prime minister, Raja Pervez

Ashraf, also under the court's pressure, wrote the letter. Less forcefully, and with less obvious results, the court confronted the military in a missing persons case and, judging the petition of Asghar Khan filed in 1996, ruled that the Chief of Army Staff and the director of the Inter-Services Intelligence (ISI) had administered an illegal fund for candidates in the 1990 election and recommended their prosecution. In this period, the Supreme Court Bar Association elected, albeit in a very close contest, Pakistan's most prominent human rights lawyer, Asma Jahangir, to be its president for a year's term. Other lawyers engaged in thuggish demonstrations against some judges,[18] and a few gained notoriety by showering the assassin of Punjab governor Salman Taseer with rose petals in January 2011. The lawyers as an organized force have continued to lose influence. But the importance of the judiciary in supporting a continuing democracy in Pakistan seems clear: retired judges manned the Election Commission that conducted the national and provincial elections of May 2013, and three of the four provincial caretaker governments in the two months before were headed by retired judges. The Supreme Court also actively participated in running the election, issuing orders on delimitations, overseas voting, and other matters. Since Chief Justice Chaudhry's retirement in December 2013, however, there has been a noticeable decline in the headline-worthy actions of the court.

JUDICIAL ACTIVISM

The judicial crisis of 2007 was probably triggered at least in part by Chief Justice Chaudhry's use—or possible overuse—of the court's *suo moto* powers to rule on the government's actions. Particular cases dealt with the privatization of the Pakistan Steel Mills Corporation and the effort to force the intelligence agencies to produce "missing persons," mainly from Baluchistan.[19] Some of the "missing" persons had been turned over to the United States as part of Pakistan's cooperation in the "war on terror," so the court's actions were seen by Musharraf to be a challenge to that part of his foreign policy.[20] According to Ghias, "by expanding the reach of judicial power to intelligence agencies, the Chaudhry Court had gone too far. Instead of the social control over dissidents and political opponents, the Court was expanding its power by taking up the popular cause of missing persons."[21] But, as Ghias notes, "the most significant threat to the Musharraf regime came not from what the Court had done, but what it could potentially do in the October 2007 presidential election,"[22] because the law required former government officials to leave their job two years before contesting. In Ghias's view, the rumors that the court would be prepared to challenge the regime on this ground as well was decisive.

It is important to note that once the Chief Justice was restored to office, in July 2007, the court resumed its judicial activism on all these fronts. Some of these steps were far-reaching, direct challenges to Musharraf's regime:

> Because of the pressure from the Supreme Court, the regime was forced to acknowledge the detention of more missing people and to release them. In addition, Chaudhry ordered the regime to release people who were not declared missing but who were being held without trial. In order to avoid appearing before the Supreme Court, the regime even released suspected "terrorists" who had been arrested but never charged.[23]

Crucially, the court blocked the implementation of the NRO that Musharraf had negotiated with Benazir Bhutto after Chief Justice Chaudhry's restoration ("in desperation" according to Ghias).[24] As that negotiation was in progress, the court decided that Nawaz Sharif was entitled to return to Pakistan, voiding his "agreement" to a 10-year period of exile, and declared the government in contempt for putting him on an airplane to Saudi Arabia when he landed in Pakistan in September.

The court did not rule directly against Musharraf on the issue of the validity of his candidacy for a second term as president in an election held before his first term ended, taking advantage of the old electoral college, formed by the legislatures elected in the rigged 2002 election, rather than wait for a new electoral college to be formed after the new elections, then scheduled for December. The Lawyers' Movement began protesting the court's inaction, even though it had placed a stay on announcing the election results. The election that duly took place gave Musharraf his second term, but the chance that the court would rule it invalid was very real. As Ghias notes, "it was in this context that Musharraf imposed [what was in effect] martial law."[25]

The new court of Musharraf-appointed judges lasted beyond the elections, because the Zardari-led PPP government refused to honor its agreement with the opposition PML-N to restore the deposed judges, who had been released in March 2008.[26] So there was a gap in the court's judicial activism, and Zardari became the revived Lawyers' Movement target. Although the PPP had moved to impeach President Musharraf, succeeding in getting him to resign in August 2008, its refusal to restore the judges forced the PML-N to withdraw from the coalition supporting the government. Zardari—now president—and the PPP were able to secure a split in the judges supporting Chaudhry. Further demonstrations by the lawyers ultimately ended with the restoration of the Chief Justice, but only once the replacement Chief Justice reached retirement on March 16, 2009, more than a year after the election.[27] The "PCO judges" were finally removed by Supreme Court order on July 31, 2009, as part of the court's judgment that the declaration of emergency in November 2007 was unconstitutional. Ayaz Amir writes: "What had restored their lordships was not the lawyers' movement, something that had already lost steam. They were restored by the dynamics of the political process, even the pressure mounted by Nawaz Sharif being an aspect of the same process."[28]

The court soon resumed its activism, inquiring into day-to-day government and ordering administrative remedies. It continued to brandish a wide range of its suo moto initiatives, holding hearings on the violence in Karachi, in August–September 2011, for example, and investigating the so-called Memogate crisis in early 2012. The court did not hesitate to intervene when it found fault in the arrangements for the May 2013 elections.

The court has also actively pushed for judicial reform more generally, building on some well-funded initiatives of the previous decade, which in turn drew on the work of judicial commissions in the past. A series of judicial conferences—beginning with the International Judicial Conference on the fiftieth anniversary of the Supreme Court in August 2006, followed by four National Judicial Conferences between 2007 and 2011, and then international ones in 2012, 2013, and 2014—featured major Pakistani and foreign experts, with the presentation of papers, speeches, and discussions leading to recommendations for reform. The Law & Justice Commission of Pakistan produced a formal judicial policy in 2009.[29]

Although "judicial reform" would seem to be an obvious positive step, it is, in fact, problematic.[30] The official idea, supported in the last decade by large infusions of aid from the Asian Development Bank and others, has been to improve the efficiency of the courts, through better infrastructure, better training, and increased staffing, with improvement measured in the reduction of the enormous backlog of pending cases.[31] Other aspects of the system, including improved legal education, have not been touched. Although the superior judiciary has reason to see itself as highly qualified, the same is probably not true of the lower courts. Ali Dayan Hasan, writing about the Aasia Bibi case, notes in passing:

It is a sobering thought that, in contrast to the two-year training programme offered to civil servants, district judges receive barely a fortnight of orientation. These judges are meant to dispense justice without any training in judicial ethics and conduct, interpretation and application of the law, or even the basics of judgment writing. And there are complaints that they lack the staple of a proper judiciary: the capacity to dispense justice devoid of personal prejudice.[32]

The view from Islamabad, however, is quite rosy:

In February 2013, the National Judicial Policy Making Committee observed that after application of National Judicial Policy, the district judiciary has decided millions of cases including 95% of Old cases [cases instituted before 31 December 2008]. This performance of judiciary has enhanced the confidence of general public in judiciary as well as in the formal justice system. The Committee observed that the results of Policy are quite encouraging, the Courts have by and large achieved the targets and the shortcoming, if any, is primarily on account of persistent shortage of required number of judges and deficient infrastructure.[33]

But others see "judicial reform" as following from the empowerment of the citizenry, both at the grassroots level and in Parliament, which would need to reform a system where the virtual monopoly of the power to appoint and promote judges has been taken by the Supreme Court. Yet others would see a "reform" as removing or at least reducing the power of the parallel Islamic law court system that was inserted into the Constitution by Zia ul Haq's military regime. The not insignificant constituency for that system, however, might see a "reform" as indicating the fulfillment of the promise of making Pakistan fully "Islamic," and thus giving the *shariat* court system more power than it now has. The increase in judicial activism, including, in particular, the emergence of public interest litigation in the mid-1980s, and within that the now routine use of suo moto powers, is seen by some as the essence of reform but by others as the emergence of a new antidemocratic claim on political power.[34] It thus remains unclear whether the existing formal legal system—particularly the superior judiciary and its attached bar associations—are the problem or the solution, when it comes to establishing a just political and social order. After all, as Siddique argues, "The pro-*status-quo* stance can and does indeed manifest in at times resistance and hostility to not just reforms that make the legal system simpler, transparent and more intelligible to the layperson, but also to any reforms that promote ideas of and mechanisms for professional accountability of judges and lawyers."[35]

The Supreme Court has made use of its suo moto powers since at least 1990, to deal with a wide range of issues, from the famous Mukhtaran Mai rape case, to the cutting down of trees along a canal in Lahore. In the use of suo moto jurisdiction, the superior courts "[free] themselves entirely from the requirements of 'petitioners' or 'aggrieved persons' and . . . are not bound by any procedural limitations. The objective to provide justice to all becomes the driving force of the proceedings."[36] Most significant, perhaps, is that the judges adopt an inquisitorial rather than an adversarial method, summoning government officers and others to court to answer the judges' questions. The Chaudhry court in its use of suo moto powers was thus not exceptional; what may have changed was the vastly increased activity of the electronic media (with film clips of violent encounters, for example), which seemingly has increased the speed with which those powers are called into play.

Some have criticized the extent to which suo moto interventions have occurred,[37] including the implication that the court—whose predecessor, PPP supporters feel, was guilty of the "judicial murder" of Zulifqar Ali Bhutto in 1979—is motivated as much by political antagonism as by a sense of justice.[38] Although these suo moto cases do grab attention, there are not that many of them: in the 2008–2012 period, there were eighty-six, with thirty-three pending as of March 2013.[39] Still, the critics argue, the court is in effect sending a signal that filing a case in the normal way and waiting in the queue for it to be decided is a second-best way of getting justice. Conversely, there are clearly some suo moto cases that have been taken up as a way for the court to consider much larger issues than resolving the immediate problem. But because the entire process of going up the ladder of courts, giving time for arguments on both sides of the issue to mature, is short-circuited by the direct access to the Supreme Court, in the form of a bench selected by the Chief Justice (who, in many of these cases, selects himself), the long-term effects of the court's decisions are more likely to be uncertain and perhaps unfortunate.[40]

JUDICIAL INDEPENDENCE AND THE SEPARATION OF POWERS

Judicial activism is perhaps one way in which the judiciary has carved out a more independent role than was anticipated when the Constitution was written. But there is a firm constitutional mandate for judicial independence, requiring the insulation of the judiciary from financial or administrative dependence on the government.[41] With the *Al-Jehad Trust* case of 1996 and the passage of the Eighteenth and Nineteenth Amendments, the Supreme Court has cemented its ability to strongly influence or even determine the appointment of the higher judiciary.[42] The court can also use its power to punish for contempt of court to force the government to obey its directives.[43]

Judicial independence does not translate automatically into the power to act autonomously. For example, it is not clear just how the court would get its orders enforced against opposition. When the court seemed poised to declare the Eighteenth Amendment unconstitutional, Najam Sethi suggested what might happen in the extreme (and unlikely) case of an explicit government-court confrontation: "The crunch will come if and when the SC [Supreme Court] orders the army to drag the [prime minister] to court or compel him to obey the court's orders. If the army obeys the court instead of the legally elected government as enjoined by the constitution, it will be nothing short of an unprecedented 'judicial coup.' If it defers to the government, the SC will have egg on its face and be stripped of all legitimacy."[44]

Khaled Ahmed used no less colorful language: "And if the army removes the PPP government—it is known that it is as unhappy with the government as the Supreme Court—then it would be time for Justice Chaudhry to either take a stand against the army or eat his words and join the gallery of dishonour of his predecessors."[45] In the event, the Supreme Court, after extensive hearings, dismissed Prime Minister Gilani (on June 19, 2012), after he had been declared in contempt of court for refusing to obey the court's order to reopen the corruption case against President Zardari relating to his Swiss bank accounts. Gilani accepted the decision and stepped down, and a new prime minister was appointed, who at first refused to "write the letter" to the Swiss government but after being threatened with dismissal in turn did so, in October 2012.[46] In February 2013, the Swiss government replied to say that the cases could not be reopened.

The court has now clearly rejected a "basic structure" argument to justify its actions vis-à-vis Parliament and Parliament's executive.[47] The language of the 1973 Constitution (clause 6 of article 239) would seem to be crystal clear: "For the removal of doubt, it is hereby declared that there is no limitation whatever on the power of the Majlis-e-Shoora (Parliament) to amend any of the provisions of the Constitution." This would follow from the sovereignty of the people, as represented in Parliament.[48] Justice Dorab Patel (who had refused to swear allegiance to Zia's PCO in 1981), writing in the mid-1990s in his posthumously published memoir, remarks, "It is clear that the [first] Constituent Assembly did not want to alter the basic structure of a democratic Constitution by conferring legislative powers on the superior Courts."[49] This point is made in Patel's discussion of *Hakim Khan v. the Government of Pakistan* (1992), in which the Supreme Court affirmed Zia ul Haq's shifting of the Objectives Resolution from the preamble to the Constitution (where it served to guide Constitution making so that nothing in the Constitution or subsequent legislation would be in conflict with Islam) to being part of article 2(A). Patel says that this did not make the Objectives Resolution into a "supra-constitutional provision."[50]

Robinson discusses decisions in 1997 and 1998 that seem contradictory, noting that "the Court has leaned both ways, at times professing a basic structure doctrine while at other times eschewing it. It has yet to be seen whether the Court will ultimately solidify or discard this doctrine."[51] In its judgment on petitions challenging the Seventeenth Amendment (2005), the five-member bench of the court, which included Justice Chaudhry, ruled:

> The superior courts of this country have consistently acknowledged that while there may be a basic structure to the Constitution, and while there may also be limitations on the power of Parliament to make amendments to such basic structure, such limitations are to be exercised and enforced not by the judiciary (as in the case of conflict between a statute and Article 8), but by the body politic, i.e., the people of Pakistan. In this context, it may be noted that while Sajjad Ali Shah, C.J., observed that "there is a basic structure of the Constitution which may not be amended by Parliament," he nowhere observes that the power to strike down offending amendments to the Constitution can be exercised by the superior judiciary.[52]

Maryam Khan, making reference to the same judgment, concluded that "if there were any residual doubts about whether Pakistani constitutional discourse could still accommodate the 'basic structure doctrine,' they were categorically put to rest in the strong language of the recent Lawyers' Forum case."[53]

Patel's discussion, however, draws our attention to another alternative to the untrammeled sovereignty of the people as expressed in the basic structure of the Constitution: the sovereignty of Allah, which must be exercised through certain individuals or groups. It does not seem that the issue of which organ of state or set of people could legitimately determine what Allah's sovereignty entails has been resolved.[54] There was certainly significant support for some kind of formal acceptance not just a system of law compatible with traditional Islamic law but rather for a precise set of statutes— though the learned in Islam did not agree on what those would be—that should be made part of Pakistani law. With the introduction of certain features of Islamic law in 1979 and the creation of the Federal Shariat Court in 1980 by General Zia, this perspective gained an institutional foothold.[55]

This view of the place of Islam in the judicial system is not necessarily ideological. A version was presented by Justice A. R. Cornelius, one of Pakistan's most esteemed judges, who served on the Supreme Court from 1953 to 1968, the last eight years as Chief Justice. Lombardi notes that "deeply frustrated by the judiciary's inability (or unwillingness) to assert the power to protect fundamental rights, . . . [Cornelius] proposed the systematic Islamisation of the Pakistan legal system."[56] According to Lombardi, Cornelius believed that fundamental rights could be secured only if the people's desire to have Pakistani law made consistent with Islamic law could be met, albeit with the judiciary acting to shape laws appropriately.[57] As Martin Lau (2006) notes:

> The judicial appropriation of Islam and its integration into the vocabulary of courts was a conscious process aimed not only at the fulfillment of a general desire to indigenise and Islamise the legal system after the end of colonial rule, but it was also a way of enhancing judicial power and independence. The Islamisation of law did, perhaps ironically, not only predate Zia-ul-Haq's regime, but was used to challenge him.[58]

Lombardi extends the argument: Lau's study provides evidence to support Cornelius's hypothesis that the public would respect a liberal interpretation of Islamic law developed by judges and that this could be used to empower the judiciary vis-à-vis the executive. Indeed, it might protect natural rights not only from predatory secular powers but from illiberal and autocratic Islamic powers.[59]

Lombardi provocatively wonders whether democracy promotion might well turn out to require Islamization, albeit *"a certain kind of Islamization."*[60] Maryam Khan, however, claims that the court has struck down attempts to use "Islam as the constitutional 'grundnorm' for a 'basic structures doctrine.'"[61] The power of the judiciary vis-à-vis the other institutions of the state thus must be based on a legitimacy that has been established politically.

THE JUDICIARY AS A POLITICAL ACTOR

The Chief Justice, by his unprecedented and courageous refusal to bow to the "necessity" of obeying the military ruler, and supported by the Lawyers' Movement, apparently made the judiciary even more securely independent of the executive. Although the court and others speak of a "separation of powers" in the classic "executive, legislative, judicial" form, those powers do not reside in separate institutions of the state dedicated to each one.[62] Rather, there now appears to be three relatively autonomous branches of the Pakistan state: Parliament (and its executive, "the government"), the military, and the judiciary.[63] The sovereignty claim of the people was triumphantly revived in the largely free and fair parliamentary elections of 2008 and 2013, but the vehement opposition of the military to the "civilian control" provisions of the Kerry-Lugar-Berman Act is a vivid indication that it sees that claim as limited.[64] The Supreme Court has claimed the power of judicial review not just over laws but also over constitutional amendments on procedural grounds. Its implied claim to evaluate substantive constitutionality in its interim order on the constitutionality of the Eighteenth Amendment was perhaps simply a bargaining chip; it did result in getting Parliament to meet its objections, in the Nineteenth Amendment. A different set of court rulings prompted the Twentieth Amendment in February 2012.

None of these branches of the state are fully unified, as they seek to exercise power vis-à-vis the others. They all exist at local, provincial, and central levels, with complicated relationships of supervision and accountability across and within those levels. The government of the day, supported by a sometimes shifting majority of Parliament, often has to struggle with its nominal "servants," a bureaucracy that sees itself with a right to rule, to get things done. The military, with the army preeminent, has significant subunits, such as the ISI. The separation of the judiciary from the executive was mandated in the 1973 Constitution for four years after it came into force but was fully accomplished only in 2009 for the lower courts.[65]

Chief Justice Chaudhry clearly saw the judiciary as the first among equal branches of the state:

I feel privileged that the Pakistani judicial system is the strongest backer of democracy which enjoys full confidence and faith of legal fraternity, other institutions as well as public at large. In recent years, the judiciary as the third pillar of [the Pakistan] State has successfully emerged as a savior and a protector of constitutional supremacy and fundamental rights.[66]

In 2008, the Chief Justice seemed to present an expansive view of the power of the judiciary:

It is not the province of the courts to step into areas that are exclusively within the domain of the Executive or the Parliament. But, if these two institutions remain indifferent to the duties entrusted to them under the

Constitution; or if they have acted contrary to the principles enshrined therein; or if their acts discriminate between the rich and the poor, or on religious, class, regional, or ethnic grounds; then judges are called upon by the Constitution, their oath and their office to act.[67]

It is hard to imagine a government so perfect that it acts entirely without discrimination; so this statement seems to give the court the right to intervene almost routinely. And the interim judgment on the Eighteenth Amendment case implies that Parliament and parliamentarians cannot be exempted from judicial scrutiny by installing a feeble and timid judiciary in the name of the sovereignty of Parliament. Both Parliament and the executive must be restrained and kept within the boundaries of the rule of law.[68]

It might be that the Chief Justice is using "the Executive" to refer to the president, who was at the time in fact independent of Parliament but has now, with the Eighteenth Amendment, been returned to the status of a virtually powerless (though not a "figurehead") head of state. As it happens, President Zardari, as the head of the ruling party, was very much the de facto leader of "the Executive." Indeed, the Lahore High Court ordered the president to relinquish his party office; a year later (in March 2013), facing a contempt charge, the president complied. The president elected after the 2013 election, Mamnoon Hussain, has no such alternate base of power. The Supreme Court's claim to some power over the executive—prime minister and president—can be seen in its efforts to get its orders in the NRO case obeyed, despite the president's constitutional immunity from court proceedings.

There is no indication that the military has yielded any ground to the judiciary's attempts to bring retired army officers, let alone serving ones, into a rule of law arena presided over by the Supreme Court.[69] Indeed, the indications are in the other direction—toward the army's implicit (or perhaps behind-the-scenes) refusal to let that happen. The protection offered to General Musharraf on his return to Pakistan in April 2013 to fight the elections, which got him out of the courtroom when the judge ordered his arrest, and the veiled warnings against "humiliating" him suggest that the military has not yielded much. Among many others, the return to the back burner of the Asghar Khan case and the "missing persons" cases, in which military intelligence was implicated, indicate that when it comes to the army, the court has been frank in its strictures, but the judicial system has not produced arrests and convictions of soldiers. True, those strictures can be impressive: the Chief Justice, in open court, told the ISI and Military Intelligence: "You're an arsonist. You have set Balochistan on fire," and, according to a news report, "said that the agencies have become 'insensitive' to the issues and referred [to] them as the 'biggest violators' of the country's law and order."[70]

It remains to be seen whether the court can enforce its decisions against the will of Parliament or the preferences of the military. In the past, the courts have acquiesced in the seizure of power, including the power of a military dictator to rewrite the Constitution in its entirety. Although they may have at times added stipulations to their approval of a government takeover—for example, requiring General Musharraf to hold elections within three years—and though a few judges have refused to swear allegiance to a PCO, on the whole they have demonstrated their lack of power.[71] The "rule of law" crisis of 2007–2009 seemed to change that, as the court, drawing on the enthusiastic and effective base of support of the lawyers in particular, strengthened its legitimacy immeasurably, in both senses of that word—that is, a great deal but in ways that are hard, if not impossible, to judge.

However, as Khaled Ahmed has pointed out, the judiciary has feet of clay,[72] and the lawyers lack legitimacy:

Before Musharraf got rid of him, the Chief Justice had piled up thousands of suo moto cases which satisfied his sense of justice as the civil servants began to be routinely humiliated by him in the Court. He had no idea that an "over-correction" was going to be the result of this in the long run and that not even justice can be administered without realism. . . . The lawyers meanwhile have showcased the muscle they have acquired during their long marches. They thrash the police whenever they can; they have thrashed the journalists trying to show their violence on TV. . . . Their ability to cow the judges into submission threatens to make them a threat to society.

With its success in getting its way on the question of appointments, the Supreme Court, if not the judiciary in general, has clearly carved out a powerful constitutional space for itself and probably no longer needs the support of the lawyers.

It remains, however, very much a political actor, and not necessarily a benign one, as the eminent lawyer Muneer Malik notes: "In the long run this is a very dangerous trend. The judges are not elected representatives of the people and they are arrogating power to themselves as if they are the only sanctimonious institution in the country. All dictators fall prey to this psyche—that only we are clean, and capable of doing the right thing."[73] The other major component of the movement was indeed the lawyers—from whom all superior court judges are ultimately selected, it should not be forgotten[74]—and there is some question of their integrity and the value of their political role.[75] Lawyers in Pakistan are not in a particularly enviable position. The various proposals for legal reform[76] have included recommendations for the improvement of legal education and by implication have endorsed the idea that the vast number of practicing lawyers include both a small number of very skilled, honest, and impressive practitioners—including those who become judges of the superior courts—and a small number of corrupt and/or violent and/or incompetent lawyers who practice in (and around) the lower courts. The most vivid recent example occurred when the assassin of Punjab governor Salman Taseer was brought to court and was showered with rose petals by some lawyers.[77] It is likely that those particular lawyers condoning the murder of Taseer represented only a very small minority of Pakistan's 90,000 lawyers,[78] if we can judge from the apparent enthusiasm for the rule of law expressed by the comparatively vast number of lawyers who turned out all over the country to mob Chief Justice Chaudhry's motorcade in the first phase of the Lawyers' Movement.[79]

Judging from their appearances in public, from the Lawyers' Movement to rowdy incidents, lawyers are—more than the average—keen participants in politics. They are not, however, a major presence in the National Assembly: in the Assembly elected in 2008, lawyers comprised only twenty of the 223 Members of the National Assembly (MNAs) who noted their occupation, in one compilation.[80] As an organized profession, however, they are very powerful. If enhancing the rule of law is to be the foundation for a new political movement toward a genuine democracy in Pakistan, then the mass of lawyers who were mobilized by the challenge Chief Justice Chaudhry posed to General Musharraf are unlikely to provide much help if there is no comparable crisis.

Chief Justice Chaudhry could not claim a legitimate explicitly political role, and after his retirement in December 2013, he has receded into relative obscurity, without much apparent political influence.[81] He may have attracted a cohort of like-minded judges, considering the proportion of judges who refused to swear (or were barred from swearing) an oath to the PCO of 2007, compared with the proportion who did so in 1999, and it is notable that the decisions of the Supreme Court under his direction had few, if any, dissenting votes. Columnist and lawyer Saroop Ijaz, with bitter sarcasm, makes the point:

> The Supreme Court is no longer just an ordinary court of law; it is a court of Justice, a modern day incarnation of the Solomonic ideal, almost a reli-

gious/mystical experience. . . . Great minds, we have been told, think alike. The unity of opinion among My Lords is unprecedented in legal history. Not one major instance of dissent by one judge immediately comes to mind (the sole notable exception being the Mukhtaran Mai case). Hence, the whining that My Lords restrict themselves to the letter of the law, etc. should stop and we should just be grateful for the wisdom imparted.[82]

Chief Justice Chaudhry's successor, Tassaduq Hussain Jillani, inaugurating the International Judicial Conference in April 2013, made a vigorous statement in support of judicial activism.[83] But the tradition that a judge must be seen to be above the political fray, which Chief Justice Chaudhry followed at the height of the Lawyers' Movement, will continue to hold. It is hard to imagine even an activist and committed judiciary acting as the explicit political leaders of a politically powerful body of lawyers.

Some judges and lawyers, while accepting the idea of democratically empowered leaders, seem to have a very harsh view of actually existing politicians and government officials. In the words of one prominent lawyer:

The large body of ignorant and semi-educated elected representatives of questionable credentials . . . are least qualified to have the last word on any subject. . . . We do not need power hungry political leaders. The country should be run by a team of good, clean and efficient administrators . . . [plus] a strong, able and efficient judiciary with no clogs on its power or jurisdiction to administer justice.[84]

When he was president of the Sindh High Court Bar Association, Muneer Malik, later a major figure in the 2007–2009 Lawyers' Movement, was part of a lawyers' agitation against President General Musharraf's Legal Framework Order of October 2002, a challenge that included a "long march" of a cavalcade of hundreds of cars converging on Islamabad from Lahore and other cities.[85] In essays published in *Dawn* in May 2007, he clearly favors a democratic politics and casts no aspersions on the political parties.[86] But in a speech to a seminar on the "separation of powers" in that same month, he notes approvingly the "oft-quoted judgment" of Justice Saleem Akhtar in the Sharaf Faridi case, which reads, "In a set-up where the Constitution is based on trichotomy of powers, the Judiciary enjoys a unique and supreme position within the framework of the Constitution as it creates balance amongst the various organs of the State and also checks the excessive and arbitrary exercise of power by the Executive and the Legislature."[87] This implied claim to legitimacy of a "juristocracy" is clearly limited.[88]

CONCLUSION

The delicate balance of securing judicial independence while avoiding the danger of the judiciary emerging as an unchecked force is something every political system, and particularly democracies, must attempt. As Helmke and Rosenbluth note, "If there is any concept of modern governance that enjoys more widespread admiration even than democracy, it is judicial independence."[89] But they discuss the wide differences in what might be called styles of judicial independence. They conclude, among other things, that "even in democracies with a system of separation of powers, the judiciary is only as independent as the political branches are unable to agree; and, partisan differences notwithstanding, judiciaries tend to reflect culturally dominant world views."[90] Quantitative measures of "judicial independence" are (so far) not persuasive,[91] so examining carefully how judicial independence, autonomy, and power appear in a place like Pakistan is important.

In Pakistan, the formal power of the judiciary is limited by Parliament's right to amend the Constitution, but the Supreme Court has successfully challenged Parliament on the issue of judicial appointment (and dismissal), in its threat to declare the Eighteenth Amendment unconstitutional unless it was amended to provide for the Supreme Court itself having the final say in these matters. Parliament duly passed the Nineteenth Amendment, following the court's guidelines, and although the court has not issued its final ruling on the matter, it seems that it was satisfied.[92] Feisal Naqvi defends this step:

> The appointment of judges and the fundamental right of access to justice are inextricably interlinked. The judiciaries of Pakistan and India decided long ago that they could not meaningfully protect their independence without the ability to ultimately control the process of the appointment of judges. There are those who stick to a doctrinaire assertion of parliamentary superiority in this context, but overall, their ranks are few. Instead, the reaction over the past 15-odd years to the Al Jehad case (and its Indian equivalent, the AOR Association case) has largely been favourable. Given that fundamental perspective, the current decision by the Supreme Court should be seen not as a power grab but as a refusal to allow the dilution of one of the fundamental pillars of judicial independence.[93]

Is the judiciary, then, the institution of the state that can ultimately "save" Pakistan from its seeming political stagnation, from the danger of another military takeover, or a destabilization by Islamic extremist forces, or other dangers to the country? The journalist Eijaz Haider poses the questions that would follow:

> Could the judiciary, no matter how powerful, address the problems of a country? Could law be applied in a vacuum, in disregard to the political, social and other realities? Could such narrow application of law go beyond the terms of a particular case and expand to embrace the bigger picture? In other words, should the brilliance of tactics be confused with the uncertainties that inform strategy and its patient application? . . . But let it be said that what the judiciary is doing, despite the judges' honourable intentions and without any reference to the specifics, is unlikely to redound either to their advantage or that of this troubled and troubling democracy.[94]

Or as Osama Siddique, a law professor, puts it:

> Constitutional norms and rules can only survive and thrive if the public reposes its faith and support to them. Hence the big risk in opposing the work of the Constitutional Committee in the name of judicial independence. "Judicial autocracy" and "judicial tyranny" are well understood concepts in international jurisprudence. As indeed are the "doctrine of political question," and also the concepts of "judicial minimalism," and "judicial restraint." They all stem from the idea that an unaccountable judiciary can crowd out democratic space, stultify democratic evolution, have its fingers burnt and get dubbed as politically partisan.[95]

Lawyer and columnist Faisal Siddiqi, writing about the crisis concerning the court's attempts to get its orders in the NRO case implemented, says: "This order signifies a possible transition from a judicially activist court to one that follows the jurisprudence of a legal empire. This new jurisprudence signifies that it is the [Supreme Court] which will determine what an honest/ameen [trustworthy, faithful, observant] democratic system should look like."[96]

Let us assume that the Supreme Court's claim to define and enforce the independence of the judiciary is, at a minimum, accepted by Parliament, even though the question of how orders of the court are to be enforced against the executive or other organs of the state is still open. This is not simply a matter of constitutional law, which is far from settled, but of political power. In effect, there are now five relatively autonomous organs of the state (whether they are usefully grouped into three "branches" with "separate powers" remains unclear): Parliament, the presidency, the judiciary, the bureaucracy, and the military. With the passage of the Twentieth Amendment in February 2012, the Election Commission may emerge as a sixth. It is worthy of note, however, that the Election Commission consists of retired judges; Mohammad Waseem calls it the "second domain of the judiciary."[97] The caretaker government, appointed in March 2013 to serve until the May election produced a new Parliament, was headed by a prime minister who is an eighty-four-year-old retired judge, and four of the five caretaker chief ministers in the provinces were also retired judges.

In order for democracy in Pakistan to be put on a firm footing, in my view, the tug-of-war between the Parliament and the presidency on the one side and the bureaucracy and the military on the other has to be "won" by the former.[98] The referee of this struggle would ordinarily be the judiciary, but the judiciary has clearly succumbed to the temptation to join in the struggle as a participant. For example, Chief Justice Chaudhry, in the course of the suo moto hearings on the violence in Karachi, remarked: "Those who impose martial law begin by saying 'my dear country men' and then play havoc with the country. Whenever martial law was imposed the deteriorating law and order situation was made its basis. We have blocked the way. We have to improve the law and order situation on our own."[99] Organizations of civil society—such as the lawyers organized into bar associations—act as supporters in reserve.

There are also, of course, informal divisions within each of the major players. If everyone in a given institution pulls in the same direction, as it were—agreeing on policy and tactics—the more institutions are aligned with each other, the greater the strength of that "team." If government and opposition are united—when it comes to controlling the bureaucracy and military—then the "flag" of crucial decisions would be pulled closer to them than if they are disunited; there should not be perceptions of a "disloyal" opposition or an "illegitimate" majority party.[100]

In a spring 2014 public opinion survey, the military had the most public support by far, followed by the "national government," with the "court system" far behind.[101] The army seems unwilling to play its usual deus ex machina role, and it is not clear that the judiciary has the capacity to be its substitute. The lawyers have subsided in their activism and no longer look like the acceptable face of a middle class–centered, civil society–led transformation of the polity. In one compilation of scenarios for Pakistan, we find a judgment that "the judiciary and the legal profession barely qualify as major factors in shaping Pakistan's future. . . . The idea of the law as supreme is not generally respected in a country where force and coercion play major roles."[102] The Supreme Court, however, has had very strong support for what it is doing: in a 2012 Gilani Poll/Gallup Pakistan survey, 62 percent of respondents agreed that the court was acting "within its mandate" (up from 57 percent two years before).[103] It is still possible that the judiciary may figure out how it can get the contestants in the tug-of-war to follow the rules that it has shaped to a considerable extent and so play a not insignificant part, at least, in putting Pakistan on the road to an effective and genuinely democratic government.

NOTES

1. This chapter was presented first to the workshop "Pakistan: The Beginning of the Dangerous Decade?" at Columbia University, October 6, 2011. My thanks to Christophe Jaffrelot, Anil Kalhan, Maryam Khan, Paula Newberg, Saeed Shafqat, and Mohammad Waseem for their careful reading and very useful suggestions, saving me from numerous errors of fact and analysis; the remaining errors are my responsibility alone.

2. Daud Munir, "Why Democracy Has Survived," *Express Tribune,* March 13, 2013. Note, however, Feisal Siddiqi's assessment: "the democratic period between 2009 and 2013 has seen the greatest growth in judicial power in Pakistani judicial history." Siddiqi, "The Judiciary & the Military," *Dawn,* January 20, 2013.

3. This phrase refers to an extensive literature on "Juristocracy" and the "judicialization of politics." See Ran Hirschl, *Towards Juristocracy: The Origins and Consequences of the New Constitutionalism* (Cambridge, Mass.: Harvard University Press, 2004); Ran Hirschl, "The New Constitutionalism and the Judicialization of Pure Politics Worldwide," *Fordham Law Review* 75, no. 2 (November 2006–2007): 721–754, for example, and articles in the *Maryland Law Review* 65, no. 1 (2006). In a superb analysis of recent developments in Pakistan, Anil Kalhan, "Gray Zone Constitutionalism and the Dilemma of Judicial Independence in Pakistan," *Vanderbilt Journal of Transnational Law* 46, no. 1 (January 2013): 1–96, provides "an understanding of judicial independence that goes beyond abstract, unqualified notions of autonomy, and instead contemplates an appropriate balance between autonomy and constraint that enables representative institutions to strengthen their governance capacities and power to rein in the military."

4. Babar Sattar, "Fading Romance," *News International,* July 31, 2010. But see his later statement that "it never became a rule of law movement after all" (Babar Sattar, "Force over Reason," *News International,* December 15, 2012). The "rule of law" is far from a simple concept, easily applied; see Ryan E. Arlin, "Rule-of-Law Typologies in Contemporary Societies," *Justice System Journal* 33, no. 2 (2012): 154–173.

5. Tayyab Mahmud, "Praetorianism and Common Law in Postcolonial Settings: Judicial Responses to Constitutional Breakdowns in Pakistan," *Utah Law Review,* no. 4 (1993): 1225–1230. See also Paula Newberg, "Balancing Act: Prudence,

Impunity, and Pakistan's Jurisprudence," in *Routledge Handbook of South Asian Politics*, ed. Paul R. Brass (London: Routledge, 2010), 177–190. Although Lau, in Martin Lau, *The Role of Islam in the Legal System of Pakistan* (Leiden: Martinus Nijhoff, 2006), 211, claims that "under the mantle of Islam, Pakistan's shariat courts have been able to circumvent virtually all constitutional mechanisms which protect legislation against judicial review," decisions of the Federal Shariat Court, established by General Zia in 1980, have not (yet?) altered this picture. See also Charles H. Kennedy, "Repugnancy to Islam: Who Decides? Islam and Legal Reform in Pakistan," *International and Comparative Law Quarterly* 41, no. 4 (October 1992): 769–787; Feisal Khan "Islamic Banking by Judiciary: The 'Backdoor' for Islamism in Pakistan?" *South Asia: Journal of South Asian Studies* 31, no. 4 (December 2008): 535–555; and Muhammad Munir, "Precedent in Islamic Law with Particular Reference to the Federal Shariat Court," *Islamic Studies* 47, no. 4 (2008): 445–482.

6. See, in particular, Hamid Khan, *Constitutional and Political History of Pakistan* (Karachi: Oxford University Press, 2001); Mahmud, "Praetorianism and Common Law in Postcolonial Settings"; Allen McGrath, *The Destruction of Pakistan's Democracy* (Karachi: Oxford University Press, 1998); Paula Newberg, *Judging the State: Courts and Constitutional Politics in Pakistan* (Cambridge: Cambridge University Press, 1995); and Newberg, "Balancing Act." The landmark cases are *Tamizuddin Khan* (1955); *Usif Patel* (1955); *Dosso* (1958); *Zia-ur-Rahman* (1973); *Nusrat Bhutto* (1977); *Saifullah Khan* (1989); *Ahmad Tariq Rahim* (1992); and *Benazir Bhutto* (1998). In 2000, a twelve-person bench of the Supreme Court essentially ratified General Musharraf's coup, although it required him to hold an election within three years (Hamid Khan, *Constitutional and Political History of Pakistan*, 936–938).

7. Hamid Khan, *Constitutional and Political History of Pakistan*, 827.

8. Ibid., 829.

9. Ilhan Niaz, *The Culture of Power and Governance of Pakistan, 1947–2008* (Karachi: Oxford University Press, 2010), 183–184. In requiring Supreme Court and High Court judges to swear an oath to a PCO, Musharraf was following the example of General Zia ul Huq, who did the same in 1981, inviting selected judges to take the oath. See Hamid Khan, *Constitutional and Political History of Pakistan*, 649–652.

10. Shoaib A. Ghias, "Miscarriage of Chief Justice: Judicial Power and the Legal Complex in Pakistan Under Musharraf," *Law and Social Inquiry* 35, no. 4 (Fall 2010): 19.

11. Inter alia, see Azmat Abbas and Saima Jasam, "A Ray of Hope: The Case of Lawyers' Movement in Pakistan," in *Pakistan; Reality, Denial, and the Complexity of Its State*, ed. Heinrich Böll Foundation; Heinrich Böll Stiftung Publication Series on Democracy, vol. 16 (2009): 140–170, www.boell.de/downloads/Endf_Pakistan _engl.pdf; Zahid Shahab Ahmed and Maria J. Stephan, "Fighting for the Rule of Law: Civil Resistance and the Lawyers' Movement in Pakistan," *Democratization* 17, no. 3 (2010): 492–513; Anil Kalhan, "Constitution and 'Extraconstitution': Colonial Emergency Regimes in Postcolonial India and Pakistan," in *Emergency Powers in Asia: Exploring the Limits of Legality*, ed. Victor V. Ramraj and Arun K. Thiruvengadam (Cambridge: Cambridge University Press, 2010), 93–96; United

States Agency for International Development (USAID), *Pakistan Rule of Law Assessment—Final Report*, prepared by Dr. Richard Blue, Richard Hoffman, Esq., and Louis-Alexandre Berg (Washington, D.C.: USAID, November 2008), 3–6, pdf .usaid.gov/pdf_docs/PNADO130.pdf. For descriptive accounts, see Muneer A. Malik, *The Pakistan Lawyers' Movement: An Unfinished Agenda* (Karachi: Pakistan Law House, 2008), for a (book-length) day-to-day account by one of the movement's leaders; Aitzaz Ahsan, "The Preservation of the Rule of Law in Times of Strife," *International Lawyer* 43, no. 1 (2009): 73–76, for another leader's view; Pakistan Institute of Legislative Development and Transparency, "Judicial Crisis," March–July 2007, Background Paper, Dialogue Group on Civil-Military Relations, www.pildat.org/Publications/publication/CMR/TheJudicalCrisis.pdf, for an analysis written mainly during the crisis and relevant legal documents; "Destroying Legality: Pakistan's Crackdown on Lawyers and Judges," *Human Rights Watch* 19, no. 19 (December 2007), for a summary and lawyers' and judges' testimony about their arrest in November 2007; Iftikhar Muhammad Chaudhry, "Pakistan: Judicial Independence Vital for Democracy," address to the New York City Bar Association, November 17, 2008, www.hrsolidarity.net/mainfile.php/2008vol18no04 /2664/; and Ghias in "Miscarriage of Chief Justice," for a thorough and creative analysis. The International Bar Association's "A Long March to Justice" (Siobhan Mullally, "A Long March to Justice: A Report on Judicial Independence and Integrity in Pakistan," International Bar Association, Human Rights Institute, 2009, available at http://ssrn.com/abstract=1615685), draws on the discussions of its high-level delegation with many lawyers and others in March–April 2009, summarized to good effect, and provides a vivid portrayal of the issues and many of the participants. See also the essays of the "Five Years Later" issue of the *Friday Times* (vol. 24, no. 5, March 23–29, 2012) and Anil Kalhan, "Gray Zone Constitutionalism."

12. Philip Oldenburg, *India, Pakistan, and Democracy: Solving the Puzzle of Divergent Paths* (London: Routledge, 2010), 203–205.

13. Ghias, "Miscarriage of Chief Justice," 21.

14. Matthew J. Nelson, "Pakistan in 2009: Tackling the Taliban?" *Asian Survey* 50, no. 1 (January–February 2010): 112.

15. Haris Gazdar, "Judicial Activism vs. Democratic Consolidation in Pakistan," *Economic and Political Weekly* 44, no. 32 (August 8, 2009): 10–11.

16. For further details, see Kalhan, "Gray Zone Constitutionalism"; and Cyril Almeida, "Controversy Over 18th Amendment," *Dawn*, April 22, 2010.

17. C. Christine Fair, "Pakistan in 2010," *Asian Survey* 51, no. 1 (January–February 2011): 101–102; Feisal Naqvi, "Not a New Debate," *Dawn*, April 23, 2010; and A. G. Noorani, "The Eighteenth Amendment," *Criterion* [Islamabad] 6, no. 1 (March 11, 2011).

18. See the set of articles titled "Legal Anarchy," *Friday Times*, October 15–21, 2010.

19. Ghias, in "Miscarriage of Chief Justice," makes a convincing and detailed argument on the transformation of the court's position and power, from the time when Chief Justice Chaudhry was a supporter of the Musharraf regime's measures that legitimated Musharraf's rule (including the one that permitted him to serve as president and Chief of Army Staff), to his tenure as Chief Justice, after 2005,

when he challenged the regime. Ghias argues that the Chief Justice had improved his position by decisions favoring the lawyers and gained support that mattered from the media. He speculates that the Chaudhry court may have been inspired by the actions of India's higher judiciary. See also Maryam Khan, "The Politics of Public Interest Litigation in Pakistan in the 1990s," *Social Science and Policy Bulletin* [Lahore, Pakistan] 2, no. 4 (Spring 2011): 2–8. For a critique of judicial overreach in India, see T. R. Andhyarujina, "Disturbing Trends in Judicial Activism," *Hindu*, August 6, 2012.

20. I owe this point to Paula Newberg.

21. Ghias, "Miscarriage of Chief Justice," 995; see also Tariq Hassan, "The Need for Judicial Activism," acceptance speech on behalf of the Chief Justice of Pakistan, *ILSA Journal of International & Comparative Law* 15, no. 1 (Fall 2008): 7–14; and *Denying the Undeniable: Enforced Disappearances in Pakistan* (London: Amnesty International Publications, 2008).

22. Ghias, "Miscarriage of Chief Justice," 996.

23. Ibid., 1011–1014.

24. Ibid.

25. Ibid., 1014.

26. According to a (WikiLeaked) U.S. government cable reporting on the March 10, 2008, visit of the American ambassador to Zardari, "He and Nawaz have agreed, privately, that former Supreme Court Chief Justice Iftikhar Chaudhry will not be restored and that the current Chief Justice will remain" (*Dawn*, May 24, 2011).

27. Ghias, "Miscarriage of Chief Justice," 1016–1018.

28. Amir continues, "in the massive hangover induced by the lawyers' movement the nation was introduced to a minor variation on this larger theme: the terror of legal fisticuffs," in Ayaz Amir, "The Hangover Recedeth," *News International*, October 29, 2010; also Khaled Ahmed, "Middle Class Gone Berserk," *Friday Times* 24, no. 6 (March 23–29, 2012).

29. See the web sites of the Supreme Court of Pakistan (www.supremecourt.gov.pk/) and of the Law & Justice Commission of Pakistan (www.ljcp.gov.pk/) for links to reports and papers of these conferences and to the National Judicial Policy.

30. For a comprehensive and persuasive account, on which this summary draws heavily, see Osama Siddique, *Approaches to Legal and Judicial Reform in Pakistan: Post Colonial Inertia and the Paucity of Imagination in Times of Turmoil and Change*, Working Paper 4, Development Policy Research Centre, Lahore University of Management Sciences (January 2011).

31. Asia Foundation, Pakistan, *Pakistan Legal and Judicial Reform Project*, 1999, http://www.adb.org/sites/default/files/pvr-1897-99.pdf. See also Amber Darr, "In Courts We Trust," *Dawn*, December 18, 2012.

32. Ali Dayan Hasan, "Filthy Business," *Dawn*, November 15, 2010. In addition, the lower courts have few material or legal code resources to deal with the extremely difficult terrorism cases; see Alex Rodriguez, "Pakistani Criminal Justice System Proves No Match for Terrorism Cases," *Los Angeles Times*, October 28, 2010.

33. Supreme Court of Pakistan press release, February 2, 2013, www.supremecourt .gov.pk/web/page.asp?id=1326 (accessed April 23, 2013). It would be wise to be somewhat skeptical of this assertion, given the detailed and impressive study by

Osama Siddique of the working of the district courts in Lahore. One of his conclusions is biting: "So delay seems to be as securely a part of the litigation experience as ever and its victims are cognizant of its perpetrators, perpetuators and beneficiaries as they clearly point out in responses to other related questions. These ought to have been believable statistics from the era before the grand arrival of massive delay reduction programs for Pakistani courts. That they are statistics in the era after the megareforms makes them a very tragic reading." Osama Siddique, *Law in Practice—The Lahore District Courts Litigants Survey (2010–2011)*, working paper, Development Policy Research Centre, Lahore University of Management Studies, June 2010 (*sic*; the survey was completed in January 2011), 111.

34. See Ahmed Rafay Alam, "Public Interest Litigation and the Role of the Judiciary," paper presented at the International Judicial Conference 2006 (August 11–14, 2006), www.supremecourt.gov.pk/ijc/ijc.htm.
35. Siddique, *Approaches to Legal and Judicial Reform in Pakistan*, 51.
36. Ibid. There is some debate about whether courts other than the Supreme Court can legitimately exercise suo moto powers, even though some have done so (the Lahore High Court ruling to set the price of sugar, for example).
37. Ibid., 11; Irfan Husain, "Swing of the Pendulum," *Dawn*, April 9, 2011.
38. As the International Crisis Group notes, "The NRO decision has been applied selectively," notably not targeting the MQM. *Reforming Pakistan's Criminal Justice System*, Asia Report No. 196 (December 6, 2010), 26; Ashtar Ausaf Ali, "The Exercise of Suo Moto," *Dawn*, March 30, 2010.
39. *Nation*, March 6, 2013, reporting on the answer from the minister of justice and law to a formal parliamentary question.
40. See Waris Husain, "Suo Motu: Pakistan's Chemotherapy?" *Dawn*, August 31, 2011; Ayaz Amir, "Everyone His Own Master," *News International*, December 17, 2010, who writes: "However, there is the danger of giving too wide an interpretation to Article 184(3). For when this occurs, as it increasingly has with the present [Supreme Court], it gives rise to the impression that the highest judiciary is not only intruding into the administrative sphere but also, in some instances, hampering the ability of government to discharge its functions."
41. Justice (R) Fazal Karim, *Judicial Review of Public Actions*, 2 vols. (Karachi: Pakistan Law House, 2006), 110–112.
42. While Parliament and its executive retain some representation on the bodies that appoint High Court and Supreme Court judges, they are in a distinct minority. The Chief Justice will probably be able to determine appointments, since the Supreme Court has already set a precedent that it can judicially review all such appointments made by Parliament. (I owe this last point to Maryam Khan.) The Nineteenth Amendment was passed in response to the court's October 21, 2010, interim judgment on the constitutionality of the Eighteenth Amendment. At the time of writing (August 2014), it appears that the court's interim order on the Eighteenth Amendment Case has not been replaced by a final judgment, even though the Nineteenth Amendment did not fully meet the court's demands with respect to superior court appointments (see Babar Sattar, "Judges as Legislators," *News International*, April 2, 2011). For a critical evaluation of the provisions of the

Eighteenth Amendment, see the eminent Indian lawyer A. G. Noorani's essay, "The Eighteenth Amendment."

43. See Fazal Karim, *Judicial Review of Public Actions*, 149–150, on the contempt power. Its reach became vividly clear in the NRO case in February 2012: Prime Minister Gilani was threatened with loss of office, because he refused to write to the Swiss government to reopen corruption cases against President Zardari, as the court had ordered. Tariq Hassan has argued that the court "is likely to further tilt the delicate balance of power in favour of the judiciary" in striking down the Contempt of Court Act of 2012 ("Regulating Contempt," *Express Tribune*, September 6, 2012). See also International Crisis Group, Asia Briefing 249, "Parliament's Role in Pakistan's Transition to Democracy," September 18, 2013, 5–8.

44. Najam Sethi, "Editorial: What an Extraordinary Week!" *Friday Times* 22, no. 36 (October 22–28, 2010).

45. Khaled Ahmed, "Legal Anarchy: A 'Decline and Fall' in the Offing?" *Friday Times* 22, no. 35 (October 15–21, 2010).

46. See Cyril Almeida, "Appeasing the Hawks," *Dawn*, April 29, 2012, for a vivid description of the presumed thinking of the court "doves" versus "hawks" on the Gilani contempt issue, as revealed in the court's listing of options on how to resolve the contempt issue in its judgment of January 10, 2012.

47. See Newberg, *Judging the State*, 237–247, which includes a comparison with the Indian Supreme Court's decisions, treated fully by Sudhir Krishnaswamy, *Democracy and Constitutionalism in India: A Study of the Basic Structure Doctrine* (New Delhi: Oxford University Press, 2009).

48. It is far from clear that the Supreme Court would agree; see Feisal Naqvi, "Not a New Debate"; and Feisal Naqvi, "Protecting the Independence of the Judiciary," *Express Tribune*, March 14 and 15, 2011, for example.

49. Dorab Patel, *Testament of a Liberal* (Karachi: Oxford University Press, 2000), 201.

50. Ibid., 200. A former president of the Supreme Court Bar Association, in an interview with the International Crisis Group (Lahore, May 27, 2010), makes the point forcefully that the Shariat Court's creation constitutes a violation of the "basic structure." See International Crisis Group, *Reforming Pakistan's Criminal Justice System*, 27.

51. Nick Robinson, "Expanding Judiciaries: India and the Rise of the Good Governance Court," *Washington University Global Studies Law Review* 8, no. 1 (2009): 64.

52. Supreme Court of Pakistan, Judgment on the Seventeenth Amendment and President's Uniform Case (2005), para. 56; see also Tayyaba Ahmed Quraishi, "State of Emergency: General Pervez Musharraf's Executive Assault on Judicial Independence in Pakistan," *North Carolina Journal of International Law and Commerce Regulation* 35, no. 2 (Winter 2009–2010): 516. In its judgment of January 19, 2010, which held the National Reconciliation Ordinance to be unconstitutional, the court said, quoting an earlier judgment, "We have stated in unambiguous terms in the Short Order that the Constitution of Pakistan is the supreme law of the land and its *basic features* [my emphasis] i.e. independence of Judiciary, federalism and parliamentary form of government blended with Islamic Provision cannot be altered even by the Parliament." Syed Zafar Ali Shah's case (PLD 2000 SC 869).

53. Maryam Khan, "Politics of Public Interest Litigation in Pakistan in the 1990s," 2–8. The Chaudhry court may not agree. See Babar Sattar, "People's Court," *Counselor* (2010), www.counselpakistan.com/vol-2/constitution/peoples-courts.php. A recent International Crisis Group briefing paper (No. 249, "Parliament's Role in Pakistan's Democratic Transition," September 18, 2013, p. 6), however, implies that something like that doctrine still exists.

54. See Leonard Binder, *Religion and Politics in Pakistan* (Berkeley: University of California Press, 1963), 142–149, for a discussion of the Objectives Resolution debate on this issue.

55. See Moeen H. Cheema, "Beyond Beliefs: Deconstructing the Dominant Narratives of the Islamization of Pakistan's Law," *American Journal of Comparative Law* 60 (2012): 875–917.

56. Clark B. Lombardi, "Islamism as a Response to Emergency Rule in Pakistan: The Surprising Proposal of Justice A. R. Cornelius," in *Emergency Powers in Asia: Exploring the Limits of Legality*, ed. Victor V. Ramraj and Arun K. Thiruvengadam (Cambridge: Cambridge University Press, 2010), 437.

57. Ibid., 453–460. "Cornelius went so far as to oppose laws that punished those responsible for 'honor killings.'" See Clark B. Lombardi, "Can Islamizing a Legal System Ever Help Promote Liberal Democracy? A View from Pakistan," *University of St. Thomas Law Journal* 7, no. 3 (2010): 666–669.

58. As quoted in Lombardi, "Can Islamizing a Legal System Ever Help Promote Liberal Democracy?" 688.

59. Ibid., 689.

60. Ibid., 691, emphasis in the original. This idea gains some support in Cheema, "Beyond Beliefs," 909–912.

61. Maryam Khan, "Selective Borrowings," Seminar 615, "We the People; a Symposium on the Constitution of India After 60 Years, 1950–2010," November 2010. See also Newberg, *Judging the State*, 241–244; Cheema, "Beyond Beliefs," 901.

62. It is not just the courts that are concerned. The text of the proclamation of emergency issued by General Musharraf as Chief of Army Staff on November 3, 2007, includes, in its bill of particulars justifying the declaration of an emergency and the suspension of the constitution, many charges that the judiciary has violated the separation of powers: for example, "some judges by overstepping the limits of judicial authority have taken over the executive and legislative functions; . . . [it is] of paramount importance that the Honourable Judges confine the scope of their activity to the judicial function and not assume charge of administration; . . . the law and order situation in the country as well as the economy have been adversely affected and trichotomy of powers eroded." Source: www.pakistani.org/pakistan/constitution/post_03nov07/proclamation_emergency_20071103.html.

63. Ayaz Amir, "The New Troika," *News International*, April 30, 2010.

64. Oldenburg, *India, Pakistan, and Democracy*, 169.

65. Civil service officers at the district level continue to exercise judicial powers, in their roles as district magistrate and other positions. There are also full-time career judges at the local level, appointed through a civil service exam, who are separate from the executive branch. See Ansar Abbasi, "The Judiciary May Not Welcome Revival of Magistracy," *News International*, July 15, 2009.

66. Chief Justice Iftikhar Muhammad Chaudhry, speech at the concluding session of the International Judicial Conference 2013, Islamabad, April 21, 2013, www .supremecourt.gov.pk/web/page.asp?id=1438. The Chief Justice had already said, in his inaugural address to the conference two days before, that "the lack of good governance on the part of the executive shifts the burden of responding to the deficiencies of governance towards the judiciary which is increasingly relied upon by the public for the fulfilment of their aspirations as citizens of Pakistan." See www.supremecourt.gov.pk/web/page.asp?id=1433 (accessed April 22, 2013).

67. Chaudhry, in "Pakistan: Judicial Independence Vital for Democracy." Or, as he put it more recently (Iftikhar Muhammad Chaudhry, in a keynote address at the Inaugural Session of the National Judicial Conference, Islamabad, Law & Justice Commission of Pakistan April 16–18, 2010, http://ljcp.gov.pk [accessed May 6, 2011]), "In a democratic system, none of the three organs i.e. the Executive, Legislature and the Judiciary is empowered to assume/exercise unbridled powers. An independent judicial system is a pre-requisite of a democratic society." This issue is of critical importance in India as well. As Ronojoy Sen, in "Walking a Tightrope: Judicial Activism and Indian Democracy," *India Review* 8, no. 1 (January–March 2009), 64, says, "The turf war between the judiciary and the two other branches is the most gripping bit of the story of the judiciary in independent India." It is not at all clear, though, what weight Pakistani judges give to Indian precedents: the range of views can be seen in paragraphs 45 through 59 of the Lawyers Forum case judgment, which ends with a strong rejection of India's "basic structure" doctrine. In any case, there is no consensus in India on this. While the courts have asserted a great deal of power in administrative actions and in seizing the power of appointment of judges, one can find opinions like those in a 2007 judgment by Justices A. K. Mathur and Markanday Katju, as quoted by Sen ("Walking a Tightrope," 76): "If the legislature or the executive are not functioning properly it is for the people to correct the defects by exercising their franchise properly in the next elections and voting for candidates who will fulfill their expectations, or by other lawful methods e.g. peaceful demonstrations. The remedy is not in the judiciary taking over the legislative or executive functions, because that will not only violate the delicate balance of power enshrined in the constitution, but also the judiciary has neither the experience nor the resources to perform these functions." See also Osama Siddique, *Pakistan's Experience with Formal Law: An Alien Justice* (Cambridge: Cambridge University Press, 2013), 23–25.

68. For the Chaudhry court's considered opinion, see paragraph 8, particularly, of the court's "Interim Order in Eighteenth Amendment Case," October 21, 2010.

69. On November 15, 2012 the Chief Justice convened a special meeting of the entire Supreme Court to assert "'The superior judiciary enjoys cross-cutting jurisdiction empowering it to carry out the role of oversight and ensure that no institution or department or authority may interfere in the domain of the other and further to check the unlawful or unauthorised or malafide act or exercise of authority'"; Azam Khan, "Full Court Meeting," *Express Tribune*, November 16, 2012. This news report notes that this is a response to a statement by Chief of Army Staff General Kayani on November 5, 2012, that clearly refers to the Supreme Court's judgment in the Asghar Khan case: "While individual mistakes might have been

made by all of us in the Country, these should be best left to the due process of law. As we all are striving for the rule of law, the fundamental principle; that no one is guilty until proven, should not be forgotten. Let us not pre judge anyone, be it a civilian or a military person and extend it, unnecessarily, to undermine respective institutions." Inter-Services Public Relations Press Release, November 5, 2012, www.ispr.gov.pk/front/main.asp?o=t-press_release&id=2189#pr_link2189. See Kamran Yousaf, "National Interest," *Express Tribune*, November 6, 2012.

70. Azam Khan, "Adiala Missing Inmates," *Express Tribune*, March 1, 2012. See Najam Sethi, "Supreme Court: Now or Never," *Friday Times* 22, no. 44 (December 17–23, 2010); Faisal Siddiqui, "The Judiciary & the Military," *Dawn*, January 20, 2013.

71. See, inter alia, Zia Akhtar, "A Legal Paradox: Pakistan's Constitution, Martial Law and State Necessity," *Sri Lanka Journal of International Law* 21, no. 1 (2009): 153–186. Newberg, *Judging the State*; McGrath, *Destruction of Pakistan's Democracy*; Madhulika Kanaujia and Rimi Jain, "Dawn of a New Democracy in Pakistan: Legal and Political Implications of Nadeem Ahmed v. Federation of Pakistan," *National University of Juridical Sciences* [Kolkata] *Law Review* 2 (2009): 713–738.

72. Khaled Ahmed, "Legal Anarchy: A 'Decline and Fall' in the Offing?" *Friday Times*, 22, no. 35 (October 15–21, 2010). See also Amir, "Hangover Recedeth." Justice Chaudhry (who became Chief Justice in 2005) helped legitimize Musharraf's takeover, by swearing allegiance to the PCO of 1999 in January 2000 and upholding Musharraf's coup a few months later. International Crisis Group, *Reforming the Judiciary in Pakistan*, Asia Report No. 160 (2008): 4. There have been more mundane examples also: according to a news report in *The Express Tribune*, titled "PM's Grace Bestowed on 16 SC Judges" (October 27, 2010), some sixteen Supreme Court justices were given very valuable residential plots by the prime minister's secretariat, and in June 2012 the Chief Justice's son was accused of financial impropriety, and the Chief Justice initially assigned himself to be on the bench to hear the case.

73. Quoted in Abbas Nasir ("Sanctimonious Slide into Chaos?" *Dawn*, January 28, 2012), putting it in the context of Malik's prominence in the legal profession and in the Lawyers' Movement; the quotation appeared originally in a front-page *New York Times* story on January 22, 2012. See also scholar Haris Gazdar's early assessment: "The constitutionalist pretensions of activist judges and their lawyer supporters are belied by their open political ambitions." "Judicial Activism vs. Democratic Consolidation in Pakistan," *Economic and Political Weekly* 44, no. 32 (August 8, 2009), 11.

74. The judges of subordinate courts must have a law degree. They are chosen through an exam set by the Public Services Commission and "are generally viewed as bureaucrats" (USAID, *Pakistan Rule of Law Assessment*, 12).

75. For a general overview of the weakness of the legal profession, see USAID, *Pakistan Rule of Law Assessment*, 27–29; and Mullally, "A Long March to Justice," 55–60, in relation to the Lawyers' Movement.

76. See USAID, *Pakistan Rule of Law Assessment*; International Crisis Group, *Reforming the Judiciary in Pakistan*; and Livingston Armytage, "Pakistan's Law & Justice Sector Reform Experience—Some Lessons," paper presented at the

Thirteenth Commonwealth Law Conference, Melbourne, Australia, April 13, 2003, www.educatingjudges.com/Hyperlinks/PakistanADBProjectLessonsLearned.pdf, on the Asian Development Bank's "Access to Justice" program.

77. A few months later, lawyers in Lahore "harassed" the judge who had dealt with the Raymond Davis case: "A group of lawyers gathered outside his courtroom last Thursday and chanted slogans against the judge. They also vandalised the sign bearing his name at the entrance to the courtroom, pasting 'American Court of Injustice' and 'Justice Seller' on the name plate" (*Express Tribune*, April 3, 2011). A search of *Dawn*'s web site of the terms "lawyers" and "violence" turned up many similar cases. See also the special set of articles in the *Friday Times* 22, no. 34 (October 8–14, 2010), on a particular conflict in which violence and judicial prerogatives and naked politics were significant issues. See Ardesir Cowasjee, "Lawless Lawyers," *Dawn*, October 24, 2010. Things have not improved: an editorial in *Dawn* (April 25, 2013) was titled "On the Rampage: Lawyers Run Amok," condemning behavior at a court hearing for General Musharraf. See also Babar Sattar, "Matter of Principle?" *News International*, April 27, 2013.

78. See Pamela Constable, "Pakistan's Lawyers on the Front Lines," *Washington Post*, November 19, 2007; Ali Khan, "A Lawyers' Mutiny in Pakistan," *Jurist*, May 17, 2007, http://jurist.law.pitt.edu/forumy/2007/05/lawyers-mutiny-in-pakistan.php; and Siddique, *Pakistan's Experience with Formal Law*, 26, for the number of lawyers.

79. Professor Maryam Khan (personal communication) notes that "the consensus amongst legal academics and public intellectuals is that a vast majority of lawyers in Pakistan is socially right-wing" (for example, Saroop Ijaz, "Sweet and Short," *Express Tribune*, February 19, 2012).

80. See the Pakistan Institute of Legislative Development and Transparency MNA directory, available at www.pildat.org/mna/. I did the compilation from the MNA profiles.

81. He has had to deal with charges about the alleged corruption of his son and irregularities in the 2013 elections. A month before his retirement, Asma Jahangir said, "The judiciary will stay independent but there won't be such undermining of other institutions as there is now" (*Express Tribune*, November 19, 2013).

82. Saroop Ijaz, "Beyond the Law," *Express Tribune*, February 17, 2013.

83. That Chief Justice Jillani retired two months later and has been succeeded by a Chief Justice who will retire in August 2015, however, draws attention to how unusual Chief Justice Chaudhry's eight-year term was (only three previous Chief Justices, in 65 years, have served terms of roughly that length). In the next eight years, no Chief Justice will serve more than three years.

84. From a speech of August 1999 by the then president of the Sindh High Court Bar Association. Mohammad Ali Sayeed, *Thoughts and Expressions of a Lawyer* (Karachi: Pakistan Law House, 2009): 130–131. It is impossible to judge how representative a view this is.

85. Malik, *Pakistan Lawyers' Movement*, 12.

86. Ibid., 279–294.

87. Ibid., 275.

88. However, some might disagree: "While the changes brought by a dictator are as momentary as slavery of a man who can be freed any time, the ongoing transformation

under the influence of judiciary is akin to rewriting his DNA. These changes are becoming irreversible and if the process not stopped right now to undo them, we will have to write a new constitution. If the transformation culminates into a judicial dictatorship, the relativistic spirit of democracy will be killed by a form of never-ending totalitarianism considered legitimate by many." Farrukh Khan Pitafi, "The Perils of Judicial Activism," *Express Tribune*, December 30, 2012.

89. Gretchen Helmke and Frances Rosenbluth, "Regimes and the Rule of Law: Judicial Independence in Comparative Perspective," *Annual Review of Political Science* 12 (2009): 361.

90. Ibid.

91. Julio Rios-Figueroa and Jeffrey K. Staton, "Unpacking the Rule of Law: A Review of Judicial Independence Measures," paper presented at the CELS 2009 Fourth Annual Conference on Empirical Legal Studies, April 26, 2009, http://ssrn.com /abstract=1434234.

92. Naqvi, "Protecting the Independence of the Judiciary." See also Siddique, *Pakistan's Experience with Formal Law*, 24–25.

93. Naqvi, "Protecting the Independence of the Judiciary."

94. Eijaz Haider, "Legal Anarchy: Democracy at Risk," *Friday Times* 22, no. 35 (October 15–21, 2010).

95. Osama Siddique, "Checks and Balances: A Flawed Debate," *Friday Times* 22, no. 4 (March 12–18, 2010).

96. Faisal Siddiqi, "Legal Empire," *Dawn*, January 13, 2012; Saroop Ijaz (in "Free and Independent," *Express Tribune*, January 22, 2012), another lawyer and columnist, adds that there has been a disturbing issue concerning judicial independence, namely, "the lack of dissenting judgments ever since the restoration of judiciary or even concurring judgments now." See also International Crisis Group, *Reforming Pakistan's Criminal Justice System*, 28: "Democracy and political stability depends on the rule of law—and vice versa. Public perceptions of a perpetual institutional clash between the executive and the judiciary will encumber both branches of government from consolidating the authority conferred by the restoration of democracy. While the elected government must respect judicial independence and directives, the judiciary, too, must observe constitutional limits and refrain from encroaching on the executive and the parliament's mandate."

97. Mohammad Waseem, "Elections Without a Mandate," *News International*, April 19, 2013. He remarks: "Prior to the 2013 elections, the judiciary controls the right, left and centre of the political stage, thanks to the unimaginative political leadership of mainstream parties."

98. In tug-of-war, people pulling on a rope attempt to move a flag across a center point and keep it there; here "crucial decisions" is the flag that each team (and each segment of each team) wish to bring over to their side. The tug-of-war ends fairly quickly; in life, the struggle never ends. Oldenburg, *India, Pakistan, and Democracy*.

99. As quoted in Jamal Khurshid, "Meddling by Army Blocked, Govt Should Do Its Duty: CJ," *News International*, September 9, 2011.

100. This is not just an abstract description. In March 2011, Punjab Chief Minister Shabaz Sharif suggested that all political "stakeholders"—military, judiciary, and

media, along with the political parties—convene a conference "to prepare a broad-based national agenda to steer the country out of crisis." Amir Wasim, " 'N' [Pakistan Muslim League—Nawaz] Reaffirms Judiciary, Army Proposal," *Dawn*, March 10, 2011. Najam Sethi, in "Editorial: No Fly Zone," *Friday Times* 23, no. 4 (March 11–17, 2011), provides an analysis of motives and capabilities of the various "stakeholders."

101. Pew Research Center, "A Less Gloomy Mood in Pakistan," August 27, 2014, www .pewglobal.org/2014/08/27/a-less-gloomy-mood-in-pakistan. Rating the "influence on the way things are going in Pakistan," 87 percent of respondents thought the military's influence to be "good"; for the national government it was 60 percent, and for the court system, 47 percent, with only the police (at 33 percent) lower.

102. Stephen P. Cohen, "Pakistan: Arrival and Departure," in *The Future of Pakistan*, ed. Stephen P. Cohen and others (Washington, D.C.: Brookings Institution, 2011), 33; see also the chapter in the same volume by C. Christine Fair, "Addressing Fundamental Challenges," 91–106.

103. Poll conducted January 1–7, 2012, http://site.gilanifoundation.com/?p=225 (accessed February 8, 2012). For one comprehensive explanation of the increasing power of the Supreme Court, see Faisal Siddiqi, "Why Is the SC So Powerful?" *Dawn*, October 15, 2012.

CHAPTER 4

TURMOIL IN THE FRONTIER

Mariam Abou Zahab

The rise of the Pakistani Taliban has not happened overnight. It is the product of the ideological dependence of Pakistan on religion since Partition, of the deliberate marginalization of the Federally Administered Tribal Areas (FATA), and of the instrumentalization of Islam by the state as a counterweight to the internal threat of Pashtun nationalism in the 1980s. Last but not least, in the FATA, the insurgency is also the consequence of persistent conflict across the border in Afghanistan.[1]

External factors—beyond the Afghan factor—are emphasized in studies dealing with the FATA. They played a role in the insurgency, but the local dynamics should be taken into account. The old system, which denied people social and political rights, was already dysfunctional before 9/11 and the U.S. intervention in Afghanistan acted as a catalyst for those who had long-standing grievances.

This chapter attempts to analyze the dynamics of Talibanization in the FATA with a focus on the socioeconomic factors. It begins by outlining the changes that have occurred in the last four decades in the social structure of the FATA and examines the impact of labor migration, of the Afghan war of the 1980s, and of the collapse of the Taliban regime in Afghanistan. The focus then shifts to the emergence of the Taliban, describing how the Taliban exploited the grievances of the tribal population to carve out enclaves of alternative power, and tries to identify the main socioeconomic drivers of militancy in the FATA. It then analyzes the issue of population displacement and its consequences. Finally, it describes the steps that should be taken to address the situation.

THE FATA SEEN AS FROZEN IN TIME

Since Partition, the Pakistani state has maintained in the FATA a colonial system based on patronage of a few *maliks*—tribal elders who, since the colonial era, were the mediators between their tribe and the political agent and who allied themselves with the administration to pursue personal interests.[2] The system of allowances and subsidies survived after the British left.[3] The failure to integrate the FATA has been driven by the desire to use this territory as a geostrategic space to influence events in Afghanistan. To justify the isolation of the area often referred to as *ilaqa ghair* (foreign land)—part of Pakistan and at the same time apart from Pakistan as if the real Pakistan stopped at the left bank of the Indus—and the continuation of colonial legal and administrative structures, a narrative drawing on colonial literature has been developed. Pashtun tribal identity is described as unchanging, frozen in time. Tribal Pashtuns are portrayed as inward-looking, living in self-imposed social and cultural isolation, opposed to integration, which is seen as a threat to their identity, and opposed to modern education, especially for girls. As Robert Nichols has demonstrated,[4] Pashtuns have never been an insular community; they have a tradition of circulating through the Indian subcontinent and as far as Australia in the colonial era, looking for opportunities, and their identity has always been fluid.

SOCIAL CHANGE WITHOUT POLITICAL EMPOWERMENT

Pashtun tribal society has changed rapidly in the FATA over the last 40 years, starting with tribals migrating to Karachi and the Gulf in the late 1960s and the 1970s. The Dubai chalo phenomenon attracted many young tribals, particularly from North and South Waziristan.[5] Members of minor lineages generated new wealth,[6] which challenged the social hierarchy. Then, in the 1980s, the rise of smuggling and the tremendous inflow of remittances further increased wealth in the emerging lower middle classes—predominantly the disadvantaged and traditionally subordinate segments of the rural society.[7] New inequalities based on wealth developed, which completely changed the social hierarchy and the dependence on land as the greatest source of power.

In the 1970s, Zulfiqar Ali Bhutto initiated development projects in the FATA in the context of his rivalry with the National Awami Party. But in the absence of political reforms, the main beneficiaries of these projects were the maliks (as contractors) and their children,[8] and the sense of alienation of the common people only grew deeper. Bhutto also facilitated the issuance of passports, which had far-reaching socioeconomic and political implications for the FATA.

One of the impacts of the Afghan jihad of the 1980s on the FATA was the increase in religious institutions where a whole generation was socialized in radical Islam in the madrasahs and along Afghan mujahideen. The rupture of tradition was caused by the import of the Islamist ideology in the 1980s. The Islamization of the Pashtuns was the fallout of the Afghan jihad; used to fight the internal threat of Pashtun nationalism, Islam became a politics of identity. General Zia ul Haq did not realize the impact it would have on traditional power structures. The breakdown of tribal authority began during the Afghan jihad when the agencies marginalized the maliks and used mullahs to unite the tribes against the USSR. Religious groups were empowered and became autonomous as the writ of the Pakistani state was ineffective in the FATA.

The pattern of politics was changed by the introduction in 1996 of universal adult franchise in the FATA. A total of 298 candidates stood for the eight National Assembly seats; elections were, however, held on a nonparty basis. Adult franchise was a long-standing demand of the young educated tribals and the emerging business elite. The participation of the tribals in elections further eroded the power and authority of the maliks,[9] as clerics, mostly linked to the Jamiat-e Ulama-e Islam (JUI), were elected and were thus able to transform their religious authority into political power.

Pashtun tribal society considered as classless and egalitarian has gradually changed into a class society with new social and political players challenging the tribal elite. Four categories were identified in a World Bank report:[10] first, the traditional leaders (landowning elders and maliks), who are allied with the administration to pursue their own interests and have been the sole recipients of the system, supporting the status quo; second, the new rich[11] (traders, contractors, timber merchants, transporters, drug/arms traffickers), who are the main beneficiaries of the war economy; third, the educated and professionals (doctors, teachers, engineers, journalists, students, nongovernmental organization employees, active and retired members of the military and the bureaucracy), who oppose the status quo and are the agents of social change; and fourth, the common people (farmers, share-croppers, landless peasants, artisans, workers in the transport sector, unemployed youth), who have no civil and political rights and are dissatisfied with the existing setup. A fifth category should be added: migrants settled in Karachi and in the Gulf who, just like the educated and professionals, oppose the status quo and could be agents of social change.

THE EMERGENCE OF THE PAKISTANI TALIBAN

Many young tribals who were unemployed joined the Taliban in Afghanistan from 1996 and fought against the Northern Alliance. They built links with the Afghan Taliban and foreign fighters to whom they provided safe passage and support after 9/11. Maliks and elders did not support the Afghan Taliban because the latter embodied the revenge of the young and the rural poor on the khans (landholders).

After the arrival of Al Qaeda in the FATA at the end of 2001, "tribal entrepreneurs" discovered the lucrative business of harboring foreign militants, which became a source of extra money.[12] Charismatic young men understood the change in political opportunities and used their jihadi credentials and their access to resources to compensate for their youth and their lack of tribal and religious legitimacy, and they filled the power vacuum.

Generalizations about the Pakistani Taliban act as smoke screens: the FATA is not a single entity, the reality is highly complex, and each agency has its characteristics and dynamics and a unique set of political and ideological drivers that affect the nature and level of militancy. In fact, armed groups active in the FATA are disparate entities, divided by tribal, ethnic, cultural, and political differences.[13] They are not a disciplined organization as tribal influence impedes unity among Taliban factions. The groups maintain separate command structures to avoid friction, and tribal animosities influence decisions to join one side or the other. In true Pashtun fashion, alliances in the region abruptly materialize and suddenly disappear when they are no more useful to gain advantage in local disputes.

Several wars are fought at the same time in the FATA: a "greater war" between the Taliban and the state over lost territory; a war in Afghanistan with the FATA as a safe haven for groups fighting foreign forces in Afghanistan (Waziristan, Bajaur); a sectarian war[14] between Sunnis and Shias in Kurram and Orakzai and between Deobandis and Barelvis in Khyber; tribal wars, for instance, between Wazirs and Mehsuds (South Waziristan); wars between minor and dominant clans of a tribe—examples can be found in every tribal agency—who instrumentalize external actors (the army or foreign fighters) to challenge their rivals; and factional wars over water, land, and other resources. What is happening is a series of overlapping localized civil wars. Moreover, the fault line between pro- and anti-Taliban is much less relevant than social and religious cleavages: for instance, in Orakzai, Sunni subtribes joined the Taliban because they were anti-Shia.

The initial target of the Pakistani Taliban was Afghanistan. Until 2004, their focus was on protecting foreign militants, recruiting, and training for war in Afghanistan. They were not a challenge to Pakistani authorities, who did not interfere in their activities and just looked the other way as if whatever happened west of the Indus was not a concern for the Pakistani state. Musharraf's policy, marked by inconsistency and intermittency, was one of containment rather than elimination in order to get the backing of the Muttahida Majlis-e Amal (MMA)[15] for the military regime and because the government thought the Taliban could be contained within the FATA. But the MMA provincial government (2002–2008) did not prevent spillover in settled areas, and the militants expanded their operational space to the cities, notably, Dera Ismaïl Khan, Tank, and Kohat.

A tactical change took place after the beginning of military operations in 2003: by kidnapping security and state officials, the Taliban could negotiate with the government on their own terms.[16] The army was part of the marginalization of the state and of the tribal political and administrative system when it signed peace deals with the militants in 2004 and 2005, sidelining the tribal elders and the political agent. The Taliban were empowered; by signing the deals, the army gave them legitimacy, and the huge sums paid as compensation for the destructions resulting from the military operations allowed them to consolidate themselves and to sustain patronage networks.

Another turning point was the creation of the Tehrik-e Taliban Pakistan (TTP) in December 2007 under the leadership of Baitullah Mehsud as an umbrella for dozens of local groups with local agendas and some elements of transnational militancy. The TTP's aim was to pool resources and manpower of Pakistani Taliban to fight against the security forces and to extend help to the Afghan Taliban taking part in the jihad against U.S. and North Atlantic Treaty Organization (NATO) forces. Its proclaimed objectives were to enforce sharia, to perform "defensive jihad" against the Pakistani army in the aftermath of the storming of Islamabad's Lal Masjid (Red Mosque) in July 2007, and to refuse future peace deals with the government. In fact, the TTP is not as united as it claims to be: there are intertribal and intratribal cleavages, and many factions and clans have not joined the TTP. It is not always a disciplined organization, as several recent events have shown. Moreover, the TTP has progressively transformed itself into a Mehsuddominated group.

THE SOCIOECONOMIC DRIVERS OF MILITANCY

The government refused to see the Pakistani Taliban as a product of the social and political modernization of the Pashtun belt, which emerged on the ruins of the tribal system. But it is clearly part of the story. Turmoil in the FATA is the expression of social change. The legitimacy of traditional leaders based on age and kinship relationships has become increasingly irrelevant. Militancy can be explained partly by the general weakening of tribal society at the hand of external forces and partly by the socialization of an increasing number of youth inside radical political Islam and outside of the traditional framework.

The militancy retains a strong hidden socioeconomic dimension. It has the characteristics of a social movement, and the class and generation factors should be taken into account to understand the dynamics. The Taliban are the expression of the conflict between the *hujra* (the men's house where tribal political activity was traditionally conducted, the *hujra* embodies the power of landowners and maliks) and the *masjid* (the mosque now representing the underprivileged).

Poverty is to some extent a factor, but the main factors are related to status in terms of economic and political marginalization. Having no social links, no future, is the main driver. The lack of physical protection, legal rights, and economic opportunities for largely subsistence farmers has prepared the ground for militant recruitment. Unemployed young tribals want to find employment and to obtain some status in society; both demands are fulfilled once they join the militants.[17] The perception of rising social inequality, a call for social justice and a challenge to the power-seeking elite, a sense of alienation, the slow pace of development projects, the military operations and later the drone strikes: all these factors contributed in radicalizing young tribals.

In the beginning, the Taliban capitalized on the local anger at the general lawlessness and became an alternative moral authority.[18] They exploited the issue of corruption and delays in justice as well as unemployment, social inequality, and lack of health and education facilities. They reinforced the perception of weakness of the state and of the local elite, who failed to respond to the aspirations of the marginalized in terms of security, justice, political empowerment, and socioeconomic development. They took advantage of the lack of governance and political participation in the FATA, eroded the tribal political and administrative system further—notably by killing elders to eliminate political opponents—and provoked deep-rooted class divisions. They garnered support by promising to replace the Pakistani governance and judicial system, which is widely viewed as corrupt and unjust.[19] The Taliban's strict interpretation of sharia did not appeal to everyone in the tribal agencies, but its promises of fairness and swift dispute resolution appealed to many. Unlike Pakistani civil institutions, Taliban courts delivered justice quickly and could implement punishments immediately. The process was initially successful; Taliban courts resolved disputes between tribes and clans that had dragged on for decades. The Taliban even limited corruption among some political agents. Their efforts were rewarded with broad-based political support from everyday people in the FATA.[20] Welcomed originally because they eliminated drugs, gambling, and other "immoral activities,"[21] they became unpopular when they turned to crime.[22] Moreover, the disintegration of the institutional structure has provided an open space to criminal gangs who have access to weapons and have borrowed Taliban rhetoric for their own interests.

"As long as the Taliban targeted security forces alone, the local people supported them as they believed it to be part of the jihad against the United States," said Maulana Abdul Wahid, a prayer leader in this city [Peshawar]. ". . . However, towards the end of 2005, as the Taliban launched a terror campaign against the general public, targeting mosques, marketplaces, schools and government buildings, public sympathy turned to anger," Wahid said. "We stopped supporting the Taliban after they began killing and injuring innocent and non-combatant people," Wahid said. "The people here repent the goodwill they had shown towards Taliban."[23]

DISPLACEMENT

Since 2004, massive population displacements have taken place. More than a third of the population of the FATA—estimated at five to six million—has been displaced at some point or another, in some cases several times. The causes of displacement are diverse: abuses of armed groups, tribal and sectarian conflicts, fighting between insurgents and tribes, drone attacks,[24] economic sanctions following the failure of peace deals with the militants, and, last but not least, military operations that have been planned without accounting for the consequences and that relied heavily on indiscriminate airpower and artillery.

The sociopolitical consequences of the displacement are a source of deep concern. The people of the FATA are very attached to their land and are desperate to return home, but the ongoing conflict, the poor security situation, the destruction of their homes and sources of income, and the lack of compensation for their losses prevent them from returning. The government has encouraged and, in some cases, forced them to go back, claiming that military operations had eliminated the Taliban and that the population can safely return. In many cases, the Taliban had just fled to a neighboring tribal agency, and once the army withdrew, they came back. Forced returns are sometimes accompanied with threats: the army asks the elders to raise a *lashkar* (tribal militia) to fight the Taliban and maintain law and order, while the Taliban threaten the population with reprisals.[25]

Until 2008, the displaced tribals stayed near their home in areas controlled by their tribe or their religious community. In Kurram and Orakzai Agencies, this led to the ghettoization of Shias, putting them at a greater risk from Taliban attacks. Tensions were also exacerbated in the cities between the local population and some tribes, notably the Mehsud, who are viewed with suspicion and even hostility, because they belong to the same tribe as Baitullah Mehsud[26] and Hakimullah Mehsud,[27] the leaders of the TTP. From 2008, the intensification of military operations forced people to move farther from the FATA and settle in the cities, particularly Peshawar and Karachi, where families joined the men who had been working there. Karachi, which was already the largest Pashtun city in the world, is now home to four to five million Pakistani and Afghan Pashtuns (about 20 percent of the population of the city), which means that more Pashtuns are living in Karachi than in the FATA. This massive influx of displaced tribals has reignited ethnic tensions, which have been a dominant factor in Karachi's politics since the 1980s.[28] The local chapter of the Awami National Party (ANP) claimed to be the sole representative of Pashtuns living in Karachi and exploited their grievances in its rivalry with the Muttahida Qaumi Movement over scarce resources. The ANP has been under sustained attack in Karachi, particularly since June 2012. The western part of the city, which was an ANP stronghold, is now under the control of the TTP. Leaders and workers of the ANP have been killed in revenge attacks for the army's operations in Swat (2009) or have left Karachi. Party offices have been closed, and ANP candidates were targeted during the election campaign in April–May 2013.

Tribal people do not feel safe in Karachi, where they are discriminated against and victims of ethnic violence. Hundreds have been killed in recent years just because they were Pashtuns. There is a general hostility toward displaced Pashtuns in Karachi, and particularly against Mehsud. Many Mehsud who have been displaced since the 2009 military operation would like to go back to South Waziristan, but they are not allowed by the army to do so.

The forced urbanization of the tribal population and its marginalization present serious consequences for the future. The displaced people risk lapsing into chronic poverty and experience an increased sense of deprivation. Children who have been exposed to extreme violence and deprived of education are often forced to work to support their family. Many among the displaced persons and the professional class who left the FATA to seek safety or better economic opportunities will not return to the region.

THE FRAGMENTATION OF THE TTP

A tentative peace process was initiated from February 2014 by Nawaz Sharif, who announced that his government would engage in peace talks with the TTP. Both sides named committees to represent them, but hardly any progress was made. This initiative, together with the appointment of Fazlullah as the new emir of the TTP after the death of Hakimullah Mehsud, led to a split of the TTP.

Mehsud militants who were dominant in the organizational structure and policymaking of the TTP could not accept Fazlullah as the emir, and the majority of them chose Khan Said (alias Sajna) as their leader. The TTP was seen as shifting "into a group based increasingly on ideology rather than tribal ties."[29] Fazlullah, who operates from Kunar and Nuristan (Afghanistan), has influence in Karachi, but he has lost influence, if he ever had any, in North Waziristan, South Waziristan, and Mohmand Agencies.

Another reason for the split of the TTP was disagreements about the negotiations with the government. On March 1, 2014, the TTP and the government agreed on a monthlong temporary cease-fire. A few days later, Ahrar ul Hind and Ansar ul Mujahidin, two little-known groups, carried out attacks respectively in Islamabad and Hangu, which the TTP condemned. Ahrar ul Hind is in fact a splinter group of the Punjabi Taliban (or TTP Punjab)[30] formed by those who disagreed with their leader, Asmatullah Muawiya, who was engaged in the peace talks. Similarly, Mohmand militants led by Abdul Wali (alias Omar Khalid Khurasani) left the TTP in August 2014 to form Jamaat ul Ahrar and announced their support for Lashkar-e Islam of Mangal Bagh, a group active in Khyber Agency and not part of the TTP.

The peace process quickly disintegrated. The army launched a military operation in North Waziristan (Zarb-e Azab) in June 2014 after the attack on Karachi airport. At least 1.5 million persons were displaced, and around 250,000 crossed the border into Afghanistan.

Jamaat ul Ahrar orchestrated the Wagah suicide attack on November 2, 2014, which killed over sixty people and left 110 others injured. The spokesman of the group, Ehsanullah Ehsan, claimed that the attack was "revenge for the innocent people killed by Pakistan army in North-Waziristan."

At the same time, the former TTP spokesman, Abu Umar Maqbool al Khurasani (alias Shahidullah Shahid), declared allegiance "in individual capacity" to Abu Bakr al Baghdadi along with five other "commanders." Graffiti supporting Ad Dawlah al Islamiya fil Iraq wal Sham (Daesh) and black flags appeared in different cities.

The Mehsud led by Sajna have denounced Fazlullah and are carrying on peace talks with the government through an eleven-member *jirga* consisting of Mehsud tribal elders, while the Punjabi Taliban faithful to Muawiya announced in September 2014 the cessation of subversive activities in Pakistan to focus on Afghanistan.[31] They are becoming "good Taliban" who, at the time of writing, were seen by the Pakistani army as potentially even more useful after the American withdrawal in 2014–2015.

STEPS TO ADDRESS THE SITUATION

The response of the state has been the promotion of lashkars (tribal militias), which is somehow fomenting a civil war—Pashtuns against Pashtun—as a counterinsurgency strategy. A lashkar is a traditional tribal militia, often formed on an ad hoc basis for the accomplishment of a specific purpose (e.g., to hunt down an outlaw, address a family feud that has gone out of control, or challenge a government policy) and then disbanded. Lashkars failed in 2003 and 2007 to expel Al Qaeda fighters. Since then, hundreds of tribal elders have been killed, the Taliban targeting all those who have been part of lashkars.

By arming the tribes,[32] the state is part of the process of its own marginalization. Instead of mainstreaming the FATA, it is trying to keep these areas apart. Lashkars are a way for dominant tribes or clans to get access to modern weapons and money and can be analyzed as a reaction to the Taliban threatening the old tribal structure. The sociology of these lashkars is interesting: for instance, in Bajaur, lashkars have been raised by the Salarzai, who are the dominant tribe; most of the land belongs to them, and they occupy better lands; their aim was to eliminate the Taliban, described as poor ordinary people, and restore the old tribal order.

Outlaws have also joined anti-Taliban militias, which means they can carry out their activities openly and wear arms. Finally, lashkars could get out of control and cause unending tribal feuds. They might also turn against the state.

Even if military operations were successful, as the government has claimed, the underlying conditions that created the insurgency have not been addressed. Contrary to what privileged tribal elders who have a vested interest in the status quo claim, the old order based on exploitation cannot be revived. It is discredited because it has been unable to respond to social change and did not build loyalty to the state.

The idea that tribal people want to be left alone is wrong. The government ignores the possibility of a tribal society's acceptance of nontribal norms of collective and personal behavior without the abolition of tribal relations—economic, political, and social. For instance, the jirga (council of elders) had lost credibility since the 1980s because it was not egalitarian; its membership had been restricted to men from powerful tribes; it did not provide justice to the poor; and in most cases, it favored the richer or more influential party. The Taliban redefined the concept of jirga with a prominent role for mullahs. The solution does not consist in doing away with the jirga—it can continue to exist, but it requires a change in its composition, with the inclusion of the educated middle class and the marginalized categories.

A new legitimacy based on principles of representation through elections and merit, transparency, and inclusiveness should be built in order to integrate gradually the FATA into the mainstream. In that respect, the two decrees signed in August 2011 by President Zardari are encouraging steps. Reforms were announced in 2009, but their implementation was stalled. The decrees bring amendments in the Frontier Crimes Regulations (FCR)[33] (2011) and extend the Political Parties Order (2002) to the Tribal Areas. The collective responsibility clause was amended: from now on, women, children below the age of sixteen, and elders above age sixty-five cannot be jailed, and the whole tribe will not be punished for the actions of one of its members. An appeal procedure has been set up, and the right to bail is recognized. Political parties can now legally function in the FATA, which should generate internal tribal dynamics and reduce the appeal of religious parties.[34] This should be followed by the election of representative FATA councils—with seats for women and religious minorities, among others—to fill the political vacuum that will be created by the elimination of the alternative leadership of the Taliban.

Political rights are meaningless without sustainable development and economic stability. Huge sums have been allocated to the FATA under foreign-funded development projects. The major flaw was the imposition of plans from above and through the FATA secretariat without taking the tribal population into confidence. Moreover, the lack of oversight means that donors' money has benefited the civil and military bureaucracy and FATA elites without reaching the people who need it most. The real stakeholders should be involved in development projects to ensure ownership by the people and overcome their sense of alienation. The focus should also be on services, ensuring that schools and clinics operate properly and that government employees do not avoid their duties in the FATA.

Jobs should be provided to those who are fifteen to seventeen years old to give them prospects for upward social mobility. This also means bringing madrasah graduates in the mainstream by engaging madrasahs in projects to develop market-relevant vocational training that is likely to benefit the most disadvantaged categories.

Some promising initiatives have recently been taken under the FATA Development Program—Livelihood Development and with United States Agency for International Development funding for the educated unemployed. For instance, a five-month diploma course in mining is offered by Peshawar University to develop the mineral sector in the FATA. Loans and other incentives are given to young people to start a business.[35]

Mainstreaming the FATA implies the eventual merger of the FATA with Khyber Pakhtunkhwa. The political parties have a clear interest in seeking the FATA's merger with the province, but due to the lack of confidence in the state, some people have reservations about coming under the Pakistani Constitution. Are the tribals ready to accept a new social contract under which they abandon some of their freedoms in exchange for the protection of the state and rights and privileges linked to citizenship? Can the state respect this contract?

CONCLUSION

Talibanization is not a Pashtun problem but the extension of Sunni–Deobandi militancy. As Asad Hashim has said: "There would be no Pakistani Taliban if there were no militants that Pakistan had supported over a number of years. And Pakistanis have paid a heavy price for this [in lives]."[36] As Taliban influence grew in the FATA during the past few years, sectarian groups reasserted themselves across Pakistan and they exploited the Talibanization of the FATA to expand their operational space.[37] This was again facilitated by the inaction and denial of the state, which claimed for a long time that the "Punjabi Taliban" did not exist. Khyber Pakhtunkhwa governor Awais Ghani gave this warning in September 2008: "It will be ill-advised to think that the militancy will remain confined to the NWFP. Militant activities have already shifted to the settled areas and Punjab and they have established strong links with South Punjab."

Moreover, the FCR amendments have come soon after the federal government issued two identical regulations, Action (in Aid of Civil Power) Regulation 2011 for FATA and PATA (Provincially Administered Tribal Areas), to give unprecedented powers to the armed forces operating against the militants in the conflict areas. The regulations provide legal cover to the "unlawful acts of armed forces" during military operations with retrospective effect—from February 1, 2008—and empower the security forces operating in both the FATA and PATA to keep terror suspects in custody at undisclosed location for 120 days.[38] The government claims that these regulations will specifically target militants, but there are fears of misuse.

There is no real hope that the security situation will improve soon in the FATA. Putting an end to violent insurgency through dialogue is a distant possibility. Contrary to what the military establishment thinks, the Taliban will not lay down arms when NATO leaves Afghanistan; they are fighting the Pakistani state. Normalcy in the FATA is not in the interests of the groups, local and foreign, active in Afghanistan who need safe havens in North Waziristan.

No real change and sustainable development can take place until the military ends its operations in the FATA. The people of the FATA will have to wait till their grievances are really addressed.

NOTES

1. Hassan Abbas, *Inside Pakistan's North West Frontier Province: The Political Landscape of the Insurgency* (Washington, D.C.: New American Foundation, 2010).
2. "Before the arrival of the Taliban in 2001, Pakistan's political agents in the FATA often treated their respective agencies as personal fiefdoms, doling out money and resources to the wealthy and well-connected. The government was perceived as corrupt, tribal judicial processes as unfair and too slow." Brian Fishman, *The Battle for Pakistan: Militancy and Conflict Across the FATA and NWFP* (Washington, D.C.: New America Foundation, 2010) (summary of a series of reports on the FATA published by the New America Foundation in 2010).
3. For details about the role of the political agent and the law enforcement system, see Pervaiz Iqbal Cheema and Maqsudul Hasan Nuri, eds., *Tribal Areas of Pakistan: Challenges and Responses* (Islamabad: Islamabad Policy Research Institute/Hanns Seidel Foundation, 2005).
4. Robert Nichols, *A History of Pashtun Migration* (Karachi: Oxford University Press, 2008).
5. Fazal-ur-Rahim Marwat, "The Genesis of Change and Modernization in Federally Administered Tribal Areas of Pakistan," *IPRI Journal* 7, no. 2 (2010). Tribals

from Waziristan are well represented in Dubai: in 2010, there were about 350,000 Pakistani Pashtuns in Dubai; more than half of them belonged to the FATA, particularly Waziristan.

6. "There is evidence that junior, or depressed, lineage saw employment abroad and the economic opportunities at home as an avenue of escape from their positions in society." Akbar S. Ahmad, *Resistance and Control in Pakistan* (Cambridge: Cambridge University Press, 1991), 97.

7. For details, see Mariam Abou Zahab, "Kashars Against Mashars: Jihad and Social Change in the FATA," in *Beyond Swat: History, Society and Economy along the Afghanistan–Pakistan Frontier*, ed. B. Hopkins and M. Marsden (London: Hurst, 2013), 51–60.

8. Bhutto introduced quotas for the FATA in educational institutions that benefited the children of the maliks who are settled in cities outside the FATA. He also established educational institutions in the FATA, among them the Cadet College in Razmak (which opened in 1978). The role of Razmak in creating a new elite cannot be overestimated: many, if not most, of the young educated tribals from Waziristan and adjoining settled districts studied in Razmak.

9. Previously, under the 1973 Constitution, only some 37,000 maliks and other tribal elders were entitled to cast their votes on behalf of the population.

10. *Traditional Structures in Local Governance for Local Development: A Case Study of Pakhtuns Residing in NWFP & FATA, Pakistan* (World Bank, 2004).

11. The misuse of the Afghanistan Transit Trade by the tribals and Afghan traders created a new class of businessmen in the FATA. Moreover, from the 1980s, transport became a major source of income for the tribals.

12. Abou Zahab, "Kashars Against Mashar."

13. "The universe of militants in FATA and NWFP is far more diverse than commonly understood. . . . Militant groups have very different backgrounds, tribal affiliations and strategic concepts." Fishman, *Battle for Pakistan.*

14. For details, see Mariam Abou Zahab, "'It's Just a Sunni–Shi'a Thing': Sectarianism and Talibanism in the Federally Administered Tribal Areas (FATA) of Pakistan," in *Contemporary Sunni–Shi'i Relations*, ed. Brigitte Maréchal and Sami Zemni (London: Hurst, 2013), 179–192.

15. The Muttahida Majlis-e Amal (MMA, or United Council of Action) was a coalition of Islamist parties formed in 2002 that won a majority of the seats in Khyber Pakhtunkhwa's Provincial Assembly and was part of a coalition government in Baluchistan. It failed to deliver and lost its credibility among Pashtuns and collapsed in the 2008 elections.

16. Mohammad Amir Rana, *Taliban Insurgency in Pakistan: A Counterinsurgency Perspective* (Islamabad: Pakistan Institute for Peace Studies, 2009).

17. According to Mussarat Hilali of the Human Rights Commission of Pakistan, the average Taliban recruit is "a poor man with no job, nothing, who suddenly gets sophisticated weapons, a car, a mobile and cash."

18. For details, see Abou Zahab, "Kashars Against Mashars"; and Mariam Abou Zahab, "Frontière dans la tourmente: La talibanisation des zones tribales," *Outre-terre: Revue européenne de géopolitique* 24 (2010): 336–357.

19. Fishman, *Battle for Pakistan.*

20. Ibid.

21. In the beginning, the Taliban's greatest appeal to the local population was that they were able "to right the wrong" and thus create a more egalitarian society.

22. See Gretchen Peters, *Crime and Insurgency in the Tribal Areas of Afghanistan and Pakistan* (West Point, N.Y.: Combating Terrorism Center, 2010).

23. Ashfaq Yusufzai, "Taliban Back off from Attacking Civilians," *Asia Times Online*, July 26, 2011.

24. The issue of drone attacks is very controversial, but contrary to what some people claim, the tribals generally do not support the drone attacks that have claimed dozens, if not hundreds, of civilian lives and have drawn many young men to the cause of the Taliban. The number of drone attacks had doubled in 2010 (122) compared with 2009. According to the New America Foundation, seventy-three strikes were recorded in 2011, forty-eight in 2012, and sixteen between January and July 2013. See Kathy Gannon and Sebastian Abbot, "Criticism Alters U.S. Drone Program in Pakistan," Associated Press, July 25, 2013.

25. For instance, the attack on a school bus in Matani, a village on the outskirts of Peshawar, in September 2011 was an act of reprisal for the lashkar raised by the Adezai tribe.

26. Baitullah Mehsud was killed by a drone strike in August 2009.

27. Hakimullah Mehsud was killed by a drone strike in November 2013.

28. See Mariam Abou Zahab, "Les conséquences des déplacements de populations des zones tribales pakistanaises," *Questions internationales* 50 (2011): 31–33.

29. Zia ul Rehman, "TTP Is Crumbling," *Friday Times*, November 14, 2014.

30. Zia ul Rehman, "A Profile of Ahrar-ul-Hind and Ansar-ul-Mujahidin in Pakistan," *CTC Sentinel*, June 11, 2014.

31. Rehman, "TTP Is Crumbling."

32. Traditionally, the lashkar has not been backed financially or logistically by the state, but some of the lashkars raised recently in the FATA have received weapons from the state authorities.

33. Frontier Crimes Regulations were promulgated in 1901 by the colonial administration. For a detailed study of the FCR, see Khalid Aziz, "The Reform of the Frontier Crimes Regulations (FCR) and Administration of the Tribal Areas of Pakistan," 2005, http://fatareforms.org/2005/11/22/reform-fcr-administartion-tribal-areas-khalid-aziz/.

34. The participation for the general elections of May 2013 was 37 percent. Independent candidates won six out of ten seats, PML-N won two seats, and PTI and JUI-F won a seat each.

35. Ranjit Devraj, "Gem of a Plan Against Taliban," *Asia Times Online*, August 18, 2011.

36. Asad Hashim, "Pakistan: A State Adrift," *Al Jazeera English*, September 2, 2011, http://english.aljazeera.net/indepth/spotlight/the911decade/2011/08/2011828133727518751.html.

37. For details, see Mariam Abou Zahab, "Pashtun and Punjabi Taliban: The Jihadi–Sectarian Nexus," in *Contextualising Jihadi Thought*, ed. Jeevan Deol and Zaheer Kazmi (London: Hurst, 2012), 369–387.

38. Rahimullah Yusufzai, "Some More Change for FATA," *The News*, August 16, 2011.

CHAPTER 5

INTERNAL SECURITY ISSUES IN PAKISTAN

PROSPECTS OF POLICE AND LAW ENFORCEMENT REFORM

Hassan Abbas

An effective police force is critical to modern crime fighting and countering terrorism. In Pakistan, an understaffed and underequipped police force is increasingly called on to manage rising insecurity and militant violence, and quite predictably the police performance has been far from satisfactory. This chapter evaluates the obstacles to upgrading the existing police system and recommends both traditional and innovative reform options, including major restructuring of the total civilian law enforcement infrastructure, without which the police force cannot be effectively improved. Because Pakistan's police capacity has direct implications for the country's ability to tackle terrorism, the international community would realize counterterrorism dividends by helping law enforcement efforts through modern training and technical assistance.

CURRENT CHALLENGES

For many years, Pakistan has been engaged in battling a hydra-headed insurgency in the Federally Administered Tribal Areas (FATA) and parts of Khyber Pakhtunkhwa (KP, formerly known as the North West Frontier Province). An expanding terrorist campaign targeting Pakistan's major cities is inextricably linked to this insurgency. The growing number of suicide attacks across Pakistan underscores the dangerous nature of the crisis.[1] From 2002 to 2006, the total number of suicide attacks in Pakistan was twenty-one, while over the next five years (i.e., the 2007–2011 period), the total number rose to 279. This explains the threat posed by this kind of terrorism alone. The numbers declined from 2012 to 2015, but the challenge remains serious.

Pakistan has reportedly suffered close to 50,000 casualties in the war on terror so far, and this trend continues.[2] Although those under fire are chiefly religious leaders challenging extremists, politicians associated with progressive political parties, and innocent civilians, police and security officials and government installations are also increasingly being targeted as a symbol of the state. Terrorists understand well that the military and the police are their most important enemies.

The changing tactics and targets of the various terrorist groups operating in the country pose a formidable challenge to a police force with limited resources, poor training, and inadequate equipment. Pakistan's civilian law enforcement structure has failed to develop any systematic and advanced counterterrorism strategy owing to the lack of modern investigative tools, requisite skills, and incentives. For the same reason, it is no surprise that the rate of crimes not associated with terrorism has also jumped in recent years. Law-and-order duties and VIP protection responsibilities consume a significant chunk of police resources.[3] The lack of forensic support further diminishes police effectiveness and capacity to deliver. Corruption, nepotism, and political manipulation are rampant; they damage police integrity, credibility, and public image. An additional impediment to criminal law enforcement is the ineptitude of Pakistan's judicial sector.

Police capacity is critical for tackling terrorism and controlling insurgency-infested areas. A growing body of empirical research has established that law enforcement, not military force, is the most effective tool for this task.[4] A RAND Corporation study titled *How Terrorist Groups End* also provides evidence that effective police and intelligence work, rather than the use of military force, delivers better counterterrorism results.[5] Douglas P. Lackey in a counterterrorism article goes a step further when he argues that "The killing of civilians by terrorists is not war, but murder, so the social genre of terrorism is crime, and terrorists should be classified as criminals," and from this premise he rightly deduces, "If terrorists are criminals, their natural antagonists are the police."[6] As he points out, most of the activities considered vital for any counterterrorism effort fall within the scope of standard police activity, including the forensic analysis of terrorist attack sites, gleaning information from abandoned terrorist camps, searching suspected terrorist locations, penetrating terrorist organizations through the use of undercover agents, surveilling suspicious sites, monitoring suspects, and maintaining databases of suspects. Hence, whether it is to combat insurgency or terrorism, a good police force is any state's best bet.

Military operations can substitute for police action in certain circumstances, but that creates a new set of issues, ranging from high civilian casualties to human rights violations. Most militaries, including that of Pakistan, are not trained or equipped to deal with internal law-and-order crises. Ideally, the military should act as a backup force that is ready to move in if needed in support of police action.

This chapter evaluates the capacity and performance of Pakistan's civilian law enforcement structure in relation to counterterrorism and crime fighting efforts, with a special focus on police forces. The attention to law enforcement as a whole is warranted as the law enforcement infrastructure includes all police departments (provincial and federal), various investigative organizations, specialized forces (including paramilitary units that support police work), and intelligence outfits that share information with police. The police force is the central institution in the law enforcement structure of any state, but it is not the only one, and therefore it cannot be treated in a vacuum. After a brief explanation of why police reforms in Pakistan are essential and possible, the report examines the current state of the Pakistan police force in terms of infrastructure and manpower. It then evaluates obstacles to reform and considers both (1) traditional reform options that, if implemented, could upgrade and improve the existing police system to effectively support counterinsurgency and counterterrorism measures and the goal of mitigating extremism in society; and (2) innovative reform options, including a major restructuring of existing police organizations or the creation of new police organizations to circumvent and reach beyond traditional problems. Effective remedies for the shortcomings of the police service likely depend on equally far-reaching reforms of the criminal justice system and political-administrative changes.

AN OPPORTUNITY FOR INTERNAL REFORM AND INTERNATIONAL SUPPORT

With the increasing insecurity and instability in the country, the government of Pakistan must consider making major changes to the police and other law enforcement structures and the coordination mechanisms these various entities use in their counterterrorism efforts. Some initiatives have been launched in this direction since 2009 in the shape of higher salaries for police and creation of advanced forensic laboratories.[7] Police recruitment from a pool of retired army soldiers to raise specialized counterterrorism units in each province was planned, though with little progress.[8] The police force is one of the few institutions in the country where an internal reform effort has been under way since the introduction of the Police

Act in 2002. The time is ripe for international support to Pakistan in this sphere. Some initiatives undertaken by the United States, United Kingdom, France, and Australia are bearing fruit already, but their scale is quite limited. Helping the police and civilian intelligence agencies with modern training and technical assistance would pay counterterrorism dividends for the international community.

Admittedly, the task is not easy; the obstacles on the path of police reform in Pakistan are potent and entrenched. Moreover, for Pakistan to attract international assistance, it needs to introduce concrete and well-thought-out organizational reforms in the law enforcement sector as well as in the related intelligence infrastructure. Such structural reforms have not been forthcoming thus far. Moreover, building the capacity of only one segment of the law enforcement infrastructure is impractical, as overarching reform is needed. In other words, the counterterrorism capacity of the police service cannot be improved in isolation; a comprehensive approach is necessary. Rule of law, a critical prerequisite for democracy, is also closely linked to effective law enforcement. Nevertheless, the stakes are simply too high for international partners to walk away from the challenge. It is undeniable that successful police reforms that enhance Pakistan's counterterrorism performance and strengthen the rule of law will stabilize Pakistan and improve the prospects of peace in the region.

AN OVERVIEW OF LAW ENFORCEMENT ORGANIZATIONS IN PAKISTAN

Before reform measures can be considered, a clear understanding of the present status of the law enforcement structure is essential. There are two sets of law enforcement organizations in Pakistan: those that operate under the federal government and the provincial police organizations. Nineteen major organizations operate directly under the federal government and deal with a variety of law enforcement responsibilities (including intelligence gathering, border and coast surveillance, and policing) and answer to different authorities. The total strength of all law enforcement and intelligence services' officials at the disposal of the federal government (with cross-provincial jurisdiction) is approximately 210,000.[9] Rarely do these organizations coordinate their plans and activities or strategize together. The chain of command of the organizations varies, which further complicates coordination and collective policy planning. As a result, decisions are often poorly implemented.

The nineteen federal law enforcement organizations can be grouped into four broad categories:

1. Forces under the Ministry of the Interior: These forces include five paramilitary organizations, namely, the Pakistan Rangers (Sindh and Punjab), the Pakistan Maritime Security Agency, the Frontier Corps (FC) (KP and Baluchistan), and the Frontier Constabulary and Gilgit-Baltistan Scouts, in addition to the Islamabad Police and the Federal Investigation Agency (FIA).

2. Police planning and management organizations under the Ministry of the Interior: These include the National Police Bureau, the National Police Management Board, the National Police Foundation, and the National Public Safety Commission. The National Counter-Terrorism Authority (NACTA) is the latest organization to be included in this category.

3. Other federal organizations: In this category are those organizations that are not under the direct control of the Ministry of the Interior. They include the National Highways and Motorway Police (under the Ministry of Communications), the Pakistan Railways Police (under the Ministry of Railways), the Airport Security Force (under the Ministry of Defense), and the Anti-Narcotics Force (under the Ministry of Narcotics Control).

4. Intelligence organizations: The Intelligence Bureau (IB), a civilian agency, and Inter-Services Intelligence (ISI), led by a serving army lieutenant general, are the two major intelligence outfits. They have regional and provincial offices throughout Pakistan.

A brief description of responsibilities, jurisdiction, and chain of command of some of these organizations is given in table 5.1.[10]

The second category of law enforcement infrastructure comprises the four provincial police organizations, as well as those operational in Gilgit-Baltistan and Azad Jammu and Kashmir (AJK). These provincial police organizations are all organized along similar lines and abide by the same set of laws and rules. For instance, the procedural criminal laws (i.e., the Pakistan Penal Code, the Code of Criminal Procedure, and the Qanun-e-Shahadat Order) are uniformly applicable to all parts of the country (except the FATA). The Police Service of Pakistan (PSP), a federal service whose members are recruited through the Federal Public Service Commission, provides more than 80 percent of senior supervisory officers (with the rank of assistant superintendent of police and above, who act as subdivisional police chiefs) to the provincial police departments. This cadre's recruitment, training, and career management (including transfers to provinces

TABLE 5.1 FEDERAL LAW ENFORCEMENT AND INTELLIGENCE ORGANIZATIONS

ORGANIZATION	MANDATE AND JURISDICTION	COMMAND AND STRENGTH
1. Frontier Corps (a) FC Khyber Pakhtunkhwa (b) FC Baluchistan	The Frontier Corps supports local law enforcement in maintaining law and order when requested by the federal government. The corps' primary task is to monitor and obstruct smuggling along Pakistan's borders with Afghanistan and Iran. Increasingly, these forces are involved in counterterrorism and counterinsurgency operations; FC KP is playing an especially important role in the FATA.	The inspector general, an army officer with the rank of major general, leads both organizations. The total strength of FC KP and FC Baluchistan is 90,318.
2. Rangers (a) Rangers, Punjab (b) Rangers, Sindh	This organization secures Pakistan's border with India and assists when called in by respective provincial governments to maintain law and order. Sindh Rangers also provide security to VIPs visiting Sindh and are especially active in Karachi. Both organizations regularly assist police in border regions and focus on intelligence gathering. An antiterrorist wing, trained by the army's Special Services Group, was incorporated in 2004 in both organizations.	The director general, an army officer with the rank of major general, leads both forces. Commanders of these forces closely coordinate with local military commanders in Karachi and Lahore. Deputy director generals are appointed by provincial governments. The Rangers' strength in Punjab is 19,475, and in Sindh, 24,630.
3. Northern Areas Scouts (Gilgit-Baltistan)	This paramilitary force secures areas that border Gilgit-Baltistan and provides assistance to local police forces for law-and-order duties.	It is led by a serving army brigadier, and the organization coordinates closely with military deployed in the area. Its total employees number 3,679.
4. Frontier Constabulary	This paramilitary force (formed after the merger of Samana Rifles and Border Military Police in British India), though largely drawn from KP, can be deployed anywhere in Pakistan by the Ministry of the Interior. The majority of its units operate in KP, the FATA, and Islamabad.	It is led by a senior police officer designated as commandant. The inspector general of police can request support from this force during any crisis. Its current strength is 22,817.

(continued)

TABLE 5.1 (CONTINUED)

ORGANIZATION	MANDATE AND JURISDICTION	COMMAND AND STRENGTH
5. Pakistan Maritime Security Agency (Pakistan Coast Guards)	It is responsible for enforcing maritime law, maintenance of seamarks, border control, and antismuggling operations. It is deployed in the coastal areas of Sindh and Baluchistan Provinces.	Formerly part of the Pakistan Army, it now operates under the Ministry of the Interior and is led by a serving army officer (rank of major general), and its various battalions are led by army officers (lieutenant colonel rank) seconded from the army. Its present strength is 4,067.
6. Capital Territory Police (Islamabad)	It performs standard police duties in Islamabad (divided into 13 police station areas) and operates directly under the control of the Ministry of the Interior. The total population of Islamabad is close to 2 million.	Led by an inspector general of police, its current strength is 10,995. The Police Act of 2002 has not been fully enforced in Islamabad.
7. Federal Investigation Agency (FIA)	The FIA investigates offenses committed in connection with matters that concern the federal government, are of interprovincial scope, or involve transnational organized crime. Its jurisdiction encompasses economic crimes, terrorism, cyber crimes, banking offenses, and enforcement of immigration laws and exit control lists. It also maintains a Redbook of high-profile criminals and terrorists.	It is led by a senior police officer (rank of an inspector general) designated as director general. The agency has offices in all four provincial headquarters, plus headquarters in Islamabad. Its total strength is around 3,500.
8. Anti-Narcotics Force	It is primarily tasked with eliminating the trafficking and distribution of narcotics in the country, enhancing international cooperation against drugs, and liaising with international organizations on the subject.	It is led by a serving army officer of the rank of a major general with the designation as director general. It operates under the Ministry of Narcotics Control. Its strength is around 3,100.
9. National Highways and Motorway Police	Established in 1997, it is specifically assigned traffic control functions and policing on national highways. The organization is reputed for its efficiency, integrity, and discipline.	Led by an inspector general of police, its officials are drawn from the police service as well as through direct recruitment. It operates under the Ministry of Communications, and its total strength is estimated to be around 5,000.

ORGANIZATION	MANDATE AND JURISDICTION	COMMAND AND STRENGTH
10. Airport Security Force	It is responsible for protecting all the airports in the country. Besides safeguarding the civil aviation industry, it is responsible for maintaining law and order within the limits of airports. In recent years, it has been trained for counterterrorism measures at airports.	A serving army brigadier is appointed by the Ministry of Defense as director general of ASF. The total strength of the ASF is estimated to be around 4,500.
11. Pakistan Railways Police (PRP)	The PRP is responsible for law-and-order duties on trains and at train stations across the country. Since 2008, the PRP has assumed police duties in 1,500 railway employee housing areas (covering an approximately 772-square-mile area) and in other areas owned by the Railways Department.	It is led by a senior police officer designated as inspector general. The total number of PRP employees is around 7,000 (according to 2007 records). The PRP also has a 600-strong commando unit for counterterrorism tasks.
12. National Police Bureau (NPB)	It acts as a national focal point for all police-related research and development matters. It functions as permanent secretariat for the National Public Safety Commission (NPSC), which oversees the functioning of federal law enforcement agencies, and the National Police Management Board (NPMB), which advises the federal and provincial governments about criminal justice reform, public safety, and police information technology.	Operating under the Ministry of the Interior, it is headed by a director general, an officer from the police service. NPSC has 12 members who meet periodically. NPMB, which comprises all the heads of the police and law enforcement agencies (except the FC), meets very rarely. Total NPB employees are fewer than 100.
13. National Counter-Terrorism Authority	This newly established institution will focus on preparing national threat assessment reports on extremism, terrorism, and insurgency and will help the government formulate a National Action Plan for counterterrorism. It will focus primarily on research, data collection, and analysis of terrorism-related issues, in addition to serving as a liaison with international organizations focusing on the subject.	It is led by an inspector general of police and operates under the Ministry of the Interior. The organization has three wings: Counterextremism; Counterterrorism; and the Research, Analysis, Training Wing. It is currently recruiting employees for all sectors of the organization. The total strength of the organization is 203.

(continued)

TABLE 5.1 (CONTINUED)

ORGANIZATION	MANDATE AND JURISDICTION	COMMAND AND STRENGTH
14. Intelligence Bureau	Its responsibilities include gathering intelligence (including for counterterrorism purposes) within the country and disseminating it through the Ministry of the Interior to political leadership and various police organizations.	It is led by a director general who is either a serving police officer (typically the case during periods of civilian rule) or a serving major general from the army (often the case during military rule). Its employees supporting police work total around 2,000.
15. Inter-Services Intelligence (ISI)	Pakistan's premier intelligence organization, only part of its responsibilities deal with law enforcement work. ISI's internal wing, the Counterterrorism Center, focuses on intelligence gathering and analysis and provides intelligence assessments to the government. The ISI is responsible for sharing relevant information with police organizations in the country through the federal government.	Led by a serving lieutenant general from the Pakistan Army (designated as Director General), the ISI reports directly to the prime minister of Pakistan. However, its head also sits in army corps commanders' meetings and reports to the Chief of Army Staff. Approximately 3,500 ISI employees (out of roughly 20,000 total strength) are involved in work that is linked to police work and counterterrorism.
Total number of employees of all federal organizations		209,790

and federal law enforcement agencies) are managed by the Establishment Division (federal government), though PSP officers report to provincial governments and draw their salaries from provincial budgetary provisions. These PSP officers can be assigned to any province, but lower ranks of police are permanent employees of provincial police organizations and cannot be transferred outside their respective provinces. Since the British era, this complicated service structure has created an elitist PSP. The statistics in table 5.1 indicate police strength and resources in the four provinces, AJK, and Gilgit-Baltistan.

REASONS FOR THE WEAKNESS OF THE LAW
ENFORCEMENT INFRASTRUCTURE

There is a broad consensus in Pakistan that after decades of abuse and neglect, its police force is failing to combat crime effectively, uphold the law, provide basic security to citizens, and fight growing militancy. Since its inception in 1947, despite frequent ethnic confrontations, sectarian battles, and sharp rises in criminal or insurgent activity, policymakers have never put the law enforcement and police sector at the top of their priority list for investment and reform. As a result, the overall police infrastructure is poorly organized. Many reports were commissioned to improve policing standards, but either their recommendations were too general or the governments of the day lacked the will to implement the recommended changes. Some of the major reasons relevant to police engagement in counterterrorism activities are historical handicap in the shape of decadent law, insufficient numbers and scant resources, institutional disconnect, political challenges, corruption, and lack of modernization.

HISTORICAL FACTORS AND OUTMODED LAW

Groomed as an imperial force tasked with coercing (rather than protecting) citizens in the aftermath of the 1857 uprising against the British, Pakistan inherited a police infrastructure founded on the Police Act of 1861. This framework provided for an authoritarian, unaccountable, and oppressive police force. A mere glance at its provisions shows that it is out of touch with the requirements of a modern and democratic state. Pakistan followed these laws until 2002, when a new reform-oriented police order was finally promulgated; however, frequent amending has damaged the new order's original intent and spirit.[11] Over a sixty-year period, around two dozen commissioned reports on police reform were produced, but it was very rare for any of their recommendations to be implemented.[12] Interestingly, India still uses the 1861 Police Act in many areas amid demands for change and reform.[13]

Prepared by leading police officials and legal experts under Musharraf's National Reconstruction Bureau, the Police Act of 2002 emulated the Japanese National Safety Commission system, to ensure oversight of police by both elected and nominated members at local (district), provincial, and national levels. Second, an independent prosecution service was provided to place additional checks on the police. Police complaints authorities at the provincial and federal levels were also planned for. However, police were given relative operational autonomy in administrative as well as investigative spheres, which was long overdue. Various responsibilities and tasks (ranging from investigations, intelligence, watch and ward, and guard duties) were divided among separate police departments to improve efficiency of the system.[14] However, bureaucratic as well as political hurdles came in the way, and President Musharraf and his political allies introduced many amendments in the Police Act in 2004, taking away powers of the neutral and independent safety commissions (in the sphere of recommending promotions and transfers) and awarding these back to politicians, providing them immense relief.[15] A police officer in Islamabad aptly explains the consequences of such developments by saying that "most police officers feel that, in order to secure their career prospects, they have no choice but to do the bidding of their political masters."[16]

Variations in the police laws of the four provinces are yet another issue negatively affecting interprovincial coordination in crime fighting and counterterrorism. Insightfully, Ahmer Bilal Soofi, who served as federal minister for law in the caretaker government, in 2013, maintains: "One of the most startling revelations during my brief tenure as federal law minister in the last caretaker government was that the police force in all the provinces is not governed under a uniform law and that there is serious confusion amongst the police officers in this regard."[17]

INSUFFICIENT NUMBERS AND SCANT RESOURCES

Pakistan's total population is estimated to be around 190 million, and the combined federal and provincial law enforcement forces (including paramilitary and related wings of the intelligence organizations) have a total strength of close to 655,000 personnel.[18] Thus, the police–population ratio is one police official for every 290 persons. On paper, Pakistan is in a better shape than, say, India, where according to Human Rights Watch there is on average one police officer for every 1,037 people. Asia's regional average is one police officer for 558 people, and the global average is one for every 333 people.[19] Pakistan also fares well vis-à-vis the UN standard for peacetime policing, which recommends one police officer for every 400 persons.[20] However, given the nature of the crisis in Pakistan, especially the heightened terrorist activity and insurgency situations in the FATA and parts of Baluchistan Province, coupled with rising crime figures nationwide, the numbers are not as good as they appear. Moreover, the UN standards assume an efficient, well-resourced, honest police force, which is not the case in Pakistan. And the ratio worsens if only forces directly involved in routine police work are counted and the paramilitary forces with a specific focus such as maritime and airport security, intelligence officials, and administrative personnel are excluded.[21]

In the domain of counterterrorism, despite the sharp rise in terrorist attacks across the country, little investment has been made in specialized expertise. For instance, the FIA's Special Investigation Group (SIG), which is responsible for investigating major terrorist attacks in the country, has a very limited number of terrorism specialists. Its number of investigators has only recently risen from a mere thirty-seven to eighty-seven, but it has only thirteen specialists in explosives, banking, and law.[22] SIG performed well in the 2009–2011 time period, but lately it has lost momentum due to transfer of some its stalwarts.[23]

PROVINCIAL POLICE FORCES, ISLAMABAD POLICE, AND OTHERS

Although substantial financial commitments have been made to increase the police capacity in KP, the KP administration has serious concerns about the availability of funds. For example, recruitment has increased substantially in recent years, shooting up to 107,445 in 2012 after attaining levels of roughly 78,000 in 2010 from 55,450 in 2009 and 50,892 in 2008, according to the KP government, and the financial budget for police has more than doubled over the past 5 years.[24] However, unexpectedly large increases in salaries, health care costs, and compensation for police officials killed in the line of duty have depleted the funds needed for expansion.

Fortunately, the belated but critical U.S. support for the provincial police force has helped the institution through increased resources and enhanced professional expertise to tackle terrorism. The support included specialized training for officers, the upgrading of police stations in sensitive areas, and the provision of protective gear, modern communications systems, and vehicles to KP police.[25] However, this new partnership has not proceeded without hitches: more than 3,000 bulletproof jackets given by the United States to KP police and FC languished at the Islamabad airport for months in 2010, apparently because of poor coordination between various departments, including the Ministry of the Interior, the Ministry of Commerce, and Pakistan International Airlines, which operates under the Ministry of Defense.[26]

Punjab Province has also made a significant contribution to increasing police capacity in the provincial budgets since 2009.[27] A sharp rise in terrorist attacks in Punjab, especially in Lahore, targeting religious institutions and police infrastructure, convinced the provincial government of the need to increase resources for police. However, so far the only effect has been an increase in salaries for police officials, which is a positive change but far from what is needed to transform the institution. The chief of police in Lahore, Mohammad Aslam Tareen, aptly argues that "we are in [a] transformation period where we badly need huge reforms in the police department," while emphasizing the need for "adopting a joint strategy among security agencies, police and public."[28] For example, although there are around 170,000 police officials in Punjab, there are only 82,000 weapons and 5,000 bulletproof vests for the officers.[29] After a major terrorist attack against two religious centers of the Ahmediya community in Lahore in May 2010, senior police officials admitted that the department faces a serious shortage of equipment and lacks training.[30]

In Sindh Province, although a lobby within the Sindh police in support of change has been gaining strength, no reforms of substance have been implemented. An analysis conducted by some pro-reform police officers concluded that nothing short of a "cultural transformation" in the police institutions would bear any fruit.[31] The analysis revealed the following: junior officers, who manage police stations, are unqualified for the job; ordinary police officials work between sixteen and eighteen hours a day; and an insufficient number of police in urban centers has compromised law enforcement efficiency.[32] Unprecedented levels of street crime and a consistent pattern of ethnic- and sectarian-motivated target killings in Karachi are just one indication of the nature of the challenge.

The situation in Baluchistan is even more desperate. In January 2010, in Quetta City, hundreds of police officials surrounded the governor's and chief minister's residences to protest low salaries. The protesting officers used official weapons for aerial firing, blocked various roads, damaged vehicles, and beat up civilians.[33] Though stern action was taken against senior officials, the only improvement made after the crisis ended was an increase in the compensation for police personnel killed by terrorists while on duty.

Islamabad police also suffer from inadequate force numbers. It is especially surprising in light of the nature of the threat to the capital city. As the Pakistani writer Ayesha Siddiqa points out, how can 11,000 cops effectively guard (and in some cases monitor) 81 embassies, 76 ambassadors' residences, 22 UN offices, 14 hospitals, 20 universities, 1,044 schools and colleges, 77 markets, and 305 madrasahs?[34] In addition, they have to protect the head of state, government, and other dignitaries who visit the capital. It is an impossible task.

The resource capacity of law enforcement organizations, other than the provincial police forces, is inconsistent. The National Highways and Motorway Police, established in 1997, is one of the most efficient organizations in the country and an almost corruption-free institution as a result of higher salaries, good training facilities, recruitment on merit, and the availability of modern equipment.[35] However, other federal law enforcement organizations, such as the Pakistan Railways Police and the Airport Security Force, have not been that fortunate. In recent months, the Pakistan Railways Police could not install donated scanners at two important and vulnerable stations because of a lack of funds, and its request for closed-circuit cameras in twenty-three large railway stations has not been fulfilled.[36] After a terrorist attack at Lahore railway station in 2012, it was revealed that none of the seventeen surveillance cameras installed at the station were functional.[37] Similarly, the Airport Security Force continues to use a type of bomb detector at one of the largest airports whose export from the United Kingdom was banned after it led to the deaths of 275 people.[38]

INSTITUTIONAL DISCONNECT

In accordance with the Constitution of Pakistan, which provides for a federal system of government, the four provincial governments are directly responsible for law-and-order functions. Consequently, the police are supervised at a provincial level. Police and paramilitary forces in the capital city of Islamabad and levies and khasadars (semi-official, local tribal police) in the FATA, however, are under the direct jurisdiction of the federal government. The police of AJK and Gilgit-Baltistan are managed by their respective governments (somewhat similar to the situation in the provinces), although the federal government has more direct leverage because of the special legal status of these regions. PSP officers who serve in senior supervisory positions all across Pakistan are deemed employees of the federal government even when they serve in provincial police institutions. In case of a center–province tussle, the central government can recall any PSP officer or refuse to send any requisitioned officer to a province. The federal government's discretionary authority has sometimes been misused for political ends, making the work environment for police officials very hard and strenuous.

The police forces in each of the provinces act independently of each other, and there is no nationwide integration in terms of training standards and coordination. The federal Interior Ministry exercises overall supervision, but provincial inspectors general of the police service report directly to their respective chief ministers and are funded from the provincial government. In addition, there is no standardized system of hiring, transferring, and promoting in the four provincial police departments, which creates employment disparities. Lack of coordination among provincial police services often leads to poor information sharing and ineffective monitoring of criminal and terrorist networks.

POLITICAL CHALLENGES

The police in Pakistan have traditionally been used by the state to suppress dissent and tame opposition.[39] Many senior police officers became politicized in recent decades in an attempt to remain in good standing with one political party or the other, and prized field appointments may still be based on political connections. In rural areas (almost 60 percent of the country), local police officers can influence the fate of politicians in elections by allowing or curbing rigging. Moreover, feudal elements often use police for torturing or "teaching a lesson" to their opponents, who are mostly peasants. Hence, they need influence with the police.

LACK OF MODERNIZATION AND CORRUPTION

The police in Pakistan have a terrible reputation, and ordinary people often avoid approaching police to report crime or communicate grievances.[40] There is a general perception that the institution of the police is corrupt, institutionally incompetent, and brutal. Consequently, justice is elusive, insecurity is rampant, and ordinary citizens are the victims of this system. Even internal police assessments acknowledge the police force's lack of credibility in the public eye.[41] However, in the overall scenario and in comparative terms, police performance is not much different from the functioning of customs officials, bureaucrats running the provincial and federal secretariats, and the intelligence services. Police officers get the most blame because they are visible to everyone and are expected to do everything in Pakistan, from crisis management to resolving political and legal disputes, in addition to facing the wrath of people venting their frustrations over blunders committed by the country's leadership, both political and military. Still, the police force cannot be defended for its routine excesses, violations of human rights, and inefficiency.

The police regularly use torture to elicit confessions because they lack other, more sophisticated means of investigation. Unfortunately, Pakistan's forensics capabilities are developing very slowly. Until the late 1990s, the country had only one major laboratory (located in Rawalpindi), staffed by a handful of experts, and only under "special circumstances" (i.e., in high-profile cases) could a police officer get access to this resource. In the 2002–2007 period, four additional laboratories were sanctioned, one in each provincial capital. Despite a $40 million grant from the Asian Development Bank to the Sindh police to upgrade the existing Sindh Forensic Science Laboratory in Karachi and set up two new facilities in the interior of the province, in Hyderabad and Larkana, progress has been very slow. Work on the National Forensic Science Agency headquarters and its main laboratory in Islamabad progressed at a snail's pace because federal government had stopped funding for the project in 2009.[42] One exception is the modern forensic laboratory in Lahore, which has been functional since 2012.[43] British-funded mobile forensic labs are also associated with this institution, enhancing the Punjab government's capacity to efficiently collect evidence from terrorism and crime scenes.[44]

A lack of attention to developing modern investigation and interrogation techniques is another serious issue. Most police officers vie for command positions in investigative work because the primary work of any police force is not even considered a field job,[45] which is a mandatory requirement for promotion to a senior supervisory role.[46] Only very recently has the government considered a proposal to declare service in the Investigation Wing a field posting, to encourage prime officers to work in this area. This development will remove the anomaly, which has so far deterred many professionally competent officers from serving in the Investigation Wing; officers will now be able to count their service with the Investigation Wing as a 2-year field posting.

Most police training schools are in a deplorable state due to a paucity of funds. The instructors are often officials who were removed from field duties for political reasons, and it is hardly surprising that the performance of a demoralized and sidelined faculty leaves much to be desired. Fortunately, there is some international interest in revitalizing this area. The U.S. government is supporting the KP government in building an additional police academy, which is a positive investment.[47] France is sending experts to conduct training at police academies in Pakistan, and funds from the

European Union are likely to be geared toward enhancing police training standards.[48] The Australian Federal Police is also supporting Pakistan police through its Forensic Capacity Building project.[49] Lately, Turkey has also been providing training facilities to Pakistani police officers.[50] However, on the basis of interviews with government officials in the United States, France, and the United Kingdom, it appears that much more coordination is needed among international donors involved in supporting Pakistan's law enforcement capacity, as the support currently shows some level of duplication. Perhaps Pakistan can facilitate synchronization in this sector.

COUNTERTERRORISM CAPACITY AND INTERINSTITUTIONAL COMPLEXITIES

The Pakistani police force was traditionally not trained for counterterrorism. Indeed, for reasons of lack of training and insufficient capacity already mentioned, it is barely able to operate as an entity in checking crime and carrying out basic law-and-order functions. However, current circumstances have upended the traditional model and thrust the police to the forefront of counterterrorism efforts. Lack of police expertise in countering the growing extremist menace is undermining the stability of the Pakistani state and claiming thousands of lives in terrorist attacks. This shortcoming is catastrophic, as counterterrorism will be part of the portfolio of the Pakistani police for years to come.

In the counterterrorism segment of the larger law enforcement sphere, a number of overarching problems are obvious impediments to reform efforts. Four warrant special attention, for without remedial measures to treat these major inadequacies, reform of the law enforcement sector, especially in the counterterrorism domain, cannot succeed.

DYSFUNCTIONAL RELATIONSHIP BETWEEN POLICE AND INTELLIGENCE ORGANIZATIONS

Lack of trust and coordination between the police force and intelligence outfits has been a long-standing concern for Pakistani law enforcers, and this concern is amplified by the sometimes close relationship between militant groups and the intelligence services. For example, according to a well-informed Pakistani journalist, throughout the 1990s one or two intelligence officers in each district of Pakistan were tasked to help out members of the state-supported militant groups if police "creat[ed] any problems for them."[51]

In private discussions, police officers routinely mention apprehending militants and criminals but quickly receiving "requests" from intelligence agencies (civilian or military) to let them go. Although the intensity of such practices has decreased in the post-9/11 environment, even today police hesitate to pursue militants and activists associated with groups generally known for their close relationship with the intelligence services.

Poor data collection with regard to crimes and criminals is another major lacuna in the system. Many criminals who join militant religious groups are not traced and tracked efficiently. Even banned militant organizations are not well profiled.[52] According to a senior official of NACTA, many militants currently incarcerated have not been interviewed by experts, which is critical to understanding their networks.[53] In many instances, militant organizations continue their publications, and wanted criminals and terrorists may simply change their affiliations to a group that is not under government scrutiny. All the while, the police remain clueless.

Again, a discernible lack of coordination among the police force, the civilian-run IB, and the military-run intelligence agencies lies at the heart of the problem. For instance, to get data from telephone companies (to trace calls made by criminals and terrorists), the police and the FIA must send a request to intelligence agencies, and the time delay can be crucial to the investigation. Aftab Ahmed Khan Sherpao, a renowned Pakistani politician who remained interior minister during the Musharraf years, publicly acknowledged that coordination between and among the ISI, IB, police, and the Special Branch of the police is far from satisfactory and that intelligence agencies often have information but do not share it with law enforcement agencies.[54]

Admittedly, since 2008, the army has been proactive in providing training to a select group of police officers. Such collaboration in KP has been highly praised by the inspector general of police in the province, Malik Naveed. In a television interview, he mentioned that around 5,000 police officials in KP had undergone counterterrorism and combat training by army instructors.[55] Apparently in lieu of special training, retired army soldiers were recruited by police institutions, especially in the Swat and Peshawar districts, in recent years. And subsequent to the government of Punjab's request that the army help train the provincial police force, the military operations directorate in Rawalpindi asked the Tenth Division headquarters in Lahore to support police training.[56] Thus, in principle, the army welcomes improvement in police capacity building. Perhaps this will ultimately lead to better coordination between police and intelligence services in practical terms.[57] A few examples of cooperation prove the utility of such cooperation. Good collaboration between Lahore Police and ISI after terrorist attacks on an ISI office and a police training center in Lahore in 2009 led to the dismantling of a very important terrorist network, which had established a number of big ammunition depots in and around Lahore.[58]

POOR ANALYTICAL CAPACITY

Effective police work is hugely dependent on the analytical competence of the law enforcement infrastructure as without access to relevant crime or terror data and professional expertise to interpret the underlying trends, no effective strategy can be formulated. According to FIA investigations, five major suicide bombing attacks in Islamabad in October and November 2009 were planned and conducted by former students of the Lal Masjid (Red Mosque), indicating that police utterly failed to profile these students in the immediate aftermath of the Red Mosque crisis in July 2007.[59] All those who surrendered (around 1,300 persons) were initially kept in police custody for a few weeks. Similarly, the main culprit in the October 2009 attack on Pakistan army headquarters in Rawalpindi, Aqeel (known as Dr. Usman), was reportedly arrested by police earlier and also interrogated by the officials of an intelligence organization, before being cleared. Both police and intelligence specialists failed to gauge his mind-set accurately. Worse still, the attack on the army headquarters was predicted by Punjab police based on information gleaned from a computer memory stick found on a militant in Dera Ghazi Khan, but to no benefit, either because of mistrust between the army and police or because of poor coordination.[60] An overload of intelligence information streaming in from multiple directions also plays a role in such warnings not being heeded.

INEFFECTIVE STRATEGY

The rising tide of suicide attacks all across Pakistan since 2006 has created widespread fear and insecurity. Though police officials have faced this challenge bravely, sustaining a high number of casualties in such attacks, the law enforcement agencies have not been able to disrupt the cycle in any systematic way. Complacency about the strength and operational capability of some militant groups also hinders formulation of an efficient strategy. For instance, Punjab police as well as intelligence agencies remained in denial for some time about the threat posed by militant groups based in South Punjab, which allowed the militants' networks not only to survive but to grow.[61] Ayesha Siddiqa maintains there is widespread reluctance in the security sector as well as on the part of the present Punjab government "to focus on the four main Punjab-based jihadi groups: Sipah-e-Sahaba Pakistan (SSP), Lashkar-e-Jhangvi (LeJ), Jaish-e-Muhammad (JeM), and Lashkar-e-Taiba (LeT). . . . These jihadi groups could actually be thwarted by a concerted, integrated police and intelligence operation."[62] Even though the situation has improved, because attacks in Punjab convinced the provincial government of the source of these troubles, critical time has been lost in the process. The August 2015 assassination of Shuja Khanzada, the interior minister of Punjab, in a suicide bombing attack conducted by LeJ (in collaboration with Pakistani Taliban) shows that the security challenge remains very serious.

INEFFECTIVE CRIMINAL JUSTICE SYSTEM

Inadequate and defective criminal justice systems are another critical problem. The witness protection system in Pakistan is almost nonexistent. Consequently, those who testify against powerful criminals and militants in courts receive no security. In dozens of cases, police officers investigating militants have been gunned down. The best-known case is that of Sipah-e-Sahaba terrorist Malik Ishaq, whose police charge sheet includes at least seventy murders but who has never had a conviction that has stuck;[63] those who testified in court as witnesses against him now live in fear of reprisal.[64] Judges face similar security threats, and in many instances lower court decisions in terrorism cases are supposedly pending owing to such fears. In recent months, alleged terrorists arrested for involvement in the Islamabad Marriott bombing and some major attacks in Punjab Province were released by the courts for lack of evidence. The police had to put the individuals under "house arrest" afterward to buy time before challenging the verdicts in higher courts.[65] Such inadequacies, unfortunately, have also led to extrajudicial killings as a preferred option for police, as evident in the apparently staged "police encounter" killing Malik Ishaq on July 29, 2015.

RECOMMENDATIONS FOR REFORM: TRADITIONAL VERSUS INNOVATIVE POLICING

Pakistan desperately needs reform of its law enforcement infrastructure. This need is now increasingly recognized both in the policy circles within Pakistan and among donor countries, especially the United States and the European Union.[66] Over the years, the government of Pakistan has attempted to introduce various reforms to control rising crime and violence, but all such attempts—made half-heartedly and reluctantly—have had only marginal impact. Additionally, a change of government in Pakistan often leads to abandonment of initiatives of the previous head of state. Reform efforts in different provinces are also uncoordinated. For instance, the Punjab government has been working on formulating special legislation to govern police functioning in the province (Punjab Police Act, 2010), but Sindh as well as Baluchistan appear to have moved in an opposite direction.[67] As Pakistan's highly reputed former senior police officer, Tariq Khosa, maintained: "In pure rush of blood and compelling parochial interests, Balochistan Government has succumbed to machinations of a service group in reviving the 19th century Police Act of 1861 by calling it the Balochistan Police Act of 2011. This is like putting old wine in a new bottle."[68]

The scale and extent of the problem are such that the limited and disjointed reform efforts such as those described can have little impact on the overall situation. Lack of resources is a big obstacle, but merely throwing money at the problem is unlikely to bear dividends. Technical issues and the need for modernization in police investigations are only one aspect of the challenge. Remedies for police shortcomings depend on equally far-reaching reforms of the judicial and court systems. All this requires extreme political will. As Frederic Grare, a leading French expert on Pakistan, points out, "Capacity building and the political will to fight terrorism cannot be separated. Should political will or real determination to fight terrorism be missing, capacity building will inevitably end in failure, regardless of the amount of foreign assistance invested."[69]

There may be no better moment to press ahead with far-reaching law enforcement reforms in Pakistan, given the emerging public consensus against militancy and extremism, especially since the December 16, 2014, terrorist attack on Army Public School in Peshawar that killed around 150 children and teachers. This trend has provided leaders the political space to make tough, reform-oriented choices.

The recommendations for police reform can be divided into two broad categories, traditional and innovative reforms. Traditional police reforms generally include provision of better salaries and basic facilities, professional training, modern equipment, and readily available forensic support, in conjunction with strengthening of the prosecution sector. Community policing and refinement of the legal framework governing police organizations also fall in this category. There are no two views about the necessity of these measures in Pakistan, and the country has embarked on this path lately, though without much coordination between provinces and with meager resources. In this domain, technical and training support from the international community can make a difference.

RECOMMENDATIONS FOR TRADITIONAL REFORMS

The following recommendations can help the traditional reform aspects:

Implement the original 2002 Police Act nationwide. All the 2004 amendments to the 2002 Police Act, which reintroduced tools of political manipulation, should be discarded, and the new ideas introduced in the Punjab Police Act of 2010, which make police more accountable and encourage a community policing model, should be incorporated into the original 2002 Police Act. All the four provinces, the FATA, the Azad Kashmir region, and Gilgit-Baltistan should be governed by a common police act.

Increase public awareness. The level of public awareness about the changes introduced with the 2002 reforms was very low. As a result, the new mechanisms for ensuring police independence and opportunities for redress of grievances against police high-handedness remained largely unimplemented. A public information campaign focusing on citizens' rights and police accountability can help this cause. Lately, the independent broadcast media in Pakistan have started exposing police brutality and are making an impact nationwide. The government of Pakistan needs to understand that an effective and independent police service will add to the legitimacy of democratic governance.

Focus on junior officers. Investigative fieldwork is done primarily by junior ranks, whereas most of the international training facilities currently are offered to senior supervisory officers. This pattern needs to be reversed so that junior officers have significant training opportunities.

Provide training support and equipment. Pakistan has a poor track record in utilizing international aid, especially when it comes in the form of financial handouts. Corrupt officials in Pakistan and foreign private contractors from donor countries often benefit most from such aid. Support for investigative training and help in the acquisition of modern equipment (e.g., small weapons, scanners, bulletproof jackets, armored vehicles) will be more effective. Moreover, police training academies are often overlooked by international donors, an oversight that needs correction.[70] Finally, foreign donors should avoid framing everything in the context of counterterrorism, as Pakistani public opinion is likely to be more appreciative of international help in this arena if it is seen as enhancing the crime-fighting capacity of police.

Help NACTA in analytical and research work. This fledging organization needs both internal and external help in attracting experienced experts and analysts who can focus on scientific and statistical studies dealing with crime patterns and develop databases useful for counterterrorism. For effective counterterrorism and counterinsurgency efforts, the law enforcement model also needs nonpolicing corrective measures, such as developing public awareness about the nature of the threat through the media and incorporating counterextremist discourse into the public schools curriculum. Decommissioning the brigades of militants and terrorists will require well-resourced and well-devised deradicalization programs. NACTA can spearhead such initiatives if given requisite funds and independence from bureaucratic channels. Unfortunately, NACTA has already been the victim of political turf battles; its first director general, Tariq Pervez, resigned shortly after taking up the position because of the opposition in some quarters to placing NACTA directly under the prime minister (as opposed to the Ministry of the Interior). The Nawaz Sharif government, which took office in June 2013, has made a public commitment to empower and strengthen NACTA. However, the previous government had made similar declarations, but it took them around 4 years to pass the NACTA legislation in March 2013.[71] Time is of the essence for Pakistan's counterterrorism efforts to take some concrete shape.

Streamline counterterrorism strategy. The following measures suggested by the 2012 Rabat Memorandum on Good Practices for Effective Counterterrorism Practice in the Criminal Justice Sector[72] should be diligently followed by Pakistan:

- Protect victims, witnesses, informants, undercover agents, juries, investigators, prosecutors, defense counsel, and judges in counterterrorism cases.
- Encourage cooperation and coordination among domestic government agencies that have responsibilities or information relevant to counterterrorism.
- Provide a legal framework and practical measures for electronic surveillance in counterterrorism investigations.
- Provide for the lawful exercise of pretrial detention of terrorist suspects.
- Develop practices and procedures to encourage international cooperation in counterterrorism matters.

RECOMMENDATIONS FOR INNOVATIVE REFORMS

As is evident from the half-hearted implementation of the 2002 reforms and predictable governmental dithering for reasons of short-term political expediency, traditional reforms by themselves are rarely enough. They need to be coupled with innovative reforms. Two critical ones are described below.

Restructuring of law enforcement organizations. Though Pakistan must resist the temptation to create new specialized antiterrorism structures that marginalize the country's already existing institutions, establishment of a central organization on the pattern of the Department of Homeland Security in the United States will go a long way toward improving coordination between various law enforcement agencies in the country. As explained earlier, the chain of command for various organizations is complicated and dispersed. A restructuring of the overall command setup that brings all the federal institutions under one umbrella can help system effectiveness considerably. Provincial police chiefs, operating under the executive control of chief ministers, can be increasingly involved in policy planning at the central level through this new organization. Staunch proponents of provincial autonomy will likely be the strongest opponents of such a reorganization. One way to alleviate their concerns is to involve all stakeholders in the decision-making process and ensure that the new institution focuses on co-ordination rather than on controlling. The fact that such experienced hands as retired Lieutenant General Moeen-ud-din Haider, who remained minister of interior under General Musharraf, support the creation of such an institution indicates that many well-informed voices can be counted on to support such a major overhaul of the system.[73]

Reform of the criminal justice system. The credibility of Pakistan's higher judiciary has increased in recent years with the judiciary's defiant response to former president Musharraf's arbitrary removal of senior judges and in the aftermath of the popular Lawyers' Movement. Consequently, at the level of the Supreme Court and the provincial High Courts, the judiciary is increasingly independent, though it is also going through a learning curve. However, police performance faces its first test in the lower courts, which are in poor shape, largely for reasons similar to those that plague police work—limited resources, lack of professionalism, and incompetence. Through a new National Judicial Policy, the higher judiciary has already begun introducing major reforms for the lower courts, but considerable financial support will be needed from the government to carry this initiative to fruition. According to Pakistan's highly respected former senior police officer, Tariq Khosa, police accountability through an independent judiciary is one of the most effective ways to ensure improvement in police performance.[74] This idea deserves attention. Another critical issue within this domain is witness protection for which police and judicial institutions need better coordination and cooperation. Many criminals and terrorists have evaded punishments because they were able to scare—and in many cases eliminate— important legal witnesses.

CONCLUSION

Pakistan's law enforcement and police system is by no means too flawed to fix. Moreover, at least within the police service, there is a discernible desire to improve performance. In comparative terms, better performance by the National Motorway Police (Highways Police) and a few effective counterterrorism operations in the late 1990s show that improvement and reform are indeed possible. The laudable performance of Pakistani police officers and junior officials while serving in various UN peacekeeping operations also shows promise. Lately, many police officials across Pakistan have shown bravery in facing suicide bombing attacks. Courageous police officers like Malik Saad and Safwat Ghayur, who sacrificed their lives while leading from the front, have inspired many young police officers in Pakistan.[75] The KP Province is lately witnessing some positive trends in police performance owing to decline in political interference in police affairs. Establishment of new training institutions (specifically focusing on investigations based on forensic evidence and intelligence training), required commando training for promotion eligibility, and transparency in the promotion process are the critical steps being taken in this direction.[76]

For reform to take root across the country along the lines suggested in the recommendations, however, Pakistan must first overcome internal lacunae: political appointments must end; postings, recruitment, and promotions must be made on merit alone; and corrupt officers must be punished publicly. No financial resources are required to accomplish these goals. Second, Pakistan has to start investing its own funds in enhancing overall law enforcement capacity. International donors must understand that supporting the larger police and law enforcement reforms is the only effective way to enhance Pakistan's capacity to fight terrorism. Such support, besides strengthening the rule of law and democracy in the country, will improve interagency coordination for intelligence sharing and joint investigations with donor countries, which have acquired increased importance in recent times.

NOTES

1. For year-over-year data, see www.satp.org/satporgtp/countries/pakistan/database /Fidayeenattack.htm.
2. Mudassir Raja, "Pakistani Victims: War on Terror Toll Put at 49,000," *Express Tribune*, March 27, 2013.

3. The budget for VIP protection varies in urban and rural areas but on average consumes around 30 percent of the police budget for operations. It is estimated to be around 50 percent in major urban centers of the country.

4. For instance, see *How Terrorist Groups End: Lessons for Countering al Qa'ida* (Washington, D.C.: RAND, August 2008), www.rand.org/pubs/monographs/2008/RAND_MG741-1.pdf. See also Kelev I. Sepp, "Best Practices in Counterinsurgency," *Military Review*, May–June 2005, 8–12, www.au.af.mil/au/awc/awcgate/milreview/sepp.pdf.

5. *How Terrorist Groups End.*

6. Douglas P. Lackey, "The Good Soldier Versus the Good Cop: Counterterrorism as Police Work," *Jerusalem Philosophical Quarterly* 55 (January 2006): 66–82.

7. "Salary Raise for Police," *Dawn*, April 20, 2009; Staff reporter, "South Asia's Best Forensic Lab Being Built in Lahore," *Pakistan Today*, January 10, 2011.

8. This is especially the case in the North West Frontier Province's troubled Swat District. For details, see Amanda Hodge, "Elite Force to Police Swat Valley," *Australian*, July 18, 2009.

9. A few estimates are used here as updated information about the total number of employees of various organizations is not available publicly. It should also be noted that intelligence agencies perform a range of standard functions, some of which are unrelated to law enforcement work, and the figures provided here are an approximation, especially in regard to the number of intelligence officials who are directly involved in counterterrorism work (see table 5.1 for details).

10. For a useful and informative source on the subject, see Asad Jamal and Sanjay Patil, eds., *Police Organizations in Pakistan* (Lahore: Human Rights Commission of Pakistan and Commonwealth Human Rights Initiative, 2010), www.humanrightsinitiative.org/publications/police/police_organisations_in_pakistan.pdf.

11. For an overall assessment of old law and new challenges, see Mushtaq Ahmed Sukhera, Syed Mubashir Raza, Huma Chughtai, Muhammad Aslam Tareen, and Syed Tassaduq Hussain Bokhari, "Police Reforms: Emerging Issues and Challenges," Syndicate Research Paper 84, Advanced Course in Public Sector Management (Lahore: National Institute of Public Administration, December 2003).

12. These included the Police Commission headed by Mr. Justice J. B. Constantine (1961–1962), the Police Commission led by Major General A. O. Mitha (1968–1970), the one-man committee of Mr. G. Ahmed (1972), the Foreign Experts Committee composed of Romanian police experts (1976), the Police Reforms Committee chaired by Mr. Rafi Raza (1976), the Police Committee headed by Mr. Aslam Hayat (1985), and, finally, the Police Reforms Implementation Committee under M. A. K. Chaudhry (1990). Not one of the major recommendations put forward by these committees was put in place until 2002. For further details, see "Feudal Forces: Democratic Nations: Police Accountability in Commonwealth South Asia," Commonwealth Human Rights Initiative, New Delhi (2007).

13. For details of the Police Act 1861 and its use in India, see Maja Daruwala, G. P. Joshi, and Mandeep Tiwana, "Police Act, 1861: Why We Need to Replace It?" Commonwealth Human Rights Initiative, New Delhi (July 2005).

14. See the Police Order, 2002 (with amendments and updates) (August 2007). Available at www.nrb.gov.pk/publications/Police_order_2002_with_amendment_ordinance_2006.pdf.

15. For details, see "Reforming Pakistan's Police," International Crisis Group Asia Reports, no. 157 (July 14, 2008).

16. Ibid., 8.

17. Ahmer Bilal Soofi, "Police Challenge," *Dawn*, June 27, 2013.

18. This figure does not includes civilian administrative staff of the Federal Ministry of the Interior, four provincial Home Ministries (which oversee law enforcement organizations), and relevant offices in Azad Kashmir, Gilgit-Baltistan, and FATA—around 10,000 employees altogether.

19. Human Rights Watch, "Broken System: Dysfunction, Abuse, and Impunity in the Indian Police," August 2009, 7, www.hrw.org/sites/default/files/reports/india 0809web.pdf.

20. Madhur Singh, "Can India Reform Its Wayward Police Force?" *Time*, August 10, 2009; "City Has Lowest Police-Public Ratio," *Hindu*, March 27, 2010.

21. For instance, see statistics in Imran Ayub, "KARACHI: City's Police–Population Ratio Abysmally Low," *Dawn*, November 24, 2008.

22. For the latest figures, see the FIA web site, www.fia.gov.pk/prj_sig.htm.

23. Interview with an FIA official, Washington, D.C., May 30, 2012.

24. Ismail Khan, "Govt's Writ Weakening in NWFP, Tribal Areas," *Dawn*, March 29, 2007.

25. Police officials in telephone or e-mail discussion with the author, Islamabad and Peshawar, January–February 2010. See also "Bomb-Proof Police Station Set up in Peshawar," *Dawn*, March 3, 2010.

26. For details, see "Bulletproof Jackets Not to Be Handed Over," *Dawn*, March 10, 2010.

27. Shabbir Sarwar, "Punjab Gears up for Rs 585 Billion Budget," *Daily Times*, June 13, 2010. For latest figures up to 2011, see www.punjabpolice.gov.pk/system/files /Police%20Budget.pdf.

28. Jam Sajjad Hussain, "Social Crime Ratio in Punjab More Than Balochistan, Sindh: CCPO," *Nation*, June 10, 2010.

29. Figure quoted on Geo TV's prime-time talk show *Jirga*, hosted by journalist Saleem Safi on June 7, 2010.

30. Shahnawaz Khan, "Attacks Expose Shortcomings of Police Department," *Daily Times*, June 7, 2010. See also Sebastian Abott, "Ill-Equipped Police Lack Funds, Intel to Combat Rising Militancy in Pakistan's Heartland," Associated Press, July 5, 2010.

31. Imtiaz Ali, "Overhaul of Sindh Police," *The News*, January 18, 2010.

32. Ibid.

33. "Quetta Handed Over to FC as Police Strike Continues," *Daily Times*, January 27, 2010.

34. Ayesha Siddiqa, "Perils of Policing," *Dawn*, November 20, 2009.

35. For instance, see "ADB Declares Motorway Police a 'Miracle,'" *Daily Times*, July 12, 2008.

36. "Pakistan Railway: Lack of Security Measures," *Eastern Tribune*, December 22, 2009. For other issues faced by Railway Police, see "Steel Mills Purchase Stolen Property of Railways," *Dawn*, July 12, 2009.

37. "Railway Station Attack: 'Bomb Trigger Found in Flush Tank,'" *Express Tribune*, April 29, 2012.

38. Hasan Abdullah, "Lives at Airport Threatened by Bogus Bomb Detectors," *Dawn*, January 26, 2010; "Man Bypasses Airport Security, Sneaks in Weapon," *Daily Times*, March 15, 2010. See also Kim Sengupta, "Inquiry into Sale of Fake Bomb Detectors Expanded," *Independent* (UK), June 8, 2010.

39. See "Authoritarianism and Political Party Reform in Pakistan," International Crisis Group Asia Reports, no. 102, September 28, 2005.

40. For instance, see *Crime Report*, Geo TV, November 26, 2010.

41. Jam Sajjad Hussain, "Police Plan Steps to Restore Public Confidence," *Nation*, November 2, 2010.

42. "Govt Stops Funding to Forensic Agency," *Daily Times*, February 15, 2009. For updates on the project, see www.nfsa.gov.pk/index.html.

43. For details, see the organization's official web site: http://pfsa.gop.pk/.

44. British High Commission Islamabad, "Foreign Secretary Visits UK-Supported Mobile Forensic Lab in Lahore," July 18, 2013, www.gov.uk/government/world -location-news/foreign-secretary-visits-uk-supported-mobile-forensic-lab-in -lahore.

45. A field job in the Pakistan police service means direct policing responsibilities, separate from administrative tasks.

46. "Proposal for Improving Police Investigation System," *Daily Times*, August 10, 2009.

47. Interview with a U.S. official, New York, October 2010.

48. "France Provides Pakistan Advanced Security Equipment," *China View*, July 25, 2009.

49. Source: www.sadaewatansydney.com/hcdinner-afp.htm.

50. See Faisal Ali Ghumman, "Turkish Experts Arrive to Train Counter-terror Force," *Dawn*, December 6, 2014, http://www.dawn.com/news/1149088/turkish -experts-arrive-to-train-counter-terror-force.

51. Khaled Ahmed, in discussion with the author, Washington, D.C., May 2006.

52. Telephone interview with an official of the Federal Investigation Agency, March 2007.

53. Interview with a senior NACTA official, Islamabad, July 2010.

54. Comments of Aftab Sherpao made in a talk show, *Jirga*, on Geo TV on June 7, 2010. The report of the United Nations Commission of Inquiry into the facts and circumstances of the assassination of former Pakistani prime minister Mohtarma Benazir Bhutto also raises critical questions about the interference of intelligence organizations in police work.

55. Malik Naveed, NWFP inspector general, Dawn TV, December 2, 2009.

56. "Punjab Police Seeks Army's Help in Anti-Terror Training," *Daily Times*, November 22, 2009.

57. For details, see "Police Need Immense Support from Intelligence Services," *News on Sunday*, May 10, 2009.

58. Interview with a senior police officer in Lahore, February 2012.

59. The Red Mosque (Lal Masjid) in Islamabad was stormed by Pakistan's military in July 2007 after its leaders and students led a months-long "antivice campaign" that included the kidnapping of police officials and forced takeover of government property. Hundreds, including civilians, died in the gun battles between security forces and extremists operating from the mosque complex.

60. For details, see "Punjab Police Predicted GHQ Attack on July 15," *The News*, October 10, 2009. See also Sabrina Tavernise and Waqar Gillani, "Frustrated Strivers in Pakistan Turn to Jihad," *New York Times*, February 27, 2010.

61. For details, see Hassan Abbas, "Defining the Punjabi Taliban Network," *CTC Sentinel* 2, no. 4 (April 2009): 1–4.

62. Ayesha Siddiqa, "Pakistan's Second Front," *Newsweek*, October 21, 2009.

63. For details, see Sabrina Tavernise and Waqar Gilani, "70 Murders, yet Close to Going Free in Pakistan," *New York Times*, August 5, 2009.

64. For details, see Asad Kharal, "First the Sorrow, Now the Fear," *Daily Times*, April 22, 2010.

65. "Four Marriott Bombing Accused Put Under House Arrest," *Daily Times*, May 7, 2010.

66. U.S. and French officials in discussion with the author, Paris and Washington, D.C, October–November 2009. For details, see "Law Enforcement and Criminal Justice Program: Pakistan," Bureau of International Narcotics and Law Enforcement Affairs, U.S. Department of State, May 3, 2010, http://www.state.gov/j/inl/rls/fs/141578.htm.

67. The draft Punjab Police Act of 2010 is available at http://www.nipsa.in/uploads/country_resources_file/1036_punjab_police_act_2010_draft.pdf.

68. Tariq Khosa, "Balochistan Blindly Follows Sindh Towards 19th Century Policing," *The News*, August 25, 2011.

69. Frederic Grare, "Political Dimensions of Police Reform in Pakistan," Policy Outlook (Washington, DC: Carnegie Endowment for International Peace, July 14, 2010).

70. For an estimate of the financial support needed to upgrade one academy, see Imran Asghar, "Rs 102m Projects for Sihala Police College Modernization," *Daily Times*, August 10, 2009.

71. Imran Mukhtar, "Senate Passes NACTA, Elections Laws Bills," *Nation*, September 6, 2013.

72. Complete text of the memorandum is available at www.thegctf.org/documents/10162/19594/Rabat+Memorandum+on+Good+Practices+for+Effective+Counterterrorism+Practice+in+the+Criminal+Justice+Sector.

73. Lieutenant General Moeen-ud-din Haider, Geo TV, July 11, 2010. The former home secretary of Sindh Province, retired Brigadier General Ghulam Mohammad Mohtarram, also supported this idea in the same program.

74. Tariq Khosa, in discussion with the author, Islamabad, July 2009. See also his comments on the subject at www.mohtasib.gov.pk/site/Projects/spgrminterface/exhibition/exhibition/PDF%20Conference%20Report%20SPGRM%20UNDP.pdf, pp. 21–22 (accessed December 1, 2014).

75. Malik Saad, the Peshawar police chief, widely respected for his competence, died in a suicide attack in Peshawar on January 27, 2007. Safwat Ghayur, commandant of the Frontier Constabulary and another senior police officer highly regarded for his integrity and counterterrorism efforts, was killed by a suicide bomber in Peshawar in a targeted attack on August 4, 2010.

76. For details, see Tariq Khosa, "Police Restructuring," *Dawn*, July 20, 2014; interviews with police officers serving in Khyber Pakhtunkhwa Province, Islamabad, October 14–15, 2014.

CHAPTER 6

PAKISTAN'S ECONOMY

DOMESTIC DISSENT AND FOREIGN RELIANCE

Shahid Javed Burki and Adnan Naseemullah

Pakistan's economy—which has been struggling with fiscal deficits, high inflation, declining dollar reserves, and the drying up of foreign direct or portfolio investment that could finance current account deficits—continues to depend on external support.[1] In September 2013, the International Monetary Fund (IMF) approved a three-year conditional extended facility loan of $6.6 billion to Islamabad. The IMF program was supplemented in March 2014 by a $1.5 billion loan from Saudi Arabia—not to say anything about the resilient American aid (see chapter 8).

Economic activity has been affected in 2013 by an acute power crisis, including widespread blackouts throughout the country that continued into the tenure of the Pakistan Muslim League—Nawaz (PML-N) government. The year 2014 yielded some better news in terms of growth, but the underlying structural weaknesses of an externally dependent economy remained. For Pakistan to return to a sustainable path of growth and development, after nearly a decade of insurgent violence, political instability, and growing international isolation, both the lack of internal consensus and an overreliance on foreign largesse needs to be addressed.

Pakistan is now the sick man of South Asia. If current trends continue, the country may well become the most stagnant in the subcontinent; Bangladesh's growth rate is now twice that of Pakistan (table 6.1).

This chapter argues that powerful proprietary groups in Pakistan, from the salariat to the landed elite to the military, have been unwilling or unable to come to agreement on basic political and economic accommodations that would limit their claim to the national fisc and allow for investment-enabling expenditure and space for domestic growth and development. As a result, Pakistan has over several decades been reliant on external sources of economic support to fund domestic fiscal and current account deficits,

TABLE 6.1 COMPARATIVE GROSS DOMESTIC PRODUCT GROWTH RATES IN SOUTH ASIA, CONSTANT PRICES (PERCENT)

COUNTRY	2010	2011	2012	2013	2014 (P)	2015 (P)
India	10.2	6.6	4.7	5.0	5.6	6.4
Bangladesh	6.0	6.5	6.2	6.1	6.2	6.4
Sri Lanka	8.0	8.2	6.3	7.3	7.0	6.5
Pakistan	2.6	3.6	3.8	3.7	4.1	4.3

NOTE: P = PROJECTED.

SOURCE: INTERNATIONAL MONETARY FUND, *WORLD ECONOMIC OUTLOOK*, APRIL 2012. PLEASE SEE WWW.IMF.ORG/EXTERNAL/PUBS/FT/WEO/2012/01/PDF/TEXT.PDF, 195.

particularly in exchange for Pakistan's commitments as a U.S. ally in the Cold War and the war on terror. Such foreign assistance, never guaranteed at the best of times, seems further in doubt given continued economic stagnation in the West and the decreasing relevance of Pakistan to international security, as international intervention in Afghanistan draws to a close.

PAKISTAN'S POTENTIAL IN COMPARATIVE PERSPECTIVE

Pakistan could certainly be more successful and more economically self-reliant. It is not hugely different, in terms of its endowments, from the "BRIC" countries of Brazil, Russia, India, and China and emergent economies like Indonesia and South Africa (table 6.2).

What distinguishes the BRIC countries from the rest of the developing world is their size (population and gross domestic product (GDP)), their dominance in the region to which they belong, their recent rates of economic growth, and their economic potential. Pakistan meets three of these four criteria. It has now a large population, approaching 200 million, less than that of China, India, Indonesia, and Brazil but more than that of Russia and South Africa.

It is furthermore located in the region that has high growth potential. Several countries in its neighborhood have vast energy resources. Some, such as Afghanistan, have recently discovered large mineral deposits, which may well extend into the Pakistani province of Baluchistan. Pakistan could become a key node of cross-country commerce between India to the east and southeast, China to the northeast, the Middle East in the west, and

TABLE 6.2 BRIC AND PAKISTAN GROSS DOMESTIC PRODUCT ANNUAL GROWTH RATE, CONSTANT PRICES (PERCENT)

COUNTRY	2002	2003	2004	2005	2006	2007	2008	2009	2010	2011	2012	2013	2014
Brazil	2.7	1.1	5.7	3.2	4.0	6.12	5.1	-0.3	7.5	2.7	1.0	2.5	0.3
Russia	4.7	7.3	7.2	6.4	8.2	8.5	5.2	-7.8	4.5	4.3	3.4	1.3	0.2
India	3.8	7.9	7.9	9.3	9.3	9.8	3.9	8.5	10.2	6.6	4.7	5.0	5.6
Indonesia	4.5	4.8	5.0	5.7	5.5	6.3	6.0	4.6	6.2	6.5	6.3	5.8	5.2
China	9.1	10.0	10.1	11.3	12.6	14.2	9.6	9.2	10.4	9.3	7.7	7.7	7.4
South Africa	3.7	2.9	4.6	5.3	5.6	5.5	3.6	-1.5	3.1	3.6	2.5	1.9	1.4
Pakistan	3.1	4.7	7.5	9.0	5.8	5.5	5.0	0.4	2.6	3.6	3.8	3.7	4.1

NOTE: BRIC = BRAZIL, RUSSIA, INDIA, AND CHINA.
SOURCE: WORLD DEVELOPMENT INDICATORS.

Afghanistan and the Central Asian republics in the north. Its rich human resource base should provide what the demographers call the "window of opportunity" that will remain open for a period longer than that for the BRIC countries.

Its diaspora, estimated at 4 percent of the national population, is located in several parts of the world; remittances from emigrants are a key source of capital inflows. Remittances have slowly increased the stock of foreign currency reserves in recent months, even as other sources of foreign finance have dried up. Diaspora populations are also untapped sources of other kinds of capital. They could potentially provide valuable managerial, financial, and other skills for reforming and transforming the economy.

The country has a rich agricultural sector supported by one of the world's largest irrigation systems, developed initially under colonial rule but expanded later by Pakistani investment, as well as the successful implementation of Green Revolution technologies. Agricultural production of cash crops such as cotton as well as a range of foodstuffs serves to provide for international trade in these commodities, to spur the industrial production of textiles and processed foods, and to stabilize domestic food supplies. These are some of the endowments that could be counted on to produce a better economic future. Compared with the BRIC countries, the only area where Pakistan has performed poorly is in terms of the rate of economic growth in recent years. This was not always the case. In fact, the country has experienced a number of growth spurts over the last half century. In the 1960s, the 1980s, and the early 2000s, the rate of GDP growth reached between 6 and 7 percent a year for extended periods.

These high-growth periods have meant respectable increases in per capita incomes. One consequence of this has been the emergence of a sizeable middle class, numbering between forty and fifty million people. This is large enough to give the economy a sustained push toward a higher rate of growth and economic modernization.

Why has the country done poorly compared with its potential? It is important to emphasize the link between economic development and the political environment in explaining Pakistan's roller coaster economic performance.[2] Had the country known greater and more consistent political stability, it would have arguably had a more consistent record of economic performance. The country has tried several different models of political governance and economic management. The military ruled for 33 years out of the 65 years of postindependence Pakistan. Moreover, during some periods of democratic rule, the military has maintained an influence on policymaking. This constant back-and-forth between military and civilian rule has adversely affected economic development. Certain periods of political instability produced uncertainty about the country's economic future.

Economies seldom do well in an environment marked by political uncertainty, but this uncertainty is a manifestation of something deeper: the inability of political groups in Pakistan to reach agreement on the allocation of rents and resources between groups, within a constitutional framework that regulates the alternation and distribution of power based on electoral success and that prevents the exercise of power by the military. As a result, political parties march on the capital with disheartening frequency, the military often intervenes in civilian politics, and individual political leaders are often as interested in looting the state as formulating and implementing growth-enhancing policy. The capacity for increased public and private (foreign and domestic) investment in value-added activities is dependent on a stable environment in which no one group is able to threaten public order in order to acquire a greater piece of the pie through contentious means. Yet Pakistan's politics leave us with little indication that such an environment, and the political compact that would allow for it, is forthcoming. The lack of sustained domestic resource mobilization and investment means that Pakistan's economy relies on foreign inflows, in terms of official aid, emergency loans, and remittances to keep the economy afloat while maintaining its external obligations. Such domestic contention and such external reliance have truncated Pakistan's potential as an economic power.

THE FOUNDATIONS OF PAKISTAN'S POLITICAL INSTITUTIONS, 1947–2008

The civilian rule for the first eleven years after independence was in a constitutional vacuum. Unlike India, Pakistan's sister state, which constructed an enduring constitutional framework within four years of gaining independence, Pakistan struggled for almost a decade before agreeing on a basic framework for governance. The 1956 constitution gave the country a parliamentary form of government and a federal structure. Yet this constitution survived for only six years and was never put to the electoral test. The first general election was scheduled for late 1958, but in October 1958, General Mohammad Ayub Khan declared martial law. The military government abrogated the constitution and promised a new political order.

Ayub Khan introduced a new system of governance under the constitution adopted in 1962. This was a highly centralized presidential system, with members of the national and provincial assemblies indirectly elected by an electoral college of 80,000 "basic democrats," themselves either elected from the population or appointed by the state. This created considerable distance between those who governed over those they ruled. Ayub Khan's fall came when some of the citizens who felt that they had not benefited from the high rates growth of the period came out on the streets. The army stepped in to restore public peace.[3] In 1969, General Yahya Khan, the army chief of staff, abrogated the 1962 constitution and removed Ayub Khan from office.

The new military president governed under the "Legal Framework Order" (LFO). The LFO provided the framework for holding the country's first general elections based on adult franchise, in December 1970. The seats in the National Assembly were distributed on the basis of population, which meant that East Pakistan (today's Bangladesh) received a larger share than West Pakistan (today's Pakistan), a departure from the principle of "parity" between the two wings that was the basis of the two previous constitutions. The elections produced a majority for the Awami League, a party based almost entirely in East Pakistan. Its leader, Sheikh Mujibur Rahman, had campaigned on the demand for considerable increase in autonomy for East Pakistan. His "six point program" would have transferred most authority to the two provinces, leaving the central government responsible only for defense, monetary policy, and international commerce. Had the results of the election been accepted, power would have transferred to the Awami League. That outcome was not acceptable to Zulfiqar Ali Bhutto, the chairman of the Pakistan Peoples Party (PPP) with strength among urban workers and Sindhi landed elites, which had won the majority of the seats in the western wing. The result of this standoff was a bitter civil war in which the Indian army, siding with the Bengali freedom fighters, defeated the Pakistani army and established the independent state of Bangladesh.

A defeated and morally devastated Pakistan turned to Bhutto, now president, to lead the country out of this crisis. He launched a number of projects aimed at restoring the confidence of his defeated people. These included the framing of a new constitution, initiating a nuclear weapons program, representing the country as a leader of the Islamic Conference, and expanding the role of the government in managing the economy. The constitution of 1973 envisaged a federal parliamentary structure with a fair amount of autonomy granted to the four provinces of Punjab, Sindh, North West Frontier Province (now Khyber Pakhtunkhwa), and Baluchistan.

Bhutto subverted many aspects of his constitution after taking over as prime minister, showing little respect for the constitution's federal provisions. The promise that the provinces would be allowed greater autonomy was not fulfilled; he was also intolerant of the rule by the opposition parties in the provinces in which his PPP did not have a commanding presence. When he called for another election, there was an impression that he was looking for a more solid majority in the national legislature that would allow him to amend the constitution toward a more centralized presidential system. The elections held in 1977 showed a massive victory for the PPP, but the opposition argued that there was widespread electoral fraud and took to the streets, leading to deadly violence between opposition activists and security forces. The postelection political violence and instability provided a pretext for military intervention by General Zia ul Haq, Bhutto's handpicked chief of the army. Two years later, on April 4, 1979, General Zia ordered the execution of Bhutto, who had earlier been sentenced to death by the Lahore High Court on the charge that he was involved in a conspiracy to assassinate a political opponent.

General Zia did not abrogate the constitution as his two predecessors had done but rather set it aside, promising to restore it after six months, yet it was eight years before elections were held under the constitution. Unlike the 1970 and the 1977 elections, political parties were banned and candidates were to run as individuals. This National Assembly passed the Eighth Amendment to the constitution; its most important clause was the infamous article 58.2(b), which gave the president the authority to dismiss the prime minister, dissolve the National Assembly, and appoint a "caretaker" administration responsible for supervising the next general election. With these powers in hand, President Zia handpicked Mohammad Khan Junejo, a Sindhi politician, who had risen to prominence during the period of Ayub Khan. But Zia misread Junejo; the prime minister proved to be independent, proceeding in a different direction from the president. The two clashed over Afghan policy. From 1979, Pakistan had partnered with the United States to launch the mujahideen insurgency to expel the forces of the Soviet Union from Afghanistan. The prime minister opposed the conflict and the toll it was taking on Pakistan. The president wanted more time during which Pakistan should take the responsibility for transferring power to a system of governance that would be durable and bring stability and security. Junejo prevailed, and in February 1988, Pakistan signed the Geneva Accord with Afghanistan, which was guaranteed by the Soviet Union and the United States.[4] Three months later, Zia dismissed Junejo, invoking article 58.2(b) of the amended constitution. Three months later, General Zia was killed in an airplane crash that remains unexplained.

All through the time that he ruled the country as president, General Zia continued to hold the position of the Chief of Army Staff (COAS). General Aslam Beg, the deputy chief at the time of Zia's death, did not take over as president but instead invited Ghulam Ishaq Khan, the chairman of the Senate, to take over as acting president. Khan, immediately after assuming his office, ordered that elections be held in October 1988, as required by the constitution. The PPP, led by Benazir Bhutto, won a majority, and Bhutto was invited to become prime minister. But Bhutto was unable to exercise all the authority guaranteed by the constitution. She was constrained by an informal extraconstitutional "troika" arrangement, in which the president and the COAS shared power with the elected prime minister, effectively the junior member.

In the 1990s, presidents, with the backing of the COAS, freely used article 58.2(b) of the constitution to remove elected prime ministers. Ghulam Ishaq Khan fired two prime ministers by using this constitutional provision, Benazir Bhutto in 1990 and Nawaz Sharif in 1993. His successor, Farooq Leghari, used it against Bhutto in November 1996 to cut short her second tenure. This period of quasi-civilian rule was to prove as turbulent as the eleven-year period immediately after independence, from 1947 to 1958. Seven prime ministers were in office during the 1988–1999 period, only four of whom were elected, with the remaining three appointed under various "caretaker" arrangements. Mian Nawaz Sharif tried to bring stability to this chronically unstable arrangement by dismissing General Pervez Musharraf from office as COAS. The attempt failed, and the army took power on October 12, 1999; Musharraf designated himself first as chief executive and then as president following a rigged referendum. Following the precedent of General Zia ul Haq, Musharraf remained in uniform until the fall of 2007, when he appointed General Ashfaq Pervez Kayani as COAS. Truly democratic rule has been established only since 2008, following protests that forced Musharraf from the presidency, elections that brought the PPP back to power and Asif Ali Zardari to the presidency, and the passage of the Eighteenth Amendment in 2010, which removed the president's ability to dismiss Parliament.

Can we draw from this political narrative a theory to explain Pakistan's political evolution from the time of its birth to the time when democracy came to be established in an unsteady way as the preferred system of governance? Several scholars have made such an attempt, most recently Anatol Lieven in his masterly work, *Pakistan: A Hard Country*.[5] Pakistan, an invented country, was faced with more challenges than was the case with its neighbor, India. Where India succeeded, Pakistan failed, because the nation-building efforts in the two countries had different objectives. In the case of India, the effort was to create a political order that could encompass a population of enormous religious, ethnic, and linguistic diversity. In the case of Pakistan, the idea was to make a nation out of a common religious identity. Posed this way, nation-building efforts should have been at least as onerous for India as they were for Pakistan, yet the absence of durable institutions from which a political order can be built in the latter severely constrained the efficacy of state building. Moreover, the assertion of groups from the military to minority groups to landed classes placed added burdens and obligations on a state unable in the first instance to place these particularistic concerns within a common political order.

As a result, there remain a number of unresolved group conflicts in Pakistani society. To begin with, the interests of the military, as a highly organized and centralized centripetal institution, have to be reconciled with those of the many centrifugal political organizations that act from diverse but parochial interests in cities and towns, representing industries, sectors, professions, languages and dialects, biradari communities, and religious sects. These interests provide both resilience and weakness to the political system and provide the context for the sustained distributional conflicts that characterize Pakistan's political economy.

PAKISTAN'S POLITICAL ECONOMY, 1947–2008

When Pakistan achieved independence, it did not have the capacities of a functioning state. That was not the case for India, which could simply take over central institutions from the British Raj. They inherited a well-developed capital city, a well-staffed central government, a central bank, and a treasury to handle government's finance. The British left foreign exchange reserves to the partitioned states, 17 percent of which were to be given to Pakistan as its share of these "sterling balances." Yet none of these were immediately available to Pakistan. It had to create a new state out of nothing. Karachi was chosen as the capital largely because it was the birthplace of Mohammad Ali Jinnah, Pakistan's founding father, and it had some facilities for housing the government because it was then the capital of Sindh, a province of British India. But Karachi's "physical plant" was not adequate to accommodate a national government. It was for this reason that the decision was taken to maintain the military establishment in the garrison town of Rawalpindi a thousand miles to the north, from where the British had run their "northern command." This separation of the civilian and military capitals was to profoundly affect the country's political and economic development. It took the new government almost a year before a central bank was established in Karachi; Jinnah, as governor-general, inaugurated the new State Bank of Pakistan on July 1, 1948, a few weeks before he died. Even then, India did not deliver Pakistan's share of the sterling balances; it took a trip to New Delhi by Prime Minister Liaquat Ali Khan and intervention by Mountbatten and Gandhi, before the Indian government released the reserves Pakistan was owed.

Compounding these problems was the arrival of eight million refugees from India, while six million Hindus and Sikhs emigrated to India. At the time of Partition, the provinces that became Pakistan had a population of thirty million; thus, twenty-four million people had to accommodate eight million immigrants, many of them poor farmers and urban dwellers forced to migrate from eastern Punjab and cities in northern and western India due to the sectarian violence that accompanied Partition.[6] In terms of GDP growth, the country initially performed poorly, when the national product increased by only 3 percent a year, close to the rate of increase in population.

Pakistan's economic performance was transformed under General Ayub Khan. In the "development decade" of the 1960s, a number of Western scholars regarded the country as the model of economic development that could be followed by other developing countries.[7] During Ayub Khan's eleven years in power, GDP increased at an average annual rate of 6.7 percent, with the economy more than doubling during this period. The inequitable distribution of the fruits of development would, however, lead by the end of the decade to resurgent Bengali nationalism against the central state, the 1971 war, and the independence of Bangladesh.

In addition to bringing political stability, Ayub Khan's approach to economic management had a number of salutary features that enabled economic growth. Ayub Khan brought a highly centralized approach to political and economic management. This had both positive and negative results. To help the government manage the economy, Ayub Khan strengthened the Planning Commission, appointing himself as its chairman. A full-time manager was hired from among the senior officers of the Civil Service of Pakistan to run the Commission. The Commission was given the task of writing and implementing five-year development plans. The Second Plan, which covered the 1960–1965 period, remains to this day the most successful planned effort by Pakistan.[8] The second important feature of the model was its emphasis on the development of the private sector. The government actively cultivated investment from migrant trading and banking communities in order to create an industrial bourgeoisie and facilitated it with the help of a trade and credit policy that provided some protection to domestic producers while providing them with capital through publicly managed industrial credit agencies.[9] Value added in the manufacturing sector increased by an impressive 17 percent a year during the Ayub Khan period.

The third part of the model was to bring discipline to the use of public sector resources by the development agencies responsible for launching and implementing a variety of government-funded projects. The most successful example of this was the Water and Power Development Authority, which carried out massive irrigation and power projects funded by international development agencies.

The rate of growth in GDP picked up because of the increase in the rate of investment; it increased by 8 percentage points between the 1950s and the 1960s. This spurt in investment was possible because of the large flow of external finance, the result of Pakistan's Cold War alignments with the United States. Pakistan joined a number of U.S.-led defense alliances and was rewarded with large amounts of aid. This was to set a pattern followed in the future. The easy availability of foreign finance has meant that the country made little effort to increase domestic resource mobilization, with tax collection averaging 10.6 percent of GDP since 1991. Dependence on external capital flows also made the country highly vulnerable and subject to the strategic interests of foreign powers, which has contributed to Pakistan's recent economic crisis, after a breakdown in relations between Islamabad and Washington in 2011 and a shift in U.S. strategic focus, on which more below.

The model, emphasizing rapid industrial growth, neglected its distributional affects. Many felt that a narrow, Karachi-based economic elite had captured much of the benefits of state-led industrialization.[10] This feeling of relative deprivation contributed to a mass movement that demanded participation by the citizenry in both the political and economic life of the country. Zulfiqar Ali Bhutto, a former foreign minister under Ayub, exploited this sentiment and launched a new political party, the PPP, which promised to bring "Islamic socialism" to the country.

Bhutto came to power in December 1971 and challenged the Ayub economic model on distributional grounds.[11] He largely dismantled the institutions Ayub Khan had constructed, reversing most of the policies of industrial promotion. His populist policies nationalized large-scale private enterprise, bringing under the control of the government industrial, financial, and commercial enterprises of significant size. Public-sector corporations were given the authority to manage these enterprises and also to make new investments in the sectors for which they had responsibility.

Bhutto did not limit his nationalization policies with the real sectors of the economy. He also brought under government's control a number of private-sector educational institutions, to bring equality in the delivery of social services. The prime minister believed that these institutions only bred elitism that retarded the progress toward his Islamic socialism. Bhutto's policies and divisive politics did a great deal of damage to the economy and to the development of the country's large human resources. The rate of GDP growth declined by almost 3 percentage points and came close to the rate of increase in population. Moreover, the incidence of poverty increased during the period. But the Bhutto years encouraged a winner-takes-all conflict over political power and economic resources, as Bhutto himself diverted enormous resources to favored clients while punishing other groups through expropriation of resources and even coercion.

President Zia ul Haq relied on technical managers to rescue the economy from the difficulties created by the Bhutto administration, even while his government favored his own clients, including Punjabi industrialists like Mian Muhammad Sharif. Under technocratic finance ministers Ghulam Ishaq Khan (1977–1985) and Mahbubul Haq (1985–1988), Pakistan essentially went back to the mixed model of economic growth it had followed during the period of President Ayub Khan. The rate of growth in GDP went back to 6.7 percent a year and the rate of increase in income per head of the population to nearly 4 percent per annum. As was the case during the period of first military rule, the United States provided large amounts of foreign aid in exchange for its support against the Soviet Union in Afghanistan.

President Zia ul Haq's death coincided with the pullout by the Soviet Union from Afghanistan and the consequent loss of strategic interest by the United States in supporting Pakistan economically. In response to IMF and World Bank conditionalities in the 1990s, Pakistan had begun to implement "Washington Consensus"–consistent structural reforms. This put private enterprise at the forefront while the economy was opened up to global trade and foreign investment. This shift in policy stance should have pleased the officials in Washington, but the nuclear tests in 1998 under the premiership of Nawaz Sharif led to the imposition of economic sanctions. Denied access to foreign capital, the rate of growth plummeted to less than 4 percent a year at the end of the decade.

Further, weak democratic governments, alternating between Nawaz Sharif's PML-N and the PPP under Benazir Bhutto, in the 1990s further calcified the conflict between proprietary groups over political power and economic resources. The military refused civilian oversight and fought for control over a substantial portion of the state's resources, and the economic clients of the various political parties at national and provincial levels competed over the nonimplementation of reform measures, public investment in private ventures, and other forms of endemic corruption that characterized the period. Even as conflict over resources increased, the external support to the state stagnated; the gradual withdrawal of U.S. development aid throughout the decade led to multiple balance-of-payments crises and World Bank–IMF adjustment programs, most of them not seriously implemented.

General Pervez Musharraf's coup against the Sharif government further decreased the legitimacy of the Pakistani state in the eyes of the United States. President Clinton's spring 2000 visit to South Asia almost completely bypassed Pakistan, and the president refused to shake hands with Musharraf. After the attacks of September 11, 2001, there was a dramatic improvement in Pakistan's economic situation as the Musharraf regime aligned itself with the United States as a frontline state in the global war on terror.

For the third time in its history, the rate of growth in the economy picked up, averaging close to 7 percent a year. Pakistan's realignment led the United States to renew its economic commitments. Not only did large amounts of aid begin to flow into the country, but Washington also helped Pakistan with debt forgiveness, which significantly lowered its repayment liabilities. The IMF also came in with a large program with comparatively soft conditions. Along with generous capital flows, the country's economy was reasonably well managed by a group of technocrats, some of whom were called in from abroad when General Musharraf assumed political control. The inflow of these resources enabled the Musharraf regime to paper over the group conflict over economic resources that had been institutionalized in the 1990s.

This broad overview of the institutional foundations behind Pakistan's economic performance leads one to conclude that the country is structurally able to produce reasonably high rates of economic growth if it is competently governed, political conflicts are managed, and significant amounts of foreign capital inflows are available. As we will see from the analysis offered in the following section, none of these conditions are now evident, which suggests that lowered rates of growth, along with their attendant social and political impacts, may be present for some time to come.

TOWARD A NEW POLITICAL ORDER
AND ITS ECONOMIC COST, 2008–2014

Although the parties that had relentlessly opposed rule by the military won the election held in February 2008, the armed forces did not immediately pull back to the barracks. General Pervez Musharraf tried to stay in power as president. But he was eventually persuaded to leave the presidency in part because the new military commander made it clear that the president did not have his support.

Asif Ali Zardari, Benazir Bhutto's widower, acted to build a political coalition in order to take control of the presidency. He first cultivated Nawaz Sharif, the head of the rival PML-N, to work with him to oust Musharraf. Sharif was even more opposed to Musharraf following the 1999 coup and his decade-long exile under threat of anticorruption charges in Pakistan. He joined a "grand coalition" organized by Zardari when Yusuf Raza Gilani, his choice for premiership, was sworn in as prime minister. The PML-N was given several important portfolios, including that of finance, but the coalition quickly fell apart. In May 2008, the PML-N left the government, leaving the PPP, along with junior partners, such as the Awami National Party (ANP) and the Muttahida Qaumi Movement (MQM), fully in charge. By that time, the PPP cochairman had received the indication that the military would not support Musharraf's continuation in office. Musharraf, now threatened with impeachment, resigned in late August and entered exile in London. Zardari was elected president a month later.

There was an expectation when the democratically elected government replaced military rule in March 2008 that it would uphold the rule of law (table 6.3). That was the spirit behind the Charter of Democracy signed on May 14, 2006, in London by the leaders of the two main political parties. Political parties joined the civil society movement for the restoration of Chief Justice Iftikhar Chaudhry, who had been removed by Musharraf. Once returned, the Supreme Court controversially held that the National Reconciliation Ordinance, an order of amnesty for politically motivated corruption charges that Musharraf had signed in 2007 in order to allow a restoration to power, was unconstitutional.

The Supreme Court's decision implied the revival of these cases, including one pending in a Swiss court, which implicated Bhutto and Asif Ali Zardari in a kickback case in which it was alleged that the couple had received tens of millions of dollars in return for the grant of a large contract. The court instructed the government to write to the Swiss authorities to restore the case. Prime Minister Gilani refused to comply, maintaining that the Constitution gave Zardari, as president, immunity against prosecution. This led to the launch of contempt proceedings by the Supreme Court against the prime minister.

On April 26, 2012, the court convicted the prime minister of having committed contempt, but Gilani again defied the court by not resigning his

TABLE 6.3 PAKISTAN'S RANKING IN CORRUPTION PERCEPTION INDEX (CPI)

YEAR	SCORE	RANK
1995	2.25	39/41
1996	1	53/54
1997	2.5	48/52
1998	2.7	71/85
1999	2.1	87/99
2000	—	—
2001	2.3	79/91
2002	2.6	77/102
2003	2.5	92/133
2004	2.1	129/145
2005	2.1	144/158
2006	2.2	142/163
2007	2.4	138/179
2008	2.5	134/180
2009	2.4	139/180
2010	2.3	143/178
2011	2.5	134/183
2012	2.7	139/174
2013	2.8	127/177

NOTE: VERY CLEAN = 9.0–10; HIGHLY CORRUPT = 0.9–2.0.

SOURCE: TRANSPARENCY INTERNATIONAL, ALL ISSUES OF CORRUPTION PERCEPTION INDEX FROM 1995 TO 2014.

office. The court acted again on June 19 and ordered his removal, issuing a "short order" that instructed the chief election commissioner to remove the prime minister from membership of the National Assembly and also instructed the president to convene the National Assembly to elect a new prime minister. This time the PPP government chose to comply but in a manner that further plunged the country into political chaos and economic uncertainty.

The nomination of Raja Pervez Ashraf, a former power minister accused of several incidents of corruption as party leader and prime minister, by President Zardari on June 21 did nothing to improve the president's tarnished image or to begin the process of bringing the country out of deep political and economic crisis. Ashraf went on to receive 211 votes, a majority in the National Assembly. The opposition was generally appalled by the president's move. According to an assessment by the *Financial Times*, "in a move that observers said would do little to arrest the mounting political crisis in the South Asian country, Raja Ashraf stepped down last year as water and power minister amid allegations of corruption and failure to end the country's chronic electricity shortages."[12] The press had begun calling Ashraf "Raja rental," a reference to the rental power scam investigated first by the Asian Development Bank and subsequently by the Supreme Court. The newspaper *Dawn* summed up the reaction to Ashraf's election in an editorial: "The nomination of Raja Ashraf was a snub to millions of citizens who are suffering long hours of load shedding in the Pakistani summer. In the face of electricity cuts, the former water and power minister was an insensitive choice—and an unwise one, in an election year—sending a signal that the PPP is unconcerned about one of the nation's most painful problems. Political considerations were obviously at stake."[13]

The perceived corruption and incompetence of the PPP coalition government placed the party at historically low levels in public opinion in the months before general elections in May 2013. Political pressure on the government in early 2013 was increasing through mass rallies by Imran Khan and his Pakistan Tehreeke Insaaf (PTI) party and a march on Islamabad organized by the charismatic antigovernment cleric Tahirul Islam Qadri. In March, the tenure of the National Assembly ended, and the Election Commission, on the recommendation of a parliamentary committee, appointed the retired judge Mir Hazar Khan Khoso as caretaker prime minister. The election campaign over April and May was marred by violence in the northwest and in Karachi, with the Taliban targeting candidates and rallies of the PPP, the ANP, and the MQM. The elections themselves, held on May 11, presented an anti-incumbent wave, with the PML-N winning seats just short of a full majority, and the PPP decreasing its representation in Parliament to less than a quarter of its previous seat strength, though still managing to outperform Imran Khan's PTI.

The 2013 elections in Pakistan represented a watershed in the resilience of emergent democratic institutions; this was the first time in Pakistan's history that a democratically elected government relinquished power and another took up power. Following parliamentary elections, the PML-N candidate for president, Mamnoon Hussain, was elected after Zardari relinquished office in July 2013, two months ahead of the end of his term. General Kayani, the COAS, retired from the army in November 2013 in favor of the next in line, Raheel Sharif, thus presenting an instance of orderly succession in military leadership as well.

The political system in Pakistan is currently not without its challenges; each province is governed and represented in Parliament by a different party or set of parties, and the tensions between Pakistan and the United States over the drone program continue. But the political system has cleared a number of serious hurdles over the course of the year, even though recent institutional resilience has yet to translate to perceptions of political order and economic upturn, as key economic crises—particularly over power—and political conflict with outgroups, such as the protests of Imran Khan and Tahirul Qadri, continue.

ECONOMIC PERFORMANCE, 2008–2014

Restoration of democracy after decades of military rule was expected to cure Pakistan of many of its economic ills. The military had not governed without interruption, as it had in many other Muslim countries in the second half of the twentieth century. In Pakistan's case, it had ruled in three long spurts—1958–1971, 1977–1988, and 1999–2008—a total of 33 years. Even when it was not in power, it continued to exercise a considerable amount of influence on the making of public policy. When the military was directly in control, the economy did relatively well; its three growth spurts were all under the martial rule. Yet one of the important reasons for the economy's superior performance during these periods was undoubtedly the large inflows of external capital, coinciding with the early Cold War, the Soviet invasion of Afghanistan, and the global war on terror.

This was possible as the military rulers were able to take advantage of international crisis and quickly align the country with Western powers, particularly the United States. This happened during the first military presidency (1958–1968) when Ayub Khan brought Pakistan into a number of defense pacts with the United States following the Korean War and the freezing of the early Cold War decades. It happened again under General Zia ul Haq (1977–1988) when Islamabad agreed to assist Washington in the latter's effort to expel the Soviet Union from Afghanistan. And it happened for the third time under General Pervez Musharraf when practically overnight Pakistan did 180-degree turn and gave up its support for the Taliban regime in Afghanistan and became the United States' partner in throwing the Islamic regime out of Afghanistan.[14] In each case, Washington rewarded the country through the provision of copious amounts of economic and military assistance, which enabled Pakistan to avoid facing distributional conflicts between increasingly assertive political groups.

The provision of these external resources may have contributed to a problem of moral hazard, with Pakistani policymakers, sure of their country's strategic importance, implicitly relying on bailouts in times of crisis. In Pakistan's case, this has happened repeatedly, with the United States, China, Saudi Arabia, the United Arab Emirates, and the IMF coming to the country's rescue at different times in its troubled economic history. An IMF bailout was arranged in September 2013, in order to help Pakistan out of economic difficulties brought on by a current account deficit that is unfinanced by foreign capital inflows.

The first eighteen months of the PML-N tenure has brought growth up above 4 percent and above-target performance in manufacturing but underperformance in agriculture and services. Balance-of-payments crises have abated somewhat: foreign direct investment has more than doubled to $2.9 billion, and there was an external account surplus of $1.9 billion in July 2013–April 2014, as opposed to a worrying deficit the year before.[15] While Pakistan has survived the crises of 2013, in large part due to assistance from the IMF and Saudi Arabia, economic growth is still lackluster and does not signify progress toward the structural reforms required for sustained growth in the medium term.

Pakistan also remains overreliant on external support and not immune to exogenous shocks that could plunge the country back into economic crisis. Of much concern is Pakistan's foreign debt, accumulated over decades of economic relationships with the United States, the rest of the Paris Club of creditor countries, and the IMF and amounting to $65.4 billion in the summer of 2014. External debt servicing in 2014 reached $6.8 billion, which was 80 percent of central bank reserves for the year.[16] Combined external and domestic debt servicing of over $11.5 billion constitutes about a third of the country's total revenues and exceeds tax revenues when adjusted for provincial shares.[17] The State Bank of Pakistan further warns of a debt servicing trap, with weak tax revenues leading to greater fiscal deficits and an even greater share of revenues committed to debt repayment and servicing. The dual challenges of the inability to create a domestic settlement that involves taxing resources in order for the government to function and overreliance on external aid (largely in the form of loans) means that economic instability and fiscal pressure will be reproduced through debt servicing requirements for many years to come.

Why was the promise of 2008, when democracy returned to the country in a stable form, not fulfilled? This question assumes a set of premises: that democracy is good for development and sustainable economic growth; that it is good for the more equitable distribution of the fruits of growth; that it is good for giving people with diverse and seemingly irreconcilable interests and objectives the opportunity to resolve their differences; that it is good for providing the citizenry with institutional outlets they can use to express their frustrations; and that it helps those states that practice it to live in peace with their neighbors. If these premises hold, we should expect that Pakistan would have benefited materially in several different ways from the return of democracy. The move from a political system explicitly dominated by military priorities to one that is more open and governed by representatives of an active electorate should have produced greater welfare, confidence, investment, and economic growth. Yet such promises have not come into fruition a half decade from the transition to democracy.

Of the five benefits of democracy listed above, only one has thus far produced satisfactory results for Pakistan. And Pakistani citizens have used democratic institutions to express their frustrations and anxieties about their circumstances. Most citizens today are worse off than they were five years ago, when the political system began to change. Yet there is no widespread rebellion against the state. The extraconstitutional agitations of Imran Khan's PTI and Qadri's Pakistan Awami Tehreek, with implicit support from the military,[18] might have damaged the credibility of the current government but have thus far been unable to overturn it. Citizens of Pakistan seem to differentiate between the validity of Imran Khan's charismatic critiques against corrupt public institutions and the political practices of his political party and that of Qadri in challenging the democratic system.

The other four potentially positive outcomes are still not evident. In terms of the democratic peace dividend, after relatively stable relations between India and Pakistan over the last decade, tensions have increased again over Kashmir, with Prime Minister Narendra Modi publicly committing to a policy of no tolerance with regard to insurgents with ties to Pakistan. These recent tensions have stalled the ongoing pursuit of arrangements that put greater emphasis on producing economic benefits for both sides, through trade.

Second, even after an election in which the government changed hands to a more pro-business party, the economy is in very bad shape. The rate of growth has slowed down to the point where it is not much more than the rate of increase in the country's population. This means that not much is being added to the national product and that those who occupy lower rungs of the income distribution ladder cannot draw benefits from the little economic change that is occurring. In fact, the distribution of income has worsened since 2008. There is an increase in both interpersonal and interprovincial inequality. Two of the country's four provinces, the Punjab and Sindh, have done relatively well, while the other two, Baluchistan and Khyber Pakhtunkhwa, have been left behind (table 6.4).

Even in the better-performing provinces, there are districts that have fallen behind. And there is growing violence in the country, a consequence of both the inability of state agencies to interdict violent actors and perhaps of the people not being able to—or not willing to—solve their differences through democratic institutions. Karachi, a city with close to twenty million people, is the most ethnically, linguistically, culturally, and religiously diverse city in the country. It has twice exploded into violence since the return of democracy.

Does this mean that democracy has failed in Pakistan; that for some reasons peculiar to the makeup of the country, democracy has not delivered? The short answer to this question is no. But the question needs a longer answer on why democracy seems to be failing to provide material benefits to Pakistan. First, although democracy has been established in Pakistan, it has not been fully consolidated in such a way as to guarantee that democratic institutions have a legitimate monopoly over policy formulation and implementation.[19] Significant aspects of the Pakistani polity are beyond the reach of the democratic authority of elected governments and subordinate administrators, from governance in the tribal agencies to oversight of the overseas

TABLE 6.4 ALLOCATION OF FUNDS TO PROVINCES

PROVINCE	ALLOCATION (%)
Punjab	51.74
Khyber Pakhtunkhwa	14.62
Sindh	24.55
Baluchistan	9.09

NOTE: PERCENTAGE OUT OF RS 1,728,113 ALLOCATED FOR PROVINCES IN 2013–2014 BUDGET.

SOURCE: FEDERAL BUDGET 2011–2012, MINISTRY OF FINANCE, GOVERNMENT OF PAKISTAN. PLEASE SEE WWW.FINANCE.GOV.PK /BUDGET/BUDGET_IN_BRIEF_2012_13.PDF, 14 AND 19.

assets of the richest Pakistanis. Second, political institutions in Pakistan must become more inclusive if they are to be effective and produce sustained economic development.[20] As more individuals and organized groups are brought into the policy process, there will be less exit and resistance and more scope for the policies and practices of the state to make a difference in the lives of the Pakistani population. Ultimately, Pakistan needs a more durable and comprehensive political settlement among powerful political groups in order to both consolidate democracy and ensure that an economically enabling environment is not challenged by winner-takes-all politics.

There is hope that the reshaping of the structure of government following the passage of the Eighteenth Amendment and the rebalancing of federalism will improve the quality of governance by bringing the state closer to the people. But there is also anxiety that the devolution of authority to the provinces could cause disruption in a number of areas. There is a particular concern that unless the process of devolution is managed carefully, it could result in the deterioration of public services to the poorer segments of the population.[21] More broadly, these institutional reforms could form the basis of a broader settlement that allows for more resources for public and private investment while delimiting the power and resources of powerful groups, but this requires both political will and flexibility that is not evident in this government, reliant as it is on a particularly narrow slice of the Pakistani political universe.

CONCLUSION

The 2013 IMF program presents the first real opportunity for addressing structural problems in the country, such as chronic fiscal deficits due to rampant tax evasion and productivity-sapping inequity in the provision of key social and economic inputs, such as foodstuffs and energy. The PML-N government will have to address the issues of the limited capacity of the state to raise sufficient resources for delivering public goods, provide sufficient energy resources for industrial output as well as household consumption, and at the same time reduce income inequalities across classes and regions, control inflation, and improve the security situation to increase confidence in the country. The 2013 elections represented the electorate's feeling that the PPP coalition was incapable of addressing these many problems, and it remains to be seen whether Nawaz Sharif's administration will be more effective over the long term, particularly after shocks to its legitimacy brought on by the PTI/PAT agitation.

Yet the capacity of the Pakistani state to implement such reforms is questionable, given historical experience of powerful groups successfully resisting reform and the narrowness of public debate. In addition, the adjustment program has not been embedded in a broader strategy of economic development that engages a broader range of stakeholders in society.[22]

Pakistan is still missing a durable political order, in which powerful groups agree to delimit their extraconstitutional agitations and outsized grabs for state resources, in order to enable public and private investment and create a politically stable institutional environment. Absent such a compact that would allow for sustainable national development, Pakistan remains dangerously dependent on the support of bilateral and international institutions and their calculations that Pakistan is "too big to fail." And yet, as Pakistan has seen time and time again, such external support is both fickle and politically costly, especially in terms of state sovereignty.

In the future, the nature of this dependence may also change. As the current American military focus on Afghanistan wanes and Pakistani commitment toward stability has increasingly been brought under scrutiny by Congress, economic aid is begrudgingly provided by an international community that recognizes that Pakistan is, in terms of international security and regional politics, simply too big to fail, and by Gulf donors who seek their own political interests in South Asia. In the course of time, this evolution may have major geopolitical implications.

NOTES

1. "Pakistan Gets $6.6 Billion Loan from IMF," *IMF Survey*, September 4, 2013, http://www.imf.org/external/pubs/ft/survey/so/2013/car090413a.htm.
2. Shahid Javed Burki, *Changing Perception, Altered Reality: Pakistan's Economy Under Musharraf, 1999–2006* (Karachi: Oxford University Press, 2007).
3. For a discussion of this period, see Herbert Feldman, *From Crisis to Crisis: Pakistan in 1969* (Karachi: Oxford University Press, 1972).
4. For a study of the Soviet Union's withdrawal from Afghanistan, see Diego Cordovez and Selig Harrison, *Out of Afghanistan* (New York: Oxford University Press, 1995).
5. Anatol Lieven, *Pakistan: A Hard Country* (New York: Public Affairs, 2011).
6. For more on Partition migration, see Vazira Zamindar, *The Long Partition and the Making of Modern South Asia* (New York: Columbia University Press, 2007).
7. One example of this is Gustav F. Papanek, *Pakistan's Development: Social Goals and Private Incentives* (Cambridge, Mass.: Harvard University Press, 1967).

8. For a description of the strategy behind the Second Five-Year Plan, see Mahbubul Haq, *The Strategy of Economic Planning: A Case Study of Pakistan* (Karachi: Oxford University Press, 1967).

9. Mushtaq Khan, "Political Economy of Industrial Policy in Pakistan, 1947–1971," working paper, School of Oriental and African Studies, University of London, http://eprints.soas.ac.uk/9867/1/Industrial_Policy_in_Pakistan.pdf.

10. Lawrence White, "Pakistan's Industrial Families: the Extent, Causes, and Effects of Economic Power," *Journal of Development Studies* 10 (April–July 1974): 274t.

11. For a detailed discussion of politics and economic management of the Bhutto era, see Shahid Javed Burki, *Pakistan Under Bhutto, 1971–77* (London: Macmillan, 1980).

12. Rahul Jacob and Farhan Bokhari, "Ex-Minister Elected Pakistani PM," *Financial Times*, June 24, 2012.

13. "Editorial: PM election," *Dawn*, June 23, 2012.

14. For a detailed account of the reason for the dramatic shift in Pakistan's position, see Pervez Musharraf, *In the Line of Fire* (New York: Simon & Schuster, 2006).

15. *Pakistan Economic Survey 2013–14* (Islamabad: Ministry of Finance, 2014), http://www.finance.gov.pk/survey_1314.html.

16. Shahid Iqbal, "$7 Billion Debt Servicing a Challenge to the Economy," *Dawn*, September 14, 2014.

17. "Domestic and External Debt," *State Bank of Pakistan Annual Report, 2013–14* (Islamabad: Statbank of Pakistan, 2014), http://www.sbp.org.pk/reports/annual/arFY13/Debt.pdf.

18. Christophe Jaffrelot, "Painted Into a Corner," *Indian Express*, August 20, 2014.

19. For more on the concept of consolidation, see Larry Diamond, "Towards Democratic Consolidation," *Journal of Democracy* 5 (July 1994): 4–17.

20. For more on this argument, see Daron Acemoglu and James Robinson, *Why Nations Fail* (New York: Random House, 2012).

21. "State of the Economy: Devolution in Pakistan," Fourth Annual Report, Institute of Public Policy, Beaconhouse National University, April 2011, http://ippbnu.org/AR/4AR.pdf.

22. Sakib Sherani, "Programmed to Fail?" *Dawn*, November 1, 2013.

PART II

THE INTERNATIONAL DIMENSIONS

CHAPTER 7

PAKISTAN–AFGHANISTAN RELATIONS SINCE 2001

THERE ARE NO ENDGAMES

Avinash Paliwal

O n December 16, 2014, nine heavily armed militants, affiliated with the Tehrik-e Taliban Pakistan (TTP), attacked the Army Public School in Peshawar. An umbrella organization of various Islamist networks, the TTP had trained its guns against the Pakistani state and vowed to impose sharia throughout the country. Within a few hours, the militants had killed 145 people, of whom 132 were children.[1] Sending shock waves across the world and outraging the Pakistani public, the attack put unparalleled pressure on the Pakistani government, particularly the armed forces, to tackle terrorism. In response, Pakistani Prime Minister Nawaz Sharif ordered a military crackdown on TTP hideouts, and special military courts were set up to deal with captured Taliban fighters.[2] Remarkably, Islamabad dispatched its Chief of Army Staff, General Raheel Sharif, and the head of its directorate of Inter-Services Intelligence (ISI), Lieutenant General Rizwan Akhtar, to Afghanistan the day after the attack. Their aim was to seek help from Ashraf Ghani, Afghanistan's new president, to crack down on the TTP's sanctuaries in Afghanistan.[3] But more specifically, Pakistan wanted Afghanistan to hand over Mullah Fazlullah (also known as Radio Mullah), the alleged mastermind of the attack.[4] Refraining from engaging in hot pursuit of the TTP in Afghan territory out of respect for Afghanistan's sovereignty, Raheel Sharif had delivered a strong message of keeping all options open were Kabul not to cooperate. Ostensibly, this was simply a crisis meeting between two countries discussing counterterrorism. However, in essence, a new chapter had begun in the history of the tormented relationship between Afghanistan and Pakistan.

Similar to Pakistan, which used various militant Islamist outfits including the Lashkar-e-Taiba (LeT) and the Haqqani Network as strategic tools to put pressure on India and Afghanistan, Kabul had built covert capacities against Pakistan by 2015. If Pakistan was hosting the Quetta Shura and other Taliban leadership on its territory, Afghanistan had some influence over the TTP that operated from its territory. In fact, Rahmatullah Nabil, the chief of the National Directorate of Security, Afghanistan's intelligence agency, openly accepted that the National Directorate of Security have infiltrated enemy networks. According to a *New York Times* report, "Afghan spies have turned some of the region's most notorious militants into sources and potential proxies, and the intelligence agency has clandestinely taken its fight across the border, targeting Taliban leaders sheltering in Pakistan."[5] In this context, Raheel Sharif's visit to Kabul, somehow, testified to the strategic impact of Nabil's (and his predecessor's) covert tactical successes. Though the weaker of the two countries, Afghanistan has struggled to develop strategic parity with Islamabad on the negotiation table. Wanting to make sure that the security and political transition after the drawdown of U.S.-led North Atlantic Treaty Organization (NATO) forces from Afghanistan does not plunge the country into another round of civil war, Kabul has persistently sought Islamabad's support in clamping down on the Haqqani Network and to curb the LeT's activities in Afghanistan. In fact, before the Peshawar attack, Ashraf Ghani, to Pakistan's delight, had publicly embraced talks with Islamabad and visited Pakistan in November 2014.[6] Differences between the two countries, however, remain far from getting resolved anytime soon. In fact, the reality check came sooner than expected. Mullah Omar, the Amir-ul-Momineen of the Afghan Taliban, was declared dead in July 2015,[7] and so was Jalaluddin Haqqani, leader of the Haqqani Network.[8] Resulting in an ugly scramble for power between the different factions of the Afghan Taliban, a spectacular rise in deadly bombings across Afghanistan, and a rising profile of the Islamic State of Iraq and the Levant (ISIS) in Afghanistan, Omar's unceremonious exit lay bare the shortcomings—both in terms of intent and capacities—of the peace process between Afghanistan and Pakistan.[9]

This chapter documents the trajectory of Pakistan–Afghanistan relations since 2001, their ups and downs, and how the two countries, joined at the hip, stand at the cusp of a critical transition in 2015. In order to do so, the first section briefly explains the historical and structural context to Pakistan and Afghanistan's contemporary relations. The second section documents bilateral relations between the two countries between 2001 and 2006. Focusing on the 2001 Bonn Conference and its outcomes, this section shows how events immediately after 9/11 altered the bilateral relations between Afghanistan and Pakistan and what impact the Taliban's resurgence by 2005 had on their bilateral ties. The third section details how the idea of reconciliation with the Taliban got debated and what role Afghanistan and Pakistan had in making or breaking this process. The fourth section details the impact of the drawdown of coalition troops on the bilateral dynamics, with the presence of India increasing steadily. For Kabul, Pakistan had supported the Taliban and was ready to adopt a forward approach to shape Afghan politics in a way that suited its interests. For Pakistan, however, Afghanistan was getting unimaginably hostile and dangerously close to India. As this section explains, the years between 2011 and 2014 witnessed policy realignments both in Kabul and Islamabad toward each other, until the December 2014 Peshawar school attack. The chapter concludes that there are no endgames between Afghanistan and Pakistan, only new beginnings, better or worse.

HISTORICAL AND STRUCTURAL CONTEXT

The partition of 1947 affected not only India and Pakistan but also Afghanistan's relations with Pakistan. The two neighbors have been at odds with each other over various issues ever since. A historical mapping of bilateral contentions between Afghanistan and Pakistan, barring the structural ruptures of the Soviet intervention, the 1990s civil war years, and the U.S.-led NATO intervention, lead to three key enduring themes. First, there exists a strong sense of historical wrong among Afghans vis-à-vis the Durand Line and the illegitimacy of its widely accepted border with Pakistan.[10] Though the relevance of this issue has fluctuated over the years, it remains a serious contention that is far from getting resolved anytime soon. Carved to delineate the British Raj's zone of influence and secure its frontiers, the 1893 Durand Line Agreement, somewhat controversially, determined the fate of Afghanistan's contemporary territorial construct. It not only incensed the leadership in Kabul, which felt cornered by the imperial disrespect for Afghanistan's territorial integrity and political sovereignty, but also divided the Pashtuns living in the frontier region. Culminating in the Third Anglo-Afghan War of 1919, conflict over the Durand Line and the illegitimacy of the same in Afghan eyes, became an integral part of Afghan nationalism. The outcome of the war, however, remained unclear on this boundary question. Though Afghanistan won independence from British Indian influence on its foreign policy, it had to accept the frontiers of British India as demarcated by the Durand Line. According to the Treaty of Rawalpindi (1919), the "Afghan Government accepts the Indo-Afghan frontier accepted by the late Amir [Abdur Rahman, as decided in 1893]."[11]

The late Amir Abdur Rahman had not wanted to give up control over the northern Mohmand tribal agencies and also viewed Peshawar as an Afghan city. Both of these had gone to British India and were inherited by Pakistan without substantial discussions with Afghanistan. In Afghan eyes, this was not just a political affront to Kabul but also a social challenge to the deeply rooted sense of Pashtun nationalism in the tribal areas and South and East Afghanistan. The impact of Pashtun nationalism at the time of Partition was reflective most in the mobilization of the Khudai Khidmatgar movement in the North West Frontier Provinces (NWFP) led by Khan Abdul Ghaffar Khan, also known as Badshah Khan or Frontier Gandhi. Opposed to the idea for a separate Pakistan, as advocated by the All India Muslim League (AIML), Badshah Khan was close to the Indian National Congress (INC) and wanted the NWFP to be a part of India. However, if such a union was not possible, then he sought a separate Pashtunistan. Much to the dismay of Badshah Khan, neither the outgoing British nor the INC favored a further division of the subcontinent by creating Pashtunistan. India's first prime minister (PM) Jawaharlal Nehru, in fact, had lost faith in the idea of a separate Pashtun nation during his first visit to the NWFP as the head of the interim government of India, in October 1946.[12] With the movement of his convoy marred by violent disruptions, Nehru lost patience and publicly deplored the local mullahs of Waziristan as "petty pensioners," sparking further protests.[13] The AIML, with support from the local British authorities and mullah, had shown considerable political capacity and activism in the tribal areas during Nehru's tour to make the future Indian PM believe that the NWFP was a lost cause. For the Pashtuns of the frontier areas, this was a betrayal. Capturing the mood of the moment, a mood that has persisted until today in Afghanistan, were Badshah Khan's last words to his former ally Gandhi: "You have thrown us to the wolves."[14]

Feeling cheated and stung by the fact that the outgoing British had carved a new state next door without discussing potential boundary disputes, and that Karachi (then the capital of Pakistan) accepted the territorial limits of the erstwhile British Raj unconditionally, Kabul refused to recognize Pakistan at the United Nations in 1947. The otherwise strong cultural and social links between the two neighbors did little to overcome political differences. In fact, adding fuel to fire, Kabul signed the Treaty of Friendship with New Delhi in 1950, signaling its political warmth for India. Around the same time, in 1950, Pashtun tribesmen, with support from Afghan troops, attacked the northern border of Pakistan and entered thirty miles northeast of Chaman in Baluchistan.[15] Border skirmishes between Afghanistan and Pakistan only grew in the 1950s and early 1960s, under the premiership (1953–1963) and presidency (1973–1978) of Mohammed Daud Khan.[16] Aggressively promoting the separatist agenda, Daud increased armed activity against Pakistan along the border areas during his reign.[17] According to a U.S. government report, "In 1960 Daoud sent troops across the border into Bajaur in a foolhardy, unsuccessful attempt to manipulate events in that area and to press the Pashtunistan issue, but Afghan military forces were routed by the Pakistan military. During this period the propaganda war, carried on by radio, was relentless."[18] Daud even reached out to India in order to put military pressure on Pakistan's eastern border, only to be refused by New Delhi.[19] Determined to wrest back what it viewed as Afghan territory, Kabul had clearly expressed its intent on waging a long but limited war along its border regions with Pakistan. On September 6, 1961, Afghanistan and Pakistan severed diplomatic relations.

The Durand Line issue has very strong resonance in Afghanistan even today. That contemporary Afghan elite and masses view the border as illegitimate is best reflective in the fact that no Afghan government, including the Taliban regime (1996–2001) that was dependent on Pakistan for its survival and international exposure, conceded on the Durand Line question to Pakistan. The border was meaningless for the Afghan Taliban for the simple reason that there should be no borders between Muslims. Not surprisingly, the Taliban regularly sent official delegations to the Pakistani side without any clearance from Islamabad. For instance, two months before 9/11, a ninety-five-member armed delegation of the Taliban visited the Mohmand Agency in the Federally Administered Tribal Areas (FATA) region. Welcomed heartily by the local chieftain, the Taliban decided to hoist its flag in defiance of Pakistan's authority in the area. The visit, and the flag hoisting, according to the Pakistani media, "revived Afghanistan's claim on the area and left Islamabad shocked."[20] Though the issue has remained dormant since the U.S.-led NATO intervention in 2001, there remains a strong undercurrent of reclaiming Afghan territory or demanding a separate Pashtunistan even today.

The second enduring theme of this relationship is the fact that the persistence of the Durand Line dispute and the Pashtunistan issue coupled with its conflicts with India has aggravated Pakistan's territorial insecurities. Islamabad's approach toward Afghanistan, to the most extent, is determined by the need to quell Kabul's revisionist demand on the border issue. Though many academic works correctly link Pakistan's Afghanistan policy to its military's notion of gaining "strategic depth" against an Indian military onslaught, there is more to this relationship. As Khalid Nadiri argues, "Pakistan's [Afghanistan] policy is the result not only of its enduring rivalry with

India, but also of historically rooted domestic imbalances within Pakistan and the Pakistani state's contentious relationship with Afghanistan."[21] Pakistan remains consistently worried that a strong Pashtun government in Kabul will revive the demand for Pashtunistan and undertake military action similar to that of Daud Khan. It is in this context that former Pakistani PM Zulfiqar Ali Bhutto responded to Daud Khan's border provocations by militarily supporting antigovernment Islamists like Gulbuddin Hekmatyar, Ahmad Shah Massoud, and Burhanuddin Rabbani.[22] Aiming to build strategic parity with Kabul by supporting dissidents, Pakistan wanted to make sure that its western border does not flare up. Having already lost half of its territory and more than half of its population in the 1971 war with India over the creation of Bangladesh, there was no way Pakistan was letting go more territory in the west.

The concept of "strategic depth," with all its nuances, complexities, and evolution over time (when examining Pakistan's approach toward Afghanistan), gained precedence in the wake of military dictator Zia ul Haq's rise to power in 1977 and the Soviet Union's military intervention in Afghanistan in 1979.[23] With clandestine support from Washington, Islamabad decided to increase its support to the mujahideen figures fighting the Soviets. Islamabad's success in bogging down the Soviet forces in Afghanistan and making the mujahideen dependent on Pakistan made it believe that it could alter its geostrategic situation by installing a friendly regime in Kabul and by fomenting an insurgency in Kashmir. The ouster of former Afghan president Mohammad Najibullah (a fierce critic of Pakistan) and the rise of the mujahideen in 1991 were, in many ways, positive returns of an investment that Pakistan had made during the Daud Khan years. These events also marked the beginning of Pakistan's direct military interventionism in Afghanistan. Having failed to secure allegiance from all mujahideen factions and its influence over Ahmad Shah Massoud's Jamiat-e-Islami fading fast, Pakistani security agencies decided to support Hekmatyar to capture Kabul using force in the first phase of the Afghan civil war. However, it was not until September 25, 1996, when Kabul fell to the Taliban, that Pakistan reached closest to achieving strategic depth vis-à-vis India in Afghanistan. The Pakistani military, a highly politicized body with its own set of interests, thus came to present itself not only as the defender of Pakistan's territorial integrity regionally but also as the vanguard of the idea of Pakistan. This drive to support a political and military force in Afghanistan that will not raise the Durand Line issue, at worst, and support Pakistan in its conflicts with India, at best, has resulted in Islamabad's constant support to the Afghan Taliban and other factions like the Haqqani Network throughout 2001 until 2015.

The third enduring theme of this bilateral relationship is the popular mistrust of Pakistan among a majority of Afghans. Despite housing more Pashtuns on its soil than Afghanistan itself does, and despite sharing a common history of fighting the Soviets, Pakistan could not build strong links with different Afghan factions and ethnic groups. Caught in its own web of geostrategic reasoning and partisan engagement, Pakistan lost touch with the changing realities of Afghanistan—it needed to connect with the people of Afghanistan. Instead, it first supported the mujahideen against Najibullah, then supported Hekmatyar against Massoud and Abdul Rashid Dostum, then threw its lot behind the Taliban, and, finally, resuscitated the Afghan Taliban and armed the Haqqani Network against the Karzai government and the U.S.-led NATO forces. Negative publicity did not deter Pakistan from pursuing such interventionist policies vis-à-vis Afghanistan. As the following sections demonstrate, Islamabad played an important role in undermining not only the Karzai government but also the coalition forces and their efforts in bringing the Taliban to heel. Nonetheless, there has been a dual impact of Pakistan's determined interventionism in Afghanistan. While it came to be perceived as a bad neighbor popularly, it also tore Afghanistan's policymaking circles on the other. For instance, despite accepting Islamabad's intrusion in domestic Afghan politics, some policymakers in Kabul advocated an accommodative approach toward Islamabad. Others, however, remained staunchly averse to Pakistan and advocated a forward military approach of taking the war across the border into Pakistan. As noted earlier in this chapter, the current Afghan chief of intelligence, Rahmatullah Nabil, belonged to the second camp even though his president, Ashraf Ghani, had made Pakistan his top foreign policy priority. The following sections show how this bilateral relationship evolved after 2001 and where it stands today.

MANAGING SURVIVAL AND STRATEGY

The ghastly events of 9/11 and the subsequent American military response in Afghanistan came as a serious setback to Pakistan's Afghanistan policy. With the Taliban in power, despite differences, Pakistan had managed to secure a foothold in Kabul. In its dealings with India, for instance, Pakistan was able to negotiate the release of three militants from the Harkat-ul-Mujahideen active in Kashmir, by facilitating the hijack of flight IC 814 en route from Kathmandu to New Delhi at Kandahar.[24] Moreover, Pakistan's ISI was successfully running militant camps in South and East Afghanistan, training fighters for Kashmir.[25] Entry of the United States in Afghanistan threatened to bring these activities to an abrupt halt. Targeting Al Qaeda as well as the Taliban, the United States had chosen to support the anti-Taliban United Front (UF) in December 2001, which had an acrimonious relationship with Pakistan. Not surprisingly, Islamabad, then under a military regime run by Pervez Musharraf, revised its policies and accepted all the conditions put forth by Washington, namely, that Pakistan would stop supporting the Taliban and target militant sanctuaries on its territories. As former Pakistani foreign minister Abdul Sattar puts it, "We agreed that we would unequivocally accept all US demands, but then we would express our private reservations to the US and we would not necessarily agree with all the details."[26] This "yes, but" approach became the hallmark of Pakistani foreign policy toward Afghanistan since 2001. A tectonic shift in the bilateral relations between Kabul and Islamabad, thus, came about in the Bonn Conference in December 2001, where the new Afghan administration was instituted, and Hamid Karzai was chosen as the president of the Afghan Interim Authority.

Attended by the Rome Group, the Cyprus Group, the Peshawar Group, and the United Front, the conference was arguably the biggest gathering of different Afghan political factions that remained at odds with Pakistan. Former Afghan king Zahir Shah, a Durrani Pashtun and supporter of the Pashtunistan issue, headed the Rome Group. The Cyprus Group was close to Iran, and the Peshawar Group was mostly representing the Gailani family, known for its secular royalist credentials, despite having lived in Pakistan.[27] The UF, a conglomerate of various armed factions dominated by non-Pashtuns, enjoyed India, Russia, and Iran's support in their fight against the Taliban before 2001. And as for Karzai, his belief that the ISI was behind his father's assassination in 1999 made him unsympathetic to the Pakistani establishment even though his political links with India, where he completed his university education, were limited. Almost every group at the conference was averse to Pakistan's interventionist policies toward Afghanistan. This aversion had strong precedent: between 1994 and 1999, "an estimated 80,000 to 1,00,000 Pakistanis trained and fought in Afghanistan," along with the Taliban against the UF.[28] However, such Pakistani presence mattered little at Bonn. All those groups whom Pakistan had supported—the Hizb-e-Islami (Gulbuddin Hekmatyar), Hizb-e-Islami (Yunus Khalis), the Haqqani Network, and Mullah Omar and other Taliban figures—were missing from the conference.[29]

Even after the conference, relations between Pakistan and Afghanistan were anything but conciliatory. The first step in Pakistan's "yes, but" approach toward Afghanistan had occurred in November 2001 itself. Islamabad, with clearance from Washington, had evacuated most of its military and intelligence personnel from Afghanistan in an airlift from an airstrip in Kunduz in northern Afghanistan. What was little known to the world at that point was that senior Taliban figures were evacuated in the same airlift. Walking a tightrope, Musharraf was facing the brunt of the consequences of siding with the United States. Former militant groups including the Jaish-e-Mohammad, previously very close to the Pakistani army, undertook multiple assassination attempts against Musharraf.[30] Reconciling the domestic fallout of siding with the United States and its purported interests in Afghanistan with the need to support Washington, Pakistan began a covert campaign of providing sanctuary to the Taliban leadership and other militant organizations in the FATA and Baluchistan. In fact, when the Pakistani army, under American pressure, began operations in the FATA in 2002, it did not target the Afghan Taliban leadership and the Haqqani Network. Rather, it provided them with support and shelter to regroup and reorganize. The impact of this support became blatantly visible from 2005 onward when the Afghan Taliban started engaging the foreign forces in a campaign of asymmetric warfare. They would enter Afghanistan, target NATO installations, and return to their sanctuaries in Pakistan. And later on, even that would change as the Taliban started gaining a strong foothold within Afghanistan itself and continued to harass the Afghan and Western forces.[31] Not surprisingly, this dual policy of supporting the United States on the one hand and fueling the insurgency in Afghanistan on the other did not improve relations between the two countries. Kabul remained averse toward Pakistan, with senior UF leaders in important governmental posts guiding policy. Even President Karzai, a Pashtun who had a complicated relationship with the UF leadership, did little to calm the bilateral situation. Apart from ordering the Afghan army to engage in combat on the border areas with Taliban fighters crossing over into Afghanistan, he reinforced Afghanistan's territorial sensitivity on the Durand Line by calling the border "a line of hatred that raised a wall between the two brothers."[32]

Pakistan's determined support to the Afghan Taliban, however, had split Afghanistan's political camp. Despite being publicly averse to Pakistani interventions, and critical of the ISI's support to the Taliban, the reality was that Afghanistan was the weaker of the two neighbors. Though with support from American and NATO the Taliban could be kept at bay for some years, it was clear to Kabul that this may not be the case once the Western forces left Afghanistan. Though this debate got acute only after 2011 when the drawdown of Western troops loomed large, two strands of tactical thought emerged in Kabul early on during the war. According to one line of thought, Afghanistan should develop capabilities and adopt a forward diplomatic and military posture toward Pakistan. Supporting anti-Pakistan insurgents like the TTP and the Baluchistan Liberation Army would be one option. Developing asymmetric capabilities to gain strategic parity vis-à-vis Islamabad was the key point. In this context, friendship with India becomes an insurance against Pakistani aggression. The second line of thought was to advance measured diplomatic engagement with Islamabad and prioritize Pakistan over other regional countries, including India. Pashtunistan as a political issue has little resonance in this scenario. Stemming from the fact that Pakistan is militarily strong and confrontation with Islamabad is not viable, this idea entailed a defensive approach toward Islamabad rather than an offensive approach. Though there were few takers of the conciliatory line between 2002 and 2006, Pakistan's active diplomacy and the changing nature of Afghanistan's domestic politics, as the next sections show, pushed many political leaders in Kabul to advocate, though silently, a more accommodative line toward Islamabad.

The period from 2002 to 2006, however, was also a time when, much to Pakistan's chagrin and Kabul's delight, Islamabad's regional rival, India, was making strides in Afghanistan. Having supported the UF throughout the Taliban rule in Kabul between 1996 and 2001, New Delhi made a spectacular diplomatic reentry in Kabul after the Bonn Conference in 2001. Capitalizing quickly on changed circumstances, India became the first country to open diplomatic links with Kabul in December 2001 itself.[33] It reopened its embassy in Kabul and its old consulates in Kandahar and Jalalabad and also expanded its consular presence in Mazar-e-Sharif and Herat. Identifying its partnership with Afghanistan as a "developmental partnership," India started giving huge amounts of economic aid to Kabul and launched several big infrastructural projects.[34] These included the building of the Zaranj-Delaram Highway, the Salma Dam in Herat, a power transmission line that provided electricity for Kabul, and a Parliament Building.[35] In 2005, India also started investing money in providing small development projects (SDPs) to Afghanistan. With its bigger projects often coming under attack, the SDPs gave India an additional reach in the Afghan countryside. Within a few years, India had become the most loved country in Afghanistan and had developed tremendous social capital in the country. In addition to gaining a foothold in the country, India was also trying to balance its image in Afghanistan. Having been seen to be supportive of the Soviet intervention and then siding with the largely non-Pashtun UF, India had lost political capital among the Pashtun communities of Afghanistan. Ever since the Bonn Conference in 2001, New Delhi had been determined to change its image in Afghanistan and build strong political constituencies across Afghanistan. Although this remained largely unproblematic between 2002 and 2007, India's presence became more visible afterward and increasingly complicated the bilateral relations between Afghanistan and Pakistan.

DIFFERENT TYPES OF RECONCILIATION

The situation in Afghanistan deteriorated rapidly after 2006. The 2007–2010 phase saw very high levels of violence and Taliban activity.[36] The situation developed on three different planes. First, the Taliban was back in full force, and coalition forces were quickly realizing that they were losing the war. In this context, London floated the idea of reconciliation with the Taliban and reintegration of these fighters, with support from Pakistan.[37] Second, relations between the United States and Islamabad got increasingly worse. Held responsible for supporting the Afghan Taliban and its different offshoots, Pakistan found little convergence with Washington on Afghanistan. The only common ground between the two countries was the U.S. and NATO reliance on Pakistani land routes to transport supplies into Afghanistan and Islamabad's financial dependence on the United States given that the Pakistani economy was under severe strain. And third, more specifically for Pakistan, India's presence had become increasingly pronounced in Afghanistan. This generated concerns in Islamabad that Kabul and New Delhi would get together and undermine its security in Baluchistan and the FATA. With the TTP training its guns against the Pakistani army, Islamabad's security concerns were genuine to a large extent but also a result of its own militarized policymaking.[38] Not surprisingly, Indian assets in Afghanistan, ranging from its embassy in Kabul to its consulates and personnel, came under consistent attacks every year beginning in 2008. With the war becoming a nightmare for the West, bilateral relations between the two countries remained fraught with tensions.

The main point of disagreement between Kabul and Islamabad emerged on the idea of reconciling with the Afghan Taliban. For Pakistan, it was important that it played an important role in the reconciliation process and could set the terms of talks. Having supported the Afghan Taliban, Islamabad wanted to make sure that any future political dispensation in Afghanistan accommodates Pakistan's interests and does not bring up the border issue. In order to maintain its influence over the process, Islamabad arrested

Taliban figures like Mullah Baradar, who had established direct contact with the Kabul government. Given the realities of Afghanistan–Pakistan relations and the fact that most of the Taliban leadership was based out of Pakistan, the coalition members accepted that Islamabad will have to play an important role in facilitating the reconciliation. Interested mostly in managing a smooth transition and withdrawal, it was imperative for both Washington and London to seek Pakistan's cooperation with the reconciliation. For Afghanistan, however, this did not bode well. Kabul was concerned it would not be able to have a truly Afghan-led reconciliation with the Afghan Taliban if Pakistan were to intervene in the process. Karzai, with help from his intelligence chiefs, had been trying to reach out to various Taliban figures clandestinely, but with limited success. Moreover, Pakistan's intervention, from an Afghan perspective, also meant that Kabul would never be able to exercise real autonomy and sovereignty in its relations with its neighbors were it to give into Pakistan's pervasive presence during the talks. Kabul wanted face-to-face talks with the Afghan Taliban without the ISI watching over their backs. New Delhi, for its part, supported Kabul's perspective and criticized the reconciliation as advocated by London.[39]

Nonetheless, reconciliation got institutionalized at the London Conference on Afghanistan in 2010. According to some portrayals, Pakistan was firmly seeking a foothold in Afghanistan and was important for ensuring a peaceful withdrawal of U.S. and NATO forces.[40] However, instead of allowing the process to go forward in the shape and form envisioned during the London Conference, Karzai organized an Afghan Peace Jirga in June 2010 to steal the initiative away from London. By September 2010, he had also engineered the formation of the Afghan High Peace Council (HPC), whose sole aim was to promote reconciliation on Afghan terms, and not those set by Pakistan. Anyone who wanted to give up arms, accept the Afghan constitution, and reintegrate with the Afghan society could do so via the HPC. Ranging from low-level fighters to the higher-ups in the Taliban hierarchy, anyone could have taken this offer up. In fact, according to various Afghan sources, many Taliban fighters and commanders were indeed keen on negotiating directly with Karzai, despite their perception that he was an American "puppet."[41] This, however, could not happen due to Pakistani coercion. Either the ISI would arrest the person who wanted to negotiate with Kabul, or it would keep his family hostage.[42] In the worst-case scenario, his family would be killed.[43] Islamabad, thus, maintained a forward diplomatic and military approach toward Afghanistan between 2007 and 2010. It had made sure that both Kabul and the coalition members did not undermine its domestic and regional interests. As for Kabul, it kept debating how to resolve differences with Islamabad in a scenario where there was no way of expecting any change in Pakistan's interventionist policies. This was all the more so because, by now, Pakistan had started blaming India for fomenting insurgency in Baluchistan and the FATA from Afghanistan.[44]

India's presence in Afghanistan, as mentioned in the previous section, grew rapidly throughout this phase. And the more India made inroads into Afghanistan, the more Pakistan got concerned. Having created a space for its own with its developmental projects and economic assistance, India had space to maneuver its policy and advocacies. In fact, it became a fierce critic of the reconciliation process as envisioned by London and supported by Washington. Every Indian ambassador to Afghanistan, in fact, registered his disagreement over how the reconciliation process was proceeding and supported Karzai's move of instating the HPC in order to facilitate an Afghan-led, Afghan-owned reconciliation process. In fact, according to former Indian foreign secretary and national security advisor Shivshankar Menon:

We never accepted the idea [of reconciliation] the way it was presented by Britain. Never. The idea that reconciliation per se as reconciliation qua reconciliation is good, we never accepted that idea. We have always accepted the idea of reconciliation on certain basic terms i.e. accepting the Afghan constitution, and that they [the Taliban] will have to come back to the mainstream, and that the fighting and the weapons had to stop. Now there is a chicken and egg problem here. The British approach has always been that these are the end results of reconciliation. We have said how can you reconcile with somebody who is still carrying weapons, waging war against a state, does not accept the constitution or the legality of the government, and disenfranchises half the country—all the women—what are you reconciling with here? That's not reconciliation . . . it's capitulation.[45]

Similarly, the former Indian ambassador to Afghanistan Gautam Mukhopadhaya thought that there were two models of reconciliation, the Afghan model and the Western model. While the Afghan model was the one initiated by Karzai and had Mukhopadhaya's support, the Western model remained contentious:

The Western Model has nothing to do with Afghanistan's interests if you ask me. . . . After initially trying [to negotiate] through Tayyab Agha [and that] thing not working out, [the West] . . . finally [said] that Pakistan is essential to Afghanistan. And this argument almost seemed difficult to oppose. But it also meant giving Pakistan a front seat and eventually—

either its proxies or it and both probably—once again a hand in Afghanistan to control things from inside. And that is flawed.[46]

Though India had little impact on how the actual reconciliation took place, it did provide the moral and diplomatic support that Kabul needed when it came under severe attack from Washington and other Western capitals, as well as Pakistan, for not cooperating. In fact, the reconciliation process failed within a couple of years. Burhanuddin Rabbani, the first head of the HPC, was assassinated in September 2011. Kabul blamed the Quetta Shura (indirectly Pakistan) for the assassination but continued the process. By 2013, however, whatever hopes were left for the reconciliation to proceed, be it the Afghan model or the Western model, had faded. Washington had decided to cut its losses and wrap up its mission by the end of 2014 and had initiated an independent dialogue with the Afghan Taliban, incensing both Afghanistan and Pakistan.

DRAWDOWN AND SECURITY DILEMMAS

Seeking a political solution to the war, the Afghan Taliban opened an office in Doha, Qatar, in January 2013.[47] Mostly aimed at the United States and the United Kingdom, the Taliban wanted to gain political legitimacy as the coalition forces withdrew from Afghanistan. A direct line of communication between the coalition members and the Afghan Taliban, however, meant that Pakistan's and Afghanistan's role would become marginal. Nonetheless, this was a model, as Mukhopadhaya noted, that suited the coalition forces. That the Doha process weakened Kabul's hand in dealing with the Afghan Taliban was not lost on Washington. However, with domestic public opinion staunchly against continuation of combat, the United States had decided to go ahead with it. As a result, Karzai, already on bad terms with his Western patrons, who had once installed him to power, canceled all talks with the Afghan Taliban from his side. Adding insult to injury, he even refused to discuss, let alone sign, the Bilateral Security Agreement (BSA) with the United States.[48] The BSA was critical for various reasons. To the United States, it provided a comprehensive political framework for the stationing of troops in Afghanistan after 2014. Additionally, it provided American soldiers with immunity from the Afghan legal system. Karzai's refusal to engage on the BSA was surprising for many, including Pakistan. While some analysts thought that Kabul was undertaking brinkmanship diplomacy, others thought that the question of legacy and what he left Afghanistan with after stepping down directed Karzai's behavior. The reality, however, was that the Afghan government, despite its many successes, did not have the financial, political, and military capacity to run Afghanistan without Western aid. Struggling to pay salaries to its public-sector employees, the Afghan government was facing severe internal problems, which, if left unaddressed, could lead to the breakdown of the state system. Moreover, all other opposition political leaders in Kabul were open to signing the BSA.

As Karzai's relations with Pakistan and the United States deteriorated over the signing of the BSA, he got support from India and China. This was despite New Delhi's and Beijing's conviction that, in the short term, the BSA was critical for maintaining stability and security in Afghanistan. Such support was critical for Karzai given that Pakistan, and even Washington, had started to blame him for being the ultimate "obstacle" to peace and reconciliation in Afghanistan.[49] To aggravate Karzai's political situation further, Islamabad was aggressively opening channels with his opponents, including Abdullah Abdullah, Abdul Rashid Dostum, Ahmad Zia and Ahmad Wali Massoud, Haji Mohammad Mohaqiq, and other mainstream political leaders of Afghanistan. In 2013, Ahmad Wali Massoud described the position of various political factions that formed the UF before 2001, toward Pakistan, as such:

> Pakistan at the moment is lobbying enormously to make friends with all the northerners. Enormously. . . . And we feel that we are in a very vulnerable situation as the international community is leaving and our leaders [Karzai] are not as good. So we accept whatever policy they [Pakistan] have. So they are very active on the contrary [to India], very very active. And you don't hear many voices from those [former UF] leaders about Pakistan. Because they [Pakistan] come not illogically, they come with logic.[50]

If in 2002 Kabul was debating its approach toward Pakistan, and the former UF factions opposed an accommodative approach, by 2014 the tables had turned. Karzai's political opponents, including previous UF faction leaders, were now open to negotiating with Pakistan and accommodating its interests. Though legitimizing this publicly would have been difficult, the political undercurrents in Afghanistan were evolving quickly. Adopting a combative approach toward Pakistan started to lose its sheen in the light of the drawdown. In fact, Islamabad's active diplomacy had almost convinced Karzai's political opponents that negotiating an arrangement with Pakistan was in the best of their interests. There were two reasons for this. First, as Massoud noted, the drawdown of coalition troops had increased existential anxieties among different political factions. If the Afghan Taliban were set to make a reentry into Afghanistan, it was best to keep them away from the northern areas and Kabul. Second, there was another critical sociopolitical reason for these realignments. Most former UF members or non-Pashtun political factions had already secured their political and military bases. There was little to gain from a rivalry with Pakistan. The Pashtunistan issue had little resonance among non-Pashtuns, and recognition of the Durand Line was not necessarily a taboo subject for these groups and communities. However, such was not the case for Pashtun leaders. Not only were the Pashtun-dominated South and East Afghanistan economically poor, but they had also faced the biggest brunt of war. In this context, if negotiating with Pakistan was not an option for Karzai's domestic political posturing among Pashtuns, combating Islamabad was not necessary for factions that had a non-Pashtun regional base.

There were valid reasons for Kabul to debate or reorient its policies toward Pakistan and reduce its links with India. On May 23, 2014, before the results of the Afghan national elections, four heavily armed militants from the LeT attacked the Indian consulate in Herat in West Afghanistan.[51] In the lengthy battle that ensued, the Indo-Tibetan Border Police soldiers guarding the consulate with support from the Afghan security forces killed all assailants. A clear political signal from Pakistan to India, the attack came three days before Narendra Modi, the new PM of India from the Hindu nationalist Bharatiya Janata Party, took oath to office. The latest in a series of attacks on Indian assets in Afghanistan since 2008, the attack captured India's and Pakistan's exacerbating security dilemma in Afghanistan as the coalition forces withdrew. For one, Pakistan's message was straightforward, that is, it was averse to India's growing presence in Afghanistan. An attack on the Indian consulate in Herat also showed that Pakistan had capabilities to undertake covert coercive action all over Afghanistan and not just in the Pashtun-dominated southern and eastern provinces. For India, the choices were becoming increasingly stark. Maintaining a civilian and diplomatic presence in Afghanistan was getting costlier—both in terms of money and lives—and removing personnel would mean compromising national interests. To complicate matters further, New Delhi suspended bilateral talks with Pakistan on Kashmir in August 2014.[52] Soon after, the South Asian rivals exchanged unprecedented artillery and small-arms fire along the Line of Control.[53] In early December 2014, the LeT successfully executed a daring attack on an Indian army garrison in Kashmir in which eleven Indian soldiers were killed.[54] All the while, Afghanistan itself was witnessing a frightful increase in suicide attacks organized by the Haqqani Network.[55]

Emergence of Ashraf Ghani as the president of Afghanistan in September 2014, after many rounds of negotiations in what was considered a highly tainted national election, unraveled Afghanistan's regional and domestic priorities.[56] An economist by training who had spent most of his life in the West, Ghani not only was open to signing the BSA—which he did soon after taking office—but was open to engaging with Pakistan to resolve bilateral differences. His first round of international trips, not surprisingly, were to Saudi Arabia, China, and Pakistan. India, for now, was off his list. In fact, just before visiting Islamabad, reports started pouring in that Ghani had shelved a request for lethal arms from New Delhi that Karzai had made in 2013.[57] Kabul was now openly courting Islamabad with the hope of ensuring stability in Afghanistan. Pakistan, Ghani hoped, would do this by halting support to elements like the Haqqani Network and the Afghan Taliban based on Pakistani soil. In return, Kabul would make sure that Afghan territory is not used by anti-Pakistan elements. Ghani was addressing Pakistan's concerns of Afghanistan being used by India to destabilize Baluchistan. Nonetheless, in reality, Kabul was witnessing a fearful increase in violence as 2014 came to an end. And Pakistan itself saw a steady increase in attacks by the TTP, with the Peshawar school attack being one of the most spectacular and inhuman.

MULLAH OMAR NO MORE: CRISIS OR OPPORTUNITY?

The situation in Afghanistan evolved on four different, but deeply interconnected, axes in 2015. First, domestic Afghan politics stabilized somewhat after the turbulence of the 2014 national elections. Ashraf Ghani, with strong international support—both financial and political—was able to assert his authority in Kabul. Though his predecessor, Hamid Karzai, challenged Ghani's pro-Pakistan approach,[58] their differences were ironed out quickly if not completely.[59] Second, divisions within the Afghan Taliban were getting increasingly acute. Commanders—Mullah Abdul Qayum Zakir and Mullah Akhtar Mansour—and their followers were getting increasingly uncomfortable with each other. Both Zakir and Mansour were old timers in the Afghan Taliban and had been close to Mullah Omar at different points in time. Lately, however, it was Mansour who had been communicating messages of the Amir-ul-Momineen to the latter's followers and to the world. Mansour also had the ear and blessings of the ISI. The Afghan Taliban's Doha office, on the other hand, became increasingly irrelevant. Unabated attacks all over Afghanistan made it clear that the representatives in Qatar had little control over their military counterparts.

Third, bilateral relations between Afghanistan and Pakistan improved considerably in the wake of Ashraf Ghani's experimental and cautious outreach toward Pakistan. With support from the United States and China, a low-key (though not entirely secret) meeting between Afghan officials, select Afghan Taliban figures, and Pakistani officials was held in Urumqi in China on May 19–20.[60] Interestingly, the spy agencies of Afghanistan and Pakistan—considered to be enemies for decades—also signed a Memorandum of Understanding (MoU) on intelligence sharing that shocked many observers within and outside Afghanistan.[61] The success of this experiment, however, depended on Pakistan's willingness and capacity to bring different Afghan Taliban factions to the table, not all of whom were interested in talking. Essentially, Pakistan had to convince not just any Afghan Taliban faction, but had to bring on board those factions that were militarily potent.

And fourth, amid all these developments, a new player was emerging on the geopolitical landscape of South Asia and Afghanistan: the Islamic State of Iraq and Levant (ISIS), also known as Daesh. The presence of ISIS was both a curse and a blessing. Curse, because it would add another layer of security challenge for most South Asian countries, including India. Blessing, because it would offer a platform for Afghanistan and Pakistan—and potentially, despite the odds, even India and Pakistan—against a common enemy. Not surprisingly, in an astute move, Ashraf Ghani began to change the narrative by labeling ISIS as the "biggest threat" to stability and security in Afghanistan and the world.[62] Whether ISIS in the Middle East had any operational linkages with militants in Afghanistan and South Asia, remained unexamined. The situation was evolving on predictable lines on all these axes during the first half of 2015. Then all hell broke loose.

In late July 2015, news leaked out that Mullah Omar, the elusive leader of the Afghan Taliban, had been dead since April 2013. Soon after, the death of Jalaluddin Haqqani also broke out in the news wires. Two stalwarts of the Afghan insurgency, one real and the other mythical, were out of play simultaneously. Occurring soon after the first round of what became known as the "Murree Peace Process," the unceremonious revelation of the deaths of Mullah Omar and Jalaluddin Haqqani disturbed all the four axes mentioned above. Mullah Omar, a myth of great proportions, was also a figure whose existence glued different Afghan Taliban factions together, despite his operational irrelevance. Confirmation of Omar's death made the rifts between Zakir and Mansour factions highly apparent, and more brutal. Clashes between members of the two factions increased as the Zakir faction, with support from Mullah Omar's son Mullah Yacoob, challenged Mansour's rise as the leader of the Afghan Taliban and castigated him for keeping Omar's death a secret for more than two years. In fact, Mansour's elevation with help from the ISI, and the rise of Sirajuddin Haqqani (Jalaluddin's son) as his second-in-command, made him anathema in many Afghan Taliban circles.[63] For the faction led by Mullah Zakir, Mullah Yacoob was the legitimate heir of Mullah Omar, despite the latter's inexistent credentials as a leader. Even Tayyab Agha, the Afghan Taliban representative who had been acting as the spokesperson of the Taliban from Doha, resigned in protest. Such protests, however, failed to make any impact.

Mullah Mansour's and Sirajuddin Haqqani's contested rise made it amply clear that the "Murree Peace Process" was Pakistan-led and Pakistan-owned, and not Afghan-led nor Afghan-owned. Pakistan had been able to convince some Taliban factions—namely those led by Mullah Mansour—to come to the negotiations table (only for a brief while). Rawalpindi would now have to make sure that these factions remained militarily strong but continue to engage in a dialogue. This was a dilemma in itself, since if the Mansour faction was strong militarily and remained confident of defeating the Afghan forces (as they had already demonstrated in many parts of Afghanistan), then why would they talk? However, a senior Pakistani officer, soon after the first round of talks in the Pakistani hill station of Murree, said, "There are people who want to talk and there could be people who would want to fight. But the group that has the largest number of fighters on the ground and is able to make an impact will have the sway. And that is the mainstream group that is holding the talks."[64] The Afghan Taliban—specifically the Mansour faction—had made strenuous efforts to strengthen its territorial control in Afghanistan before coming to the negotiation table in Murree. In fact, by May 2015, the Afghan Taliban had come to dominate a large swath of territories in South, East, and pockets of north Afghanistan. The scenario looked heartbreakingly similar to that of the late 1980s and early 1990s, when the mujahideen and the Afghan communists fought pitched battles to capture big cities. Some of the worst fighting, in fact, took place in and around the city of Kunduz, about 310 miles north of Kabul.[65] However, in contrast to the post-Soviet scenario, this time around the situation on the ground was much more complex. Also, again unlike the post-Soviet scenario, in which Pakistan had had some degree of influence on and limited legitimacy among different mujahideen factions, this time around, Pakistan had very little of either. Despite the illusion of control over the faction led by Mullah Mansour and Sirajuddin Haqqani, Pakistan was unable to deliver what Ashraf Ghani had been seeking desperately—a reduction in violence in Afghanistan. All this happened despite Kabul's targeting of those TTP and ISIS elements—Hafeez Sayeed, Gul Zaman, and Shahidullah Shahid—on Pakistan's request.[66]

On August 10, 2015, a massive bomb blast rocked Kabul, killing scores of people.[67] This blast was one of many that had come to wreak havoc in Afghanistan, but its intensity had shocked most Afghans. The attack showed that if Pakistan was expecting to convert Mullah Omar's death into an opportunity to consolidate its control over the Afghan Taliban and then get them to talk to Kabul, it was failing miserably. Soon after becoming the chief, Mansour made a statement seeking continuation of armed attacks in Afghanistan.[68] The intensity of the blast and the high number of casualties broke the fragile but developing Afghanistan–Pakistan bilateral axis. In a public address, Ashraf Ghani caustically told his neighbors:

> In the middle of the night, at 1:30 a.m., doomsday descended upon our people. It wasn't an earthquake, it wasn't a storm, it was human hand. . . . I ask the people and the government of Pakistan: If a massacre such as the one that occurred in Shah Shaheed had happened in Islamabad and the perpetrators had sanctuaries in Afghanistan, had offices and training centers in our major cities, how would you react?[69]

Was there an implicit threat in Ghani's statement? The answer to this question will become clearer in the coming months or years. What is evident, however, is the failure of the experiment that Ghani undertook—at huge domestic political risk—in engaging with Pakistan without any preconditions. More worryingly, all those militants in Afghanistan who are getting disillusioned with their leadership are finding a credible platform—ISIS— to preach Islam and practice war. The death of Mullah Omar, critically, liberated the situation from hard questions over operational linkages between the actual ISIS and militants in Afghanistan and Pakistan.

What was India doing all this time? With its own bilateral relations with Pakistan spiraling downwards, India maintained a studious silence on the Afghanistan issue. Despite having supported Ashraf Ghani's government, New Delhi remained skeptical at best of his outreach to Pakistan. While no official denunciation was made, senior officials in the Ministry of External Affairs and the Prime Minister's Office made their reservations clear in unofficial channels. "We would like a strong, sovereign, and stable Afghanistan that does not bow down to external blackmail. If Kabul wants to achieve this by engaging with Pakistan, then so be it. Despite our reservations about this process, we cannot interfere in Afghanistan's domestic affairs," said a serving Indian official.[70] According to many analysts, India had effectively been sidelined as the Afghanistan–Pakistan dialogue took momentum with support from international powers including China, Russia, and the United States.[71] With the international community encouraging talks, India's criticism that the process was not "Afghan-led and Afghan-owned" lost its impact. On the contrary, Pakistan succeeded in keeping India at bay as New Delhi meekly watched from the margins. Though correct, this analysis describes only part of the full picture.

India did not want to be a part of this Afghanistan–Pakistan peace process from the very beginning. Despite its silence, New Delhi was far from being a mute spectator in Afghanistan. On the contrary, it had been consolidating its relations with those political factions within Afghanistan who had doubted this process from the start, such as Hamid Karzai, as well as those Afghan Taliban figures who had been left out in the cold. While some officials in New Delhi genuinely wanted a dialogue between Kabul and Islamabad (or Rawalpindi), there were others who had been waiting for the precise moment when Pakistan would take the lead in the talks, and then fail. According to retired Indian intelligence officials, ISI will not be able to control or manipulate all factions of the Taliban, whereas India has the wisdom to wait and exploit.[72] As mentioned earlier in this chapter, India did not believe in a process where the terms of talks were not set at the beginning—an approach British officials had abided by religiously. Abiding by such a process—in which one party had expressly sought India's disappearance from the Afghan landscape—was unacceptable to New Delhi. The Indian approach toward Afghanistan was best articulated by one of its top strategic analysts, C. Raja Mohan, a week before the Kabul bombing:

> The Pakistan army may not have either the material resources or the political vision to construct an inclusive and durable state structure in Kabul. The gap between Pakistan's strategic ambition in Afghanistan and its national capability might inevitably set the stage for the next round of blood-letting on India's northwestern frontiers.[73]

CONCLUSION

Many South Asia analysts predicted a less than promising security scenario for South Asia and Afghanistan in 2011. In 2015, unfortunately, this prognosis stands vindicated. As the West wraps up its military presence in Afghanistan, a fresh chapter of conflict and violence is opening up between Afghanistan and Pakistan. Even India and Pakistan remain at odds, with border clashes on the rise. Two questions emerge from these recent historical trends: First, will Pakistan, despite its current inability to deliver on the peace process, cooperate with a politically and economically weak Kabul in the coming years? A fierce debate rages on this question. For some, Pakistan's policy of interference in Afghanistan's domestic affairs will not change regardless of Kabul's offers. If Pakistan did not give up support to militant groups while the West was militarily engaged in the region, why will it do so now? With its core interests remaining the same—to legitimize the Durand Line as an international border and have a friendly government in Kabul that maintains distance from New Delhi—there is little scope for an overhaul in Pakistan's strategic calculus vis-à-vis Afghanistan. The Pakistani security establishment's support to the Haqqani Network and its role in resuscitating the Taliban insurgency in Afghanistan since 2003 are considered definite markers of Pakistan's intent in Afghanistan. Adding potency to this argument is Pakistan's skillful management of its Afghanistan policy despite being under tremendous pressure from the West to tame or attack the Taliban. The costs of targeting militants that Pakistan had created in the first place (to target India and Afghanistan) are too high (more so than burning bridges with Washington). Making enemies with all these radical elements, which have their own ideological and organizational complexities and dynamism, is beyond the capacity or intent of the Pakistani military. As a result, Pakistan targets only those militants that it sees as a direct threat to the Pakistani establishment. These included some select factions of the TTP. Nonetheless, the counterargument is of a paradigm shift in the Pakistani military's threat perception. On June 15, 2014, Pakistan launched Operation Zarb-e-Azb in North Waziristan against the TTP, and other militant factions operating from the FATA region, including the Lashkar-e-Jhangvi, the East Turkestan Islamic Movement, Jundullah, Al Qaeda, the Islamist Movement of Uzbekistan, and the Haqqani Network.[74] For the short term at least, Pakistan did not see India as its main threat. Its focus shifted to internal instead of external threats, as the operation advanced. On the basis of these facts, the argument runs that Pakistan may be forced to reconsider its strategy vis-à-vis Afghanistan and India and reduce its support for nonstate militant actors. Such limiting of support for elements whom the Pakistan's security establishment has traditionally considered its "strategic assets" is yet to be seen. As relations with India deteriorate, the logic of not retaining armed proxies does not hold strategic rationale. But this also depends on how India conducts itself in Afghanistan and with Pakistan.

India's policy toward Afghanistan and Pakistan has evolved rapidly since 2011. Despite having signed the Strategic Partnership Agreement (SPA) with the Karzai government in 2011, India remained reluctant in providing lethal weaponry to Kabul when requested. According to analysts, New Delhi's reluctance on this front was primarily to address Pakistan's anxieties of Indian influence in Afghanistan.[75] There were, however, tactical issues of India's limited defense capacities and Kabul's ever-changing list of weapons requirements that further delayed this process. Moreover, the structural dynamics of the region and Kabul's defense requirements have not changed significantly. Thus, Ghani's shelving of this request may just be a tactical diplomatic move to assess how Pakistan responds to it. Nonetheless, India's marginalization in Afghan political affairs after Karzai's departure is apparent. Ghani's overtures to Pakistan and primacy to China made sure that India was not at the top of Kabul's agenda in the winter of 2014. The arrival of Modi in New Delhi with a decisive democratic mandate did little to convince Kabul of maintaining a pro-India posture. Also, India continues to pursue a wait-and-watch approach; the debate of whether to expand or contract its strategic presence in Afghanistan is far from resolved in New Delhi. Although it is bound under the SPA to support the Kabul government, the costs of doing so may be exorbitant if Pakistan decides to up the ante of attacks against Indian assets in Afghanistan. Will India respond with force or by maintaining a low profile? Only time will tell. Though New Delhi would like to build on its positive relations with Kabul and, at least, maintain its current levels of presence in Afghanistan, a lot will depend on Pakistan's actions, the West's commitment to stay the course till 2024, and Kabul's handling of its internal political differences.

The second question is, how will Afghanistan deal with Pakistan now that its diplomatic courting of the Pakistani military and Islamabad seems to be failing? According to recent reports, Kabul seems to have found a solution to this question. Rather than debating whether to accommodate Pakistani demands or to adopt a combative stance, Kabul is doing both simultaneously. As discussed at the beginning of this chapter, if President Ghani was engaging Islamabad diplomatically and sidelining India publicly, his chief of intelligence, Rahmatullah Nabil was building capacities, not so covertly, to strengthen his diplomatic hand vis-à-vis Islamabad. Case in point was his cultivation of Latif Mehsud, number two in the TTP hierarchy, as a source and potentially a proxy.[76] When the Americans discovered Nabil's links with Latif Mehsud, they promptly intervened and handed him over to Pakistan in late 2013, infuriating Kabul. Instead of denying his role, Nabil told Washington that "just like any other intelligence agency, we have the right to have sources."[77] He added, "I think it is very important just to be very frank."[78] He wanted to show Pakistan that Kabul can do exactly the same things on Pakistani soil (i.e., intervene using proxies) that Islamabad has fostered in Afghanistan. Whether Kabul will be able to develop a credible deterrence at an asymmetric level in its dealings with Pakistan still needs to be seen. Given the financial strains of the Ghani government and internal political fissures in Kabul, developing a coherent strategic thought vis-à-vis the neighborhood will be challenging. What is amply clear, however, is that though the West's war in Afghanistan ended in December 2014, there seems to be no endgame in sight for either Pakistan or India in Afghanistan.

NOTES

1. Sophia Saifi and Greg Botelho, "In Pakistan School Attack, Taliban Terrorists Kill 145, Mostly Children," CNN, December 17, 2014, http://edition.cnn.com/2014/12 /16/world/asia/pakistan-peshawar-school-attack/.
2. "Pakistan to Use Army Courts for Terror Cases," Al Jazeera, December 20, 2014, www.aljazeera.com/news/asia/2014/12/pakistan-military-courts-terrorism -20141224215542372724.html.
3. Ismael Khan and Azam Ahmed, "Pakistan Urges Afghans to Help Find Taliban Leaders Behind Massacre," New York Times, December 17, 2014, www.nytimes .com/2014/12/18/world/asia/pakistan-premier-lifts-death-penalty-moratorium -following-school-massacre.html?_r=1.
4. Mateen Haider, "Gen Raheel Visits Kabul, Seeks Handover of Mullah Fazlullah," Dawn, December 17, 2014, www.dawn.com/news/1151412.
5. Matthew Rosenberg, "Afghan Spy Chief Defies Labels, Usefully," New York Times, January 16, 2015, www.nytimes.com/2015/01/17/world/asia/afghan-spy-chief-defies -simple-label.html?_r=0.
6. Jon Boone, "Ashraf Ghani Visit May Mark New Chapter in Afghan-Pakistan Relations," Guardian, November 14, 2014, www.theguardian.com/world/2014/nov /14/ashraf-ghani-visit-pakistan-afghanistan.
7. Bilal Sarwary, "Mullah Omar Dead: Afghan Taliban Struggles to Maintain Unity in the Wake of Leader's Death—as Exclusively Seen Letters Clearly Reveal," The Independent, July 31, 2015, http://www.independent.co.uk/news/world/middle -east/mullah-omar-dead-afghan-taliban-struggles-to-maintain-unity-in-the -wake-of-leaders-death—as-exclusively-seen-letters-apparently-reveal-10428847 .html.
8. "Afghan Militant Leader Jalaluddin Haqqani 'has died,'" BBC News, July 31, 2015, http://www.bbc.co.uk/news/world-asia-33740337.
9. Pamela Constable, "Angry Afghan Leader Assails Pakistan as Haven for Deadly Taliban Attacks," Washington Post, August 10, 2015, https://www.washingtonpost .com/world/car-bomb-strikes-near-kabul-airport-amid-wave-of-taliban -violence/2015/08/10/78106f28-3f4b-11e5-8d45-d815146f81fa_story.html.

10. Amin Saikal, *Modern Afghanistan: A History of Struggle and Survival* (New York: I. B. Taurus, 2012).

11. Article V, Treaty of Rawalpindi, August 8, 1919.

12. Rajmohan Gandhi, *Ghaffar Khan: Non-Violent Badshah of the Pakhtuns* (London: Penguin, 2008).

13. Letter from Sir O. Caroe (NWFP) to Field Marshall Viscount Wavell (Governor's camp, Parachinar), October 23, 1946, in *The Transfer of Power, 1942–47,* vol. 8, *The Interim Government,* Foreign and Commonwealth Office, Great Britain.

14. Mukulika Banerjee, *The Pathan Unarmed* (Santa Fe: School of American Research Press, 2000), 189.

15. Daveed Gartenstein and Tara Vassefi, "The Forgotten History of Afghanistan-Pakistan Relations," *Yale Journal of International Affairs* 7, no. 1 (March 2012): 38–45.

16. George L. Montagno, "The Pak-Afghan Détente," *Asian Survey* 3, no. 12 (December 1963): 616–624.

17. Daoud as Prime Minister, 1953–1963, U.S. Library of Congress, http://countrystudies.us/afghanistan/26.htm

18. Ibid.

19. Author's interview with Lalit Mansingh, former foreign secretary of India (1999–2001), New Delhi, January 25, 2013.

20. G. Rauf Roashan, "The Unholy Durand Line, Buffering the Buffer," Institute for Afghan Studies, August 11, 2001, www.institute-for-afghan-studies.org/Contributions/Commentaries/DRRoashanArch/2001_08_11_unholy_durand_line.htm.

21. Khalid Nadiri, "Old Habits, New Consequences: Pakistan's Posture Towards Afghanistan Since 2001," *International Security* 39, no. 2 (2014): 133.

22. Saikal, *Modern Afghanistan.*

23. For details on strategic depth, see Christine Fair, *Fighting to the End: Pakistan Army's Way of War* (New York: Oxford University Press, 2014).

24. For more on the IC 814 hijacking, see Neelesh Mishra, *173 Hours in Captivity: The Hijacking of IC 814* (New Delhi: HarperCollins, 2000).

25. Steve Coll, *Ghost Wars: The Secret History of the CIA, Afghanistan, and Bin Laden from Soviet Invasion to September 10, 2001* (London: Penguin, 2005).

26. Cited in Ahmed Rashid, *Descent Into Chaos: The World's Most Unstable Region and the Threat to Global Security* (London: Penguin, 2009), 32–33.

27. Satinder K. Lambah, "Graveyard of Empires, Crucible of Coalitions," *Outlook,* December 26, 2011, www.outlookindia.com/article.aspx?279342.

28. William Maley, *The Afghanistan Wars* (New York: Palgrave Macmillan, 2009), 288.

29. For details on the 2001 Bonn Conference, see Mark Fields and Ramsha Ahmed, *A Review of the 2001 Bonn Conference: An Application to the Road Ahead in Afghanistan* (Washington, D.C.: National Defense University, 2011), www.fes-asia.org/media/Peace%20and%20Security/Untitled_attachment_00031.pdf.

30. "Jaish Behind Attempt to Kill Musharraf," *Daily Times,* January 1, 2004, http://archives.dailytimes.com.pk/national/01-Jan-2004/jaish-behind-attempt-to-kill-musharraf.

31. See Antonio Giustozzi, *Koran, Kalashnikov, and Laptop: The Neo-Taliban Insurgency in Afghanistan* (New York: Columbia University Press, 2009); and Sami

Yousafzai, "The Taliban's Oral History of the Afghanistan War," *Newsweek*, September 26, 2009, www.newsweek.com/talibans-oral-history-afghanistan-war-79553.

32. Selig S. Harrison, "The Fault Line Between Pashtuns and Punjabis in Pakistan," *Washington Post*, May 11, 2009, www.washingtonpost.com/wp-dyn/content /article/2009/05/10/AR2009051001959.html.

33. Author's interview with Satinder Lambah, former prime minister's special envoy to Afghanistan, New Delhi, March 26, 2013.

34. Ministry of External Affairs, Government of India, *India and Afghanistan: A Development Partnership*, January 1, 2009, http://mea.gov.in/Uploads/PublicationDocs /176_india-and-afghanistan-a-development-partnership.pdf.

35. Ibid.

36. For details on the number of attacks and deaths in the Afghanistan over the years, see Susan G. Chesser, *Afghanistan Casualties: Military Forces and Civilians*, Congressional Research Service, December 6, 2012, www.fas.org/sgp/crs /natsec/R41084.pdf.

37. Richard Norton-Taylor, "UK Pressing Karzai to Negotiate with the Taliban, Says Leaked Memo," *Guardian*, November 13, 2009, www.theguardian.com/politics /2009/nov/13/uk-karzai-negotiate-taliban.

38. Nadiri, "Old Habits."

39. Author's interview with Gautam Mukhopadhaya, former Indian ambassador to Afghanistan (2010–2013), Kabul, April 11, 2013.

40. Jane Perlez, Eric Schmitt, and Carlotta Gall, "Pakistan Is Said to Pursue Foothold in Afghanistan," *New York Times*, June 24, 2010, www.nytimes.com/2010/06/25 /world/asia/25islamabad.html?pagewanted=all.

41. Author's interview with an Afghan official, A., who wanted his/her identity to remain undisclosed, 2013.

42. Ibid.

43. Ibid.

44. "India Using Afghan Soil to Carry out Attacks on Pakistan: Sartaj Aziz," *Times of India*, January 12, 2015, http://timesofindia.indiatimes.com/world/pakistan /India-using-Afghan-soil-to-carry-out-attacks-on-Pakistan-Sartaj-Aziz/article show/45852506.cms.

45. Author's interview with Shivshankar Menon, former national security advisor (2010–2014) and foreign secretary (2006–2010) of India, London, November 24, 2014.

46. Mukhopadhaya interview.

47. "Afghan Taliban Opens Qatar Office, Says Seeks Political Solution," *Reuters*, June 18, 2013, www.reuters.com/article/2013/06/18/us-afghanistan-taliban-opening -idUSBRE95H0NU20130618.

48. "As Taliban Opens New Office in Doha, Hamid Karzai Calls off Talks with U.S. on Security Agreement," *Reuters/IBNlive*, June 20, 2013, http://ibnlive.in.com /news/as-taliban-opens-new-office-in-doha-hamid-karzai-calls-off-talks-with -us-on-security-agreement/400232-2.html.

49. Mehreen Zahra-Malik, "Pakistan Sees Afghanistan's Karzai as Obstacle to Peace with Taliban," *Reuters*, March 24, 2013, www.reuters.com/article/2013/03/24/us -pakistan-afghanistan-idUSBRE92N0KJ20130324.

50. Author's interview with Ahmad Wali Massoud, younger brother of Ahmad Shah Massoud, now leading the Hizb-e Nahzat-e Melli-ye Afghanistan (or National Movement of Afghanistan), Kabul, April 29, 2013.

51. The LeT is an avowedly anti-India Islamist outfit and a "strategic asset" of the Pakistani ISI. See "LeT Responsible for Attack at Indian Consulate in Herat: U.S.," *Hindu*, June 26, 2014, www.thehindu.com/news/international/world/let-responsible -for-attack-at-indian-consulate-in-herat-us/article6151009.ece.

52. Maneesh Rahman and Jon Boone, "India Calls off Pakistan Talks After Envoy Invites Kashmiri Separatists to Tea," *Guardian*, August 18, 2014, www.theguardian .com/world/2014/aug/18/india-pakistan-talks-off-kashmir.

53. Deeptiman Tiwari, "India's Tough Posture on the Border Has Been in Place Since June," *Times of India*, October 9, 2014, http://timesofindia.indiatimes.com/india /Indias-tough-posture-on-border-has-been-in-place-since-June/articleshow /44733824.cms.

54. "Enough Evidence to Show LeT, Pakistan Hand in Uri Attack: Army," *Indian Express*, December 8, 2014, http://indianexpress.com/article/india/india-others /enough-evidence-to-show-let-pak-hand-in-uri-attack-army/.

55. Rod Nordland, "Taliban Press Attacks Against Afghan Targets," *New York Times*, November 28, 2014, www.nytimes.com/2014/11/29/world/asia/taliban-attacks -increase-in-afghanistan.html?_r=0.

56. The two sides—one represented by Ashraf Ghani and the other by Abdullah Abdullah—could not reach a settlement for months after the second round in June 2014. Differences between factions only grew after a deal was struck that Ghani would be the president and Abdullah the chief executive officer under the National Unity government.

57. Praveen Swami, "Upset with Delay, Kabul Shelves Request for Arms from Delhi," *Indian Express*, October 30, 2014, http://indianexpress.com/article/india/india -others/upset-with-delay-kabul-shelves-request-for-arms-aid-from-delhi/.

58. Jon Boone, "Hamid Karzai: Afghanistan in Danger of Sliding 'Under Thumb' of Pakistan," *Guardian*, March 9, 2015, http://www.theguardian.com/world/2015 /mar/09/hamid-karzai-if-we-give-up-control-of-our-foreign-policy-pakistan -taliban-ashraf-ghani-india.

59. Mirwais Adeel, "Ghani and Karzai Meets to Resolve Differences, Mainly on NDS-ISI MoU," *Khaama Press*, July 15, 2015, http://www.khaama.com/ghani-and-karzai -meets-to-resolve-differences-mainly-on-nds-isi-mou-1288.

60. Petr Topychkanov, "Secret Meeting Brings Taliban to China," originally published in Russia and India Report, Carnegie Endowment for International Peace, May 28, 2015, http://carnegieendowment.org/2015/05/28/secret-meeting-brings -taliban-to-china/i95e.

61. Rezaul H. Laskar, "Pak's ISI, Afghan Spy Agency NDS Signs MoU on Intelligence Sharing," *Hindustan Times*, May 19, 2015, http://www.hindustantimes.com/world -news/pakistan-s-isi-afghan-spy-agency-nds-sign-mou-afghan-mps-slam-pact /article1-1348631.aspx.

62. Eric Bradner, "Afghan President: 'Terrorists Neither Recognize Boundaries nor Require Passports," CNN News, March 25, 2015, http://edition.cnn.com/2015/03 /25/politics/afghanistan-ghani-congress-speech/.

63. Shereena Qazi, "Taliban Leaders Dispute Appointment of Mullah Mansour," *Al Jazeera*, August 04, 2015, http://www.aljazeera.com/news/2015/07/taliban-leaders -dispute-appointment-mullah-mansoor-150731151533576.html.

64. Quoted in Ismail Khan, "Afghan Govt, Taliban Resume Peace Talks in Murree on Friday," *Dawn News*, July 29, 2015, http://www.dawn.com/news/1197087.

65. Harriet Alexander, "Afghan Troops Fight Taliban to Hold on to Key City," *Telegraph*, May 7, 2015, http://www.telegraph.co.uk/news/worldnews/asia/afghanistan /11589620/Afghan-troops-fight-Taliban-to-hold-on-to-key-city.html.

66. Ismail Khan, "ISIS Leaders Reported Killed in Drone Strikes in Afghanistan," *New York Times*, July 9, 2015, http://www.nytimes.com/2015/07/10/world/asia/us-drone -strike-said-to-kill-gul-zaman-and-shahidullah-shahid-of-islamic-state.html.

67. "Afghanistan: Taliban Suicide Bomb Attack near Kabul," *BBC News*, August 10, 2015, http://www.bbc.co.uk/news/world-asia-33845326.

68. Jibran Ahmed, "Taliban Leadership Struggle Fuels Wave of Attacks in Afghanistan," *Reuters*, August 12, 2015, http://www.dailymail.co.uk/wires/reuters/article -3195106/Taliban-leadership-struggle-fuels-wave-attacks-Afghanistan.html.

69. Mujib Mashal, "After Kabul Attack, Afghan Leader Points Finger at Pakistan for Failing to Stop Taliban," *New York Times*, August 10, 2015, http://mobile.nytimes .com/2015/08/11/world/asia/suicide-car-bombing-kabul-airport.html.

70. Author's interview with senior Indian official, who wanted his/her identity undisclosed, New Delhi, January 2015.

71. Kabir Taneja, "China, Pak Court Taliban on Afghan Talks, India Sidelined," *Sunday Guardian*, March 21, 2015, http://www.sunday-guardian.com/investigation/china -pak-court-taliban-on-afghan-talks-india-sidelined.

72. Based on the author's discussions with a series of former and serving Indian intelligence officials in 2015, none of whom wanted to be identified.

73. Raja Mohan, "Raja-Mandala: After Mullah Omar," *Indian Express*, August 4, 2015, http://indianexpress.com/article/opinion/columns/after-mullah-omar/.

74. There is ambiguity on whether Pakistan targeted the Haqqani Network. According to many authoritative sources, it did not target the Haqqanis. See "U.S. Commander Commends Zarb-e-Azb for Disrupting Haqqani Network's Ability to Target Afghanistan," *Express Tribune*, November 6, 2014, http://tribune.com.pk /story/786641/us-commander-commends-zarb-e-azb-for-disrupting-haqqani -networks-ability-to-target-afghanistan/.

75. Sandra Destradi, "India: A Reluctant Partner for Afghanistan," *Washington Quarterly*, June 1, 2014, http://twq.elliott.gwu.edu/india-reluctant-partner-afghanistan.

76. Matthew Rosenberg, "Afghan Spy Chief Defies Labels, Usefully," *New York Times*, January 16, 2015, www.nytimes.com/2015/01/17/world/asia/afghan-spy-chief-defies -simple-label.html?_r=0.

77. Ibid.

78. Ibid.

CHAPTER 8

U.S.–PAKISTAN RELATIONS UNDER OBAMA

RESILIENCE OF CLIENTELISM?

Christophe Jaffrelot

It is the start of something new. Our countries have had our misunderstandings and disagreements in the past and there are sure to be more disagreements in the future, as there are between any friends or, frankly, any family members.

HILLARY CLINTON, 2010

We acknowledge to ourselves privately that Pakistan is a client state of the U.S. But on the other hand, the U.S. is acting against Muslim interests globally. A sort of self-loathing came out.

PERVEZ HOODBHOY, 2010

The U.S.–Pakistan relations that have developed with ups and downs over the last six and an half decades can probably be best characterized as a security- (or military-) related form of clientelism.[1] French political scientist Jean-François Médard defines clientelism as "a relationship of dependence . . . based on a reciprocal exchange of favours between two people, the patron and the client, whose control of resources are unequal."[2] A clientelistic relationship does not imply any ideological sympathy but is purely instrumental.[3] Despite the mutual dependence it establishes, its asymmetric nature gives the patron a clear advantage—up to a point. The patron is in a position to get things done by the client, the client paying allegiance to the patron in exchange for benefits, including protection.[4]

During the Cold War and the anti-Soviet war in Afghanistan, Pakistan played the role of client state of the United States: in exchange for considerable civil and military aid, the country participated in the containment of communists in Asia. But already at the time the terms of the countries' cooperation were clearly circumscribed from two standpoints: first, Pakistan—as a sovereign state—wanted to maintain substantial room for maneuver; and second, each time the United States demonstrated too close an alliance with India, the Land of the Pure behaved less as Uncle Sam's obedient intermediary than as a pivotal state using its geopolitical position to further its national interests by partnering with other powers. The second war in Afghanistan, which began after the September 11, 2001, attacks, although at first it looked like it would repeat the scenario played out in the combat against the Soviets, in fact marked a turning point. Barack Obama's policy on Pakistan, the focus of this chapter, far from bringing the two countries closer together again after they had drifted apart toward the end of the Bush years, has not been able to fully defuse bilateral tensions.

A CYCLICAL CLIENTELISTIC RELATIONSHIP

The U.S.–Pakistan relations that crystallized in the 1950s were not based on deep political, economic, or societal affinities and ties: Pakistan has been governed by the army more often than not, something Washington at times found embarrassing; there were no intense economic relations between both countries, nor were there any person-to-person relations, partly because the Pakistani diaspora in the United States was very small and not very well integrated.

Geopolitical considerations and strategic mutual interests were the main reasons the United States and Pakistan became "friends." As early as 1947, Karachi (the then capital of the country) asked the United States for support in order to cope with the so-called Indian threat. In December, Pakistan asked the United States for a $2 billion five-year loan for economic development and security purposes.[5] President Truman, who was as yet unsure whether the United States should get closer to India or Pakistan, committed to a much smaller amount—$10 million—and invited Nehru to Washington. Liaquat Ali Khan immediately announced that he would pay a visit to Moscow shortly thereafter. Truman invited him to the United States as well. Nehru's visit to the United States in October 1949 was not a success from Washington's point of view, given the Indian prime minister's rejection of the polarization of world politics along two blocs. Liaquat Ali Khan—who did not go to Moscow—visited Washington in May 1950. He solicited the United States on two related fronts: arms procurements and $510 million in aid for development and military purposes. Truman remained noncommittal.

Things changed soon afterward in the context of the deepening of the Cold War and the hot episode of the Korean War—which started one month after Khan's visit—and definitely after Eisenhower took over power in Washington in 1953. The United States then decided to use Pakistan to counter Soviet expansion in the region. Karachi was prepared to play this new version of the "Great Game" so long as this strategy was useful against its archenemy, India.[6]

On the one hand, Pakistan joined both the Central Treaty Organization and the Southeast Asia Treaty Organization and in 1957 gave the Americans access to an air base from which U2s could spy on the USSR.[7] On the other hand, the United States was prepared to give Pakistan very substantial aid and to sell the country millions of dollars in arms so that it would be better equipped than India. Pakistan became a client state as much from a developmental point of view as from a security perspective. Only 25 percent of the nearly $2 billion it received in American assistance between 1953 and 1961 was in military aid.[8] As Akbar Zaidi points out: "By 1964, overall aid and assistance to Pakistan was around 5% of its GDP and was arguably critical in spurring Pakistani industrialization and development, with GDP growth rates rising to as much as 7 percent per annum."[9] At that time, few countries were supported by the United States to such an extent.[10]

However, the security dimension of this relationship largely explains why military coups have never presented a problem for the world's oldest democracy. In fact, to have generals at the helm made things easier for the United States in the 1950s, as evident from the personal equation between Eisenhower—an ex-army man himself—and Ayub Khan, who described Pakistan as the United States' "most allied ally."[11]

INTEREST-BASED AND (THEREFORE) UNSTABLE
U.S.–PAK RELATIONS

A BONE OF CONTENTION, INDIA; AND A NEWCOMER ON STAGE, CHINA

U.S.–Pakistan relations were clearly built on a quid pro quo that both countries decided to cultivate. Whereas the United States relied on Pakistan against the USSR—and, increasingly, China—not worrying about the lack of amity with India,[12] Pakistan looked to America for help against India and was not averse to aligning against the USSR as well as against China until the Sino-Soviet split.

But the fact that both countries did not have exactly the same enemies made their relations inevitably complicated. A bone of contention that was bound to recur was the nature of relations between the United States and India—that country overdetermining Pakistan's worldview. In the early 1960s, President John Kennedy came to office "determined to pursue closer relations between the U.S. and India, a country he viewed as pivotal in the struggle between East and West, without undermining the alliance between the U.S. and Pakistan."[13] He approved a two-year commitment of up to $1 billion in support of India's economic development in 1961,[14] which complicated U.S.–Pakistan relations—all the more so as the U.S.-led consortium that was supposed to mobilize resources in favor of this country could not raise much money. Although in 1961, the United States delivered twelve F-104 jet fighters to Pakistan in the framework of an agreement signed the year before, one year after, Washington sold arms to India during the 1962 war initiated by China.

That was an important episode for the U.S.–Pakistan relations. When Nehru turned to Kennedy for help after the Chinese attack, the prompt, positive response he received was all the more disturbing for Pakistan as Islamabad was not informed in advance of the latter's decision to provide arms to the former (something that allegedly contravened a secret bilateral deal signed in 1959). Considering that America pursued a policy "based on opportunism and . . . devoid of morality,"[15] Ayub Khan (and his new foreign minister, Zulfiqar Ali Bhutto) turned more decisively to China—a clear indication of the need for a patron that Pakistan always felt was necessary to cope with India and of both the importance of the Indian factor and the interaction between U.S.–Pakistan relations on the one hand and Pakistan–China relations on the other. In 1964, Ayub Khan invited Chou En Lai to Pakistan, a visit that was to be followed by many others. Playing the game of a pivotal state, Ayub Khan declared in 1965 that he now knew "how to live peacefully among the lions by setting one lion against another."[16]

And 1965 also marked the next step in the souring of relations between Washington and Islamabad, as the United States did not intervene on Pakistan's side in the war with India and—even worse—cut off aid to both sides (which hurt Pakistan more than India). Afterward, the United States kept aid shut off until Nixon made a "one-time exception" to supply arms in 1969.

However, the U.S.–Pakistan partnership experienced a tactical renaissance because of its very clientelistic quality. In the early 1970s, Islamabad became a key intermediary between Washington and Beijing when Nixon and Kissinger wanted to make an overture to the Chinese. Nixon, in exchange, resisted the U.S. Congress condemnation of the savage repression of the Bangladeshi movement—and the correlative demand for the suspension of American aid.

But the Indian factor resurfaced soon after. First, the United States did not help Pakistan during its war against India, which resulted in the traumatic birth of Bangladesh, except by sending the aircraft carrier the U.S.S. *Enterprise* to the Bay of Bengal. Second, Jimmy Carter—a Democratic president like Kennedy—not only was particularly concerned by Pakistan's nuclear program (as evident from the sanctions he imposed on the country in accordance with the Glenn and Symington amendments), but he promoted a new—short-lived—U.S.–India rapprochement that was perceived by many Pakistani leaders as directed against them. Indeed, in January 1978, Carter was the first American president not to visit Pakistan before or after a visit to India, a decision naturally related to his boycotting of the new master of Pakistan, General Zia, who had deposed Bhutto the year before. In 1979, Carter suspended American aid as a response to what the United States considered Pakistan's covert construction of a uranium enrichment facility.

FROM AFGHANISTAN TO AFGHANISTAN

President Carter discarded most of his reservations vis-à-vis Pakistan the moment the Soviets invaded Afghanistan. Pakistan was immediately selected as the frontline state that the United States would use in the old military-clientelistic perspective. Carter suggested that the 1959 security agreement that was the brainchild of Eisenhower and Ayub Khan should be reactivated, and he cleared the sale of military aircraft to Pakistan.

While Carter's initiative remained limited, his successor, Ronald Reagan, considerably amplified this change. Not only did he not object to the development of Pakistan's nuclear program as much he could have done despite the Pressler amendment,[17] but the United States gave Pakistan about $4 billion in 1981–1986 (half for military purposes and half for civilian purposes) and sold sophisticated weapons to its military. In 1987, Reagan and Zia negotiated another new six-year aid budget of $4 billion, in which 43 percent of the expenditures were to be security related, mostly earmarked for the Pakistani army. Reagan's successor, George Bush Sr., routinized this security-centered clientelistic relationship.

The war against the Soviets, however, gave a new flavor to the old clientelistic equation. When the United States subcontracted the war to Pakistan, the Inter-Services Intelligence (ISI) was given a great deal of autonomy to select which groups of mujahideen were to fight in Afghanistan. Shaping the jihad, the ISI channeled the aid flows to the groups it favored, and in fact the Central Intelligence Agency (CIA) was asked to help these groups in such a way that the patron lost some of its authority.

A security-oriented clientelistic relationship is neither value based nor rooted in economic ties or in societal affinities and is therefore less stable. U.S. attention and "interest" in Pakistan rose recurrently in times of crisis when Pakistan could help the United States combat the USSR. But it was bound to sink below the active-engagement level each time diplomacy-by-the-rule-book took over, relegating Pakistan to an unimportant position again, as attested by the less-than-first-rank diplomats posted there as well as the studied inattention it received after the Soviets were defeated in Afghanistan.

In the late 1980s, after the Soviet withdrawal from Afghanistan, the United States lost interest in Pakistan—or more exactly, the interest that Pakistan represented for the United States diminished and considerations based on values and other interests filled this vacuum. The nuclear prolif-eration issue suddenly gained new prominence, resulting in some Ameri-can sanctions:[18] $300 million in aid was cut and the United States announced that the F-16s that Pakistan had already paid for in 1989 would not be delivered—but Pakistan was allowed to buy other material at market price (Islamabad disbursed $120 million for military equipment in 1991–1992).[19]

Bill Clinton maintained this line of conduct in the mid-1990s, softening the sanctions in two different ways. First, civil aid reached $2 billion in 1995. Second, in 1996, $368 million worth of military equipment, the delivery of which had been frozen by virtue of the Pressler amendment, was shipped to Pakistan, and $120 million was refunded for prepaid material that the United States refused to sell. If U.S.–Pakistan relations remained on a (rather low) plateau until the late 1990s, the Pakistani 1998 nuclear tests (like the Indian ones) resulted in new sanctions. A few months later, the Al Qaeda attacks on the U.S. embassies of Dar Es Salaam and Nairobi led to more ac-rimony, all the more so as the missiles that the American fleet in the Indian Ocean fired on Al Qaeda camps in Afghanistan killed militants among whom were Pakistanis. The following year, the Clinton administration attributed the Kargil war in Jammu and Kashmir to Pakistani military adventurism. On July 4, Prime Minister Nawaz Sharif went to the White House, where he was requested to order "his" generals to withdraw behind the Line of Con-trol. Only months afterward, as a sequel to this fiasco, Chief of Army Staff General Musharraf orchestrated a military coup, which persuaded the

United States to impose additional sanctions on Pakistan. The U.S. attitude was all the more resented in Islamabad as Washington at the same time was forming closer ties with New Delhi. In March 2000, this divergence was caricatured in the contrast between the Clintons' festive five-day visit to India and Bill Clinton's five-hour stopover in Islamabad—during which he spent most of his time lecturing the Pakistanis on television and asking Musharraf to spare the life of Nawaz Sharif.[20]

A year and a half later, in the wake of 9/11, Washington turned to Islamabad—where Musharraf was ready to play the military-clientelistic game. For George Bush, Pakistan was once again the frontline country par excellence. It could provide military logistic bases to fight this new Afghan war and share intelligence. Musharraf, who had to convince the army cadres to join hands with the United States against the Taliban whom they had supported so far, argued in favor of including Pakistan in "the coalition of the willing" that Washington was putting together for the "global war on terror." First, Bush had told him that if Pakistan was not "with" the United States, it would be considered as being "against" the United States. Second, Musharraf believed that the war would not annihilate the Taliban's influence and that Pakistan would be able to maintain some relationship with them. Third, India was asking to be a U.S. partner as well—and Pakistan could only lag behind its arch-enemy at its own risk. And last but not least, Pakistan was not in a position to refuse, even if Bush had been less pushy, given the country's diplomatic isolation and its economic situation.

Focus is warranted on this last aspect that is so important for the clientelistic dimension of U.S.–Pakistan relations. Pakistan's lost decade—the 1990s—ensnared the country in a spiral of debt. In only five years, between 1995–1996 and 1999–2000, total debt had risen from Rs 1,877 billion to Rs 3,096 billion, with service of the debt reaching 45 percent of budget spending and 63 percent of receipts in 2000. At the same time, the army still needed a huge amount of money. Military expenditure represented 21 percent of the budget spending in 2001–2002—despite an artificial reduction due to the transfer of military pensions under the heading of "general administration."

By joining hands with the U.S.-led coalition against terror, Pakistan killed two birds with one stone. First, it was reintegrated with the concert of nations. Musharraf made a tour that took him to Tehran, Istanbul, Paris, London, and New York, where he had his hour of glory while addressing the United Nations on November 12, by George Bush's side, as the two men issued a joint statement emphasizing the friendship uniting both countries "for fifty years."[21] Second, Pakistan received preferential treatment in terms of aid, the

United States paving the way for other countries. Washington lifted all sanctions connected with the nuclear issue (from the 1978 Symington amendment to the 1985 Pressler amendment and the Glenn amendment of 1998) and those that had been decided in the wake of Musharraf's military coup[22]—which allowed the country to obtain loans from the United States and send officers there for military training, neither of which had been possible since 1990.

THE BUSH–MUSHARRAF AXIS AND ITS LIMITS

Musharraf was in a position to repeat Zia's achievements during the previous Afghan war. He could persuade the United States to legitimize his military rule, extract funds from them, and acquire American weapons.

THE "MOST ALLIED ALLY" PATTERN REVISITED?

In the 1980s, Zia had asked one of his generals to tell Secretary of State Haig that "we would not like to hear from you the type of government we should have."[23] Haig had responded: "General, your internal situation is your problem."[24] History was repeating itself a dozen years later. Although in late 2001 Musharraf committed to holding elections the following year, he pointed out, in New York, on November 13, that he would remain in office regardless of the results. The American media had prepared the ground for this kind of declaration. *Newsweek*, for instance, commented on Musharraf's rule in explicit terms: "We should certainly be happy that Pakistan is run by a military dictator friendly towards us, rather than that the country try try to be a democracy that could have been hostile."[25] Hence the bitterness of progressive Pakistani editorialists. Zaffar Abbas lamented in the *Herald*, "The problems of democracy and human rights have very clearly been relegated to a lower level while the U.S.A. returns to the cold war philosophy according to which 'our dictator is a good dictator.'"[26]

The United States developed an increasingly benevolent attitude vis-à-vis Musharraf in the early 2000s for two main reasons. First, he facilitated their war in Afghanistan. Pakistan allowed the United States to use its airspace and fly sorties from the south; it gave U.S. troops access to some of its military bases (for nonoffensive operations only); Pakistani soldiers ensured the protection of these troops and of some American ships in the Indian Ocean; in terms of logistics, Pakistan not only provided vital components such as fuel for the fighters, but it also gave access to its ports (including Karachi) and roads (including the Indus Highway, which became a jugular vein) for the delivery of most of the supplies North Atlantic Treaty Organization (NATO) forces required in Afghanistan; last but not least, "Islamabad provided Washington with access to Pakistani intelligence assets in Afghanistan and Pakistan."[27]

Second, Musharraf to some extent delivered in the fight against Al Qaeda. The capture of Abu Zubeida in Faisalabad on April 6, 2002, of Sheikh Ahmed Saleem in Karachi in July, of Khalid Shaikh Mohammed, one of bin Laden's lieutenants who had been the architect of 9/11, in Rawalpindi on March 1, 2003, and of Tanzanian Al Qaeda leader Ahmed Khalfan Ghailani—one of the chief accused in the blast of the American embassies in Nairobi and Dar Es Salaam in 1998—on July 27, 2004, in Gujrat was very much appreciated in Washington.[28] By 2004, about 700 Al Qaeda suspects had been killed or captured in Pakistan according to a report prepared for Congress.[29]

In addition to his fight against Al Qaeda, Musharraf seemed prepared to fight against all Islamist organizations, as suggested in his January 12, 2002, speech propounding what became known as "enlightened moderation" and the subsequent ban of several Islamist groups. In exchange, the United States was rather complacent over the nonproliferation issue and resumed its aid on an unprecedented scale. Washington denounced Pakistan transfer of nuclear technology to North Korea in October 2002, but nothing happened until late 2003, when the matter became public. Even then, the United States seemed to take it rather lightly. In December 2003 and January 2004, nuclear scientists from Kahuta Laboratory suspected of having sold nuclear technology to foreign countries were detained and interrogated by the police. On January 31, A. Q. Khan himself, founder of the Kahuta Laboratory and father of the Pakistani bomb, was accused of similar acts regarding Iran, North Korea, Iraq, and Libya. While under house arrest, he admitted on television, in February 2004, that he had organized such exchanges in an individual capacity, and his supporters immediately mobilized in great numbers.[30] Musharraf pardoned A. Q. Khan straightaway, feting him as a national hero.[31] Interestingly, the U.S. administration offered no protest whatsoever: Washington obviously needed Pakistan so badly that on March 18, 2004, it declared Pakistan one of its non-NATO allies.

More important, in August 2004, Pakistan received the first of three yearly installments of the $3 billion the United States had promised Musharraf during his June 2003 visit to America.[32] Out of these $600 million, $300 million was earmarked for military procurement and the other $300 million for development and civil expenditure. In addition, in 2007 the U.S.

government granted an additional $750 million as the first disbursement of a five-year plan for the development of the Federally Administered Tribal Agencies (FATA). The United States gave $12 billion in aid and military reimbursements to Pakistan between 2002 and 2008—out of which $8.8 billion was security related (table 8.1). The Pakistan army received about $1 billion a year for seven years—in other words, roughly a quarter of the country's yearly defense budget in the mid-2000s.[33] The ISI depended even more on American financial support. The CIA's contribution to the agency's budget allegedly amounted to one-third of the total.[34]

YET ANOTHER DISENCHANTMENT: WHO IS THE BOSS AFTER ALL?

By the end of Bush's second term, the U.S. administration had realized that Musharraf and the Pakistani army had not been fully reliable allies and Congress became even more critical of the president's strategy.

First, not only was it clear in 2008 that no Al Qaeda leader had been either caught or killed since 2004, but in September of that year, the United States was alerted that "Pakistan's top internal security official conceded that Al Qaeda operatives moved freely in this country."[35] Second, the United States noted that the FATA had become a major safe haven for militants who were striking the NATO troops in Afghanistan—one-third of the attacks they faced were coming from that side[36]—and the Afghan Taliban had apparently found another sanctuary in Quetta where their Shura (Council) could meet safely.[37] Third, "by the close of 2007, U.S. intelligence analysts had amassed considerable evidence that Islamabad's truces with religious militants in the FATA had given Taliban, Al Qaeda, and other Islamist extremists space in which to rebuild their networks."[38]

The "FATA issue," therefore, was bound to dominate U.S.–Pakistan relations. As mentioned above, the Taliban and Al Qaeda operatives had found there a safe haven during the 2001 Afghan war. Since then, the U.S. administration had put pressure on the Pakistani army for it to deploy troops in this area. In 2002, the army launched Operation Meezan, "thus entering FATA for the first time since the country's independence in 1947."[39] About 24,000 military and paramilitary troops were deployed. A second operation, code-named Kalusha, took place in March 2004. Both failed. Not only were the tribes hostile to these military incursions and the well-trained militants were heavily armed, but the Pakistani army, lacking basic expertise in counterinsurgency techniques, further alienated the tribal leaders by causing

TABLE 8.1 OVERT U.S. AID AND MILITARY REIMBURSEMENTS TO PAKISTAN (2002–2014)
(ROUNDED TO THE NEAREST MILLION DOLLARS)

PROGRAM OR ACCOUNT	2002	2003	2004	2005	2006	2007	2008	2009	2010	2011	2012	2013	2014
Section 1206 of the National Defense Authorization Act					28	14	56	139					
Counternarcotics funds				8	24	49	54	47	43	39	1	8	
Coalition support funds	1,169	1,247	705	964	862	731	1,019	685	1,499	1,118	688	1,438	861
Frontier Corps training and equipment							75	25					
Foreign military financing	75	225	75	299	297	297	298	300	294	295	296	280	280
International military education and training	1	1	1	2	2	2	2	2	5	4	5	5	5
International narcotic control and law enforcement	91	31	32	32	38	24	22	88	170	114	75	57	57
Nonproliferation, antiterrorism, demining, and related	10	1	5	8	9	10	10	13	24	25	20	11	11
Pakistan Counterinsurgency Capability Fund								400	700	800	452		
Total security	1,346	1,505	818	1,313	1,260	1,127	1,536	1,699	2,735	2,395	1,537	1,799	1,214

(continued)

TABLE 8.1 (CONTINUED)

PROGRAM OR ACCOUNT	2002	2003	2004	2005	2006	2007	2008	2009	2010	2011	2012	2013	2014
Coalition support funds (nonmilitary)	14	16	26	21	28	22	30	34	30	28			
Development assistance	10	35	49	29	38	95	30						
Economic support fund	615	188	200	298	337	394	347	1,114	1,292	919	905	724	477
Food aid	5	28	13	32	55		50	55	124	51	96	81	30
Human rights and democracy fund	1		2	2	1	11					<1		
Migration and refugee assistance	9	7	6	6	10	4		60	91	43	54	9	
International disaster assistance					70	50	50	103	232	145	12	20	
Total economic related (percent of the total)	654 (32.7)	274 (15.4)	296 (26.6)	388 (22.8)	539 (30)	576 (33.8)	507 (24.8)	1,366 (44.6)	1,769 (39.3)	1,186 (33.1)	1,067 (40.9)	834 (31.7)	507 (29.5)
Grand total	2,000	1,779	1,114	1,701	1,799	1,703	2,043	3,065	4,504	3,581	2,604	2,633	1,721

SOURCES: FOR 2002–2006, SUSAN B. EPSTEIN AND K. ALAN KRONSTADT, PAKISTAN: U.S. FOREIGN ASSISTANCE, CONGRESSIONAL RESEARCH SERVICE, CRS REPORT FOR CONGRESS, OCTOBER 4, 2012, HTTPS://WWW.FAS.ORG/SGP/CRS/ROW/R41856.PDF. FOR 2006–2009, U.S. DEPARTMENTS OF STATE, DEFENSE, AND AGRICULTURE; U.S. AGENCY FOR INTERNATIONAL DEVELOPMENT; HTTP://IFPC.STATE.GOV/DOCUMENTS/ORGANIZATION/196189.PDF. FOR 2010–2014, "DIRECT OVERT U.S. AID APPROPRIATIONS FOR AND MILITARY REIMBURSEMENTS TO PAKISTAN, FY2002–FY2015: PREPARED BY THE CONGRESSIONAL RESEARCH SERVICE FOR DISTRIBUTION TO MULTIPLE CONGRESSIONAL OFFICES, DECEMBER 22, 2014," WWW.FAS.ORG/SGP/CRS/ROW /PAKAID.PDF.

collateral casualties while resorting to indiscriminate bombing. They decided to negotiate peace deals with the militants.

The first one was signed with Wazir tribesman Nek Muhammad, the most popular—and even charismatic—fighter, in Shakai, South Waziristan. This agreement, in exchange for the militants' commitment to abstain from fighting the Pakistani government and NATO forces in Afghanistan, made provisions for the release of 163 prisoners, financial compensations to the victims of military operations, and the safety of the foreign mujahideen who were allowed to stay in the FATA, provided they were registered. This last clause was a bone of contention that resulted in the relaunching of military operations in June 2004. Negotiations took place again, and another agreement was signed in February 2005 between the Pakistani authorities and Baitullah Mehsud (who had somewhat taken over from Nek Muhammad, killed in 2004, and was to become the first chief of the Tehrik-e Taliban Pakistan). It again stipulated that the militants should neither attack Pakistani civil servants or property nor support foreign fighters. In exchange, the army pledged not to take action against Mehsud and his companions because of their previous activities. Mehsud scrapped the deal in August 2007 "in reaction to increased patrols by Pakistan's army."[40] A similar deal had been made in North Waziristan in September 2006. It also collapsed in 2007.[41]

Last but not least, the United States had to admit, again in 2007, that it had relied far too exclusively on Musharraf and his army. In fact, the personal equation that Bush and the Pakistani president had developed had become a liability. With the rise of anti-Americanism that followed the U.S.-led 2001 war (which the Pashtuns were not the only Pakistanis to resent), the United States had given Musharraf a bad name (literally speaking, since he was often called "Busharraf").[42] Musharraf in turn had damaged his image in the United States by his growing authoritarianism, manifest in the hijacking of elections, repression of the judiciary, and, eventually, declaration of the state of emergency in November 2007. The State Department's Country Report on Human Rights Practices released in March 2008 emphasized that Pakistan's record in this domain had worsened because of the increasing number of extrajudicial killings, disappearances, and cases of torture.[43] As Hussain Haqqani, who was to become Pakistan's ambassador in Washington, stated before the House Armed Services Committee on October 10, 2007,

The United States made a critical mistake in putting faith in one man—General Pervez Musharraf—and one institution—the Pakistani army—as instruments of the U.S. policy to eliminate terrorism and bring stability to the Southwest and South Asia. A robust U.S. policy of engagement with Pakistan that helps in building civilian institutions, including law enforcement capability, and eventually results in reverting Pakistan's military to its security functions would be a more effective way to strengthening Pakistan and protecting United States policy interests there.[44]

Bush policy was well in tune with the traditional security-centered clientelistic relationship that the United States and Pakistan had cultivated with occasional hiatuses since the 1950s. But it was time for review, since this strategy was clearly not delivering. Alternative voices could now not only speak up but also be heard. Experts such as Bruce Riedel and Teresita Schaffer as well as members of Congress regretted more vehemently than ever before that the Bush administration did not make any significant effort to promote democracy in Pakistan or to alienate President Musharraf.[45] This approach could no longer be ignored after elections were held in Pakistan in February 2008, putting a civilian government back at the helm of Pakistan.

It is in this context that in July 2008 Senators Joe Biden and Dick Lugar introduced the Enhanced Partnership with Pakistan Bill (S. 3263) in order to break with what they called the "transactional"—I would say clientelistic—perspective and to promote "a sustained, long term, multifaceted relationship with Pakistan."[46] Such an agenda implied a tripling of nonmilitary American assistance to $1.5 billion per year over the 2009–2013 period. Simultaneously, military aid and arms transfers would be conditional on two developments: first, the army should show that it made "concerted efforts" in its fight against Islamist groups; and, second, it should not interfere with political and judicial processes. While the overtone of the bill was critical of the army, it also reflected a sense of introspection. Biden and Lugar wanted to "reverse a pervasive Pakistani sentiment that the United States is not a reliable ally."[47] This feeling, which originated in the way the United States had left the region after the withdrawal of the Soviets from Afghanistan, was shared not only by Musharraf—who said publicly in January 2008 that Pakistanis felt that they had been "used and ditched"[48]—but also by his successor, President Zardari, who was elected democratically in September 2008. In a January 2009 op-ed in the *Washington Post*, Zardari wrote, "Frankly, the abandonment of Afghanistan and Pakistan after the defeat of the Soviets in Afghanistan in the 1980s set the stage for the era of terrorism that we are enduring"[49]—a very personal reading of history.

Barack Obama took office at almost the same time as Zardari, and he was to pursue the nascent attempt at breaking with the old pattern of security-centered clientelism while capitalizing on the new civilian rule in Pakistan.

WHAT HAS CHANGED WITH OBAMA?

During the 2008 election campaign, Obama emphasized the need to look at the Afghan issue in a larger perspective. He was convinced that the problem of Kashmir and the FATA should be dealt with simultaneously and that the relaxation of Indo-Pakistani tensions would prepare the ground for Islamabad to transfer more troops to positions along the Afghan border. In December 2008, after being elected, he said, "we can't continue to look at Afghanistan in isolation. We have to see it as a part of a regional problem that includes Pakistan, includes India, includes Kashmir, includes Iran."[50] Such statements caused so much protest in India that he immediately gave up the idea of addressing the Kashmir issue. But the "AfPak" concept remained after Obama took office.

PAKISTAN AS A LONG-TERM PRIORITY: THE AFPAK NOTION AND THE KERRY-LUGAR-BERMAN ACT

Introducing the "AfPak" concept, Obama bracketed together Afghanistan and Pakistan because, for him, Afghanistan could not be "solved" without "solving Pakistan." That move was made explicit with the appointment of Richard Holbrooke as the president's special envoy for Afghanistan and Pakistan. The idea was not only to use Pakistan vis-à-vis Afghanistan but to highlight the fact that the Islamist problem lay in Pakistan—something the Bush administration had not been unaware of but did not pay much attention to either. Obama considered that Pakistan was as important as Afghanistan, if not more so, for American strategy and interests. When he said that the "cancer"[51] that destabilized the whole region was in Pakistan, one wondered whether he was not even shifting from AfPak to PakAf.

One year after his 2008 election, Obama continued to think in these terms. In his December 2009 West Point address, when he announced "the surge," the sending of 30,000 additional American troops to Afghanistan, he made it clear that "an effective partnership with Pakistan" was one of the "core elements" of the U.S. strategy. But he did not want to view this partnership in the narrow, security-centered, and clientelistic perspective of the past:

> In the past we too often defined our relationship with Pakistan narrowly. Those days are over. Moving forward, we are committed to a partnership with Pakistan that is built on a foundation of mutual interest, mutual

respect, and mutual trust. We will strengthen Pakistan's capacity to target those groups that threaten our countries, and have made it clear that we cannot tolerate a safe haven for terrorists whose location is known and whose intentions are clear. America is also providing substantial resources to support Pakistan's democracy and development. We are the largest international supporter for those Pakistanis displaced by the fighting. And going forward, the Pakistan people must know America will remain a strong supporter of Pakistan's security and prosperity long after the guns have fallen silent, so that the great potential of its people is unleashed.[52]

Stressing America's long-term, non-security-related commitment to Pakistan, Obama was evidently eager to dispel the pervasive impression among Pakistanis that the United States was unreliable and would let them down, just as it had let them down after the war against the Soviets in Afghanistan, as soon as they won (or claimed to have won) their global war against terrorism. To that end, Obama wanted to work with the democratically elected governments in Afghanistan and Pakistan to fight the Islamist groups that were posing a threat to them as much as to the United States. As president-elect, he had declared:

What I want to do is to create the kind of effective, strategic partnership with Pakistan that allows us, in concert, to assure that terrorists are not setting up safe havens in some of these border regions between Pakistan and Afghanistan. So far President Zardari has sent the right signals. He's indicated that he recognizes this is not just a threat to the United States, but it is a threat to Pakistan as well. . . . I think this democratically-elected government understands that threat and I hope that in the coming months we're going to be able to establish the kind of close, effective, working relationship that makes both countries safer.[53]

The Enhanced Partnership with Pakistan Act was passed in this context to move away from a military-centric relationship. Initiated by Senators Biden and Lugar, it was taken up by John Kerry and Lugar after Biden became vice president—hence its initial name, the "Kerry-Lugar Bill." This piece of legislation was passed in 2009. The first three articles of the "Statement of Principles" section are worth quoting:

1. Pakistan is a critical friend and ally to the United States, both in times of strife and in times of peace, and the two countries share many common

goals, including combating terrorism and violent radicalism, solidifying democracy and rule of law in Pakistan, and promoting the social and economic development of Pakistan.

2. United States assistance to Pakistan is intended to supplement, not supplant, Pakistan's own efforts in building a stable, secure, and prosperous Pakistan.

3. The United States requires a balanced, integrated, countrywide strategy for Pakistan that provides assistance throughout the country and does not disproportionately focus on security-related assistance or one particular area or province.[54]

The Kerry-Lugar Bill was intended "to promote sustainable long-term development and infrastructure projects, including in healthcare, education, water management, and energy programs."[55] Supporting a bill that was passed unanimously by the Senate in September 2009, Senator Lugar dwelled on the fact that its objective was to shift from a security-centric to a development-oriented paradigm: "We should make clear to the people of Pakistan that our interests are focused on democracy, pluralism, stability, and the fight against terrorism. These are values supported by a large majority of the Pakistani people."[56]

The aid that Washington committed to giving in the framework of this act amounted to $1.5 billion a year over the 2010–2014 period. The United States was no longer trying to pay (or equip) Pakistan so that the country would implement a certain security-related policy, but it was prepared to pay for Pakistan to make development a priority.

This approach was also different because it reflected a longer-term perspective—which was badly needed to correct the (not-so-wrong) impression prevalent among many Pakistanis that Washington was not a reliable partner because it was inconsistent. They had become a "disenchanted ally" (to paraphrase the title of Dennis Kux's book) of the United States after they were let down by Washington in the 1990s, once the Soviets had left Afghanistan.

But the new American policy was a long-term one for another reason as well. The Obama administration considered that Pakistan was "the most dangerous country in the world." This formula—which was first used by Bruce Riedel, a Brookings expert—was taken up several times during the 2008 presidential campaign by Joe Biden, the vice presidential candidate.[57] What was at stake was not only nuclear proliferation, military expenditure, and adventurism but also the related issue of the rise of Islamism, something only a long-term effort to educate Pakistanis and make them richer could defuse. While the Bush administration—including his neoconservative hawks—had tried to fight terrorism by democratizing the Greater Middle East, Obama's team concentrated on the country that mattered the most according to them and tried to support the democratization process by a special aid package.

One must not underestimate the affinities between the Bush administration and the Obama administration on that front. In both cases, there was a realization—resulting to a large extent from 9/11—that the real enemy was the Islamists. Holbrooke, in a Huntingtonian perspective, said about the Lashkar-e-Taiba (LeT), Al Qaeda, and the Taliban: "Their long-term objective is to destroy the Western civilization."[58] In *Obama's Wars*, Bob Woodward cites James L. Jones saying similarly: "It's certainly a clash of civilizations. It's clash of religions. It's a clash of almost concepts of how to live."[59] But in contrast to the Bush administration, Obama wanted to combine short-term security objectives with long-term support for the development of a democratic civil society in Pakistan.

In the Kerry-Lugar Bill, emphasis on the nonmilitary dimension of the U.S.–Pakistan relations to be promoted found its clearest expression in the last page of the bill where it was stressed that the allocation of the funds were conditional on the submission to Congress of a Semi-Annual Monitoring Report comprising "an assessment of the extent to which the Government of Pakistan exercises effective civilian control of the military, including a description of the extent to which civilian executive leaders and parliament exercise oversight and approval of military budgets, the chain of command, the process of promotion for senior military leaders, civilian involvement in strategic guidance and planning, and military involvement in civil administration."[60]

This provision was unacceptable to the Pakistani generals who protested that the bill encroached on the country's sovereignty.[61] Other Pakistanis reacted more positively, even though many comments reflected a deep trust deficit.[62] For many, it could be interpreted as a return to "colonial governance."[63] Daniel Markey attributes these reactions to the manner in which the bill had been rewritten by Representative Howard Berman for the bill to be passed in the House of Representatives—hence its abbreviation "KLB," for "Kerry-Lugar-Breman."[64] For Markey, "the KLB rollout was a diplomatic disaster that hurt the U.S. effort to build ties with Pakistan."[65] It was, indeed, a failure but mostly because the United States was in a position neither to deliver civilian aid nor to reduce the security dimension of their collaboration.

THE MORE IT CHANGES . . . : THE RESILIENCE OF THE SECURITY
PARADIGM (2009–2011)

Obama's Pakistani policy immediately ran into a major contradiction: while it was apparently intended to focus more on development, it remained security oriented. The Pakistani army continued to be the main interlocutor of the United States—by default, given the weakness of the civilian authorities, but also by design, as security issues remained a priority.

IGNORING WEAK CIVILIAN LEADERS—AND MAKING THEM EVEN WEAKER

The Pakistani leaders, whom Obama had singled out as partners to build this new relationship, have been ineffective. Zardari—to whom Obama had sent a long letter offering that Pakistan and the United States become "long-term strategic partners"[66] in November 2009—quickly lost most of his credibility due to his reputation for corruption and nepotism as well as his inability to relate to the Pakistani people, a problem partly resulting from his lifestyle and partly because of his fear of being killed by Islamists, which has transformed him into a recluse. According to a Pew Center survey, only 11 percent of interviewees had a favorable view of Zardari in 2011, compared with 20 percent in 2010, 32 percent in 2009, and 64 percent in 2008.[67]

But even when Zardari still enjoyed some degree of popularity, he was unable to prevail over the military. He did not manage to bring the ISI under civilian jurisdiction; he was not able to twist the arm of the army after he had offered to share intelligence with India about the 2008 Mumbai attacks—something the military bluntly refused; and he was unable to resist the demand of the Chief of Army Staff (COAS), Pervez Kayani, the successor of Musharraf, to obtain a three-year extension. Civilians were in office, but the army continued to rule—at least in key domains such as Pakistani policy toward Afghanistan, India, and nuclear weapons, all of which had major implications. As early as 2009, Hillary Clinton, the then secretary of state, "supported democracy in Pakistan but found the civilian government adrift,"[68] an impression that was reinforced by the way with which "Zardari answered Obama with a wandering letter that the White House concluded must have been composed by a committee dominated by the Pakistani military and ISI."[69] Zardari spoke more and more like the military anyway.[70]

In any case, Hussain Haqqani had come to the conclusion that "On issues that mattered to the Americans, the civilians were simply unable to deliver."[71] What were these matters? All were security related, especially after the failed Times Square bomb blast on May 1, 2010, to which we shall return below.

Retrospectively, we may think that Washington should have resisted the temptation to adjust to the balance of power resulting from the growing assertiveness of the military at the expense of the civilians. But it did not happen and gradually, civilians (Richard Holbrooke, Hillary Clinton, Robert Gates, and Joe Biden) started talking to General Kayani—even when civilians were sitting at the table—and this practice precipitated the decline of civilian authority in the U.S.–Pakistan relations (and beyond). This attitude reflected the need for the Obama administration to deal with effective Pakistani leaders, but it was also an indication of the strong links between the Pakistani army and the Pentagon, which have always played a major role in this bilateral relation. These affinities were evident from the frequent—and apparently friendly—meetings between Kayani and Admiral Michael Mullen, chairman of the Joint Chiefs of Staff from 2007 to 2011. They both met twenty-six times.

NEGOTIATING WITH THE PAKISTANI ARMY

The weakness of the Pakistani civilian government made the paradoxical character of Obama's strategy even more obvious, but there was anyway an intrinsic contradiction in this strategy. On the one hand, the Obama administration aspired to build a civil society that would sustain a more democratic regime in the long term. But its short-term priorities were of a completely different nature: like his predecessor, he wanted first to capture bin Laden and dismantle Al Qaeda and second to protect American troops fighting the Taliban in Afghanistan from attacks originating in Pakistan. To achieve these objectives, the Obama administration needed to rely on the Pakistani army, which was well trained in the art of bargaining with the United States about scores of issues to get "its due."[72]

During the first year of his administration, Obama realized that the peace deals that the Pakistani army was making with militants in the FATA and adjacent areas did not offer any solution but gave these militants much needed respite to regroup before launching new offensives. The Pakistani army admitted that such an assessment was correct in 2009 when militants took over the Swat Valley. This time it reacted on a large scale and regained the upper hand in the valley.[73] Then it launched an operation in South Waziristan, where it deployed about 28,000 soldiers, partly under American pressure, in late October 2009. The ratio to take on about 10,000 militants was so low that Richard Holbrooke wondered whether the Pakistani army wanted to "disperse" or "destroy" the enemy.[74]

Although the United States appreciated the military operations the Pakistan army launched in Swat and to a lesser extent in South Waziristan, it urged army leaders to do the same thing in North Waziristan, where they believed not only Al Qaeda leaders but also Taliban and the Haqqani Network were now based, sometimes after fleeing South Waziristan. These groups—especially the Haqqani Network—were allegedly planning not only strikes against NATO forces in Afghanistan but also terrorist attacks in the West as well—including on U.S. soil. The American military commander in Afghanistan, General Stanley McChrystal, exerted additional pressure on the Pakistani army in May 2010 after American investigators discovered that the failed bomb attack in Times Square had been plotted in the FATA.[75]

The Pakistani army, which had already lost thousands of soldiers in the FATA, was still reluctant to act. First, the Pakistani army and paramilitary were probably not in a position to fight successfully in a very difficult terrain—where civilians had already suffered considerably, giving the Pakistani state a bad name in the region. Second, the Pakistani army and the ISI were not willing to attack groups they considered useful allies to regain their lost influence in Afghanistan after the NATO forces would leave—especially since December 2009, when Obama announced not only the troop surge but that withdrawal of American troops would start in July 2011. Pakistan thus had to prepare for the Afghan transition, and groups such as the Haqqani would at that time be useful to reinstall the Taliban in Kabul to keep India at bay. Third, army operations in the FATA were widely considered the main reason for retaliation in the form of terrorist attacks in the main cities of Pakistan—where suicide attacks had never been as frequent as in the years 2009–2010.

As a result, the United States gradually came to the conclusion that they should ask the Pakistanis to let them handle the job themselves, with as much Pakistani support as possible. The American administration longed for the Pakistanis to allow them to undertake hot pursuit in the tribal area. They were rebuked by Islamabad, whose leaders—civilian as well as military—considered that such moves would encroach on the country's sovereignty. But the United States obtained significant concessions in 2009–2010.

According to cables released by WikiLeaks and published in 2011 by the Karachi-based newspaper *Dawn*, as early as May 2009, the American ambassador in Islamabad, Anne Patterson, wrote to the State Department that the United States had "created Intelligence Fusion cells with embedded

U.S. Special Forces with both SSG [Special Services Group] and Frontier Corps (Bala Hisar, Peshawar) with the Rover equipment ready to deploy. Through these embeds, we are assisting the Pakistanis to collect and coordinate existing intelligence assets. We have not been given Pakistani military permission to accompany the Pakistani forces on deployments as yet."[76] But by September, joint intelligence activities had been expanded to include army headquarters: "Pakistan," Patterson said, "has begun to accept intelligence, surveillance, and reconnaissance support from the U.S. military for COIN [counterinsurgency]. In addition 'intelligence fusion centers' had been established 'at the headquarters of Frontier Corps and the 11th Corps and we expect at additional sites, including GHQ and the 12th Corps in Baluchistan.'"

In addition to these developments regarding intelligence sharing, in the late 2000s the United States obtained what it had dearly wished for: an intensification of drone strikes (a key point to which I'll return below). The Pakistan army did not authorize the United States to strike on its territory explicitly and did not share intelligence in any open, unambiguous, and constant manner. On the contrary, in the spirit of a true client state, it extracted as much compensation as it could in terms of financial support and arms.

Arms delivery was an important concern to the Pakistani generals, at a time when the military collaboration between Islamabad and New Delhi was increasing. To have access to American weapons was a key component of their country's credibility vis-à-vis India, and it was a prestige issue. Many deals were finalized under George W. Bush, but naturally, they spilled over into Obama's first term. According to a congressional report, "in 2002, the United States began allowing commercial sales that enabled Pakistan to refurbish at least part of its fleet of American-made F-16 fighter aircraft and, three years later, Washington announced that it would resume sales of new F-16 fighters to Pakistan after a 16-year hiatus."[77] But F-16s were only the most symbolic items on the Pakistani shopping list. According to the Pentagon, sales agreements between both countries amounted to $4.55 billion over the years 2002–2007, the F-16s and related equipment representing a large fraction of this. In fact, the F-16 deal could be broken down into three components: eighteen new F-16C/D block 50/52 combat aircrafts with an option for eighteen more, amounting to $1.43 billion; about sixty midlife updated kits for F-16A/B, representing $891 million; F-16 armaments (including 500 air-to-air missiles and 1,450 2,000-pound bombs), representing $667 million. Other major defense supplies included eight P-3C Orion maritime patrol aircrafts and their refurbishment (worth $474 million), 100 Harpoon anti-ship missiles (worth $298 million), six C-130E transport aircraft, and twenty AH-IF Cobra attack helicopters (worth $163 million). The State Department had to justify these sales when they were paid for using American aid in the form of foreign military financing, on the grounds that they were "solely for counterterrorism efforts, broadly defined."[78]

Members of Congress were skeptical about such arguments.[79] In June 2006, the Pentagon notified Congress of arm sales worth up to $5.1 billion, including the eighteen newly built F-16s mentioned above. Members of Congress objected that these aircraft "were better suited to fighting India than to combating terrorists"[80]—to no avail. Two years later, a congressman belonging to the Indian caucus, Gary Ackerman, protested again that F-16s could hardly be used as counterinsurgency weapons—all the more so as some of these F-16s had been refitted to carry nuclear bombs).[81] The State Department official who responded argued that this aircraft has become "an iconic symbol" of U.S.–Pakistan relations.[82] Indeed, as Craig Cohen and Derek Chollet have rightly pointed out, "Although foreign military financing is often justified to Congress as playing a critical role in the war on terrorism, in reality the weapons systems are often prestige items to help Pakistan in the event of war with India."[83] This means that U.S.–Pakistan relations are again (or rather still) structured around forms of military cooperation intended, from Islamabad's point of view, to cope with India.[84] When the first batch of F-16 jets arrived in Pakistan in July 2010, one of the officials receiving them commented upon this delivery in unambiguous terms, "Look at the rival [India]. How many fighter jets they are purchasing?"[85]

Although the Obama administration would have probably been less inclined to sell as many arms as its predecessor did, especially given Congress's growing objections, it delivered them—in early 2010, the United States approved the delivery of twelve Lockheed Martin F-16Cs and six F-16Ds—and finalized other agreements that the Pakistani army greatly appreciated. For the Pakistani generals, in addition to military equipment, the fact that some of their officers could receive training in the United States was very much valued. In 2009–2010, eight Pakistani air force members spent ten months in Arizona to be trained to fly the new F-16s.[86] These pilots were the first Pakistani officers to receive training in the United States since 1983.

When Washington showed reluctance and when the growing pervasiveness of anti-Americanism in Pakistan further complicated army collaboration with the United States, Islamabad hardened its attitude. In October 2010, it claimed that the country's sovereignty had been violated by a NATO

helicopter that had crossed the Durand Line and killed two Pakistani soldiers and one paramilitary in Kurram,[87] and it decided to stop the flow of
supplies to NATO forces in Afghanistan through the Torkham area. This
move was clearly intended to remind the United States of its vulnerable position as regards its troop supply lines—all the more so as convoys attempting to use an alternative route were attacked.[88]

This "incident" and the growing tensions between the United States and
Pakistan (Islamabad was then resentful of Obama's decision to visit India
and not Pakistan the following month) precipitated the organization of a
strategic dialogue. By holding such a meeting in Washington, the U.S. government recognized that the Pakistani generals had to be its main interlocutors for all security matters it regarded as a priority. The Pakistani army
came away with a $2 billion military aid package. This amount was similar
to the $1.5 billion in security-related aid the United States already granted
Pakistan every year, but it was "a multiyear security pact," which, according
to an American official, meant a lot to the Pakistani army: "This is designed
to make our military and security assistance to Pakistan predictable and to
signal to them that they can count on us."[89] The new security pact comprised
three parts: the sale of American military equipment to Pakistan, a program
to allow Pakistani officers to study at American war colleges, and counterinsurgency assistance to Pakistani troops.

This $2 billion package came at a time when money had become an issue
between the Pakistani army and the United States. Until 2007, most of the
annual bills submitted to the United States for an amount of about $1 bil-
lion were paid without question. The rejection rate was only 1.5 percent in
2005. It rose to about one-third in 2007 and jumped to 38 percent in 2008
and 44 percent in 2009. What was at stake were "the claims submitted by
Pakistan as compensation for military gear, food, water, troop housing and
other expenses."[90] The 2010 $2 billion package was clearly intended to restore
some measure of trust between the Pakistani army and the Obama administration. This deal was important because at that time more than before, it
seemed, according to Hussain Haqqani, that "for Pakistanis, the money was
never enough. Every now and then, Pakistani officers showed up with charts
to illustrate the presumed economic loss the country suffered because of terrorism and the war against it."[91]

To sum up: one year after the Kerry-Lugar-Berman Act was passed, the
Obama administration was conforming to the old pattern defined above as
a security-oriented form of clientelism. The emphasis remained on military
cooperation. The April 2011 White House quarterly report on Afghanistan
and Pakistan devoted more space to the military agreement than to civilian

projects.[92] The paragraph regarding the agreement signed during the October 2010 U.S.–Pakistan Strategic Dialogue is worth citing in extenso:

> The [U.S.] commitment includes a request to the Congress for $2 billion in Foreign Military Financing (FMF) and $29 million in International Military Education and Training (IMET) funding over a 5-year period (Fiscal year 2012–2016). FMF provides the foundation for Pakistan's long-term defense modernization. In addition, the IMET commitment will allow Pakistani military personnel the opportunity to train alongside their U.S. counterparts, which will help create deepened personal relationships and enhance our strategic partnership. IMET funding was suspended along with other security assistance during the decade-long period of Pressler Sanctions, depriving a generation of Pakistani officers of an opportunity to attend courses in the United States that impart our values for civilian control of the military, human rights, military organization, and operational planning, among other things.[93]

The emphasis on long-term collaboration, which until then had applied to civilians, here concerns the military, with a goal of modernizing the Pakistani army—never officially mentioned before—and providing training. Ironically, the report suggests that human rights protection will be enhanced by U.S.-trained army officers. In contrast, the report admits that the civilian dimension of the U.S.–Pakistan relations is lagging behind: while the Enhanced Partnership with Pakistan Act provided for the spending of $1.5 billion a year for civilian projects, "the United States Agency for International Development [USAID] has disbursed $877.9 million in civilian assistance since the passage of Kerry-Lugar-Berman legislation in fall 2009, not including humanitarian assistance. While some new programs are underway, it will take time for other projects, particularly large infrastructure projects, to be fully implemented."[94] Ambassador Robin Raphel, who had been appointed "coordinator for nonmilitary assistance in Pakistan" in 2009, admitted two years later that "it was unrealistic to think we could spend such a large amount of money so quickly."[95] Daniel Markey attributes this failure not only to the fact that USAID was not able any more to handle such a sum but also to the tensions between this institution and Holbrooke, until his untimely death in December 2010.

The contrast between the financial effort in favor of the military and the civilian sector is obvious in table 8.1. The nonmilitary component of U.S. assistance to Pakistan represented only 33.8 percent of the total in 2007 by the end of the second term of George W. Bush, whereas it has reached about

45 percent in 2009 and about 40 percent in 2010. And with $2.735 billion in 2010, the military component was almost the double of what it was, as an average, during the second term of George W. Bush.

On the top of it, the Obama administration overlooked the conditionalities that were supposed to be part of the Enhanced Partnership with Pakistan Act. This act required the secretary of state to certify that Pakistan fulfilled certain criteria regarding noninterference with the civilian processes, sharing of intelligence with the United States regarding Islamist networks, cessation of any form of support to the Afghan Taliban, and so on. The secretary of state had to provide certification every year for the money to be disbursed. When she occupied this post, Hillary Clinton delayed the assessment exercise and, eventually, gave her certification on March 18, 2010, considering that Pakistan was in compliance with all the conditionalities—something senior American officers themselves contradicted privately, especially after the Pakistani authorities' actions taken against CIA staff members and their demand for a drastic reduction of the Special Forces (see below). The Obama administration preferred to look the other way so as not to alienate the Pakistani generals.

"MASTERS, NOT FRIENDS"? THE CRISIS OF U.S.–PAK RELATIONS (2011–2013)

The standard clientelistic model was based on a form of subcontracting: the American patron paid the Pakistani authorities in exchange for the performance of certain tasks. In this exchange, Pakistan retained a certain degree of autonomy. The country's sovereignty was admittedly encroached upon in the 1950s–1960s with the installation of U-2 bases to which Pakistani officials themselves were denied access. But Ayub Khan made sure that the Americans behaved as "friends, not masters"—a phrase he used for the title of his autobiography, which significantly devoted considerable space to U.S.–Pakistani relations.[96] As a result, after Russia identified Pakistan as the country from which the U-2s were coming, the lease granted by Islamabad for the base in Badaber was not renewed—and the base was shut down in 1968. More important in the 1980s, the golden age of U.S.–Pakistan cooperation, Islamabad had been given considerable leeway, enabling it to promote the groups of Afghan mujahideen it considered with favor. In the 2001–2008 period, the Bush administration also gave Musharraf a degree of latitude and tried to balance out the India–U.S. rapprochement by cozying up to Pakistan. Obama has behaved differently. Not only has he choked the Pakistanis by conflating them with the Afghans (at best perceived as good mujahideen but rustic tribals by the Punjabi establishment) in the expression "AfPak"—and Pakistanis resented the trilateral summits the United States hosted with Pakistan and a pro-India Afghanistan under Karzai—but furthermore, he has made no secret of his preference for India as strategic partner in South Asia and attached little importance to Pakistan's sovereignty as evident from his intensive use of drones.

DRONE ATTACKS

For many Pakistanis, the drone attacks have become a symbol of the way the United States has disregarded their country's sovereignty. These attacks had already started under the Bush administration. In fact, the WikiLeaks cables show that as early as January 2008, Kayani was asking the United States for some Predator coverage in South Waziristan while his army conducted operations against militants. According to K. Alan Kronstadt, a specialist in South Asian affairs at the Congressional Research Service, in April 2008, three Predators were "deployed at a secret Pakistani airbase and can be launched without specific permission from the Islamabad government."[97] Although the drone strikes increased in 2008, they were ramped up dramatically under President Obama. In fact, "in its first eighteen months, the Obama administration authorized more drone attacks in Pakistan than its predecessor did over two terms."[98] In 2010, these attacks focused on North Waziristan, where militants had regrouped after the South Waziristan operation the year before. The number of drone strikes in this region rose from 22 in 2009 to 104 in 2010.[99] The London-based Bureau of Investigative Journalism estimated that less than one-third (714) of the 2,400 to 3,888 persons killed by the 405 drone attacks in Pakistan from 2004 to December 2014 have been identified.[100] Indeed, most of the official American figures leave civilian casualties unrecorded.[101] According to the New America Foundation's drone database, considered the most accurate source, the number of drone strikes increased from 9 over the years 2004–2007 to 33 in 2008, 53 in 2009, 118 in 2010, and 70 in 2011. For the Foundation, "the 310 reported drone strikes in northwest Pakistan, including 27 in 2012, from 2004 to the present have killed approximately between 1,870 and 2,873 individuals, of whom around 1,577 to 2,402 were described as militants in reliable press accounts. Thus, the true non-militant fatality rate since 2004 according to our analysis is approximately 16 percent. In 2011, it was more like eleven percent."[102] Steve Coll gives similar figures so far as the civilian casualties are concerned: "In Obama's first year in office, the figure was twenty percent—still very high. By 2012, it was five per cent." But major blunders were still committed (forty-one tribal elders taking part in a *jirga* were killed by mistake in 2011, for instance). And this is one of the reasons why, by mid-2012, Obama had ordered John Brennan (the deputy national security advisor for homeland security and counterterrorism and assistant to the president) to reassess the drone policy. The number of drone strikes diminished and was further reduced after Brennan became chief of the CIA in 2013.[103] According to the New America Foundation, the number of strikes has fallen from seventy-three in 2011 to forty-eight in 2012, twenty-seven in 2013, and twenty-one in 2014, and the number of casualties has followed the same trend: 849 in 2010, 517 in 2011, 306 in 2012, 153 in 2013, and 138 in 2014.

Targeted killings were the chosen method for decimating the Islamist network—and remained so to some extent. Already in June 2004, Nek Mohammad was killed by a missile launched from a Predator. Baitullah Mehsud met the same fate in August 2009. But many civilians—and even Pakistani soldiers—died, too,[104] and civilian casualties were one of the reasons for the American unpopularity among the Pakistani people.[105] This is why the Pakistani army made a point of systematically voicing vehement protest against drone operations.

THE RETALIATION–COUNTERRETALIATION CYCLE

In addition to drone strikes, the presence of American agents on Pakistani territory has increasingly been perceived as attacks against the sovereignty of Pakistan by Islamabad and Rawalpindi. The Pakistani authorities sent a signal to the United States by leaking to the media the name of the Islamabad-based CIA station chief in December 2010. The agent immediately received death threats and left the country. CIA contractors presented an even bigger problem. The Obama administration had authorized a considerable number of CIA agents to be sent to Pakistan,[106] many of them as "contractors," dispensing Washington from having to reveal their true mission to the government in Islamabad. And Pakistan apparently issued hundreds of work visas without realizing that it was granting residency permits to American spies. (Besides CIA agents, contractors of Xe [formerly Blackwater]—a private security firm [in]famous for its role in Iraq—was active in Pakistan. In 2009 a former U.S. official revealed that Blackwater people worked on a CIA base in Baluchistan.)[107]

In January 2011, one of these CIA contractors, Raymond Davis, killed two Pakistanis who, according to him, were trying to steal something from him while he was driving in Lahore. He was arrested and the Pakistani authorities refused to release him for one month in spite of intense pressure from the American ambassador, who argued that he was protected by diplomatic immunity. He was eventually freed and allowed to return to his country, probably in exchange for financial compensation to the victims' families (even though the American authorities denied any payment) and for the American promise of reducing the number of Special Forces and CIA agents/contractors.[108]

THE OSAMA BIN LADEN RAID

On May 2, 2011, the raid in Abbottabad that ended in the killing of bin Laden showed that the Americans continued to conduct a number of activities in Pakistan that encroached on the country's sovereignty. First, it would not have been possible to locate bin Laden's residence in Abbottabad without intense activity on the part of U.S. intelligence agents that the Pakistani authorities were apparently unaware of. Above and beyond that, the CIA could secretly approach and recruit a health official, the surgeon general in Khyber Agency, Shakil Afridi, to scout out the location under cover of a vaccination campaign.[109]

Second, the operation code-named "Geronimo"—involving twenty-three Navy SEALs from the Naval Special Warfare Development Group and a half-dozen helicopters (including two MH-60 Black Hawks)—apparently left from the American base in Jalalabad, Afghanistan, and crossed the Pakistani border in secret. Certain Pakistani officials, such as the ambassador to London[110] and ISI officers,[111] claimed that their country had been involved in the operation in which bin Laden was killed, but others, higher ranked, starting with President Zardari—all too eager to seize an opportunity to criticize the army (at least for incompetence)—said they had not been informed of the operation,[112] which thus constituted a violation of Pakistan's sovereignty. Their denials can doubtless be explained by the unpopularity of such an operation in public opinion. But several American sources "confirmed" that the United States did not want to let the Pakistanis in on the secret.[113] Hillary Clinton and, more cautiously, Barack Obama, were careful not to offend the Pakistanis by suggesting that they had helped the United States to locate bin Laden,[114] but Chairman of the Joint Chiefs of Staff Michael Mullen apparently did not let Kayani in on the whole operation until three o'clock in the morning of May 2.[115] An Obama advisor even told the *New Yorker*: "There was a real lack of confidence that the Pakistanis could keep this secret for more than a nanosecond."[116] As for Leon Panetta, chief of the CIA, he clearly stated that the Pakistanis had been kept in the dark in surprisingly explicit terms: "Any effort to work with the Pakistanis could jeopardize the mission. They might alert the targets."[117]

The Pakistani authorities—who had first suggested that this operation had been jointly organized by both countries—protested against the unilateral incursion of American helicopters from Afghanistan without any official clearance,[118] claiming that it was a violation of national sovereignty. In a short communiqué, "the chief of army staff made it very clear that any similar action, violating the sovereignty of Pakistan, will warrant a review on the level of military/intelligence co-operation with the U.S."[119]

The Pakistani army reacted particularly badly to Operation Geronimo for three reasons. First, the presence of bin Laden in a city only 75 miles from Islamabad, which houses a military academy and where several retired officers reside, fueled suspicions as to possible complicity as well as allegations of incompetence: either the general staff knew and was guilty of collusion, or it did not know and doubts about its professionalism were thus warranted. Second, the civil authorities, starting with President Zardari and one of his close associates, Pakistan's ambassador to Washington, Hussain Haqqani, stood to gain from this military's fiasco (as the "Memogate" episode will show below), while pointedly congratulating the Americans.[120] Third, Operation Geronimo, if conducted as reported above, attested to the ease with which the Americans penetrated Pakistani territory, again in disregard for the country's sovereignty.

In reaction, the army arrested five Pakistanis who helped the Americans plan Operation Geronimo, including Dr. Afridi, who has been sentenced to jail for thirty-three years for high treason—the ISI wanting to make an example out of him. Pakistan also asked the United States to vacate the Shamsi Air Base in the Baluchistan desert, although it was an important location for the drone operations in the tribal area.[121]

"HOT PURSUIT" AND "FRIENDLY FIRE"

Back in the early 2000s, NATO troops wanted to pursue assailants in Afghanistan who took refuge across the Pakistani border after their attacks. The Pakistani authorities denied them permission for such "hot pursuit" actions, as they are known, because Pakistan wanted to avoid foreign military presence on its soil and to monitor on its own a border that was already extremely sensitive given Afghanistan's refusal to recognize the Durand

Line. Although incursions were rare, blunders were less so. U.S. soldiers pursuing Islamists to the "border" or merely patrolling along this imaginary line—more imaginary in this case than any frontier—have mistaken their target a number of times and opened fire on Pakistani soldiers. Each incidence of such "friendly fire" has given rise to reactions of public opinion. In the month of June 2007, opposition members walked out of the National Assembly to protest against an incursion of American troops on Pakistani soil that left thirty-two dead.

In June 2008, eleven Pakistani soldiers were killed by American "friendly fire," and in September an even more deadly operation took place in Angoor Ada, South Waziristan, where three helicopters searching for terrorists killed nearly two dozen people—including women and children—among whom there was not a single Islamist. In retaliation, Pakistan blocked convoys supplying NATO troops with gasoline for an unlimited period, which turned out to be fairly short.

Two years later, in another blunder, two Pakistani soldiers were killed. But the most serious incident took place in Salala in November 2011. This Mohmand Agency checkpoint in the FATA on the Afghan border was the target of strikes from helicopters and fighter planes that lasted several hours and left twenty-four Pakistani soldiers dead.[122] This time, the Pakistani authorities appointed a commission of inquiry and closed all NATO supply lines between Pakistan and Afghanistan.

All of the above-mentioned factors—from drone strikes to "friendly fire"—are largely responsible for the growing unpopularity of the United States in Pakistani public opinion in recent years.[123] According to a Pew Research Center study published in July 2010, 59 percent of the Pakistanis interviewed described the United States as an enemy and only 11 percent as a partner. Only 8 percent expressed confidence in Obama—a record figure, as none of the other twenty-one countries included in the opinion survey had such a poor image of the American president.[124] This anti-Americanism partly explains the rising influence of the party led by Imran Khan, former national cricket team captain turned political leader, whose opposition to the United States is his hobby horse. The common denominator for all these factors for Pakistan's rejection of the United States lies in the fear of compromising the country's sovereignty. This dread—shared by a large number of Pakistanis, even among Westernized elites—has led some of them to reconsider the Kerry-Lugar-Berman Bill in this light. Thus, the South Asia Strategic Stability Institute, a think tank with ties to the military establishment (and the ISI) came out in favor of rejecting it, not only because it limited the army's margin for maneuver, but also because it would allegedly prevent the country from defending itself. Considering that according to the terms of this law, "Pakistan is not allowed to buy any defense articles without the due approval of the President of the United States, Secretary of State or the Secretary of Defense of U.S.," accepting the bill would amount to a "freeze on the nuclear weapons program and will result in the Pakistani nuclear deterrence as irrelevant for all future conflicts."[125] The distrust of not only the hawks in the security apparatus toward Americans but many Pakistanis in general is rooted in the prevalent view that the reason for the U.S. presence in their country is less the fight against Islamist terrorism than supervision of their leaders, starting with Zardari, and even the takeover of their nuclear arsenal.

THE INDIAN FACTOR

Although the bin Laden raid, the Raymond Davis episode, and the Salala "friendly fire" badly affected U.S.–Pakistani relations in 2011, they had started to deteriorate in late 2010. At that time, one of the factors of this evolution was India related. For decades, Islamabad considered Washington as one of its key supporters in its competition with its big neighbor, but it realized in the post-9/11 context that the United States would, in fact, contribute more to the widening of the gap between India and Pakistan, instead of promoting "parity" (a key word of the Pakistani vocabulary). That conclusion became particularly clear in November 2010, during Obama's official visit to India, at a time when, according to the annual Pew survey, 53 percent of interviewed Pakistanis considered that India posed the greatest threat to their country—compared with 23 percent who said the same about the Taliban. Indeed, Pakistan was particularly antagonized by the Indo-U.S. rapprochement, which had already resulted in the 123 Nuclear Agreement (2008). The military in particular viewed "the U.S. operations in Afghanistan with suspicion, not least because they perceive the post-2002 government in Kabul as being overly friendly towards New Delhi."[126]

Obama's official visit to India in November 2010 triggered vehement reactions in Pakistan for several reasons. The American president endorsed India for a permanent seat on the United Nations Security Council, lifted export controls on sensitive technologies enacted in the wakes of the 1998 nuclear tests, and finalized an order for ten Boeing C-17 Globemaster III aircraft, worth $5.8 billion. Certainly, he invited India to resume talks with Pakistan, but he remained silent when Manmohan Singh responded that he could not have meaningful discussions with Pakistan until it shut down the "terror machine" on its territory.[127] Naturally, Obama did not mention the Kashmir issue.

The final communiqué suggested that India had now become a major global partner in a way that could only worry the Pakistanis. Indeed, in this joint statement:

> The two sides committed to intensify consultation, cooperation and coordination to promote a stable, democratic, prosperous, and independent Afghanistan. President Obama appreciated India's enormous contribution to Afghanistan's development and welcomed enhanced Indian assistance that will help Afghanistan achieve self-sufficiency. In addition to their own independent assistance programs in Afghanistan, the two sides resolved to pursue joint development projects with the Afghan Government in capacity building, agriculture and women's empowerment.
>
> They reiterated that success in Afghanistan and regional and global security require elimination of safe havens and infrastructure for terrorism and violent extremism in Afghanistan and Pakistan. Condemning terrorism in all its forms, the two sides agreed that all terrorist networks, including Lashkar e-Taiba, must be defeated and called for Pakistan to bring to justice the perpetrators of the November 2008 Mumbai attacks.[128]

Far from asking India to maintain some distance from Afghanistan—as General McChrystal had suggested in 2009, precisely to reassure the Pakistanis—President Obama seemed to invite India to get even more involved in this country, as he intended to withdraw U.S. troops and was looking for development partners in Afghanistan. This went entirely against the wishes of Islamabad, which had asked Washington to keep New Delhi at bay.[129]

Not only did Obama (along with Manmohan Singh) point his finger at Pakistan from India—something British Prime Minister Cameron had already done a few months before—but, as further humiliation, he decided not to go to Pakistan, journeying instead to Indonesia, South Korea, and Japan. That was an almost unprecedented move since up until that point, with the exception of Jimmy Carter in 1978, American presidents who had been to India had also visited Pakistan—if only for a few hours, as Bill Clinton did in 2000.

While the Pakistanis increasingly distrust the Americans, the latter have reciprocated in an increasingly overt manner.

The failed Times Square terrorist attack was probably a milestone for many Americans. On May 2, 2010, a car full of explosives was neutralized at Times Square before it could make a devastating impact. Its owner, Faisal Shazad, who was arrested trying to leave the country, had just spent five months in Pakistan. As it turned out, he had been trained there in the camps of jihadi organizations such as Jaish-e-Mohammed. Interestingly, he was the son of an ex-vice marshal of the Pakistani Air Force and had studied in the United States from 1994 onwards. As a financial analyst, he had obtained U.S. citizenship in 2009.[130] The AfPak area had remained associated with terrorism in American minds since 9/11, and the Times Square episode merely reactivated this latent representation. The incident not only fostered distrust vis-à-vis Pakistani immigrants but, according to some Washington analysts, reconfirmed the inability of the Pakistani authorities to deal with terrorist networks—or, even worse, their complacent attitude toward them.

However, the main reason for increasing American distrust came exactly one year later, when Osama bin Laden was discovered and killed by an American commando. While Obama simply said that bin Laden had probably benefited from some support structure, which needed to be identified and elucidated, the U.S. Congress—in tune with mainstream public opinion—questioned Pakistan's reliability more vehemently than ever before. Either the Pakistani authorities had some knowledge about bin Laden's hideout and therefore their duplicity was of an even larger magnitude than one could imagine before, or they were oblivious, and that meant that they could not be of much help in the global war against terror. In both cases, members of Congress argued that the United States should reconsider the huge financial support granted to the country.

The outcome of this review, less than three months later and after three other major incidents, was a reduction in aid. On May 7, the name of the new CIA station chief in Islamabad was again leaked to the media, including a daily newspaper, the *Nation*, notoriously close to the military establishment. The Americans attributed this development to the ISI.[131] Two weeks later, on May 22, an Islamist commando infiltrated the Karachi strategic naval base and resisted the army's counteroffensive for about ten hours, killing a dozen people and destroying sophisticated U.S.-made equipment. A Pakistani journalist well known for his expertise regarding the military–Islamist nexus, Syed Saleem Shahzad, revealed in the *Asia Times Online* that the attack was in retaliation for the arrest of about ten Al Qaeda members by Pakistani naval forces and, more important, that complicity within the navy itself had made it possible.

These revelations made a particularly strong impact as they came just after the humiliation of Operation Geronimo, which had deeply affected the credibility and prestige of the Pakistani army. The army generals, who were already adept at denouncing as antipatriotic the investigative journalists' exposure of breaches in the security apparatus, resorted to more radical means. According to U.S. intelligence, the ISI was behind the torturing and killing of Shahzad. Besides eliminating one of the most courageous media personalities in Pakistan, this murder aimed to dissuade his colleagues from continuing their investigations.[132] Interestingly, Admiral Mullen was among the first American officials to point an accusing finger at the ISI.

The chain of events over those six months—from the first leak of the Islamabad CIA station chief's identity to the killing of Shahzad—led Barack Obama, on July 9, 2011, to either suspend or cancel one-third of the U.S. military aid to the Pakistani army, that is, about $800 million out of $2 billion. These measures did not affect the core of the security relations between both countries as the delivery of key equipment such as F-16s was not at stake. In fact, $300 million of the cuts pertained to already problematic compensations that the United States was supposed to give Pakistan in exchange for the deployment of troops on its western border—but that they increasingly refused to pay.[133] During her daily press briefing, Victoria Nuland, spokesperson for the secretary of state, while she emphasized the continuation of civilian aid, justified the president's decision in terms showing that the United States tried to use military aid as a bargaining card: "When it comes to our military assistance, we're not prepared to continue providing that at the pace that we were providing it unless and until we see certain steps taken."[134]

The relations between Pakistan and the United States further deteriorated during the fall. On September 13, 2011, insurgents firing rocket-propelled grenades and automatic weapons and suicide bombers attacked simultaneously four targets in Kabul, including the American embassy and NATO headquarters. Immediately, the deputy chief of Kabul attributed this highly sophisticated operation, which killed seven Afghans, to the Haqqani Network. Ten days later, Admiral Mullen, chairman of the Joint Chiefs of Staff, who was to retire in a few days, confirmed this interpretation and went one step further. Admiral Mullen, who had worked hard to build a relationship of trust with the Pakistani army, and in particular with General Kayani, declared before the Senate Armed Services Committee:

The fact remains that the Quetta Shura and the Haqqani Network operate from Pakistan with impunity. Extremist organizations serving as proxies of the government of Pakistan are attacking Afghan troops and civilians as well as U.S. soldiers. For example, we believe the Haqqani Network—which has long enjoyed the support and protection of the Pakistani government and is, in many ways, a strategic arm of Pakistan's Inter-Services Intelligence Agency—is responsible for the September 13th attacks against the U.S. Embassy in Kabul.[135]

The American media interpreted this statement as announcing a policy turn, especially after the *New York Times*, five days later, published the outcome of a fine piece of investigative journalism showing that in 2007 Pakistani soldiers had killed a U.S. major and wounded three other officers who were mediating between Afghan and Pakistani troops over a border issue in Teri Mangal.[136] Certainly, it was the first time that such a high-ranking American officer pointed his finger at the connection between the Pakistani army and the Haqqani Network. But this connection was already well known, if not publicly denounced. In a 2009 secret review, Ambassador to Pakistan Anne Patterson wrote: "Pakistan's army and ISI are covertly SPONSORING four militant groups—Haqqani's HQN [Haqqani Network], Mullah Omar's QST [Quetta Shura Taliban], Al Qaeda, and LeT—and will not abandon them for any amount of U.S. money."[137]

Mullen did not say anything new in terms of policy recommendations. The idea that the United States must continue to engage Pakistan in order (1) to persuade its leaders that they are taking a huge risk in not quashing the Islamist forces they have more or less created and (2) to convince its society, through development-oriented aid, that the United States is a friend is, mutatis mutandis Obama's policy and, before him, that of the Kerry-Lugar Bill. Interestingly, the American president downplayed the alarmist dimension of Mullen's statement soon after, saying on the radio about the relation between the Pakistani army and the Haqqani Network, "the intelligence is not as clear as we might like in terms of what exactly that relationship is. . . . But my attitude is, whether there is active engagement with Haqqani on the part of the Pakistanis or rather just passively allowing them to operate with impunity in some of these border regions, they've got to take care of this problem." Asked if Mullen was correct, Obama said: "I think Mike's testimony expressed frustration over the fact that safe havens exist, including the Haqqani network safe haven, inside of Pakistan." Obama also underlined the successful aspect of the U.S.–Pakistan relations:

We've been very firm with them about needing to go after safe havens inside of Pakistan, but we've tried to also preserve the intelligence cooperation that we've obtained that's allowed us to go after al-Qaeda in a very effective way," he told the host, Michael Smerconish. "There's no doubt that the relationship is not where it needs to be and we are going to keep on pressing them to recognise that it is in their interest, not just ours, to make sure that extremists are not operating within their borders" added Obama. The U.S. president however credited Pakistan with "outstanding cooperation in going after al-Qaeda."[138]

At a ceremony marking the end of his tenure, Mullen emphasized that the U.S. relationship with Pakistan was "vexing and yet vital." "I continue to believe that there is no solution in the region without Pakistan, and no stable future in the region without a partnership." He added: "I urged Marty [Martin Dempsey, his successor] to remember the importance of Pakistan to all of this, to try and do a better job than I did."[139] Mullen told CNN in an interview: "The worst case, for me, is to see Pakistan deteriorate and somehow get to a point where it's being run by insurgents who are in the possession of nuclear weapons and nuclear weapons technology, which would mean that that part of the world would continue to deteriorate and become much more dangerous."

Congress was less accommodating. On September 23, 2011, the Enhanced Partnership with Pakistan Act (EPPA) was amended so as to stipulate that

> no aid would be available to Pakistan unless the Secretary of State certifies that Pakistan is making measurable progress towards achieving the principal objectives of U.S. assistance to Pakistan as stated in the Pakistan Assistance Strategy Report. Furthermore, in order to receive security assistance within EPPA, Pakistan would have to show demonstrable progress in combating terrorist groups, including the Haqqani Network; fully assist the U.S. in investigating bin Laden's residency in Pakistan; and facilitate entry/exit visas for U.S. military trainers and personnel for other cooperative programs and projects in Pakistan.[140]

In December 2011, in reaction to the closure of NATO supply lines to Afghanistan in the aftermath of the "friendly fire" incident in Salala, Congress passed the National Defense Authorization Act, which further tightened conditions for granting aid Pakistan. It planned "to withhold 60% of any [Fiscal Year] 2012 appropriations for the Pentagon's Pakistan

Counterinsurgency Fund (PCF) unless the Secretary of Defense reports to Congress a strategy for the use of such funds and the metrics for determining their effectiveness, and a strategy to enhance Pakistani efforts to counter improvised explosive devices."[141]

PAKISTANI (LIMITED) ACTS OF RETALIATION

In response to American reprisals, Pakistan devised its own. To counter the United States Congress, the Pakistani Parliament, after extensive debate, drew up its own roadmap entitled "Guidelines for Revised Terms of Engagement with U.S.A/NATO/ISAF and General Foreign Policy." This document, which was passed on April 12, 2012, stipulated in its first three articles:

1. The relationship with U.S.A. should be based on mutual respect for the sovereignty, independence and territorial integrity of each other;
2. The U.S. footprint should be reviewed. This means (i) an immediate cessation of drone attacks inside the territorial borders of Pakistan, (ii) the cessation of infiltration into Pakistani territory on any pretext, including hot pursuit; (iii) Pakistani territory including air space shall not be used for transportation of arms and ammunitions to Afghanistan;
3. Pakistan's nuclear program and assets, including its safety and security cannot be compromised. The U.S.-Indo civil nuclear agreement has significantly altered the strategic balance in the region[;] therefore Pakistan should seek from the U.S. and others a similar treatment/facility.

Furthermore, the Pakistani members of Parliament demanded from the Americans "an unconditional apology" for the attack in Salala, which had resulted in the "martyrdom [*shahadat*]" of twenty-four soldiers, and they specified that "no private security contractors and/or intelligence operatives shall be allowed." Negotiations were immediately engaged. Obama sent Richard Holbrooke's successor, Marc Grossman, to Islamabad—but a drone strike was launched on April 30 against the Miram Shah bazaar in the capital of North Waziristan where members of the Haqqani Network, who had launched attacks on the U.S., Japanese, and German embassies in Kabul on April 15, were believed to be hiding.[142] The negotiations—led by the Defense Committee of the Cabinet for the Pakistani side—in fact quickly excluded the drones issue and turned to the amount of compensation Islamabad requested in exchange for reopening supply routes to Afghanistan, amounts discussed privately ranging from $1.8 to $3 billion.[143]

Eventually, in early July 2012, Hillary Clinton called her opposite number, Hina Rabbani Khar, to apologize, and the Pakistani government gave up the idea of asking for $5,000 per truck (it reverted to the previous rate of $250 per truck). This deal was purely transactional: on the one hand, the United States was longing for the supply routes to be reopened, as the additional cost of using the air routes had been $100 million a month for seven months, and on the other hand, the Pakistani government needed U.S. cash. Immediately after reopening the supply routes on July 4, 2012, the United States announced that it would resume paying "coalition support funds" (which reimburse Pakistan for logistical, military, and other support provided to American military operations against militants): the Pentagon spokesman indicated that the United States had to pay $1 billion in arrears since the suspension of payments.[144] This decision has to be factored in while reading table 8.1.

BACK TO BUSINESS AS USUAL? (2013–2015)

Mullen's formula qualifying the U.S.–Pakistan relation as "vexing and yet vital" was never more true than in the years 2011–2012, when tensions between both countries peaked. But in 2013–2015, a form of normalization took place under the new dispensation marked by the election of Nawaz Sharif to the post of prime minister and the appointment of Raheel Sharif as COAS.

Certainly, during the 2013 election campaign, opposition parties, mainly Imran Khan's Pakistan Tehreeke Insaaf (PTI) and Nawaz Sharif's Pakistan Muslim League, accused the Pakistan Peoples Party–led government of undermining the sovereignty of Pakistan by permitting drone strikes. But these strikes continued after Nawaz Sharif's electoral success in May 2013, and the new prime minister was not less accommodating than his Pakistan Peoples Party predecessors. Between June 7 and December 2013, more than a dozen drone attacks took place in the FATA (mostly in North Waziristan),[145] in spite of the fact that in August Kerry had paid a visit to Islamabad—the first since 2011—to announce that the drone strikes would end "very soon."[146] He had also said that he was hopeful of a "deeper, broader and more comprehensive partnership"[147]—words that sounded well in tune with the Kerry-Lugar-Breman Bill. During this visit, Kerry also announced that the "strategic dialogue" that Pakistan and the United States had initiated in 2010, and which had been suspended in 2011, could now be resumed. The meeting took place in January 2014. Kerry then said: "The United States has no doubt that Prime Minister Sharif's policies will put Pakistan on a path towards a more prosperous future, and we fully support his goal of making Pakistan's marketplace a tiger economy for the 21st century."[148]

Members of Congress were less positive. A few days before Kerry's speech, it passed a bill binding the U.S. administration to withhold $33 million from the funds meant for Pakistan, until Shakil Afridi (the man who had helped the United States to locate bin Laden in Abbottabad) was released from prison and cleared of all charges—he had been sentenced to thirty-three years' imprisonment for treason in 2012. The bill also mentioned that none of the funds meant for Pakistan under several major headings (including "Economic support fund") could "be distributed unless the U.S. Secretary of State certifies that Islamabad is cooperating with the United States in counter terrorism efforts against the Haqqani Network, the Quetta Shura Taliban, Lashkar-e-Taiba, Jaish-e-Mohammad, al Qaeda and other domestic and foreign terrorist organisations."[149]

The Obama administration was less cautious and preferred to reset the U.S.-Pakistan ties by resorting to the old clientelistic recipes. In December 2013, Chuck Hagel assured Finance Minister Ishaq Dar that $850 million of arrears (pertaining to the coalition support fund) would be paid—something Dar considered not Pakistan's "charity, but its right."[150] Nawaz Sharif was equally eager to restore the old transactional ties. Certainly, the visit of Nawaz Sharif to Washington in October 2013 was overshadowed by the drone issue, all the more so as a few days before the UN special rapporteur on human rights and counterterrorism had released a report ahead of a debate on the use of drones at the UN General Assembly, in which it was said that about 330 drone strikes had taken place in Pakistan since 2004 and that they had killed about 2,200 people, including 400 civilians.[151] (The report also said that there was "strong evidence" that top Pakistani and military officials approved U.S. drone strikes.)[152] But although Nawaz Sharif mentioned the drone strikes during his visit, he kept a low profile on this issue. He clearly did not want to weaken his chances to reach his main objective, which was financial. Given the economic crisis that Pakistan was facing, American aid was more important than ever. First, the United States helped Pakistan vis-à-vis the International Monetary Fund (IMF). After weeks of negotiations, during the fall of 2013, Pakistan had finally been offered $6.6 billion by the IMF in exchange for the usual commitment: the country is supposed to reduce its budget deficit from 8.5 percent of the gross domestic product to 3.5 percent in 3 years. Second, Pakistan needed American money—and got some of it. While the Obama administration had already obtained from Congress the release of some aid—military and economic—since the summer, the visit of Nawaz Sharif gave the American president the opportunity to announce the revival of plans that had been blocked for months. The total amount of the support was between $1.6 billion and $2.5 billion according to the available sources.[153] Although table 8.1 shows an erosion of American aid to Pakistan, the total amount of money the United States gave to Pakistan in 2014—$1.721 billion—remained above the 2004, 2005 and 2007 figures.

These money transfers, which continue to take place at a rather high level, reflect the resilience of the old clientelistic relation—back on track once again. But Pakistan was to be rewarded even more by the United States after Islamabad gave up the idea of negotiating with the Tehrik-e Taliban Pakistan (TTP) and started to meet some of the American expectations in terms of countermilitancy. In 2013, Nawaz Sharif wanted to talk with the Pakistani Taliban and looked for a negotiated settlement with the FATA-based TTP, whereas the Americans wanted to fight this group. Both seemed to be at cross-purposes when a drone strike, in November 2013, killed Hakimullah Mehsud, the TTP chief, with whom the Sharif government had apparently initiated peace talks. The PTI immediately orchestrated a massive protest against strikes, which it accused not only of resulting in the death of innocent people but also of sabotaging peace. PTI activists blocked the trucks in charge of NATO supplies at checkpoints in the province of Khyber Pakhtunkhwa, in spite of the official policy of Islamabad that was much more conciliatory.[154] Under the PTI's pressure in the political arena, Nawaz Sharif could not come out in support of a systematic repression of the TTP.

But the United States found a new ally in Raheel Sharif, the successor of Kayani in December 2013. An expert in counterinsurgency, Raheel Sharif was immediately more determined to fight the North Waziristan militants than his predecessor. In January 2014, Pakistan air force jets and helicopters multiplied the bombing of suspected hideouts in the region (and, to a lesser extent, in the Khyber and Orakzai Agencies). According to press reports, dozens of militants were killed, including Uzbeks.[155] Then, a full-fledged ground operation was announced and prepared with the evacuation of hundreds of thousands of civilians. Immediately after it was started, former director general of the Inter-Services Public Relations (ISPR) Major General Athar Abbas and former prime minister Gilani declared separately that Kayani had been responsible for postponing any military operation in North Waziristan.[156] Hinting at a paradigmatic shift, columnist Muhammad Ali Ehsan pointed out that Musharraf and Kayani "believed in the 'sacred doctrine of strategic depth' that possibly was the reason that tied their hands behind their backs as the army continued fighting a 'stalemated war' that was being characterised more by 'firefighting acts' than any military actions of substance. General Raheel Sharif, from the outset, vouched to respond to every terrorist act with a military action."[157]

The North Waziristan operation that started officially on June 15, 2014, was given the name of Zarb-e-Azb (the name of the sword that Prophet Mohammad used in the battles of Badr and Uhud). It was massive, primarily because of the huge number of internally displaced persons that it generated. By the first week of July, 800,000 people had left their homes and migrated to Khyber Pakhtunkhwa,[158] and two weeks later, the one million mark was crossed.[159] Given these humanitarian collateral casualties, it was even more important for the army to mobilize society behind the operation. It was legitimized by the Sunni Ulema Board, which declared that it was a jihad.[160] The army claimed that it had "the support of the entire nation."[161] By early September, the army announced that 910 terrorists had been killed (whereas eighty-two soldiers had died), that dozens of hideouts and twenty-seven explosives and arms-making factories had been destroyed, and that the towns of Miramshah, Mirali, Dattakhel, Boya, and Dogan had returned to the control of the state.[162] And by mid-November, the army claimed that "1,198 terrorists have been killed, 356 injured, 227 have been arrested" (whereas forty-two officers and security forces had been killed and 155 injured). The army also claimed that "11 private jails, 191 secret tunnels, 39 IED factories, 4,991 various types of ready-made IEDs, 132 ton explosive material, 2,470 sub machine Guns, 293 machine Guns, 111 heavy machine Guns have also been recovered during the operation."[163] Senior journalist Zahid Hussain, who went to Miramshah and Mirali in November 2014, underlined the magnitude of the North Waziristan operation, which, according to him, was "unique in many ways," among other things because "The role of intelligence has contributed hugely to the targeting precision of militant sanctuaries."[164] The army also claimed that the Haqqani Network had not been spared,[165] something Washington was bound to appreciate.[166]

Indeed, Lieutenant General Joseph Anderson, an American senior commander of the NATO forces based in Afghanistan, declared in mid-November 2014 to the *Washington Post* that the North Waziristan operation had "disrupted" the Haqqanis' "efforts here and has caused them to be less effective in terms of their ability to pull off an attack here in Kabul."[167]

A few days later, Raheel Sharif spent one full week on an official visit in Washington—four years after the last, tumultuous visit of Kayani. He got a warm reception from civilian leaders (including Secretary of State John Kerry, National Security Adviser Susan Rice, Deputy Secretary of Defense Bob Work, and U.S. Special Representative for Pakistan and Afghanistan

Dan Feldman) as well as military leaders, including Chairman of the Joint Chiefs of Staff General Martin Dempsey and the Central Command chief General Austin, who "praised the Pakistan army for its commitment, professionalism and achievement in the fight against terror as well as ongoing Zarb-i-Azb operation."[168] During his visit, General Sharif was conferred the U.S. Legion of Merit "in recognition of his brave leadership and efforts to ensure peace in the region."[169]

The United States appreciated not only Raheel Sharif's North Waziristan operation but also his attitude vis-à-vis Afghanistan. While Islamabad was relieved, in November 2014, by the American decision not to withdraw fully from Afghanistan and to continue to fight the Taliban in 2015 in the framework of the agreement signed by the new Afghan president, Ashraf Ghani, Washington was also happy to observe some rapprochement between Kabul and Islamabad in the post-Karzai era. Now Raheel Sharif played a part in this rapprochement. On November 7, he went to Kabul to meet President Ghani and "offered the 'full range' of training courses and facilities in Pakistan's training institutions to Afghan security forces."[170] Although Pakistan had made the same offer before, this time Kabul did not turn it down. Seven days later, President Ghani's trip to Pakistan (the third country he visited after China and Saudi Arabia)—which began with a first round of discussions at Rawalpindi general headquarters, where he met Raheel Sharif again—was interpreted in Washington as a reconfirmation of the new trend, in a context where better relations between Kabul and Islamabad were perceived in the United States as key to the regional stability. On November 21, 2014, Obama made a phone call to Nawaz Sharif, not only to inform him of his forthcoming visit to India, but also to mention the Afghano-Pakistani relations. He said that he "appreciated efforts in this regard and called it pivotal for the peace and stability in the region."[171] He also expressed his will to take the U.S.–Pakistan relations "one step beyond" current levels. Three days later, an American airstrike in eastern Afghanistan targeted Fazlullah, the TTP chief, whose elimination was a Pakistani priority.[172]

The military cooperation intensified. While the United States withdrew most of its troops by the end of 2014—leaving only 10,000 soldiers behind—it handed over 14 combat aircrafts, 59 military trainer jets, and 374 armoured personnel carriers to Pakistan. In April 2015, the State Department also approved a $952 million deal regarding fifteen Viper attack helicopters and one thousand Hellfire II missiles.[173]

By the middle of 2015, however, the normalization of the U.S.–Pakistan reached a plateau. While Commander Resolute Support Mission and U.S. Forces in Afghanistan general John Campbell congratulated the efforts of

Pakistan to bring around the table, in Murree (Punjab), representatives of the Afghan Taliban and the Kabul government in July, soon after, Ashraf Gani protested that Islamabad (and Rawalpindi!) was supporting Taliban groups which were attacking Afghanistan across the Durand Line. More important, in August, the announcement that Mollah Omar had died more than two years before in a Karachi hospital reactivated the suspicion of double game that the bin Laden raid had exacerbated in 2011. The Obama administration hinted that it may not certify the effectiveness of Pakistan counterterrorism operation to Congress to enable passage of Coalition Support Fund. Washington could afford this kind of measure more easily after the withdrawal of most of the American troops from Afghanistan, which made Pakistan less useful to the United States: the American troops were small enough for being supplied via other routes or even by air.

CONCLUSION

Historically, U.S.–Pakistan relations have largely followed a clientelistic pattern. The American patron needed a regional broker to contain communism, to play the middleman vis-à-vis China, and to offer support in the post-9/11 "global war on terror." The client needed arms and money to resist India, the neighbor that continues to overdetermine its foreign policy, and to satisfy its military—a state within the state craving for a comfortable life and sophisticated weaponry. This relationship was not based on any other ideological, societal, or economic affinity, thereby contributing to make it somewhat shallow and unstable. So long as both countries had a common enemy—the USSR—or tried to have common friends—China—and did not look at India in too dissimilar ways, their relationship was supported by at least some common ground. But these common denominators have vanished one after another. First, the fact that India has become closer to the United States has indisposed the client. Second, China, Pakistan's "all-weather friend," has been perceived as a threat to an increasing number of Americans. Third, after the trauma of 9/11, the image of Pakistan has been badly affected not only by a rising, popular Islamophobia but by the close relations that some Pakistani elements have cultivated with militant Islamists.

In this context, the Obama administration and (even more clearly) congressmen including Senator John Kerry have tried to shift the emphasis from a security-centered approach to a more civil society–oriented one. But this attempt has been handicapped by the limited power of Pakistan's civilian rulers and the contradictions of its own agenda: long-term objectives in terms of development have been undermined by short-term security-centered goals, which has led the Obama administration—possibly under some pressure from the Pentagon—to recognize the Pakistani military as its main interlocutors. Once again, the military-based clientelistic pattern has prevailed, the Pakistani army being the United States' true partner, just as it was before.

But while this pattern had worked fine in the 1980s against the Soviets when the United States and the Pakistani army had a common enemy, things were clearly different twenty years later—partly because of the anti-Soviet jihad. The Pakistani army had developed strong relations with militant groups—or had acknowledged (resigned itself to?) their entrenchment in the country's social fabric. As a result, Pakistan under Musharraf and during the Kayani era was not a reliable ally of the United States in its fight against Islamists. Things have changed again, it seems, with the appointment of a new COAS, Raheel Sharif, who appears to be more prepared to fight militants, as evident from the North Waziristan campaign he initiated in 2014. As a result, U.S.–Pakistan relations seem to be somewhat back on track according to their traditional pattern: "For Washington, it remains an issue-specific and transactional relationship. They give us errands and we get paid."[174]

But would a paradigmatic shift through which the Pakistani establishment would consider Islamists as its main enemies mean a return to the old pattern? Four caveats may affect such a movement toward the business-as-usual model. First, the North Waziristan operation may not be such a turning point because the Pakistani army may continue to protect some of its old Islamic partners. According to Ken Dilanian, "Several U.S. officials said in interviews that the double game continues, because key Haqqani leaders were warned in advance about the offensive and decamped to Pakistani cities."[175] The relation between the Pakistani security establishment and the LeT seems even more resilient. In December 2014, the organization, for the first time since the 1980s, held its annual *ijtema* (congregation) in Punjab. Hafiz Saeed addressed a crowd of 400,000 people.[176]

Second, the U.S.–Pakistan relationship will not be fully back on track if the former does not respect the sovereignty of the latter more explicitly. In the past, when the United States and Pakistan worked in tandem, the former let the latter operate rather freely on its territory—as evident from the way Zia could do almost anything he wanted with the American money that was meant to be channeled toward the Afghan mujahideen. Today, drone strikes remain a bone of contention—in spite of their decreasing number—and may remain so if the Pakistani army is not handed over their responsibility (their termination does not seem a realistic perspective).

Third, the new U.S.–India relations have deeply affected the U.S.–Pakistan relations over time. George W. Bush had balanced the American–Indian rapprochement by making important concessions. Obama has not made a similar effort in this direction, as if Pakistan was, at best, a tactical partner, whereas India was a strategic partner. This is evident from the visits he made to India in 2010 and 2014—whereas he never went to Pakistan. Since Pakistan's foreign policy remains overdetermined by its fear of India, this is a major factor of estrangement between Islamabad and Washington.

Fourth, mutual distrust has reached unprecedented levels. According to the July 2014 Pew survey, 14 percent of Pakistanis gave a favorable assessment of the United States (50 percent less than in 2006),[177] while 18 percent of Americans viewed Pakistan positively.[178] While Pakistan has made no effort to reach out to Americans, the United States has tried but failed to relate to the Pakistani society the way the KLB was intended to do. In fact, this is a reconfirmation of the KLB's failure that few figures suffice to demonstrate. While the plan was entering its final year, the Pakistani government claimed that it had received only $3.8 billion, including $252 million for energy sector programs, $185 million for economic growth and agriculture, $323 million for education, and $272 million for the health care sector. A large fraction of the money, $1.157 billion, was spent on emergency and flood relief.[179] While American humanitarian aid has been appreciated (as evident from the popularity of the American rescue operations after the 2005 earthquake in Kashmir), its impact was probably less than a more sustained effort of development. Commenting on the KLB two months before the end of this program, U.S. Special Representative for Afghanistan and Pakistan Daniel Feldman declared that out of $7.5 billion, $5 billion had been disbursed but that this plan would be neither extended nor renewed. Instead, he suggested that trade should take over from aid, which meant a review of tariffs protecting the American market (in the sector of textiles in particular)— something many members of Congress may not be prepared to support.

For the four reasons mentioned above, U.S.–Pakistan relations may not return to their highest level any time soon, but even at their peak they were rather shallow and interest based. Hence the diplomatic ups and downs under Ayub Khan and Zia. The patron may resign itself to get less from its client—and may therefore give him less in exchange. But their relation will probably survive. Even if the North Waziristan operation is not initiating a paradigm shift, the United States may continue to engage Pakistan because of its role regarding the dissemination of Islamism and nuclear proliferation. The United States will probably try to maintain some presence on Pakistani territory for intelligence gathering by creating dependence (through financial aid or arms sales). Intelligence was already considered a key element by the Bush administration, which had initiated the "global war against terror" and started to rely on drones: "The drones were basically flying high resolution video cameras armed with missiles. The only meaningful way to point drones toward a target was to have spies on the ground telling the CIA where to look, hunt and kill. Without spies, the video feed from the Predator might as well be a blank television screen. . . . They were the key, in some respects, to protecting the country."[180] The key role of spies partly explains the tension that resulted from the Raymond Davis affair. At that time, "temporary American 'diplomats' got only a one-month visa, and then they had to leave the country. That crippled a plan to essentially flood Pakistan with more CIA operatives."[181]

But fighting Islamism is not the only reason why the United States needs spies in Pakistan. Nuclear proliferation is another one, the nuclear issue seen in a larger perspective being an existential issue. As the *New York Times* puts it: "walking away [from Pakistan] could make the nuclear-armed government even more unstable—a chilling prospect."[182] In 2011, Obama told his staff that the possibility that Pakistan should " 'disintegrate' and set off a scramble for its weapons . . . was his biggest single national security concern."[183]

Probably since 2010—after the Times Square episode if not before— Obama has ceased to think about U.S.–Pakistan relations as anything but a security-related affair. According to Sanger, his policy—that is known as "mitigation"—"has three goals. The first is helping Pakistan keep its arsenal safe—while improving the American ability to find and immobilize the weapons if that effort fails. The second is to keep the Pakistani civilian government from being toppled, by the army or extremists, through various forms of assistance. And the third is to keep up the pressure on insurgents and Al Qaeda operatives, mostly with drone strikes. But 'mitigation' is all about self-defense. There is not much in it for the Pakistanis. And it is easy to forget that for all its double-dealing with the Taliban and other insurgent groups, Pakistan has been a major loser in the region's wars."[184]

Indeed, such an approach may not be compatible with the pursuit of a clientelistic relation. Still, the withdrawal of the remaining American troops from Afghanistan by 2015–2016 might not bring Washington and Islamabad back to the positions they had finally carved out in the 1990s. Unlike in the 1990s, the temptation to show indifference (or even conduct a policy of sanctions) will probably be offset by the fear of seeing Islamism gaining momentum in the AfPak region and of Pakistan's nuclear arsenal—the fastest growing in the world[185]—falling into Islamist hands.[186]

Conversely, there is no doubt today that Pakistan is seeking to shed its "client" status with respect to the United States, ultimately to become a pivotal state. This notion was developed in the 1990s by analysts seeking to define the criteria for a second circle of U.S. partners outside of NATO.[187] At the time, the authors included both Pakistan and India in their list of nine states they considered could relay American influence, as if Washington could rely on both these countries at once. This is not the only contradiction that can be detected in their use of the concept. The most significant lies elsewhere, in their underestimation of these countries' ability to "pivot," that is, to hedge their bets by replacing one partner with another depending on the circumstances, or even to exercise their nuisance capacity.

The fact that Pakistan aspires to become a pivotal state is evident from the recommendations passed by Parliament on April 12, 2012, attesting to this, as they indicate Pakistan's intention to strengthen relations with the European Union, Russia, the Muslim world, the Association of Southeast Asian Nations, and especially China to escape the United States. Although Beijing is certainly an all-weather friend of Pakistan, it is not clear today that it is prepared to support its protégé (at least financially) as much as the United States does today. In 2008, when Islamabad went bankrupt, the Chinese refused to bail it out. Things may change since Pakistan is an important country for President's Xi Jinping's "one route, one belt" project. Beijing has announced $46 billion of investment in Pakistan in this framework.

NOTES

1. This chapter is based on a wide range of conversations and interviews in Islamabad and Washington. I am especially grateful to the following persons: Hassan Abbas, Shahid Amin, Shahid Javed Burki, Christine Fair, Frederic Grare, Nazir Hussain, Zahid Hussain, Alan Kronstadt, Khalid Mahmood, Tanvir Ahmad Khan, Ali Sarwar Naqvi, Vali Nasr, Jamshed Marker, Maqsudul Hasan Nuri, Philip Oldenburg, George Perkovich, Aqil Shah, Ayesha Siddiqa, Ashley Tellis, Akram Zaki, and Akbar Zaidi.

2. Jean-François Médard, "Le clientélisme politique: De la relation de clientèle à l'analyse politique," *Revue française de Science Politique* 26, no. 1 (February 1976): 103–131. See also by the same author "Political Clientelism in France: A Re-Examination of the Centre-Periphery Nexus," in *Political Clientelism, Patronage and Development*, ed. R. Lemarchand and S. N. Eisenstadt (New York: Sage, 1980); "The Underdeveloped State in Tropical Africa: Political Clientelism or Neo-

Patrimonialism?" in *Private Patronage and Public Power: Political Clientelism in the Modern State*, ed. C. Clapham (New York: St. Martin's, 1982). See also Herbert Kitschelt and Steven Wilkinson, eds., *Patrons, Clients and Policies: Patterns of Democratic Accountability and Political Competition* (New York: Cambridge University Press, 2007).

3. See two other French authors, Jean Leca and Yves Schemeil, "Clientélisme et patrimonialisme dans le monde arabe," *International Political Sciences Review* 4, no. 4 (1983): 455–494.

4. U.S.–Pakistan relations are sometimes described not as clientelistic but as "transactional," a word that captures the bargaining dimension but does not reflect the intention of the American patron, clearly interested in getting something done by its "client" (and which literally pays for the service).

5. Dennis Kux, *The United States and Pakistan, 1947–2000: Disenchanted Allies* (Baltimore: Johns Hopkins University Press, 2001), 20–35.

6. Selig Harrison, *The Widening Gulf: Asian Nationalism and American Policy* (New York: Free Press, 1978).

7. The Badaber base was located in the North West Frontier Province near Peshawar.

8. K. Alan Kronstadt, *Pakistan–U.S. Relations: Report for Congress* (Washington, D.C.: Congressional Research Service, 2009).

9. S. Akbar Zaidi, "Who Benefits from U.S. Aid to Pakistan?" *Carnegie Policy Outlook*, September 21, 2011, 3. See also S. Akbar Zaidi, "Who Benefits from U.S. Aid to Pakistan?" *Economic and Political Weekly* 46 , no. 32 (2011); and Nancy Birdsall, Wren Elhai, and Molly Kinder, "Beyond Bullets and Bombs: Fixing the U.S. Approach to Development in Pakistan," in *Report of the Study Group on a U.S. Development Strategy in Pakistan*, Center for Global Development, June 2011, www.cgdev.org/files/1425136_file_CGD_Pakistan_FINAL_web.pdf.

10. Carol Lancaster, "Quel avenir pour l'aide américaine à l'étranger," *Revue Tiers Monde* 151 (July–September 1997): 542.

11. Robert Nolan, "Pakistan: The Most Allied Ally in Asia," Foreign Policy Association, www.fpa.org/newsletter_info02583/newsletter_info_sub_list.htm?section =Pakistan%3A%20The%20Most%20Allied%20Ally%20in%20Asia (accessed 23 July 2011). Cited in http://pakistan-encyclopedia.blogspot.fr. Interestingly, this quote is sometimes attributed to Eisenhower. See Kronstadt, *Pakistan–U.S. Relations*, 32.

12. John Foster Dulles once said about India: "neutralism is immoral."

13. *Foreign Relations of the United States, 1961–1963*, ed. Glenn W. LaFantasie, vol. 6, *South Asia*, ed. Louis J. Smith (Washington, D.C.: United States Government Printing Office, 1996).

14. Yet the ideological compatibility with Pakistan's more market-oriented economic programs, reinforced by a substantial U.S. expert presence and guidance, stood in stark contrast with a pervasive dislike of India's chosen path, even under Kennedy, when plans for a U.S. collaboration on a steel plant were shot down. See George Rosen, *Western Economists and Eastern Societies: Agents of Change in South Asia, 1960–1970* (Baltimore: Johns Hopkins University Press, 1986).

15. Cited in Kux, *United States and Pakistan*, 150. Ayub Khan uses such harsh words in spite of the fact that the United States had voted in favor of a Pakistani resolution

regarding Kashmir in June 1962 at the UN Security Council—a resolution that India criticized and that was vetoed by the USSR.

16. Ibid., 153.

17. The Pressler amendment was passed in 1984 under pressure from congressmen such as Senator John Glenn. It subordinated arms sales to yearly presidential certification that Pakistan did not have nuclear weapons. Reagan did it from 1985 onwards, even though intelligence reports were more and more alarming on that front. Many questions remain unanswered in this regard: Did Reagan not object, thinking that nuclear nonproliferation was less important or that his nonobjection was an acceptable price to pay for the alliance? Did the Pakistanis make (official) assurances that they had stopped nuclear development? Did the United States know well that they had not? On the U.S. complacency regarding the Pakistani nuclear program, see Adrian Levy and Catherine Scott-Clark, *Deception: Pakistan, the United States, and the Global Nuclear Conspiracy* (New York: Atlantic Books, 2007).

18. Farzana Shaikh convincingly argues that the United States not only let Pakistan acquire the nuclear weapon but in fact pushed the country in this direction by refusing "a formal security agreement upgrading the 1954 Mutual Defence Assistance Agreement and with clear and unambiguous guarantees ratified by Congress." Farzana Shaikh, *Making Sense of Pakistan* (London: Hurst, 2009), 197. See also A. Z. Hilali, *U.S.–Pakistan Relationship: Soviet Invasion of Afghanistan* (London: Ashgate, 2005), 69–70.

19. As in the 1960s, Pakistan turned to China, and Peking sold M-11 ballistic missiles to Islamabad.

20. It seems that the Pakistanis pleaded with Clinton to visit—it was not at first scheduled—and he in effect allegedly said, "You want a visit—I'll give you a visit!"

21. At the United Nations, in a joint communiqué, fifty-four Asian countries expressed their assurance that Pakistan would get a seat on the Security Council when the next rotation of nonpermanent members took place in 2003.

22. See Sumit Ganguly, "Pakistan's Never-Ending Story: Why the October Coup Was No Surprise," *Foreign Affairs*, March–April 2000.

23. As a variation on the theme of "most allied ally," in 2007 Deputy Secretary of State John Negroponte called Pakistan an "indispensable" ally of the United States, which is the word Obama used to describe India during his visit in 2010.

24. Cited in Kux, *United States and Pakistan*, 257.

25. Cited in Robert Fisk, "Farewell to Democracy in Pakistan," *Independent*, October 26, 2001.

26. Zaffar Abbas, "Pakistan's Great Gamble," *Herald*, October 2001, 22.

27. Craig Cohen and Derek Chollet, "When $10 Billion Is Not Enough: Rethinking U.S. Strategy Towards Pakistan," *Washington Quarterly* 30, no. 2 (Spring 2007): 10.

28. In September, the police raided two religious seminaries in Karachi and arrested twenty foreign students (thirteen Malaysians, six Indonesians, and one Burmese). More important, they arrested Gun Rusman Gunawan, an Indonesian madrasah student who is supposedly the younger brother of the chief of the Jemaah Islamiyah—the movement responsible for the Bali bomb attack. On October, two Yemenis were arrested in Faisalabad; one of them was apparently a top aid of bin

Laden. Observers have argued that Pakistan kept tabs on these people and delivered them one at a time to Washington whenever there was a bad patch in relations or Pakistan wanted something special.

29. Kronstadt, *Pakistan–U.S. Relations*, 9.

30. On January 23, the Pakistan Bar Council organized a countrywide strike to express solidarity with the nuclear scientists and protest against the government's humiliating attitude toward them. The same day, Muttahida Majlis-e Amal (MMA) militants demonstrated against the debriefing of the nuclear scientists and ongoing army operations in the Pashtun Belt.

31. In 2008, A. Q. Khan alleged that one shipment of uranium enrichment equipment to North Korea was "supervised by the Pakistani army with the consent of the then Army chief Musharraf," who accused Khan of lying (Kronstadt, *Pakistan–U.S. Relations*, 63). But it beggars belief that A. Q. Khan could have arranged the transport of such goods without active army approval.

32. The personal affinity between Bush and Musharraf played a role there. When they met at the White House in September 2006, the former said about the latter: "When he looks me in the eye and says . . . there won't be a Taliban and won't be Al Qaeda, I believe him, you know?" Cited in Cohen and Chollet, "When $10 Billion Is Not Enough," 8.

33. David Rode, Carlotta Gall, Eric Schmitt, and David E. Sanger, "U.S. Officials See Waste in Billions Sent to Pakistan," *New York Times*, December 24, 2007.

34. Greg Miller, "CIA Pays for Support in Pakistan," *Los Angeles Times*, November 15, 2010.

35. Kronstadt, *Pakistan–U.S. Relations*, 65.

36. Ibid., 11.

37. The State Department's Country Reports on Terrorism 2007 released in April 2008 mentioned that "the United States remained concerned that the Federally Administered Tribal Areas (FATA) of Pakistan were being used as a safe haven for Al Qaeda terrorists." See http://www.state.gov/s/ct/rls/crt/2007/103709.htm.

38. Kronstadt, *Pakistan–U.S. Relations*, 55.

39. Hassan Abbas, "An Assessment of Pakistan's Peace Agreements with Militants in Waziristan (2004–2008)," in *The Afghanistan–Pakistan Theatre: Militant Islam, Security and Stability*, ed. Daveed Gartenstein-Ross and Clifford D. May (Washington, D.C.: FDD Press, 2010), 9. The following paragraphs draw from this excellent source.

40. Ibid., 12.

41. The role of the MMA government of Peshawar in these repeated failures needs to be examined in greater detail.

42. In a videotaped address to the Pakistanis, the Al Qaeda leader Ayman al-Zawahiri accused Musharraf of selling out their country to the United States in August 2008.

43. Kronstadt, *Pakistan–U.S. Relations*, 78.

44. Ibid., 91.

45. See Sandy Berger and Bruce Riedel, "America's Stark Choice," *International Herald Tribune*, October 9, 2007. For an account of Teresita Schaffer's statement before the Senate Foreign Relations Committee, see "Democracy Gets Small Portion of U.S. Aid," *Washington Post*, January 6, 2008.

46. Cited in Kronstadt, *Pakistan–U.S. Relations*, 85.

47. Ibid.

48. In his address before the Royal United Services Institute, London, Musharraf declared: "The strategic ally, Pakistan, strategic ally of the West for forty two years—47 to 89 was ditched and the people of Pakistan in these streets, the men in the street thought that we have been used and ditched." Available at http://presidentmusharraf.wordpress.com/2008/01/06/rusi-london/.

49. Asaf Ali Zardari, "Partnering with Pakistan," *Washington Post*, January 28, 2009. It is surprising that the United States voiced no objections to the victimization discourse. However, it should be kept in mind that the U.S. back down was a condition of the agreement with the USSR that both would withdraw their military presence and aid from their respective sides and that the United States in effect gave Pakistan a free hand in backing Hekmatyar in the post-Najibullah struggles and looked the other way as the Taliban emerged and succeeded. A fair question to the Pakistanis would have been: Would you have preferred the United States to maintain its pre-1989 "engagement" with all the pressure and leverage that it entailed?

50. President (elect) Barack Obama, *Meet the Press*, December 7, 2008, transcript at http://www.msnbc.msn.com/id/28097635.

51. "We need to make clear to people that the cancer is in Pakistan," he declared during an Oval Office meeting on November 25, 2009. Bob Woodward, "Obama: 'We Need to Make Clear to People That the Cancer Is in Pakistan,'" *Washington Post*, September 28, 2010, www.washingtonpost.com/wp-dyn/content/article/2010/09/28/AR2010092805092.html.

52. "Obama's Address to the Nation on the Way Forward in Afghanistan and Pakistan, December 2009," Council on Foreign Relations, www.cfr.org/pakistan/obamas-address-nation-way-forward-afghanistan-pakistan-december-2009/p20871.

53. See the December 7, 2008, *Meet the Press* transcript at http://www.msnbc.msn.com/id/28097635, 20/10/2012.

54. Details about the Kerry-Luger Bill, available at www.ibitians.com/2009/10/03/full-text-kerrylugar-bill-details-conditions/ or http://pakistaniat.com/2009/10/07/full-text-kerry-lugar-bill/.

55. From the text of the Kerry-Lugar Bill. Ibid.

56. Cited in "US Senate Passes Kerry Lugar Bill to Triple Aid to Pakistan," *Times of India*, September 25, 2009, http://timesofindia.indiatimes.com/world/us/US-Senate-passes-Kerry-Lugar-Bill-to-triple-aid-to-Pakistan/articleshow/5053865.cms.

57. "Biden, Palin at One on Pakistan Danger," *Dawn*, October 4, 2008.

58. "'Few Steps' by Pakistan, Not Enough Says U.S.," *Hindu*, July 23, 2010.

59. Bob Woodward, *Obama's Wars* (New York: Simon & Schuster, 2010), 127.

60. From the text of the Kerry-Lugar Bill.

61. In order to defuse the concerns of many Pakistanis, including the military, promoters of the Enhanced Partnership with Pakistan Act had to produce a "Joint Explanatory Statement" where it was made clear that the act intended "to demonstrate the American people's long-term commitment to the people of Pakistan. . . . The legislation does not seek in any way to compromise Pakistan's sovereignty, impinge on Pakistan's national security interests, or micromanage

any aspect of Pakistani military or civilian operations." John Kerry and Howard Berman, "Joint Explanatory Statement, Enhanced Partnership with Pakistan Act, 2009," Council of Foreign Relation, www.cfr.org/pakistan/joint-explanatory -statement-enhanced-partnership-pakistan-act-2009/p20422.

62. Mosharraf Zaidi considered, for instance, that "The Kerry-Lugar Bill signals a dramatic shift in how American power seeks to engage with Pakistanis." M. Zaidi, "Kerry-Lugar Bill: The Fruition of 62 Years," www.mosharrafzaidi.com/2009/09 /30kerry-lugar-bill-the-fruition-of-62-years/ (accessed 28 July, 2011).

63. See, for instance, http://new-pakistan.com/2010/02/11/building-trust/.

64. Markey points out: "The legislative process that yielded KLB was an unusually messy one, reflecting clear differences between Berman's vision and that of the bill's Senate sponsors. In June 2009, Kerry publicly criticized the House version of the bill for sending the wrong message to the Pakistani public. He said it threatened to paint Pakistan's government as 'an American puppet,' and suggested this ran 'counter to some of the things that we're trying to do.'" Daniel S. Markey, *No Exit from Pakistan: America's Tortured Relationship with Islamabad* (New York: Cambridge University Press, 2013), 143.

65. Ibid., 144.

66. According to Hussain Haqqani, the then Pakistani ambassador in the United States, "The letter even hinted at addressing Pakistan's oft-stated desire for a settlement of the Kashmir dispute." Hussain Haqqani, *Magnificent Delusions: Pakistan, the United States, and an Epic History in Misunderstanding* (New York: Public Affairs, 2013), 339.

67. "Pakistani Public Opinion Ever More Critical of U.S.," Pew Research Center, June 27, 2012, www.pewglobal.org/2012/06/27/pakistani-public-opinion-ever-more -critical-of-u-s/.

68. Haqqani, *Magnificent Delusions*, 321.

69. Woodward, *Obama's Wars*, 287.

70. Ibid., 117.

71. Haqqani, *Magnificent Delusions*, 325.

72. The Pakistani army was against the Kerry-Lugar Bill not only because it gave priority to civilians over the military but also because it meant huge aid for development at the expense of security-related financial support.

73. Just before that, the effective use of an enhanced Frontier Corps in Bajaur to push back or suppress the militants tended to be viewed as a model.

74. Cited in Jane Perlez, "Pressure from U.S. Strains Ties with Pakistan," *New York Times*, October 26, 2009.

75. McChrystal, apparently, told Kayani: "'You can't pretend any longer that this is not going on. We are saying you have got to go in to North Waziristan." Jane Perlez, "U.S. Urges Action in Pakistan After Failed Bombing," *New York Times*, May 8, 2010.

76. Hasan Zaidi, "Army Chief Wanted More Drone Support," *Dawn*, May 20, 2011. See also "Government Official Urged Follow-up Drone Strikes," *Dawn*, May 20, 2011.

77. Kronstadt, *Pakistan–U.S. Relations*, 57.

78. Cited in ibid., 59.

79. Some members of Congress also feared that the Pakistani army might transfer American technology to China. See *Hearing Before the Committee on International*

Relations, House of Representatives, 109th Cong., 2d Sess., July 20, 2006, http://commdocs.house.gov/committees/intlrel/hfa28787.000/hfa28787_of.htm.

80. Kronstadt, *Pakistan–U.S. Relations*, 60.

81. Ibid., 62.

82. Ibid., 61.

83. Cohen and Chollet, "When $10 Billion Is Not Enough," 13.

84. While some members of Congress worried about the fact that "Pakistan diverted much of the funds [coming from the United States] towards a military buildup focused on India" (Kronstadt, *Pakistan–U.S. Relations*, 88), "Counterarguments contend that such purchase[s] facilitate regional stability and allow Pakistan to feel more secure vis-à-vis India, its more powerful neighbour" (Kronstadt, *Pakistan–U.S. Relations*, 108). Obviously, the counterarguments prevailed until at least the end of the last decade.

85. "Pakistan Plans to Buy 14 More F-16 Jets from USA," *Asian Defence News*, July 7, 2010.

86. A Pakistani air force wing commander considered that "This graduation is historic for US–Pakistan relations." "U.S.–Pakistan Relations Bolstered by F-16 Training," *Asian Defence News*, June 15, 2010.

87. Kurram seems to have become the place where leaders of the Haqqani networks have regrouped after they left North Waziristan as a result of drone strikes.

88. This attack was probably orchestrated by the Pakistani army itself.

89. Cited in Mark Landler and Eric Schmitt, "Meeting Pakistanis, U.S. Will Try to Fix Relations," *New York Times*, October 18, 2010.

90. Adam Entous, "Washington, Islamabad Clash Over Bills for War on Terror," *Wall Street Journal*, Europe, May 18, 2011.

91. Haqqani, *Magnificent Delusions*, 337.

92. In his March 27, 2009, speech announcing a new American strategy in Afghanistan and Pakistan, President Obama announced that "clear metrics to measure progress and hold ourselves accountable" would be developed—hence the production of quarterly reports by the White House.

93. "White House Quarterly Report on Afghanistan and Pakistan, April 2011," Council on Foreign Relations, www.cfr.org/pakistan/white-house-quarterly-report -afghanistan-pakistan-april-2011/p24600, 17.

94. Ibid., 21.

95. Cited in Daniel S. Markey, *No Exit from Pakistan*, 146.

96. Mohammad Ayub Khan, *Friends, Not Masters: A Political Autobiography* (1967; Islamabad: Mr. Book, 2006).

97. Kronstadt, *Pakistan–U.S. Relations*, 22.

98. Greg Bruno, "U.S. Drone Activities in Pakistan," Council on Foreign Relations, www.cfr.org/publication/22659/us_drone_activities_in_pakistan.

99. Eric Schmitt, "Pakistan's Failure to Hit Militant Sanctuary Has Positive Side for the U.S.," *New York Times*, January 17, 2011.

100. See www.thebureauinvestigates.com/namingthedead/?lang=en.

101. The fact that civilian casualties of drone attacks remain unreported is well documented by the Foundation for Fundamental Rights. See Steve Coll, "The Unblinking Stare," *New Yorker*, November 24, 2014, 98.

102. Peter Bergen and Katherine Tiedeman, "The Year of the Drone," New American Foundation, Counterterrorism Strategy Initiative, http://counterterrorism .newamerica.net/drones.

103. Coll, "Unblinking Stare," 107–108.

104. According to a 2009 World Public Opinion survey, 90 percent of the Pakistanis considered that the United States abused its greater power to force their country to do what they wanted (compared with 69 percent of Iraqis). See http://www .worldpublicopinion.org/pipa/articles/views_on_countriesregions_bt/623. The Pew Research Center's opinion polls have all presented the United States as one of the most unpopular countries in Pakistan. In July 2010, 59 percent of the Pakistanis interviewed described the United States as an enemy, whereas only 11 percent looked at it as a partner. Only 8 percent of the Pakistanis interviewed expressed confidence in Obama—he did not obtain such a low rating in any of the other twenty-one nations surveyed. Pew Research Center, "Public Opinion in Pakistan: Concern About Extremist Threat Slips. America's Image Remains Poor," July 29, 2010. The trust deficit is such that most of the Pakistanis believe not that the United States is in the region for honorable reasons but that its real purpose is to establish unacceptable domination over their country and in particular take control of their nuclear devices. On anti-Americanism in Pakistan, see Dietrich Reetz, "A Case Study of Pakistan," in *Anti-Americanism in the Islamic World*, ed. Sigrid Faath (London: Markus Wiener, 2006), 182–196. Among the most popular anti-American commentators on television, Zaid Hamid played a significant role in the late 2000s, for instance, attributing all of Pakistan's ills to the United States.

105. See the views of people in the FATA at http://www.newamerica.net/sites /newamerica.net/files/policydocs/FATApoll.pdf.

106. "Once in office, Mr. Obama signed off on a large increase in the number of CIA officers on the ground in Pakistan." Peter L. Bergen, "Warrior in Chief," *International Herald Tribune*, April 30, 2012, 8.

107. In April, while the date of the American withdrawal from Afghanistan was being finalized and Washington was negotiating with Kabul the development of a military base in Afghanistan to prepare the future beyond this date, Prime Minister Gilani called on Karzai to dissuade him from continuing to rely on the United States in this way. He told him that the United States not only had "imperialist designs" but also was no longer reliable due to the financial crisis it faced. He claimed that the alternative to guarantee Afghanistan's security lay in China, an emerging power that Pakistan could convince to take care of the country. This meeting, whose content was leaked to the American media (probably by Afghan officials), further strained U.S.–Pakistan relations. Matthew Rosenberg, "Pakistan Lobbies Afghans to Drop U.S. Partnership," *Wall Street Journal*, April 27, 2011, 1.

108. Declan Walsh and Ewan Mac Askill, "Blackwater Operating at CIA Pakistan Base, Ex-Official Says," *Guardian*, December 11, 2009. See also Shahid R. Siddiqui, "How Active Is Blackwater in Pakistan?" *Foreign Policy Journal*, August 30, 2010, www.foreignpolicyjournal.com/2010/08/30/how-active-is-blackwater-in -pakistan/.

109. Declan Walsh, "Fallout of bin Laden Raid: Aid Groups in Pakistan Are Suspect," *New York Times*, May 2, 2012, www.nytimes.com/2012/05/03/world/asia/bin-laden-raid-fallout-aid-groups-in-pakistan-are-suspect.html.

110. Nick Paton Walsh, "Official: Pakistan Had but Didn't Probe Data That Helped Make Raid," CNN, May 2, 2011, http://edition.cnn.com/2011/WORLD/asiapcf/05/02/bin.laden.pakistan.role/.

111. Alex Rodriguez, "Suspicions Grow Over Whether Pakistan Aided Osama bin Laden," *Los Angeles Times*, May 2, 2011.

112. Asif Ali Zardari, "Pakistan Did Its Part," *Washington Post*, May 3, 2011.

113. Jane Perlez, "Pakistani Army Chief Warns U.S. on Another Raid," *New York Times*, May 5, 2011.

114. Associated Press, "Clinton: Pakistan Helped Lead U.S. to bin Laden," *Forbes*, May 2, 2011, http://billionaires.forbes.com/article/02T93vJ2aferu?q=Pakistan.

115. "Osama bin Laden Killed in Pakistan, Says Obama," *Dawn*, May 2, 2011; Perlez, "Pakistani Army Chief Warns U.S. on Another Raid."

116. Nicholas Schmidle, "Getting bin Laden," *New Yorker*, August 8, 2011.

117. Massimo Calabresi, "CIA Chief Breaks Silence: Pakistan Would Have Jeopardized bin Laden Raid, 'Impressive' Intel Captured," *Time*, May 3, 2012. By deciding not to inform the Pakistanis about the operation, the United States apparently learned from previous mistakes. In 2007, for instance, bin Laden was allegedly tipped off by ISI agents and thus escaped capture. Eric Schmitt and Thom Shanker, *Counterstrike: The Untold Story of America's Secret Campaign Against Al Qaeda* (New York: Times Books, 2011).

118. The Foreign Ministry simply said in a short communiqué: "This operation was conducted by the U.S. forces in accordance with declared U.S. policy that Osama bin Laden will be eliminated in a direct action by the U.S. forces, wherever found in the world." ("Bin Laden Operation Conducted by US Forces: Pakistan," *Dawn*, May 2, 2011, http://www.dawn.com/news/625467/bin-laden-operation-conducted-by-us-forces-pakistan).

119. Farhan Bokhari, "Pakistan Army Warns U.S. on Repeat Strike," *Financial Times*, May 6, 2011, 2.

120. Walsh, "Official: Pakistan Had but Didn't Probe Data."

121. Haqqani, *Magnificent Delusions*, 319.

122. See the fact file published by Islamabad Policy Research Institute, a think tank that significantly puts the Salala and the Abbottabad operations on the same level: "Abbottabad and Salala Attacks 2011," Islamabad Policy Research Institute working paper 14, no. 1–2 (January–February 2012): 55–95.

123. This is especially true in the FATA. "Public Opinion in Pakistan's Tribal Regions," New America Foundation, Policy Documents, September 2010, www.newamerica.net/sites/newamerica.net/files/policydocs/FATApoll.pdf.

124. Pew Research Center, "Public Opinion in Pakistan."

125. "Kerry-Lugar Act (S-1707): Uncut," South Asia Strategic Stability Institute, Strategic Brief, October 2009, 21–23.

126. Daniel Markey, *Pakistani Partnerships with the United States: An Assessment* (Washington, D.C.: National Bureau of Asian Research, November 2009), 13.

127. S. G. Stolberg and J. Yardley, "Obama Courts Emergent India as Deeper Ally," *New York Times*, November 9, 2010, 1 and 13.

128. Joint Statement of Manmohan Singh and Barack Obama, available at http://netindian.in/news/2010/11/08/0008622/joint-statement-manmohan-singh-barack-obama.

129. Haider Ali Hussein Mulick, "Obama's Afghanistan–Pakistan Quandary Part II—Pakistan Wants U.S. Pressure on India as Condition for Cooperating Against Al Qaeda," Yale Global, April 15, 2009, http://yaleglobal.yale.edu/content/obama's-afghanistan-pakistan-quandary---part-ii. Christine Fair points out that "The lamentable reality is that U.S. Policy towards India has made Pakistan's security calculus even more paranoid, and the fact that India has been able to expand its presence in Afghanistan under the U.S. umbrella has not made Islamabad any happier." Graham Webster, "After bin Laden, Still No Choice for U.S. with Pakistan: An Interview with Christine Fair," National Bureau of Asian Research, www.nbr.org/downloads/pdfs/PSA/Fair_interview_05262011.pdf.

130. For an interesting biographical account, see Andrea Elliott, Sabrina Tavernise, and Anne Barnard, "For Times Sq. Suspect, Long Roots of Discontent," *New York Times*, May 15, 2010.

131. Jane Perlez, "C.I.A. Officer Is Unmasked as Pakistan Vents Anger," *International Herald Tribune*, May 10, 2011, 1.

132. Jane Perlez and Eric Schmitt, "Pakistan Spies Tied to Reporter's Killing," *International Herald Tribune,* July 6, 2011, 7.

133. Eric Schmitt and Jane Perlez, "U.S. Is Deferring Millions in Pakistani Military Aid," *New York Times*, July 9, 2011.

134. U.S. State Department transcript, available at www.state.gov/r/pa/prs/dpb/2011/07/168018.htm#PAKISTAN. Relations between them further deteriorated when the Federal Bureau of Investigation arrested the executive director of the Kashmir American Council, Ghulam Nabi Fai, alleging that he was an ISI spy. Ewen MacAskill and Declan Walsh, "U.S.–Pakistan Relations Worsen with Arrest of Two Alleged Spies," *Guardian*, July 19, 2011.

135. "Statement of Admiral Michael Mullen, U.S. Navy Chairman Joint Chiefs of Staff Before the Senate Armed Services Committee on Afghanistan and Iraq, September 22, 2011," https://4gwar.files.wordpress.com/2011/09/mullen-09-22-11.pdf.

136. The report read, "American officials familiar with Pakistan say that the attack fit a pattern. The Pakistanis often seemed to retaliate for losses they had suffered in an accidental attack by United States forces with a deliberate assault on American troops, most probably to maintain morale among their own troops or to make a point to the Americans that they could not be pushed around, said a former American military officer who served in both Afghanistan and Pakistan." Carlotta Gall, "Pakistanis Tied to 2007 Attack on Americans," *New York Times*, September 27, 2011, A1, A6.

137. Cited in Paul Miller, "Tracing the Path to Abbottabad," *Foreign Policy*, May 5, 2011.

138. "Obama Urges Pakistan to Tackle Haqqani Problem," *Reuters*, September 30, 2011, http://uk.reuters.com/article/2011/09/30/uk-usa-pakistan-obama-idUKTRE78T4KP20110930; "Intelligence About ISI Link Not Clear: Obama," *Dawn*, September 30, 2011, http://www.dawn.com/news/662952/intelligence-about-isi-link-not-clear-obama.

139. Karen Parrish, "Mullen Offers Advice to Dempsey on Chairman Job," U.S. Department of Defense News, September 30, 2011, http://archive.defense.gov/news/newsarticle.aspx?id=65495.

140. Susan B. Epstein and K. Alan Kronstadt, "Pakistan: U.S. Foreign Assistance," Congressional Research Service, April 10, 2010, 3.

141. Miller, "Tracing the Path to Abbottabad," 2.

142. "U.S. Drone Kills 3 in Pakistan's Tribal Belt," International Herald Tribune, April 30, 2012, 4.

143. "DCC Go-Ahead for Resetting Pak–U.S. Ties," Dawn, April 18, 2012.

144. Alex Rodriguez and David S. Cloud, "U.S. Apologizes; Pakistan to Reopen Supply Routes," Los Angeles Times, July 3, 2012.

145. International Security, "Drone Wars Pakistan: Analysis," http://securitydata.newamerica.net/drones/pakistan-analysis.html.

146. Adam Levine and Faith Karimi, "Kerry Says Pakistan Drone Strikes to End 'Very Soon,'" CNN, August 2, 2013, http://edition.cnn.com/2013/08/01/politics/pakistan-drones/.

147. Bureau of South and Central Asian Affairs, U.S. Department of State, "U.S. Relations with Pakistan," August 16, 2013, www.state.gov/r/pa/ei/bgn/3453.htm.

148. "Strategic Dialogue: Kerry Hails Pakistan's 'Tiger Economy' Potential," Express Tribune, January 29, 2014, http://tribune.com.pk/story/664333/strategic-dialogue-kerry-hails-pakistans-tiger-economy-potential/.

149. Anwar Iqbal, "U.S. Sets Benchmark: Release Afridi or Forego $33 Million," Dawn, January 16, 2014, www.dawn.com/news/1080703.

150. Shahbaz Rana, "Ambitious Plans: Every Dollar of CSF to Be Recovered, Says Dar," Express Tribune, December 12, 2013, http://tribune.com.pk/story/644228/ambitious-plans-every-dollar-of-csf-to-be-recovered-says-dar/.

151. This report made some impact in Pakistan: Sumera Khan, "UN Report Speaks Pakistan's Mind/FO," Express Tribune, October 20, 2013, http://tribune.com.pk/story/619896/un-report-speaks-pakistans-mind-fo/?print=true.

152. Sajjad Haider, "'Strong Evidence' Pakistan Military Approved U.S. Drone Strikes: UN Report," Dawn, October 19, 2013, www.dawn.com/news/1050387/strong-evidence-pakistan-military-approved-us-drone-strikes-un-report/print.

153. See "U.S. Plans Revival of Aid, to Release $1.6 Billion," Dawn, October 20, 2013, www.dawn.com/news/1050516/us-plans-revival-of-aid-to-release-16-billion/print; and Declan Walsh, "Drone Issue Hovers More Than Ever, Even as Strikes Ebb," New York Times, October 25, 2013, A8.

154. "PTI Activists Search Trucks for NATO Supplies," Dawn, November 24, 2013, http://dawn.com/news/1058267/pti-activists-search-trucks-for-nato-supplies.

155. Kamran Yousaf, "North Waziristan: TTP Shura Leader, Master Trainer Killed in Air Strike, Say Officials," Express Tribune, January 23, 2014, http://tribune.com.pk/story/662242/north-waziristan-ttp-shura-leader-master-trainer-killed-in-air-strikes-say-officials/; "Military Offensive: Over 50 Militants Killed in Waziristan, Khyber Air Blitzes," Express Tribune, January 22, 2014, http://tribune.com.pk/story/661806/military-offensive-over-50-militants-killed-in-waziristan-khyber-air-blitzes/; "40 Militants Killed in North Waziristan Aerial Bombing," Express Tribune, February 20, 2014; "Helicopter Shelling Kills Six Militants in Hangu,"

Dawn, February 22, 2014, www.juancole.com/news/the-dawn/2014/02/helicopter-shelling-militants"; "Bombing in North Waziristan Leaves 60 Dead," *Express Tribune*, May 21, 2014, http://tribune.com.pk/story/711140/bombing-in-north-waziristan-leaves-30-militants-dead/.

156. The former director general of Inter-Services Public Relations, Major General (retired) Athar Abbas declared that Kayani delayed any significant military operation in North Waziristan in order to spare the Haqqani Network, inter alia. "'Kayani Was Reluctant to Launch N Waziristan Operation,'" *Dawn*, June 30, 2014, http://tribune.com.pk/story/729162/kayani-was-reluctant-to-launch-n-waziristan-operation-three-years-ago/. See also Hafeez Tunio, "Gilani Says Decision to Launch N Waziristan Operation Was Reserved by Kayani," *Express Tribune*, July 12, 2014, http://tribune.com.pk/story/734223/pml-n-should-honour-musharraf-resignation-deal-says-gilani/.

157. Muhammad Ali Ehsan, "The Importance of the North Waziristan Operation," *Express Tribune*, June 24, 2014, http://tribune.com.pk/story/725982/the-importance-of-the-north-waziristan-operation/.

158. Zahir Shah Sherazi, "North Waziristan IDPs Figure Reaches 800,000," *Dawn*, July 8, 2014.,www.dawn.com/news/1117879.

159. Azam Khan, "1 Million IDPs and Counting," *Express Tribune*, July 23, 2014, http://tribune.com.pk/story/739664/1-million-idps-and-counting/.

160. "Fatwa Declared Zarb-i-Azb a Jihad," *Dawn*, June 23, 2014, www.dawn.com/news/1114565.

161. Capt. Kanwal Kiani, "Operation Zarb-e-Azb: Nation's War," *Hilal*, July 2014, 19.

162. "Army Says 910 'Terrorists,' 82 Soldiers Killed in North Waziristan," *Dawn*, September 3, 2014, www.dawn.com/news/1129619.

163. Mateen Haider, "Army Snubs 'Malicious' Pentagon Report on Pakistan," *Dawn*, November 15, 2014, www.dawn.com/news/1144710/army-snubs-malicious-pentagon-report-on-pakistan. See also "1,200 Militants Killed During 5-Month Offensive: Army," *Reuters*, November 16, 2014, http://in.reuters.com/article/2014/11/16/pakistan-military-offensive-idINKCN0J00AM20141116.

164. Zahid Hussain, "Battleground North Waziristan," *Dawn*, November 19, 2014, www.dawn.com/news/1145359.

165. Zahir Shah Sherazi and Mateen Haider, "Haqqani Network Also Target of N Waziristan Operation: ISPR," *Dawn*, June 26, 2014, www.dawn.com/news/1115240.

166. Tahir Khan, "Kabul Trip: Haqqani Threat Neutralised, Islamabad Assures Washington," *Express Tribune*, July 23, 2014, http://tribune.com.pk/story/739645/kabul-trip-haqqani-threat-neutralised-islamabad-assures-washington/.

167. Tim Craig, "Pakistani Army Chief's Trip to U.S. Likely to Be Marked by Greater Optimism, Trust," *Washington Post*, November 14, 2014, www.washingtonpost.com/world/asia_pacific/pakistani-army-chiefs-trip-to-us-likely-to-be-marked-by-greater-optimism-trust/2014/11/13/427374e8-6aa1-11e4-a31c-77759fc1eacc_story.html.

168. Anwar Iqbal, "COAS in US: Army Praised for Zarb-i-Azb, Fight Against Terror," *Dawn*, November 18, 2014. www.dawn.com/news/1145275.

169. Cited in Muhammad Ali Ehsan, "General Sharif's U.S. Visit," *Express Tribune*, December 8, 2014, http://tribune.com.pk/story/803597/general-sharifs-us-visit.

170. Kamran Yousaf and Tahir Khan, "Meets Ghani, Abdullah: Gen Raheel Offers to Train Afghan Security Forces," *Express Tribune*, November 7, 2014, http://tribune .com.pk/story/787130/meets-ghani-abdullah-gen-raheel-offers-to-train-afghan -security-forces/.

171. "Obama Calls Nawaz, Expresses Desire for Better Pakistan–U.S. Ties," *Express Tribune*, November 22, 2014, http://tribune.com.pk/story/795027/obama-calls -nawaz-expresses-desire-for-better-pakistan-us-ties/.

172. Ken Dilanian, "U.S., Pakistan Remain Wary but Relations Improve," *AFP*, December 5, 2014, http://bigstory.ap.org/article/a07950c2f5924f3489eb190f2795220d /us-relationship-pakistan-wary-improving.

173. *Major U.S. Arms Sales and Grants to Pakistan Since 2001*, report prepared by the Congressional Research Service for distribution to multiple congressional offices, May 4, 2015, https://www.fas.org/sgp/crs/row/pakarms.pdf.

174. Shamshad Ahmad, "Finally, 'Back on Track,'" *Express Tribune*, October 25, 2013, http://tribune.com.pk/story/622442/finally-back-on-track/.

175. Dilanian, "U.S., Pakistan Remain Wary."

176. Amjad Mahmood, "Footprints: JuD's Show of Strength," *Dawn*, December 7, 2014, http://www.dawn.com/news/1149307.

177. Pew Research Center, "Opinion of the United States," Global Indicators Database, www.pewglobal.org/database/indicator/1/country/166/.

178. Raisa Vayani, "At 7%, Pakistan's Approval Rate of Obama Lowest Among 44 Countries," *Express Tribune*, July 15, 2014, http://tribune.com.pk/story/735997 /pakistans-favorability-of-obama-lowest-among-surveyed-countries/.

179. "Pakistan Has Received Half of the Funds Earmarked Under US Aid Bill, NA Told," *Express Tribune*, January 27, 2014, http://tribune.com.pk/story/664070 /pakistan-has-received-half-of-the-funds-earmarked-under-kerry-lugar-bill-na -told/.

180. Woodward, *Obama's Wars*, 6.

181. David E. Sanger, *Confront and Conceal: Obama's Secret Wars and Surprising Use of American Power* (New York: Crown, 2012), 193.

182. "The Latest Ugly Truth About Pakistan," *New York Times*, September 24, 2011, A20.

183. Sanger, *Confront and Conceal*, 238.

184. Ibid., 281.

185. Pakistan may be in a position to produce between 110 and 120 nuclear warheads today and 200 by 2020. Gregory D. Koblentz, *Strategic Stability in the Second Nuclear Age*, Council Special Report No. 71 (Washington, D.C.: Council on Foreign Relations, November 2014), www.cfr.org/arms-control-disarmament-and -nonproliferation/strategic-stability-second-nuclear-age/p33809.

186. This dread is clearly expressed by Bruce Riedel in *Deadly Embrace: Pakistan, America, and the Future of the Global Jihad* (Washington, D.C.: Brookings Institution Press, 2011).

187. R. Chase, E. Hill, and P. Kennedy, eds., *The Pivotal States: A New Framework for U.S. Policy in the Developing World* (New York: W. W. Norton, 1998), 445.

CHAPTER 9

PAKISTAN–CHINA SYMBIOTIC RELATIONS

Farah Jan and Serge Granger

Pakistan's foreign policy from the onset was formulated along the lines of its (in)security concerns, and relations with China are framed under the same rubric. These two states share a unique relationship that has remained consistent over the years, despite variations across time and issues. In Pakistan, the perception of China is of an unfaltering "all-weather friend" and a reliable ally, regardless of regional and global circumstances. Similarly, for China, Pakistan is a "permanent friend."[1] Many scholars[2] have argued that Pakistan–China relations are inspired by their mutual rivalry with India, and more recently the argument has revolved around containing India. This chapter attempts to expand on the existing literature by arguing that Pakistan, since the very beginning, has looked to a stronger partner for protection. In the process, it has oscillated between the United States and China. Thus, two questions come to the fore in regards to this relationship: First, keeping Pakistan's security concerns in mind, why did Pakistan alternate between the two great powers, and for what kind of gain? Second, is the Pakistan–China relationship a pragmatic expression of containing India to foster China's regional supremacy?

In international politics, states with significant external threats either balance against the threatening power to deter it from attacking or bandwagon by aligning with the threatening state, in order to appease it.[3] This chapter seeks to address the above questions by situating Pakistan's alignment behavior in this literature. When reviewing Pakistan and China relations, we would be remiss to overlook the India nexus in this alliance. India plays an important role in the strategic defense aspect of this relationship.

JOINING HANDS AGAINST INDIA

From a historical standpoint, China's partnership with Pakistan emerged at a time when it was looking for support on the global stage; this partnership intensified in the 1960s during the Sino-Indian War and since then has continued to thrive even after the Sino-Indian rapprochement.[4] The vitality and durability of this relationship is what perplexes scholars and prompts us to explore the depth of this partnership. As noted by John Garver, "China's partnership with other countries, both large (USSR and US) and small (Albania, Vietnam, Algeria, and North Korea) have waxed and then waned, but with Pakistan it is indeed a remarkably durable relationship."[5] Similarly, for Pakistan, friendship with China is considered one of the cornerstones of its foreign policy. The foundation of this alliance is further grounded in economic, defense, geostrategic, and people-to-people relations between the two states. This bond is continuously cultivated by means of bilateral trade and cooperation; military-to-military exchanges and transfer of critical defense technology; and support and development of conventional weapons and other major Chinese investments in Pakistan. Despite the absence of cultural similarities and common values, this alliance has remained strong, as noted by Andrew Small: "Sino-Pakistani ties have proved remarkably resilient. . . . Across the last few decades they have survived China's transition from Maoism to market economy, the rise of Islamic militancy in the region, and the shifting cross currents of the two sides' relationship with India and the United States."[6]

It is important to highlight that it was India and not Pakistan that initially warmed up to China following the establishment of the communist regime in 1949. India, like Pakistan, had gained independence in 1947 and was emerging on the global stage. The newly established states were foraging for international support, whether that included economic, military, or diplomatic blessings. The contrast between the two states was that Pakistan was quick at latching on to the West, and India adopted a policy of nonalignment. It is at this point in history that we start seeing Pakistan looking for a strong partner to ease its security concerns. It was under these conditions that Indian Prime Minister Jawaharlal Nehru visited China. He was mindful of China's rise: as he cautioned, "A new China is rising, rooted in her culture, but shedding the lethargy and weakness of ages, strong and united."[7] Nehru's prophecy encompassed a sense of warning, which was later affirmed by the assertions of India's China expert K. M. Panikkar. Panikkar was perturbed by the new developments in China, and he noted an apparent arrogance and ruthlessness in the new masters of China.[8] Hence, in his opinion, it was important for India to extend cordial relations toward China. India, aware of its rivalry on its western border with Pakistan, aspired for friendly ties with a powerful neighbor on its northern periphery and thus hoped for an India–China axis in South Asia to pacify its own insecurities.

To appease China, the Indian delegate to the United Nations in September 1950 advocated admitting communist China's representation to the United Nations.[9] This measure had a twofold strategy: first, it aimed to strengthen India's ties with China, and second, it hoped that this maneuver would gain Chinese support in regard to Kashmir. During this period, India backed China's position on Taiwan, but China maintained an equivocal position on Kashmir.[10] The Kashmir conflict raised four concerns for Beijing. First, the conflict destabilized the border and could spark unrest in Xinjiang. Second, an Indian victory in Kashmir enhanced Indian power, which had interests in Tibet, confirmed by Nehru's intention to provide asylum to the Dalai Lama. Third, Indian pretentions on Kashmir included Aksai-Chin, a region considered essential for the Chinese who began constructing the Xinjiang–Tibet border road. Finally, an Indian victory would sever a Chinese–Pakistani land border, instrumental in putting military pressure on India.

THE PAKISTAN–CHINA–U.S. TRIANGLE—AND THE INDIA NEXUS

To explicate the variations in Pakistan–U.S. and Pakistan–China relations, Pakistan's foreign policy could be viewed in two phases: from independence until 1971 and a post-1971 era. Pakistan's alignment pattern from the very beginning has been to align with a stronger partner—alternating between the United States and China. After the postwar years, at the time of Pakistan's birth, the United States emerged as the sole superpower—albeit for a short while. Pakistan's foreign policy orientation at that time was toward England. As pointed out by a retired Pakistani ambassador, "England's orientation at that point was towards the U.S. Hence, the existing Pakistan army establishment at that point was British trained, and they were simply toeing the line."[11] One of the reasons for this pro-British attitude was the background of the policymakers. The political elites of the time were not only British educated but also served in the British government.[12] The British influence along with the security search pushed Pakistan to align itself with the West, particularly with the United States, which emerged as an indomitable power after World War II.

Ties with China were established in January 1950, when Pakistan became the third noncommunist state to recognize the People's Republic of China. Diplomatic links followed a year later, and one can argue that the first ten years of this relationship were insignificant in comparison to the later years. Pakistan in the 1950s had ascribed to the Western logic of "godless communists" and considered communism the "biggest potential danger to democracy in the region."[13] China's response was subdued, hopeful that Pakistan would follow principles of peaceful coexistence.[14] Premier Chou-En Lai put these principles forward, in 1955, at the Bandung Summit. It should be remembered that when the Five Principles of China's regional policy were institutionalized, the United States at that point was engaged in its containment policy. For China, this was a pragmatic approach to give its neighbors the impression that its policy was based on principles, whereas others were driven by self-interest.[15] China's Five Principles of Peaceful Coexistence (*Panchsheel*) are mutual respect for sovereignty and territorial integrity; mutual nonaggression; mutual noninterference in internal and external affairs; equality and mutual benefit; and peaceful coexistence.

It is important to take into account the Cold War dynamic that dominated the world stage at that time. The U.S. anticommunist coalition in Asia and the Middle East was at full throttle. It was in the 1950s that Pakistan was espoused by the United States as its ally in this mission. For Pakistan, this was an opportunity it could not turn down, considering future military gains and benefits. Accordingly, these aspirations were fulfilled when Pakistan requested assistance and President Eisenhower in 1954 extended the much needed aid.[16] Thereafter, Pakistan and the United States signed multiple bilateral defense agreements, and Pakistan joined the Southeast Asia Treaty Organization and the Central Treaty Organization. India viewed Pakistan's alignment with the West and its military fortification as a threat. China had a similar perspective on Pakistan's association with the West: Pakistan's military agreements were considered to be a threat to China, India, and the region. For Beijing, responding to the 1959 Pakistan–U.S. bilateral defense agreement, this was Washington's iniquitous design of encroachment on the region. Despite bilateral agreements, China had a sense of assurance in regards to Pakistan and did not fear aggression from Pakistan; instead, it was apprehensive of U.S. motives.[17] Furthermore, China was mindful of Pakistan's insecurity vis-à-vis India and considered Pakistan's alignment with the United States a measure to ease its anxieties in regards to its military weakness in contrast with India.

The United States in the early days of the Cold War had a political stake in the stability of both India and Pakistan, because it did not want either of these countries to come under communist influence. The United States feared worldwide repercussions and even alluded to it in the National Security Council Report in 1959: "Seriously increased political instability in either or both of these large nations could significantly increase Communist influence in the area, or alternatively, might lead to hostilities in South Asia. Either turn of events could engage great power interests to the point of threatening world peace."[18] The shift in Pakistan–U.S. relations came in 1959 when Senator John F. Kennedy advocated support toward India's development in order to balance power relations in South Asia against China. India's neutral stance was defended with parallels drawn with nineteenth-century America during its formative days.[19] This attitude was disconcerting for Pakistan and created a breach of trust with the United States. From this point onward, decision makers in Pakistan changed directions from the West to the East—from the United States and its Western allies, to China, a trustworthy guarantor.

As the decade came to an end, India–China relations deteriorated and Pakistan systematically warmed up to China. Since the early 1960s, Pakistan–China ties have remained strong and cordial, irrespective of regional and international circumstances. The isolation of China in the 1950s and 1960s nurtured a foreign policy aimed at securing allies, which would outnumber those who recognized Taiwan at the United Nations. With the movement of decolonization unrolling, ties with Pakistan became an exemplar of Chinese dialogue with new independent Muslim countries that had just obtained their independence and were en route to self-government. China was in need of diplomatic recognition to enter the United Nations and would gather more support from newly independent countries. Afghanistan recognized China in 1955; Egypt, Syria, and North Yemen did so the following year. By the late 1950s, Iraq, Morocco, Algeria, Sudan, and Guinea had also normalized relations with Beijing. Somalia, Tunisia, and South Yemen followed in the 1960s, while Iran and Turkey joined in days before the entrance of the People's Republic of China to the United Nations. China would find in Pakistan a worthy partner in vindicating it to other Muslim countries that friendly relations were possible with a communist, agnostic China, notwithstanding its rocky relationship with Indonesia, the most populous Muslim country in the world.

China's border negotiation with Pakistan was on a relatively small borderline of 310 miles, and Pakistan gained much from border negotiations. China recognized Pakistani control over parts of Kashmir, therefore thwarting India's claim on the land. Conversely, border disputes with India initiated in 1958 contributed to the Sino-Indian War of 1962. China refused to accept the boundary line drawn by the British and argued that "no treaty on the boundary has ever been concluded between the Chinese central government and the Indian government."[20] On October 20, 1962, China launched an offensive strike, which took the Indian army by surprise. Prime Minister Nehru announced in a radio broadcast a series of defeats in the battle against China. This in the view of many scholars was a cruel awakening for the newly established state well cognizant of foreign domination. After its first defeat, India asked for military help from Britain, the United States, and the Soviet Union. The United States and Britain offered and provided immediate assistance. By November 1962, Nehru publicly conceded, and a unilateral withdrawal was made on the condition that India would accept the neutralized zone delineated by China, and furthermore India was prohibited to reestablish any military posts in the Ladakh region. For Pakistan, this was a golden opportunity to condemn India, but at the same time it felt betrayed by the United States and its Western allies who provided immediate support to India. President Ayub Khan blamed the Indian government for being aggressive and not conciliatory in regards to its border dispute with China. From his perspective, the Indian ambition of becoming the great power in Asia forced the Chinese to humble them.[21] It is this critical juncture of 1962 that is considered to have set the trajectory for Pakistan–China relations for years to come.

Since the independence of Pakistan and India, South Asian history has continuously been overshadowed by the Indo-Pakistan rivalry, hence affecting regional and international policies and alliances. Whereas India fought a war with China over a border dispute, Pakistan decided to negotiate an agreement on the border between China's Xinjiang Province and Pakistan's Gilgit and Hunza areas.[22] Many Western analysts argued that the Chinese were generous in their border dispute with Pakistan, in order to "woo the Pakistanis from their Western commitments and above all to prove to the Indians how much they are missing by not coming to terms."[23] While Sino-Indian relations diverged, Sino-Pakistan relations were transformed and turned into a special alliance.

Beyond the goodwill and collective interest of both China and Pakistan, the two states also inked substantive agreements starting from 1963 onward. Border issues were settled, and Pakistan was the first noncommunist state to sign a trade agreement with China. The landmark air agreement, in which landing permission for Pakistan International Airlines was granted without conditions, was considered a major triumph for Pakistan.[24] The air agreement further contributed to strained relations between the United States and Pakistan; it was a measure against the isolation of China that the United States tried to promote.

During the Sino-Indian War of 1962, Pakistan–U.S. relations tailed off, after the United States expeditiously honored the Indian request for military assistance.[25] For Pakistan, this was a betrayal of its position as a Western-aligned state, whereas India had maintained a nonaligned status all through the Cold War. Relations with the United States were further damaged during the Indo-Pakistan war of 1965, during which Washington halted all military aid to Islamabad and New Delhi. China during this time frame patiently watched this relationship wax and wane. The aphorism "my enemy's enemy is my friend" applies fairly to this case.

It is important to highlight China's stance in the two major events ensuing after the Sino-Indian War: the Indo-Pakistan War of 1965 and the disintegration of East Pakistan in 1971. Both in 1965 and in 1971, China backed Pakistan's position over India's. In the 1965 war, China considered India to be the aggressor and held it solely responsible for the conflict. Beijing denounced and condemned the Indian attack as an "act of naked aggression."[26] China played a major role in the cease-fire dialogue between the two rivals and maintained a degree of military pressure on its borders of Sikkim, Bhutan, and the Northeast Frontier Agency for several months following the cease-fire. This measure by the Chinese was seen by many as furnishing Pakistan with a strong negotiating position vis-à-vis India.[27] The Chinese assistance during the Indo-Pakistan War symbolized a new beginning for this friendship, in which China further proved its dependability and consistency. These were the attributes that the United States failed to demonstrate, and thus it led to the divergence of paths of "the most allied allies."

The 1971 civil war situated the Chinese in a twofold predicament in which they disagreed with General Yahya Khan's brutal military actions in East Pakistan as well as with the East Pakistani rebel's ties with India. China's response to the 1971 disintegration of Pakistan was much weaker than its support in the earlier war with India. Publicly China concentrated on condemning India for "open interference in the internal matters of Pakistan." In a statement issued in April 1971, the Chinese government assured its "support for Pakistan and its people in their just struggle to safeguard state sovereignty and national independence."[28] But privately, they were very uncomfortable with the situation in East Pakistan. As John Garver noted, the Chinese were critical of the ruthless measures exercised to deal with the rebels of East Pakistan; on a public level, they did not endorse Pakistan's actions but directed critical opprobrium toward India's direct involvement and infiltration in Pakistan's Eastern Wing.[29]

China's response in 1971, compared with 1965, differed in its degree but not in its position toward Pakistan. This still leaves open the question of what led to the variation in the Chinese position. As Andrew Small noted, the 1971 episode made it clear that "China would not pull Pakistan out of the holes it insisted on digging for itself."[30] In addition, China at that point was worn out by its cultural revolution and was focused on its economic development along with a rapprochement with the United States. Although China did not militarily assist Pakistan, Beijing nevertheless provided diplomatic support at the UN Security Council by vetoing Bangladesh's application for UN membership until Pakistani prisoners of war had been returned and Indian troops had withdrawn.[31]

In response to Pakistan's serious efforts toward Sino-American détente and its role as an intermediary in the Sino-American dialogue that led to President Nixon's visit to China in 1972, China provided support to Pakistan during the post-Bangladesh crisis. The statement issued in the joint U.S.–China Communiqué of 1972 expressed "firm support for the government and people of Pakistan in their struggle to preserve their independence and sovereignty, and the people of Jammu and Kashmir in their struggle for the right of self determination."[32] This statement on the surface translates into Beijing's continued support of Pakistan's interests, but talk is cheap and actions are costly. China's lackluster support for Pakistan during the 1971 crisis set the precedent for future expectations that Beijing would not militarily intervene on behalf of Pakistan.

Pakistan's reaction to China's response was politely stated by Z. A. Bhutto during an interview: "We have not lost confidence in China's friendship, nor in China's word."[33] Bhutto was aware of the long-term gain from the Pakistan–China relationship, in which China had shown interest in Pakistan's security and respected Pakistan's domestic political situation.[34] China had become the most reliable suppliers of military equipment and also aided Pakistan's defense industry. Even during the Bangladesh crisis, China provided Pakistan with large shipments of arms in East Pakistan, along with $100 million in assistance.[35] The Russian invasion of Afghanistan would bring back American aid to Pakistan, but it would disappear once more after the Soviets had retreated and suspicion rose about Pakistan's nuclear plans involving China. During the Soviet invasion of Afghanistan, China and the United States cooperated in opposing the Soviets, but China's support was based on two reasons: the Soviets were looking for expansion in Beijing's backyard, and Soviet troops were seen primarily as a threat to Pakistani security. At that point, the policies and stances of China and Pakistan were coordinated to such an extent that General Zia declared on his visit to Beijing in 1980 that "Pakistan and China have a perfect understanding in all fields."[36]

By "all fields," Zia alluded to the greatest possible military relationship: Pakistan and China's nuclear agreement. China's involvement in Pakistan's nuclear program was crucial and "one of the most heavily guarded secrets."[37] Yet it was not Zia but Z. A Bhutto who secured the remarkable nuclear deal with Mao in 1976, when China agreed to transfers 50 kilograms of uranium to Pakistan. As Bhutto in his final days wrote, "My single most important achievement . . . is the agreement . . . concluded in July 1976, [which] will perhaps be my greatest achievement and contribution to the survival of our people and our nation."[38] After India's nuclear test in 1974, China began transferring technology and uranium to the Kahuta plant, preparing Pakistan's nuclear capacity. Although information on Pakistan's nuclear program is highly confidential and restricted, A. Q. Khan in a crestfallen state revealed that China had initially supplied highly enriched uranium along with a weapon design.[39] It has even been claimed that China tested for Pakistan its first bomb in 1990 and that this was one of the reasons for Pakistan's swift response to the Indian nuclear test in 1998.[40] After the 1998 tests, Pakistan's nuclear capacity became a fait accompli, which in turn secured Chinese interest in balancing India's dominance of South Asia.

Pakistan plays a dual role for China: it contributes in keeping India engaged on its western border and provides access to the Arabian Sea via the Gawader port along with future pipelines, rail, and road networks. This in turn furthers China's transition to being a global power. For India, a Sino-Pakistan military alliance represents a belligerent potential; as noted by K. Alan Kronstadt, Chinese support for Pakistan is considered part of Beijing's policy of "encirclement of India." In the words of former Pakistani ambassador to the United States Hussain Haqqani, "For China, Pakistan is a low-cost secondary deterrent to India, and for Pakistan, China is a high value guarantor of security against India."[41] Indeed, China has demonstrated itself to be a consistent and reliable "guarantor" for Pakistan. Since the 1960s, Beijing has unceasingly strengthened Pakistan's military capabilities, unlike the arbitrary U.S. military aid. The military dimension of this relation was added after the 1965 Indo-Pakistan War, when China supplied much needed bombers and tanks to Pakistan, including MiG-15s, IL-28 bombers, and T-59 medium-range tanks.[42]

China and Pakistan have a long history of military ties; more recently, this includes joint-venture projects that have produced the K-8 trainer, FC-1/JF-17 combat aircrafts,[43] and Al-Khalid tanks. From 2005 to 2009, China was the largest arms supplier to Pakistan, accounting for 37 percent of Pakistan's imports, whereas the United States accounted for 35 percent.[44] China continues to provide Pakistan with advanced air defense equipment as well as fighter jets, regardless of Indian protests that the Chinese measures affect the strategic defense balance. It is relevant to mention India's emerging political, economic, and military strength in the region, and the question that concerns us is, Could strong Indian opposition to Chinese policies vis-à-vis Pakistan prevent China's historic role as Pakistan's "unfaltering ally"? The answer depends on how Pakistan handles the challenge of Islamist proxies. Nevertheless, for the time being, Beijing seems to be publicly standing by Islamabad. This was evident in May 2011, when during an official state visit to Beijing, the Pakistani prime minister was promised an urgent batch of fifty advanced multirole JF-17 Thunder jets by China, despite strong Indian protests.[45] The relevance of this measure is crucial due to the fact that it came at a time when the Pakistan military establishment's credibility was at its lowest point after the bin Laden discovery by the United States. Chinese encouragement in the form of military provision to Pakistan speaks for Beijing's unrelenting support for its strategic partner and neighbor.

Historically, the Sino-Pakistan military collaboration was to strengthen Pakistan against India, but after the 1990s and particularly after the U.S. sanctions on Pakistan, China became the leading arms supplier, and the balance of interest tilted more in Pakistan's favor. Since 2004, the two countries have conducted four joint military exercises called YOUYI, meaning friendship.[46] In the YOUYI exercises, special forces along with senior military leadership from both sides have participated. Similarly, the U.S.–India joint military exercises commenced in 2004 were known as YUDH ABHYAS, which translates into "training for war." The November 2011 U.S. Department of Defense *Report to Congress on U.S.–India Security Cooperation*[47] emphasized that the defense trade relationship would enable transfer of advance technologies to India. Pakistan's insecurities are rooted in the arms race with India. As pointed out by international relations scholars, state policies that are intended to increase one state's security inadvertently decrease the security of other states.[48] Thus, the prospect of India gaining a military edge with U.S. support automatically decreases Pakistan's security (heightening existing insecurities) and further deepens the breach of trust between Pakistan and the United States.

PAKISTAN AS A PIVOTAL STATE

Pakistan is a pivotal state for both the United States and China, on the grounds of its capacity to affect regional and systemic stability. Robert

Chase, who coined the term "pivotal states," would identify a pivot on the grounds of its large population and important geographic location. Hence, a collapse of such a state would "spell transboundary mayhem: migration, communal violence, pollution, disease and so on."[49] Linking it back to the traditional security concerns, one would argue that Pakistan's security is not just a matter of Pakistani concern but also the concern of the major power players of the region, and China appears to be aware of this aspect. The stability of Pakistan is more important to China than it would be for the United States. For example, Chinese security interests in Xinjiang can be directly threatened from South Asia. A stable Pakistan diminishes the possibility of a threat from the subcontinent. Similarly, the United States is not ignorant of Pakistan's importance and that the stability of Pakistan and the region is intertwined with its security interests.

The historical narrative of Pakistan–China and Pakistan–U.S. relations shows a pattern in which relations are formed in pursuit of (greater) security. At each critical juncture, Pakistan has oscillated between the United States and China for defensive security capabilities as well as armed offensive capacity.[50] The events following September 11, 2001, changed the regional dynamics, and once again Pakistan was at the focal point for the United States. For China, this carefully devised Pakistan–U.S. nuptial presented an opportunity to further strengthen Pakistan's economic and military position (at the expense of the United States) vis-à-vis India. The following section will explore the Pakistani public perception of China, the United States, and India.

PUBLIC PERCEPTION AND SECURITY CONCERNS

The importance of public perception cannot be ignored when it comes to foreign policy matters. Historically, Pakistan's importance for the United States has been structured on a need-based arrangement, and that pattern led to deep distrust within the Pakistani public perception of the United States. China, conversely, has fared considerably well. In Pakistan, Beijing has cultivated an image of a time-tested all-weather friend, despite the lack of cultural affinities and common values, whereas Washington's perception is of a hegemonic partner, as reflected in the public opinion survey conducted by Pew Research Center (table 9.1). The U.S. image is undeviating in its negative perception from 2001 to 2013. An overwhelming 70 percent of Pakistanis perceive the United States as an "enemy," whereas, a large

TABLE 9.1 FAVORABILITY PERCEPTION FIGURES IN PERCENTAGE (2000–2013)

COUNTRY	2000	2002	2003– 2004	2005	2006	2007	2008	2009	2010	2011	2012	2013
United States	23	10	13	23	27	15	19	16	17	12	12	11
China	N/A	N/A	N/A	79	69	79	76	84	84	82	87	81
India	N/A	6	10	20	33	30	27	25	20	14	22	13

SOURCE: DATA PROVIDED FROM PEW RESEARCH, GLOBAL ATTITUDES PROJECT, *U.S. IMAGE IN PAKISTAN FALLS NO FURTHER FOLLOWING BIN LADEN KILLING*, JUNE 21, 2011, HTTP://WWW.PEWGLOBAL.ORG/FILES /2011/06/PEW-GLOBAL-ATTITUDES-PAKISTAN-REPORT-FINAL-JUNE-21-2011.PDF.

majority (87 percent in 2012) of Pakistanis consider China as a partner and friend.[51] As illustrated in table 9.1, U.S. favorability numbers are even lower than those of India.

Given the widespread skepticism and public discontent, the aforementioned numbers are not surprising but a mere reflection of the overall mood in Pakistan with regards to the United States. The more surprising statistics are the U.S. grant figures in comparison to those of China. For fiscal years 2004–2009, the average annual grant assistance to Pakistan by China was $9 million in comparison to $268 million by the United States (table 9.2).[52] Regardless of the exponential difference in assistance, China still enjoys a more advantageous position in Pakistan. Since 2004, public opinion of the United States has been significantly affected by its drone strikes in the Federally Administered Tribal Areas. China, in contrast, is perceived as a noninterfering and nonthreatening neighbor. Pakistan's overemphasized focus on China's mutual respect and noninterference policy (a component of *Panchsheel*) has also played an important role in the high favorability figures. Comments made in a speech by former prime minister Yusuf Raza Gilani stand as a good example: "One thing that is certain is that . . . Pakistan and China focus on and protect each other's core interests. Pakistan always respects the sovereignty and core interest of China, and China does the same."[53]

Recent years have seen a further decline in the U.S. perception, particularly after the incremental increase of drone strikes in 2008; the May 2, 2011, raid to kill bin Laden; and the Salala incident of November 2011. Furthermore, the U.S. war against Al Qaeda and its affiliates in Afghanistan is adjudged by the Pakistani public as a societal security[54] concern that could be translated into a crusade against Islam and the Muslim world. However surpris-

TABLE 9.2 INTERNATIONAL AID TO PAKISTAN (2001—2010)

DONORS	COMMITTED ($ MILLIONS)	DISBURSED ($ MILLIONS)
United States	4,238	3,283
Japan	1,711	982
China	3,290	857
United Kingdom	1,676	1,177
Germany	748	721
United Arab Emirates	454	103
Saudi Arabia	824	319

SOURCE: CENTER FOR GLOBAL DEVELOPMENT, "AID TO PAKISTAN BY THE NUMBERS,"
HTTP://WWW.CGDEV.ORG/PAGE/AID-PAKISTAN-NUMBERS. GRANT DATA PROVIDED BY CENTER
FOR GLOBAL DEVELOPMENT, WWW.CGDEV.ORG.

ingly, China is not viewed as a threat to Islam or the Muslim world, despite its iron fist policies in the Muslim-majority province of Xinjiang. China's use of force within its territory is perceived as legitimate and permissible.

FOR CHINA, A CONTEST FOR SUPREMACY?

The Sino-Indian rivalry that was initiated in 1958–1959 is at present not more than a border dispute.[55] However, China is a rising global power, which brings us to our second question: Is the alliance with Pakistan a result of Beijing's pragmatic expression of containing India to foster regional supremacy? The dominant actors in this puzzle are Pakistan, China, the United States, and India, and one can argue that in the twenty-first century, South Asia not only is the epicenter of the traditional Indo-Pakistan rivalry but also is crucial for U.S.–China relations. China's perception of its security is an important factor to be considered. The notion of security in this context is twofold; the traditional military–political understanding of security; and economic security, which Barry Buzan refers to as concerns in regard to access to the resources that are necessary to sustain state power.[56] Hence for China, Pakistan delivers on two fronts, as a counterweight against India and as a gateway for influencing and reaching out to other Islamic countries—the Middle East in particular as a major resource area. Despite its communist past and a glorious secular history along with a religious policy aimed at curving clergy power, China has maintained its alliance with Pakistan.

China's primary security objective with Pakistan remains the containment of India, and more recently the aim has also been to prevent sanctuaries for Uyghur separatists and to curtail Islamic extremists. Uyghur separatist groups have emerged because of Chinese colonization of Xinjiang. The Chinese Communist Party has been vigilant in squashing groups that have engaged in separatism.[57] The East Turkestan Islamic Movement[58] has links outside China, which forces China to be dependent on other countries to dismantle such a group. That Uyghur separatists receive sanctuary and training in Pakistan has been a source of tension between the two states. Pakistan has responded by clamping down on Uyghur training camps and has extradited Uyghurs to China. At the same time, Pakistani authorities have taken strict measures with regards to Chinese citizens. The Red Mosque operation[59] stands as an exemplar for the measures taken by the Pakistani establishment for the appeasement of Beijing. Pakistan has fully backed China in its handling of the 2009 Uyghur ethnic riots in Xinjiang, which left 200 people dead and 1,600 injured.[60] However, continued Uyghur attacks in China have left Beijing dissatisfied by Pakistani efforts to combat terrorism.[61] Considering the new security threats to the region, Pakistan attempts to deliver to the utmost to protect China interests and support Beijing's decisions on the international stage.

A TRADE CORRIDOR FOR GREATER AFGHAN–PAKISTANI INTEGRATION WITH CHINA

When Chinese leader Deng Xiaoping succeeded Mao, he introduced a pragmatic foreign policy focused on economic ends and means. Deng Xiaoping's foreign policy enabled China's rise through a profit-centric approach and avoided structural pitfalls that a major power faces. Beijing revisited its policies and laid down a new domestic and international modus operandi. According to the new approach, Beijing's foreign policy was grounded in the economic interest of China, with a diminished appetite for unilateralism, and heavy emphasis was placed on regional and global multilateralism with the aim of improving ties with key global trade partners in compliance with its Five Principles approach. This is what many analysts would call the marriage of *Panchsheel* with the Beijing Consensus—in other words, a Chinese soft power strategy.

China's relations with Pakistan have been formed on economic aid, military transactions, and commerce in goods and commodities. A recent example of Chinese commitment to Pakistan's economic development is the China-Pak Economic Corridor (CPEC). According to this deal, the Chinese government and finance companies will invest $45.6 billion over the course of 6 years for energy and infrastructure projects in Pakistan.[62] Likewise in 2008, the two countries signed a comprehensive trade agreement granting unprecedented market access to each other. The bilateral trade figures have exponentially increased over the years, estimated at $7 billion per annum and expected to reach $15 billion by 2015. Since Deng Xiaoping's economic reforms and more specifically the rise of economic globalization, Beijing's vision for Pakistan is more focused on economic robustness, along with its military vigor. This is perhaps more evident in the infrastructure project, including major highways, gold and copper mines, and power plants, with an estimated ten thousand Chinese workers employed in Pakistan. In 2005, Pakistan and China signed a precedent-setting Treaty of Friendship and Co-operation, pledging that "neither party will join any alliance or bloc which infringes upon the sovereignty, security and territorial integrity of either China or Pakistan." A careful examination of the terminology used in this treaty reminds us of Cold War parlance, where the contractual parties were committing to supporting each other against aggression.

Beijing's policy of handling Muslim countries translates into China's capacity to export its soft power to gain access to resources. With the withdrawal of the United States from Afghanistan, Beijing's interest in the Afghanistan–Pakistan region has become strategically important, due to its increased needs for oil, gas, and minerals. China's interest in Afghanistan's untapped reserves is geographically linked with Pakistan, because of the transportation routes. Although the Wakhan corridor connects Afghanistan to China, because of the lack of infrastructure, the Pakistan option is deemed the only conduit to act as a trade and energy corridor that can help China gain access to resources and overtake India's interest in the region. China's investment in the Aynak copper mine is a good case in point.[63]

For the past few decades, China has been constructing a series of ports around the Indian Ocean. The Gwadar port in Baluchistan is another important piece in Beijing's economic expansion and transition to being a global power. The Gwadar port is aimed at securing an alternative passage in case of Indian embargo.[64] Gwadar's strategic location provides China with access to the Indian Ocean, where it can station a naval presence capable of providing security. Gwadar also provides China with the capacity to monitor Indian naval activities. And most important, the port provides future commercial interest, especially in the field of energy. In accordance with CPEC, the Gwadar port will be linked to Northwest China.

More than 100 years ago, a French Canadian engineer proposed to use snow shoes in Gilgit to secure a passage to China.[65] His proposition was turned down by the British resident in Kashmir, saying it was impracticable and useless because trade and threats were absent. Today the same route is being financed by the Chinese government as an economic corridor, which could be used to import oil, gas, minerals, and goods. The development of the Gwadar port was considered by many as the beginning of a long-term planned corridor that would make Chinese energy imports safer by avoiding the Malacca Strait—which could be blocked by the United States and its allies.[66] This also dampens India's investment in its naval strength and renders it unable to block or intercept the Chinese ships navigating in the Indian Ocean.

CONCLUSION

The trajectory of the Sino-Pakistan relations has remained on course, unwavering and determined since its formative days in the 1950s. The watershed moment for this alliance was the Sino-Indian War of 1962, consequently positioning China on its "all-weather friendship" path to Pakistan. Since then, this relationship, along with the greater South Asian region, has seen many changes, but the strength of this alliance has remained consistent, thus making the Sino-Pakistan alliance unique, even though the two states have never signed any formal alliance or defense pact. In this chapter, we have emphasized the security aspect of this relationship over the course of sixty-plus years. At the turn of the present decade, this relationship was once again confronted with important regional issues: for example, the scaling down of U.S. military aid; the upsurge in militant nonstate actors; and the attacks in Kashgar (Xinjiang Province) coordinated by militants trained in Pakistan. Thus, the options and alternatives are there for both China and Pakistan.

China has increasingly invested in Pakistan, and a retreat of U.S. involvement in the region pushes China to engage more intensively in Pakistan for multiple reasons. First, China acutely needs oil and commodities, which have traditionally come from the Middle East via the Indian Ocean, to arrive through alternative routes, thus deeming China more control in relation to India. Therefore, insecurity in Pakistan and the region would surely postpone the layout of infrastructure (such as the Sino-Pakistan corridor) required to transport the much needed resources. Second, insecurity also creates a challenge for economic development in Afghanistan and Pakistan, particularly when China has invested billions of dollars in both countries. Third, by engaging in Pakistan, China enhances its power against India and the United States. Finally, instability in Pakistan would mean trouble along the border in Xinjiang. Considering this rationale and calculating the costs and benefits, China does need Pakistan as much as Pakistan needs China. Nevertheless, this situation can change if the circumstances around the alliance are transformed—primarily if the attacks in Xinjiang persist by militants trained in Pakistan. Political instability and Pakistan's failure to crack down on militant training camps from its tribal belt could lead to a radical shift in its relations with China.

The future course of the Pakistan–China alliance is contingent on what China's national interest and strategic goals are in the region. For Pakistan, this decade has been one of unforeseeable events. The question is, Could this be the juncture in history where the paths of these "time-tested partners" diverge? The key to this challenge is subject to the course of action adopted by Pakistan. This alliance could be seriously harmed if Uyghur militants continue to launch attacks in Xinjiang. Another prospect that can affect this alliance is Pakistan–India rapprochement. Over the years, we have seen changes in relations between China and India, China and the United States, and Pakistan and the United States relations, but the Pakistan–India rivalry has remained consistent. The probability of Indo-Pakistani rivalry termination is weak, but it is impossible to ignore the prospect of it in the future. The intriguing question would be, Where and how would the Sino-Pakistan alliance position itself without "the India nexus"? Would the tour de force of this alliance wane in that situation, or could it give rise to a much stronger regional alliance? To give an idealistic perspective, one would argue that a nonantagonistic atmosphere in South Asia could lead to regional alliance, between China, Pakistan, and India—creating a very different situation than the current realpolitik environment.

Alliances in the international arena are configured and structured on the interests and motives of the states involved. Although the interests and motives may somewhat vary, the goals and strategies are invariably structured on a cost–benefit analysis, with the maximum possibility of favorable outcomes in their desired goals and objectives. The Sino-Pakistan alliance was structured on a common goal, the containment or encirclement of India, but the interests and motives for both were different. The motivation for Pakistan is rooted in its insecurities vis-à-vis India, and China seeks to maintain its strategic position of being the dominant economic and military power in the region. The India threat factor plays the role of an explanatory variable in this relationship. We would like to conclude by quoting a strategy postulated by Deng Xiaoping, which has Machiavellian undertones and sheds light on Beijing's grand design:

Observe calmly;
Secure our [Chinese] position;
Cope with affairs calmly;
Hide our [Chinese] capacities and bide our time;
Be good at maintaining a low profile;
And never claim leadership;
Make some contribution.[67]

This is realpolitik par excellence, and it resembles the Chinese game *wei qi* (a game of encirclement). Pakistan in this equation is one of the strategic pieces for China in its game to contain or encircle India and gain regional or ultimately global supremacy. The turn of this decade will prove the mettle of this alliance and Pakistan's strategic importance for China.

Cordial feelings are mutual on both sides of the border and have remained strong since its inception at the Bandung Conference in 1955. But whereas in the beginning security concerns were on the forefront for both China and Pakistan, China's national interests and objectives diverged after the 1979 economic reforms of Deng Xiaoping. Pakistan to this day continues to be perturbed by its perpetually constructed security dilemma, whereas China has adopted a pragmatic course focused on economic development and prosperity. However, despite the divergence in national objectives, this relationship has thus far maintained the initial essence of mutual trust and cooperation. Recent affirmations from Beijing have further validated this sentiment, particularly at a time when Pakistan's credibility and reputation were at its lowest ebb, following the May 2, 2011, raid by the United States and killing of Osama bin Laden in the vicinity of Pakistan's elite military academy. Beijing's sympathetic reaction to this sensitive affair was a testament to its sixty years of unwavering support for Pakistan.

NOTES

1. Chinese Premier Wen Jiabao's address to the joint parliamentary session in Islamabad, December 19, 2010. In his words, "Time flies, but true friendship remains. . . . China and Pakistan are brothers forever."

2. M. Ayoob, "India as a Factor in Sino-Pakistani Relations," *International Studies* 3 (July 1967): 279–300; Wayne Wilcox, "Chinese Strategic Alternatives in South Asia," in *China's Policies in Asia and America's Alternatives*, 2 vols., ed. Tang Tsou (Chicago: University of Chicago, 1968), 433–444; John Garver, *Protracted Contest: Sino-Indian Rivalry in the Twentieth Century* (Seattle: University of Washington Press, 2001); Samina Yasmeen, "Pakistan's Cautious Foreign Policy," *Survival* 36 (1994): 2.

3. Stephen M. Walt, "Testing Theories of Alliance Formation: The Case of Southwest Asia," *International Organization* 42, no. 2 (Spring 1988): 278.

4. Garver, *Protracted Contest*, 187–188.

5. Ibid.

6. Andrew Small, *The China–Pakistan Axis* (London: C. Hurst, 2015), 2.

7. Wayne Wilcox, *India, Pakistan, and the Rise of China* (Ann Arbor: University of Michigan Press, 1964), 47.

8. Ibid., 48.

9. Abraham Meyer Halpern, *Policies Toward China: Views from Six Continents* (New York: McGraw Hill, 1965), 496.

10. Ibid., 206.

11. Author's interview with a retired Pakistani ambassador in Islamabad, April 2012.

12. Latif Ahmed Sherwani, *Pakistan, China and America* (Karachi: Council for Pakistan Studies, 1980), 22. Sherwani mentions that M. A. Jinnah trained as a barrister and practiced law in England, Liaquat Ali Khan was educated at Oxford, and Foreign Minister Zafrullah Khan was educated in England and was knighted for his loyal services.

13. Prime Minister Mohammad Ali Bogra's statement at the Indo-China decolonization summit at Colombo, in 1954.

14. Abdul Sattar, *Pakistan's Foreign Policy, 1947–2009* (Karachi: Oxford University Press, 2010), 76.

15. Garver, *Protracted Contest*, 21.

16. Anwar Hussain Syed, *China and Pakistan: Diplomacy of an Entente Cordiale* (Amherst: University of Massachusetts Press, 1974), 33–34.

17. On two different occasions (the Manila Conference and the Bandung Conference), the Pakistani prime minister and ambassador assured Chou-En Lai that Pakistan hoped for happy and harmonious relations with China. Khalid Bin Saeed in Halpern, *Policies Toward China*, 234.

18. Department of State, S/S–NSC Files: Lot 63 D 351, NSC 5909 Series, https://history.state.gov/historicaldocuments/frus1958–60v15/d6#fn1.

19. Sattar, *Pakistan's Foreign Policy*, 69.

20. Ibid., 83.

21. Wilcox, *India, Pakistan, and the Rise of China*, 75.

22. Halpern, *Policies Toward China*, 238.

23. Syed, *China and Pakistan*, 89.

24. Ibid., 94.

25. Ibid., 34.

26. Ibid., 110.

27. Ibid., 130.

28. Garver, *Protracted Contest*, 209–210.

29. Ibid., 210–211.

30. Small, *China–Pakistan Axis*, 15.

31. Ibid., 16.

32. Shanghai Communiqué signed by President Richard Nixon and Chairman Mao Tse-Tung on February 27, 1972.

33. Niloufer Mahdi, *Pakistan's Foreign Policy, 1971–1981: The Search for Security* (Lahore: Ferozson, 1999), 199.

34. When General Zia took over power and Bhutto was removed and later hanged, Sino-Pakistan relations remained as usual.

35. Small, *China–Pakistan Axis*, 16.

36. Mahdi, *Pakistan's Foreign Policy*, 210.

37. Feroz Khan, *Eating Grass: The Making of The Pakistani Bomb* (Stanford, Calif.: Stanford University Press, 2012), 171.

38. Zulfiqar Ali Bhutto, "If I Am Assassinated," Supreme Court of Pakistan Criminal Appeal No. 11 of 1978, in Small, *China–Pakistan Axis*, 31.

39. Pervez Hoodbhoy, *Confronting the Bomb: Pakistani Indian Scientists Speak Out* (Karachi: Oxford University Press, 2013), 70.

40. Ibid. Hoodbhoy notes the work of former U.S. Air Force secretary Thomas Reed. Reed argues that the Chinese did extensive training of Pakistani scientists and provided them with a weapon design (CHIC-4) that was easy to build. Hoodbhoy notes that Pakistani scientists deny this claim (*Confronting the Bomb*, 70–71).

41. Council on Foreign Relations, "China–Pakistan Relations," www.cfr.org/china /china-pakistan-relations/p10070.

42. P. R. Kumaraswamy, *China and the Middle East: The Quest for Influence* (New Delhi: Sage, 1999), 95.

43. The FC-1 (Fighter China-1) Xialong, designated by the Pakistan air force as JF-17 (Joint Fighter-17) Thunder, is a jointly developed fighter jet. Pakistan began the production of JF-17 Thunder fighter jets in 2005 at Pakistan Aeronautical Complex and holds the exclusive rights of 58 percent of the airframe coproduction work. For details see www.pac.org.pk/jf17.html.

44. Stockholm International Peace Research Institute yearbook (Stockholm: Oxford University Press, 2010), 288.

45. "Sky Wars: Pakistan, India and China," *Dawn*, May 24, 2011.

46. Inter-Services Public Relations, Pakistan, press release, November 14, 2011, http:// ispr.gov.pk/front/main.asp?o=t-press_release&id=1897#pr_link1897.

47. U.S. Department of Defense, *Report to Congress on U.S.-India Security Cooperation* (November 2011), 3–4, http://www.defense.gov/Portals/1/Documents/pubs /20111101_NDAA_Report_on_US_India_Security_Cooperation.pdf.

48. John Herz, "Idealist Internationalism and the Security Dilemma," *World Politics* 2 (January 1950): 157–180; Herbert Butterfield, *History and Human Relations* (London: Collins, 1950), 19–20, cited in Robert Jervis, "Security Regimes," *International Organization* 36, no. 2 (Spring 1982): 358.

49. Robert Chase, Emily Hill, and Paul Kennedy, *The Pivotal States: A New Framework for U.S. Policy in the Developing World* (New York: W. W. Norton, 1989), 153.

50. The most notable critical junctures were the Indo-Pakistan War of 1965, the disintegration of East Pakistan in 1971, and the Soviet invasion of Afghanistan in 1979.

51. Pew Research Center, "U.S. Image in Pakistan Falls No Further Following bin Laden Killing," June 21, 2011, http://pewglobal.org/2011/06/21/u-s-image-in-pakistan-falls-no-further-following-bin-laden-killing/5/.

52. Center for Global Development, "Aid to Pakistan by the Numbers," www.cgdev.org/section/initiatives/_active/pakistan/numbers (accessed September 17, 2012).

53. "Pakistan Takes China as Best Friend, Time-Tested and All-Weather, Says PM," http://news.xinhuanet.com/english2010/china/2011-05/21/c_13886156.htm.

54. Societal security concerns are defined as the "ability of societies to reproduce their traditional patterns of language, culture, association and religious and national identity and customs within acceptable conditions for evolution." Barry Buzan, "New Pattern of Global Security in the Twenty-First Century," *International Affairs* 67, no. 3 (July 1991): 433.

55. The heading of this section is borrowed from Aaron Friedberg's book, *A Contest for Supremacy: China, America, and the Struggle for Mastery in Asia* (New York: Norton, 2011).

56. Buzan, "New Pattern of Global Security," 433.

57. Rémi Castets, "Uyghur Islam, Caught Between Foreign Influences and Domestic Constraints," in *China and India in Central Asia: A New "Great Game"?* ed. Marlène Laruelle, Jean-François Huchet, Sébastien Payrouse, and Bayram Balci (Hampshire, UK: Palgrave Macmillan, 2010), 215–233.

58. "Xinjiang Riots Hit Regional Anti-terror Nerve" *Xinhua*, July 18, 2009, http://news.xinhuanet.com/english/2009-07/18/content_11727782.htm.

59. In the summer of 2007, Chinese citizens were kidnapped in Islamabad on the basis of running a brothel. The kidnappings sparked an angry reaction from Beijing, and in response the Pakistani army launched a military operation on the Red Mosque, where the militants were hiding.

60. Preeti Bhattacharji, "Uighurs and China's Xinjiang Region," Council on Foreign Relations, May 29, 2012, http://www.cfr.org/china/uighurs-chinas-xinjiang-region/p16870.

61. Brian Spegele, "China Points Finger at Pakistan Again," *Asian Wall Street Journal*, March 7, 2012.

62. "China Commits $45.6 Billion for Economic Corridor with Pakistan," *Express Tribune*, November 21, 2014, http://tribune.com.pk/story/794883/china-commits-45–6-billion-for-economic-corridor-with-pakistan/.

63. In 2007, a state-owned metallurgical group (CMGC) bid $3.4 billion, $1 billion more than any other competitors from Canada, Europe, Russia, and the United States. This will give them the rights to mine copper for the next 25 years, yielding an estimate of eleven million tons of copper. Michael Wines, "China Willing to Spend Big on Afghan Commerce," *New York Times*, December 29, 2009, http://www.nytimes.com/2009/12/30/world/asia/30mine.html?pagewanted=all&_r=0.

64. Thrassy N. Marketos, *China's Energy Geopolitics: The Shanghai Cooperation Organization and Central Asia* (New York: Routledge, 2010), 109.

65. National Archives of India, Foreign Department, Gilgit Frontier, December 1894, nos. 1–10.

66. Thierry Kellner, "Géopolitique de l'énergie La politique pétrolière de la République populaire de Chine: Stratégies et conséquences internationales," in *L'éveil du dragon*, ed. Frédéric Lasserre (Ste-Foy: Presses de l'Université du Québec, 2006), 454.

67. Deng Xiaoping, "The 24 Character Strategy," in Annual Report to Congress, Military Power of the People's Republic of China (2007), http://www.globalsecurity .org/military/library/report/2007/2007-prc-military-power.htm.

CHAPTER 10

PAKISTAN BETWEEN SAUDI ARABIA AND IRAN

ISLAM IN THE POLITICS AND ECONOMICS OF WESTERN ASIA

Sana Haroon

T his chapter traces the development of economic, political, and religious ties between Pakistan and Iran and Saudi Arabia from 1947 to the present. This discussion is intended to link the debate about religious ties between Pakistan and other parts of the Muslim world to a broader body of scholarship and evidence of Pakistan's regional ties as deriving from trade, migration, diplomacy, and geopolitics.

The religious politics of Western Asia are often analyzed through the dichotomy of Iran's Shia revolutionary state and Saudi Arabia's Sunni monarchical one. Pakistan's relations with Iran and Saudi Arabia over sixty years, from 1947 to 2014, suggest ways in which a variety of ideologies have been received politically, diplomatically, and through nonstate actors and the manner in which Pakistan has tilted in favor toward the Arab world and Sunni Islam in spite of the geography, history, and language that link it to Iran.

The first section of the chapter sets up a periodization for the consideration of Pakistan's relations in Western Asia by exploring diplomatic relations between Pakistan, Saudi Arabia, and Iran from 1947 to 2013.[1] I will explore a substantial body of scholarship that proposes that Pakistan's policy position toward a postcolonial Middle East emerged slowly as a product of Cold War alliances managed by Ayub Khan from 1952 to 1968. Ayub Khan's position was altered by the politics of Zulfiqar Ali Bhutto from 1968 to 1977, a period during which, I will argue, the course of Pakistan's current relations with the Middle East was set. The era of Zia ul Haq's dictatorship from 1977 to 1988, followed by the governments of Benazir Bhutto and Nawaz Sharif from 1988 to 1999, constitute a third period in the development of Pakistan's foreign policy. This phase was deeply influenced by the revolution in Iran and the Soviet occupation of and then withdrawal from

Afghanistan. This section builds on the work of Shahid Amin, Hasan Askari Rizvi, S. M. Burke, and others who have broadly framed the study of Pakistan's relations in the Middle East in the regional security context and through the idea of an "Islamic" cultural continuum.

The second section of the chapter builds on this periodization to explore the movement of goods, capital, and labor between Pakistan, Iran, and Saudi Arabia from 1947. This analysis of published economic data and sources describing the development of Islamic finance and sharia-based economics suggests the mainstays of Pakistan's economic and financial links in Western Asia. The third and fourth sections explore cultural relations between Pakistan and Saudi Arabia and Iran since 1979 and transnational Islamism, arguing for a better understanding of Pakistan's participation in a Sunni regionalism. The chapter concludes with a brief discussion of events since 2008.

PAKISTAN'S DIPLOMATIC RELATIONS WITH SAUDI ARABIA AND IRAN

British colonialism had disrupted many of the transfers of people, capital, and ideas across borders and in the maritime region.[2] Prior to 1947, India's governmental relations with the Arab world and Iran were mediated through the Foreign and Political Office of the Government of India.[3] The primary issues of concern for colonial Indian relations with the Gulf were the limitation of "piracy" for protection of crown shipping routes and, later, the laying of telegraph lines across Iran, under the shallow waters of the Persian Gulf, and into India.[4] By the early twentieth century, colonial officials had become concerned by reports of gunrunning and smuggling between Afghanistan, colonial India, and Iran and into the maritime Gulf region from the Makran coast.[5] Relations with the Hijaz were affected by colonial concerns about the loyalty of British Indian subjects during World War I.[6] After the war, the Government of India used passport restrictions to discipline hajj pilgrims, embarrassed by the apparent poverty and itinerancy of Indian travelers to Mecca.[7]

Decolonization opened the door for relations of a more meaningful and mutually beneficial nature. As early as 1947, Pakistani statesmen championed the cause of nationalism and self-determination for colonized Muslim states in testimonials in the United Nation's General Assembly. Despite such nationalist passions, it took time for Pakistan to put together its Foreign Service, and diplomatic relationships evolved slowly. With a piecemeal inheritance of the apparatus and tools of diplomacy in postwar Asia, the state strove to put a diplomatic service and strategy in place. The new government of Pakistan took account of those of its citizens who had received exposure in the colonial civil service, assigning them to key relationships with the United States, Britain, and China. Other posts were filled by young college graduates who completed two-year courses in diplomacy at the Fletcher School, funded through Fulbright fellowships.[8]

Chaudhuri Khaliquzzaman, then president of the Muslim League, set out on a two-month tour of the Middle East barely two years after Partition, attempting to cobble together a national foreign policy position. S. M. Burke writes that he began to envisage a "United Islamistan" in the course of his travels, and his wide publicizing of this agenda did more harm than good for Pakistan's image in the West and accomplished nothing among the Arab states, which seemed unmoved by Pakistan's efforts on behalf of Palestine at the United Nations.[9]

Shortly after Pakistan's entry to the United Nations, the delegation voted with the Arab bloc and Iran to oppose the creation of Israel. In 1949, the International Islamic Economic Conference met in Karachi, attended by delegates from across the Muslim world. Ghulam Muhammad asked that members imagine themselves part of an "organic whole," thereby creating a basis for "collective bargaining."[10] In 1951, the first foreign minister, Zafrulla Khan, continued to address Pakistan relations with the Middle East only in the most general terms, writing of Iran and Saudi Arabia as countries and people that shared the bitterness of the colonial legacy and the geography of an Islamic front against communism.[11]

The United States positioned Pakistan as an ally as the influence of the USSR increased in the Middle East and in Afghanistan. The alliance with Pakistan was justified on the basis that East Pakistan and West Pakistan would each offer bases in the case of a major war, thereby allowing the United States to "close" a "world engirdling circle of influence,"[12] and U.S. spy planes were stationed at Pakistani airbases in the northwest. Hence, when Ayub Khan joined Muhammad Ali Bogra's government as defense minister in 1954, he managed Pakistan's entry into the Mutual Defense Assistance Agreement and then the Baghdad Pact in 1955 (later renamed the Central Treaty Organization, or CENTO).[13] This period marked the beginning of Pakistan's foreign relations with countries of the Middle East— relations that privileged anti-Soviet defensive arrangements with Turkey, Iran, and, for a short time, Iraq, over alliances with Saudi Arabia, Egypt, Jordan, and other Arab states.

During the early years of Pakistan's existence, Saudi Arabia was openly critical of the Pakistan government. When Maulana Maududi of the

Jamaat-e-Islami was sentenced to death for his involvement in the movement against the Ahmadi community, Saudi Arabia threatened to sever
diplomatic ties with Pakistan.[14] During the 1956 Suez crisis, King Saud met
with Nehru and openly criticized Pakistan's position in the Baghdad
Pact.[15] Bhutto later claimed that the Arab world's grievances toward Pakistan were personal and that Ayub Khan's coup in 1958 "noticeably improved" the attitude of the United Arab Republic (the polity representing
the briefly united governments of Syria and Egypt).[16]

Ayub Khan attempted to reverse some of the damage caused by his entry
into the Baghdad Pact in a 1960 visit to Saudi Arabia and the United Arab
Republic. He enunciated his support of the Arab position against Israel,
sought economic assistance from Saudi Arabia, and received assurances of
consideration of his request.[17] The following year, Riyadh agreed to represent Pakistan's interest in Afghanistan in view of rapidly deteriorating relations between the governments of Kabul and Islamabad.[18]

The relationship between Pakistan and the Saudis began to improve after
the 1960 visit, at the expense of relations with other Arab countries and
peoples. In 1961, Pakistan began to supply Saudi Arabia with weapons (rifles
and ammunition), which were "passed on to royalist forces in Yemen" fighting against the newly established republican government.[19] In 1967, Ayub
Khan signed an agreement whereby Pakistan would train the Saudi Armed
Forces.[20] During the 1971 war, when there was a U.S. embargo on military
sales to Pakistan, it was rumored that Libya and Jordan provided American-
built combat aircrafts to Pakistan in return for services rendered by Pakistani pilots in "different Arab air forces."[21]

Conversely, relations with Iran were cordial at the outset of the bilateral
relationship. In 1947, the demarcation of the Pakistan–Iran border necessi-
tated an early diplomatic engagement between the two countries. The border
demarcation was amicably concluded in 1958 and included a gift of territory
from Pakistan to Iran, to protect Iran's oil drainage in the region.[22] The
Baghdad Pact opened up early relations between Pakistan and Iran.
When Iraq exited the pact in 1959, the shah positioned Iran as a regional
center, opening the Baghdad Pact Nuclear Center at Tehran University for
"cooperation and training in the use of radioactive isotopes."[23] That year,
Ayub Khan addressed the Iranian Parliament in a declaration of friendship,
and a stamp was printed commemorating his visit to the country. In 1964,
Iran, Pakistan, and Turkey entered into an agreement establishing the
Regional Cooperation for Development.

During the 1965 war, Iran provided medical supplies, fuel, and aid as well
as facilities for repair and refueling of Pakistani air force fighter planes.[24]

Trained Irani nurses were also sent to help treat the wounded.[25] After the war, Iran was thought to be aiding Pakistan in the purchase of West German jet fighter aircrafts despite the U.S.-imposed sanctions on arms sales to Pakistan.

Zulfiqar Ali Bhutto had been an influence on Pakistan's foreign relations as early as 1957 when he was appointed as a delegate to the United Nations. He then became a cabinet minister in Ayub Khan's government after the coup of 1958 and became foreign minister in 1963. During this time, he articulated his commitment to the politics of nonalignment and remained in favor of cultivating relations with an Islamic bloc. Bhutto wrote that the sharpening of Pakistan's commitments to the Arab world came in 1960 with the revelation of German agreements to arm Israel.[26]

During and after the 1965 war, Bhutto was the primary engineer of Pakistan's foreign policy. He led Pakistan in the Tashkent peace negotiations brokered by the USSR but then broke with Ayub Khan's government and toured the country speaking in public rallies against the government. This movement escalated alongside growing anger in East Pakistan and brought down the Ayub Khan regime in 1969.

In the well-studied events that followed, Pakistan's first direct elections in 1970 gave an absolute majority to the East Pakistani party Awami League led by Sheikh Mujibur Rahman. However, Zulfiqar Bhutto, whose party, the Pakistan Peoples Party (PPP), had dominated the elections in West Pakistan, was asked to convene the assembly.[27] The civil war that followed led to the separation of East Pakistan into the nation-state of Bangladesh. In December 1971, a few days after the end of the war, Bhutto was appointed president of Pakistan as the Constituent Assembly set to work drafting a new constitution.

Championing the politics of the people, Bhutto nationalized key industrial sectors in Pakistan and passed land reforms months after coming to power. He also appeared to take up the cause of Arab socialism, renaming Lahore Stadium in honor of Muammar Al-Qaddafi for "the friendship Libya had shown Pakistan."[28] Bhutto's actions provoked the suspicion of many of the monarchs of the Middle East, and he keenly felt the need for validation of his government, particularly in light of ongoing hostilities with India over Kashmir. He made several visits to the Middle East and North Africa in 1972, soliciting statements of support from Turkey, Iran, Morocco, Egypt, Tunisia, and Libya (in addition to the USSR and China) for implementation of the UN General Assembly Resolution for the cessation of hostilities, repatriation of prisoners of war, and withdrawal to cease-fire lines.[29] As the scheduled peace meetings with India approached, Bhutto embarked on a whirlwind tour of Abu Dhabi, Kuwait, Iraq, Lebanon, Jordan, Saudi Arabia, and Iran in addition to Nigeria, Somalia, Ethiopia, Mauritania, and Turkey in late May 1972.

Bhutto's politics did not overturn the earlier terms of engagement with the Middle East. Military Staff College in Quetta had trained officers from British colonial armies across the Middle East since the 1920s. The Pakistani military offered its services in Jordan from the 1960s and extended these arrangements to the newly independent emirate of Abu Dhabi, and presumably to Saudi Arabia, after 1972. Bhutto continued to barter the skills of the Pakistan army for aid, preferential ties, and camaraderie and the creation of a front against India. However, Bhutto augmented these relations by opening up commercial and economic bilateral agreements with the Middle East and North Africa, solidifying Pakistan's position in a Western Asian and North African economic sphere. During the 1972 trip, Bhutto set the ground for an agreement between Pakistan International Airlines and Saudi Airlines to jointly operate all hajj flights between these countries,[30] and Karachi's shipyards began to manufacture harbor tugs and coastal craft for Abu Dhabi.[31]

It was as an extension of this vision of a regional economic order that Bhutto proposed that the convention of the second summit of the Organization of the Islamic Conference be held in Lahore. The summit had been called to discuss the aftermath of the Arab-Israeli War and the oil embargo and was to be bankrolled by Saudi Arabia, flush with petro-dollars in the aftermath of the embargo by the Organization of Petroleum Exporting Countries (OPEC).[32] The Islamic Summit openly and somewhat transparently set an agenda for Pakistan's policy position toward the Middle East, something I will discuss in more detail in the next section.

At a different level, the events of 1972–1974 allowed Bhutto to initiate personal relations with heads of Muslim states. Bhutto struck up close relations with Sheikh Zayed of the newly independent United Arab Emirates and King Faisal of Saudi Arabia. As chairman of the Islamic Conference, Bhutto was able to receive more controversial heads of state, including Muammar Al-Qaddafi (only recently come to power in Libya in 1969) and Yasser Arafat, the head of the Palestinian Liberation Organization.[33] Where Ayub Khan provided King Hussain of Jordan with military support in putting down the Palestinian Liberation Organization in Jordanian refugee camps,[34] Bhutto gave commitments of military support to Arafat and, in 1976, flew air ambulances and military support in to the Palestinian enclaves in Lebanon, in response to a request for help directed through the embassy staff in Beirut.[35]

Bhutto began to develop Pakistan's nuclear weapons program. Gordon Corera describes the beginning of the quest for nuclear weapons as an aspect of the showmanship of Bhutto in a post-1971, defeated Pakistan.[36] The inception of the nuclear program was concurrent with Bhutto's attempts to reach out to Middle Eastern countries and gain monetary support for his government and his programs. Corera surmises that support for and interest in the bomb could have encouraged the monetary support committed by Saudi Arabia as well as Libya and other Gulf states in this sensitive period.[37]

Economic aid began to flow into Pakistan from the Middle East after 1974. General Muhammad Zia ul Haq—judge, jury, and executioner of Bhutto and his politics—took control of this relationship as the Afghan jihad began. In 1979, Iran and Pakistan agreed that in light of the failure of the organization to maintain peace in the region, their continued membership in CENTO did not serve national interests.[38] The period that followed, 1979–1999, marked an era of economic growth, urban development, and institutional transformation in the Gulf and Saudi Arabia. Conversely, the revolution in Iran, the imposition of sanctions, and the Iran–Iraq War isolated it from the wave of labor migration and capital flows, which brought Pakistan into closer relations with the Arab states.

In 1981, Zia ul Haq first engaged diplomatically with postrevolutionary Iran in an official state visit. Following this visit, reports of Iran using "backdoor" trading routes through Pakistan to import essential goods began to filter into the press.[39] Pak–Iran relations remained on an even keel through the period of the Iran–Iraq War, harmonized through their policy toward Afghanistan. As the Afghan war drew to a close, Pakistan and Iran signed trade agreements that doubled Pakistan's oil import from Iran in return for increased rice, wheat, and sugar exports. The two governments also agreed to raise a previous cap on transit trade across the Baluchistan border.[40]

In 1982, Pakistan signed a protocol with Saudi Arabia by which Pakistani troops would be stationed in Saudi Arabia to defend the holy sites.[41] The troops remained there until 1987, when Saudi Arabia sent back the 20,000 Pakistani soldiers troops stationed there because they included Shias, and the Saudis were not comfortable with this presence in the aftermath of the events of the hajj of 1987.[42] Saudi Arabia was said to have supported the Sunni politics of the Jamaat-e-Islami in the 1988 elections in which Benazir Bhutto came to power. Her election heralded the beginning of a period of relatively cool relations between the two countries, which ended in 1990, when Saudi followed Iran in issuing a statement of support for Pakistan's position on the escalating conflict in Kashmir. Benazir Bhutto made a visit to Saudi in the same year and discussed increased Saudi aid for Pakistan.[43] After Iraq's invasion of Kuwait in 1990, Pakistan sent a mechanized brigade of close to 6,000 men to Saudi and another 1,000 to the United Arab Emirates under the 1982 agreement.[44] However, over time, Saudi Arabia's own internal recruitment and training made it less dependent on this sort of military assistance.[45]

Pakistan's return to democracy after the death of Zia ul Haq marked the next phase of relations between Pakistan and the Middle East. Benazir Bhutto's first and second terms as prime minister of Pakistan were positive periods of engagement with Iran. In 1995, in her second term, Benazir Bhutto visited Iran and opened discussions on the import of natural gas from Iran as a feasible alternative to import from Qatar and Turkmenistan.[46] Later that year, an agreement was signed to build a gas pipeline connecting the South Pars gas field to Pakistan and potentially onward to India. In 1996, discussions began over pricing of the gas, finance, and building of the pipeline. Both countries remained committed to the project, although the dimensions and viability of the project, including the question of whether it would link to the Indian market, continued to be debated.[47] During the same period, Iran acquired designs that allowed the country's nuclear scientists to build a pilot centrifuge. The UN International Atomic Energy Agency later discovered that the designs were from Pakistani laboratories and were received as early as 1995.[48] The extent to which the army (under General Mirza Aslam Beg) and the government were involved in these transfers remains unclear.[49]

During Nawaz Sharif's second term as prime minister, from 1997 to 1999, tensions between Iran and Afghanistan began to escalate as the Taliban extended their control across Afghanistan. In September 1998, forty Iranian citizens, including diplomatic staff, disappeared in the violent Taliban capture of Mazar-i Sharif. Pakistan's mediation led to the release of five Iranian truck drivers, but the nine diplomats were later found dead. Pakistan's continued support of the Taliban during this period soured Pakistan–Iran relations.[50] Pakistan's insistence on the right to host the Organization of the Islamic Conference (OIC) summit meeting in 1997 at the 50th anniversary of Pakistan's creation was also seen as a deliberate snub to Iran, whose turn it really was.[51] However, enhanced U.S. sanctions on Iran and U.S. strikes in Afghanistan in 1998[52] may have muted Iran's position toward Pakistan at this time.

Saudi Arabia and the United Arab Emirates' relevance for Pakistani domestic politics took a new turn in the 1990s when political leaders chose these countries as their homes during periods of exile. Benazir Bhutto set up her base in Dubai after the dissolution of her first government in 1990 and after her second ousting in 1996. Nawaz Sharif chose Saudi Arabia as his home in his period of exile from Pakistan from 1999 to 2007. Pervez Musharraf made his first out-of-state visit to Saudi Arabia to seek legitimization after the coup in which he overthrew Nawaz Sharif. Asif Zardari also spent time in his personal residence in Dubai after his release from jail in 2004.

In 2008, the PPP led by Asif Ali Zardari took power, completing a full term amid allegations of corruption but also overseeing the passage of the Eighteenth Amendment to the Constitution. Whereas the PPP strongly maintained the importance of diplomatic and economic ties with Iran, the 2013 elections, which brought Nawaz Sharif in as prime minister for a third term, were followed almost immediately by announcements of government intentions to seek financial support from Saudi Arabia.[53]

As the subsequent section will explore, Pakistan's diplomatic ties with Saudi Arabia and Iran developed alongside the economic vision of successive governments. This economic relationship, affected by events such as the end of the Cold War, provided opportunities both for Saudi Arabia and the United Arab Emirates to step into a role of patrons of Pakistan's political elites and for the imagining of large collaborative projects, such as the Iran–Pakistan gas pipeline.

TRADE, CAPITAL, AND MIGRATION

During the colonial period, trade between South Asia, Iran, and Saudi Arabia was channeled through British maritime shipping routes and land trade routes, taxed at the colonial borders of India, and denominated in pounds sterling. Oil was transported between Iran and Saudi Arabia and the Indian colonial market by British- and U.S.-owned oil marketing companies. In the early years of Liaquat Ali Khan's and then Khwaja Nazimuddin's leadership, Pakistan determined its national developmental agenda. From early on, no less than fifty percent of total revenue was allocated to defense and the remainder to railways, electric power, agriculture, telecommunications, and new industries. Commonwealth membership, commodity aid from the United States, and the demand for Pakistani products during the Korean War[54] led Pakistan to continue to focus on trade relations with the United Kingdom and United States in the early years after Partition.

Between 1947 and 1957, Pakistan imported petroleum products from a variety of sources, including Iran, the USSR, Malaysia, and Burma, but the bulk was imported from the United Kingdom.[55] Owing to the controls on the price of oil, Pakistan's low level of industrialization and electrification, and limitations on the use of foreign exchange to finance imports, petroleum products accounted for under 10 percent of total imports up to 1973. The OPEC embargo on oil in 1973 multiplied the cost of oil in the budget of the government of Pakistan while simultaneously transforming the economic position of the oil-producing countries. Zulfiqar Ali Bhutto's management of the OIC summit at this crucial moment directly linked Pakistan to the economies of the oil-producing countries of the Middle East.

The OIC summit allowed for the continuation of a debate that had begun in 1970 at the Karachi conference of Foreign Ministers of Muslim Countries. Then, the participants had opened up the discussion of economic, social, and cultural cooperation between Muslim countries and agreed to explore the creation of a regional system of banking based on Islamic methods for the management of "Moslem capital." The Egyptian economist Mohamed Hassan al Tohami went on to write a study entitled "Egyptian Study on the Establishment of an Islamic Banking System (Economics and Islamic Doctrine)." This paper was the basis for the establishment of the Islamic Development Bank in Riyadh in 1973.[56] Al Tohami served as secretary general of the 1974 OIC summit in Lahore at which he presented his ideas about the "Islamic economy," which would "safeguard the interests of Islamic countries and their peoples" and allow for the "investments by states and individuals alike of surplus capital . . . with the purpose of augmenting it for the good of all Islamic states and people."[57]

The idea of the Islamic economy was based on three principles. The first was that many Muslim countries were economically strong but might enter the world economy on disadvantageous terms. The second was that morality demanded that surplus capital of wealthy countries be invested to benefit all Islamic states and people. The third was that Muslim financial ethics differentiated Muslim peoples and Muslim states within the world economy, and these ethics were best understood through the sharia.

As secretary general of the OIC summit, Tohami called for development and planning that would allow for the investment of surplus capital in the region, thereby shoring up the economies of poorer Muslim states and upholding the moral principles of Islam by creating interest-free banking models. This proposal was a reversal of Pakistan's earlier position on leadership in the Muslim world as from 1947 Pakistan had claimed to champion Islam in the postcolonial world. From 1974, Pakistan deferred to Saudi Arabia, the United Arab Emirates, Iran, and Libya—the Arab oil-producing countries—stating that they were the rightful guardians of Islam and of the umma.[58]

The Islamic Summit set the stage for a new era of professional and economic alliances between Pakistan and the Arab world. Up to 1972, the only
Arab Gulf country that extended loan facilities to Pakistan was Kuwait.[59]
Between 1973 and 1978, Pakistan received aid commitments of $971 million
from Libya, Iran, Abu Dhabi, Qatar, Saudi Arabia, and the OPEC fund.
These funds were used for balance-of-payments support for petroleum
imports, for setting up oil refineries, and for other communications and
capital investment projects.[60]

The most important relationships that grew out of these aid commitments were those with the United Arab Emirates and Saudi Arabia. Largely
owing to the increase in price of oil, imports from Saudi Arabia accounted
for close to 60 percent of total petroleum imports in 1973–1974, whereas they
had accounted for only 11 percent of imports in 1970–1971. Pakistan began
importing oil from the United Arab Emirates in the same year, supported
by a $100 million loan facility received from Abu Dhabi and a $15 million
facility for the import of crude oil from Abu Dhabi National Oil Corporation (ADNOC).[61] Iran made aid commitments of $580 million in 1974 and a
further $150 million in 1976.[62]

Earlier balance-of-payments and project support had come from the
United Kingdom, United States, USSR, and China. Arab aid commitments
of the 1970s led to the establishment of several jointly funded projects
including the Pak-Arab Refinery and Pak-Arab Fertilizer Project at Multan,
funded by Abu Dhabi; the Tarbela hydropower project, funded by OPEC;
and fertilizer, cement, and thermal power plants, funded by Saudi Arabia.
Joint investment and holding companies were also set up with financial
commitments from Kuwait and Libya.[63] Earlier refineries, such as Pakistan
Refinery, incorporated in 1960, and National Refinery, incorporated in 1963,
were built to refine Iranian crude oil. In contrast, the Pak-Arab Refinery
Limited, 60 percent owned by the Abu Dhabi National Oil Corporation and
finally completed in 2000, was built to refine the Abu Dhabi and Saudi Arabian crude products.

Saudi Arabia's (and the United Arab Emirates') economic growth and urban development onward had great implications for Pakistan. Pakistani
migrant workers in Saudi were remitting over $500 million annually—over
40 percent of total foreign remittances—from the late 1970s.[64] By the turn
of the century, an equal amount was being remitted from the United Arab
Emirates.[65]

In addition to direct economic assistance, a second profound influence
on Pakistan's economics emerged in the growth of capital markets and
banking in the United Arab Emirates and Saudi Arabia. The Dubai Islamic

Bank was established in 1975 in the United Arab Emirates and was owned by the Dubai government, and the Islamic Development Bank was established in Saudi Arabia in 1975 through a joint declaration by member countries of the OIC.[66] Both organizations were intended to create sharia-compliant banking models that could serve investors and borrowers through the region. Professionals also built on the access to capital to fund banking, commercial, infrastructural, and financial projects in Pakistan.[67] The Bank of Credit and Commerce International set up by Pakistani banker Agha Hassan Abedi and funded by the Abu Dhabi royal family has been relegated to ignominy,[68] but more recent collaborations have been closely regulated under international trade and banking laws and are, by all accounts, successful enterprises. Together, these influences suggest a prevailing vision of a morally construed Islamic region within which a mutually profitable mobilization of capital is seen as possible.

The idea of the Islamic economy influenced taxation and banking practices in Pakistan as well. In February 1979, Zia ul Haq declared that Pakistan was going to follow an interest-free finance model, applying the principle to the activities of public-sector investment corporations.[69] The assessment of *zakat* was to follow the example of Saudi Arabia, which had been levying zakat since 1956, as is suggested in an 1980 Urdu publication, translated from a 1977 work by a scholar of the Abdul Aziz University (of Sharia) in Riyadh. The author argues that zakat must be applied equally to savings and assessed on commerce and industry.[70] The book also accounts for the history of zakat regulation through oversight, banking, and auditing in Saudi Arabia, suggesting the methods by which zakat could be assessed and charged by the government in Pakistan.[71]

The interest-free models of banking, first developed by Faisal Islamic Bank and ADNOC, have been picked up by international banks operating in the region[72] and have, since 2001, inspired the extension of "sharia-compliant" banking services by a number of Western and local banks in Pakistan, overseen by the State Bank of Pakistan.[73]

Although the burgeoning of sharia-compliant banking services suggests that Pakistanis are ethically interested in the Islamic finance model, the low rate of governmental collection of zakat funds and almost negligible value of voluntary zakat payments into the government fund establish that governmental regulation of this sector is not widely appreciated by the Pakistan public.[74] The idea of the Islamic economy therefore has its greatest salience for the private sector rather than for a state-sponsored Islamism.

The events of the 1970s led to an increase in imports from Iran as well, but trade with Iran both before and after the revolution of 1979 occupied a more modest portion of Pakistan's trading account than that with Saudi Arabia (table 10.1). The trading relationship with Iran has always had important consequences for the economy of Baluchistan, where an undocumented trade in fuel subsidizes the local economy.[75] Documented and undocumented trade in dry goods, vegetables, fruit, livestock, electricity, and labor fills the markets on both sides of the border. The Iranian government has shown a great interest in the border relations with Baluchistan, and many of the projects funded by Iran in the 1970s supported industry based in Baluchistan.

At a national level, Pakistan imported petroleum and petrochemicals as well as food and ore from across the border. Imports from Iran to Pakistan were encouraged through loan agreements and trade agreements in the pre-1979 era, but the trade relations of the 1980s were far more significant because of the international trade sanctions on Iran, under which Iran exported oil and imported essential commodities from across the Pakistan border. Between 1981 and 1983, total imports from Iran increased from Rs 23 million to Rs 1.1 billion, and exports to Iran increased from Rs 823 million to Rs 4.2 billion. In 1986, the two countries set up a Joint Economic Commission to manage trade across the border.[76] After a period of tensions over Pakistan's Afghan policy in 1997–2001, Pak–Iran trade was renewed along with efforts to regularize the undocumented economy.[77]

In 2003, diplomacy toward actualizing the Iran–Pakistan gas pipeline was renewed, and in 2010, a deal was signed to start construction of the route.[78] Despite overt U.S. pressure and threats to extend sanctions against Iran to any financier of the project and the withdrawal of a Chinese consortium, which was going to lead the financing, both countries remained committed to building the pipeline, and it became a key point in the articulation of regional self-interest and defiance of the United States under the PPP government of 2008–2013.

Between 1973 and 2000, two different sets of interests came to define Pakistan's relations with the Arab world and relations with Iran. Relations with the Arab world had ballooned with the petrodollar economy. Relations with Iran, while also deeply significant for regional economic growth and resource sharing, were not seen as buoyant or as lucrative and were sidelined, particularly after the end of the Iran–Iraq War. Yet the benefit to Pakistan's domestic economy from economic ties with Saudi Arabia and the Gulf has yet to be fully quantified. While remittances of foreign exchange strengthen the domestic economy, other ties may be detrimental to Pakistan's national interest. Arab investors have blocked attempts to develop coal-fired power plants, encouraging Pakistan to remain dependent on expensive

TABLE 10.1 PAKISTAN TRADE WITH SAUDI ARABIA AND IRAN, 1955–2010

IMPORTS/EXPORTS	1955–1956	1965–1966	1966–1967	1971–1972	1974–1975	1978–1979	1979–1980	1988–1989	1992–1993	1996–1997	1999–2000	2000–2001	2009–2010
Imports from Saudi Arabia	17.29	2.40	0.70	51.10	1,559.10	1,962.00	3,235.00	5,541.00	14,083.00	27,793.00	47,790.00	73,359.00	282,364.58
Exports to Saudi Arabia	Not reported	20.60	31.40	47.40	620.90	945.00	1,269.00	2,128.00	8,280.00	8,452.00	11,121.00	11,438.00	38,818.99
Imports from Iran	17.50	28.90	124.30	63.80	116.80	59.00	95.00	1,932.00	4,601.00	11,177.00	6,746.00	16,784.00	Not reported
Exports to Iran	Not reported	13.60	17.30	20.70	594.20	464.00	1,040.00	1,452.00	1,130.00	622.00	595.00	833.00	Not reported
Imports from UAE				39.60	244.00	1,319.00		1,890.00	7,870.00	37,879.00	46,993.00	54,868.00	143,953.76
Exports to UAE		108.20	147.04	265.29	476.00	615.00		3,680.00	10,592.00	15,611.00	25,513.00	25,028.00	144,358.00
Total mineral oil/petroleum imports					256.50	3,333.60	3,710.70	10,685.00	18,509.00	40,066.00	88,353.00	145,238.00	
Total imports for the year	1,439.80	4,208.30	5,192.30	9,602.00	3,495.40	20,925.00	26,102.90	46,929.00	135,841.00	258,643.00	465,001.00	627,000.00	2,910,975.00
Total exports for the year	1,728.90	2,691.00	2,870.90	3,371.40	10,286.00	11,635.80	23,410.00	90,183.00	177,028.00	325,313.00	539,070.00	8,190.00	1,617,458.00
Oil as a percentage of total imports	7.51	3.49	8.71		7.34	15.93	14.22	22.77	13.63	15.49	19.00	1,512.58	23.02

Loans (in $ millions)

Saudi Arabia				100.00	130.70	260.70						
Loan					130.00							
Export credit					0.70							
Iran				778.64							0.00	
Loan												
Export credit												
Saudi oil as a % of total oil import	15.98	1.63	6.86	19.92	46.77	52.87	30.28	29.94	35.15	31.46	32.90	50.82

Workers remittances (in $ millions)

Iran				2.39	26.85	16.49	1.34	0.31	Not reported	Not reported	Not reported	Not reported
Saudi Arabia				17.26	594.38	795.46	819.95	748.36	613.03	309.85	304.43	354.15
UAE					22.34	205.75	191.37	135.89	164.39	147.79	190.04	1,497.24

NOTE: THIS TABLE IS BASED ON INFORMATION FROM THE PAKISTAN ECONOMIC SURVEYS FROM 1956 TO 2011. MANY HISTORIC FIGURES ARE REVISED FROM YEAR TO YEAR TO ACCOUNT FOR CHANGES IN EXCHANGE RATES OR TO CORRECT ERRORS. BECAUSE THIS TABLE DOES NOT ADJUST ALL THE FIGURES TO CURRENT EXCHANGE RATES, IT SHOULD BE UNDERSTOOD TO INDICATE GENERAL TRENDS.

imports of furnace oil. Saudi Arabia made a credit facility for oil purchase available to Pakistan on a deferred payment basis just after the nuclear tests in 1998. These aid relations became more complicated under the PPP government when Saudi Arabia refused to sell oil to Pakistan on anything other than commercial terms despite the crisis state of the Pakistani power sector during the recent PPP tenure.[79]

PLACING ISLAM IN REGIONAL RELATIONS

Ideas about the political salience of a transnational Islamic community in a world of nation-states first began to be articulated in the late nineteenth century. This idea—that Muslims of the world constitute a composite called the *umma*—inspired both Shia and Sunni political-religious movements. In addition to invoking the idea of a moral community, the idea of the umma relies on a shared regard for the history, languages, knowledge, and sites of Islam. For Sunnis, these are the Arabic language, the Hanafi, Hanbali, Shafi, and Maliki legal traditions as certain hadith compilations, and the sites of Islam in the Arab world, including Mecca, Medina, and Al Aqsa. For Shias, this list includes the Persian language, the legal compendium of Imam Jafar, and the sites of Karbala and Najaf in Iraq and Qom in Iran.

Intellectual relations between South Asian Muslims and Iran and Saudi Arabia are rooted in a long history of travel and learning. Both before and after 1947, some Sunni scholars in South Asia often traveled to Mecca and Medina for initiation into hadith and fiqh studies and Arabic language study,[80] and Shia scholars often traveled to Iraq.[81] This sort of training was received in addition to knowledge traditions and education from South Asian teachers. Students would spend several years in Saudi Arabia participating in study circles and sometimes setting up their own. They studied and taught in ethnically diverse groups of students linked by their subject of study and the language of study, which was Arabic. In the late colonial period, Sunni scholars from the organization called the Ahl-i Hadith and those connected to the madrasah Darul Ulum Deoband most often traveled to Saudi for study. This continued in the postcolonial period, and some Pakistani scholars who came to great prominence remained in Saudi Arabia as teachers or in other professional capacities.[82] The same is presumably true of the teaching and learning experience of Shia scholars in Najaf and later in Qom.[83]

Pakistan's cultural relations with the Muslim world have been affected by the fault line between Arab Sunnism and Iranian Shiism. Pakistan's earliest relations with Iran were premised on its historic cultural connections to the Persianate cultural world while Pakistani ulama looked toward the institutions of Islamic legal studies in Saudi Arabia.

During the period of the CENTO accords, Iran sought collaborations in petrochemicals research and development and engineering,[84] while Pakistan sought to enhance a Persianate cultural heritage through education programs and sharing of expertise about art, archaeology, anthropology, and architecture. Iranian cultural centers were established in cities across Pakistan, including Quetta, Peshawar, Islamabad, Karachi, and Lahore, and an Iran–Pakistan Language Authority was established in 1969 to foster Persian research, writing, and publishing in Pakistan.[85] Iran sponsored a cultural center and digital library mostly focused on manuscript preservation at Punjab University Library,[86] and the Iran–Pakistan Persian Research Center, established in 1971 and now located in Islamabad, maintains a collection of manuscripts and a research library.[87]

Both before and after 1979, Pakistan and Iran have had agreements for student exchange programs. The earliest of these involved each country offering ten postgraduate scholarships to the other.[88] Under more recent agreements, Pakistan reserves small quotas at public universities for Iranian students, and Iran does the same for Pakistani students. Pilgrims intending to visit Sufi shrines and Shia sites in Iran (or, for that matter, in India) have not received the same attention as hajjis, although visa policies for religious tourists have been discussed between the two states. Instead, travel to holy sites in Iran is managed by private tour operators.

It was only after 1979 that Qom became a major center for Shia theological study, and the example of Iran began to inspire Shia intellectualism and politics in Pakistan.[89] A recent publication from Islamabad's Al Basirah Trust, a research organization for the study of Islam in the light of ijtehad, describes this inspirationalism as pivoting on the personality and then memory of Imam Khomeini and the possibilities for engaging in scholarly and political debates in a religious idiom.[90] Equally, Iran's clerics have regularly spoken out in the Iranian press about the condition of Pakistan's Shia and have extended moral and personal support to Pakistan's Shia activists.[91]

Mariam Abou Zahab's work on the "new Shias" inspired by postrevolutionary Iran describes the politicization of the Shia identity through the emergence of transnational connections between Shia clerics in Pakistan and those in the Middle East (including Lebanon) and through the establishment of new teaching and congregational spaces in Pakistan, which transferred a distinctly Iranian Shiism into Pakistan.[92]

In contrast, the Arab world has long occupied an undisputed position as a cultural, intellectual, and moral wellspring for Sunni Islam. In overt attempts to bolster this position, Saudi Arabian ulama have sought to modernize religious institutions in Saudi Arabia in line with other educational and institutional developmental objectives. Muhammad Qasim Zaman's recent work, *Modern Islamic Thought*, identifies the national and transnational ambitions of Salafi ulama in institutionalizing the loci for issuing fatwa.[93] Modern colleges offering government-recognized degrees for the study of sharia and the Arabic language were set up in Riyadh in 1951 and Medina in 1961 in an attempt to institutionalize and monitor religious study. In 1953, the Dar al-Ifta was established and grew to be a single centralized source of religious interpretation and injunction in the Saudi state.[94] These colleges and institutions enroll international students and invite theologians from around the Muslim world, including Pakistan.

Patronage of Pakistani ulama by Saudi ulama is suggested by regular visits of Saudi theologians to Pakistan. Such visits are strongly encouraged in Pakistan and both official and unofficial levels. When the imam of Mecca's Grand Mosque visited Pakistan during the Lal Masjid crisis, he was allowed to meet with Abdul Rashid Ghazi and heard his demands for the establishment of Saudi-style sharia.[95] In other cases, meetings between the religious parties and Saudi officials have been facilitated by Pakistani politicians.[96] Saudi Arabia provided the campus for the International Islamic University established in Islamabad in 1980. In 1985, three Islamic and Arabic studies centers funded by and named for Sheikh Zayed, president of the United Arab Emirates, were opened at the University of Karachi, Peshawar University, and Punjab University.[97]

Official cultural relations opened possibilities for Pakistan to receive other forms of religious support as well. In the 1960s, King Faisal provided funds to build the Faisal Mosque in Islamabad to which he added $10 million to support the creation of an Islamic educational center on the mosque grounds.[98] The International Islamic University was set up in 1980 through this donation,[99] and the mosque was completed in 1986.

Other instances of expansive Arab financial support for projects in Pakistan seem greatly inspired by personal interests, connections, and largesse on the part of Arab royals. The Sheikh Zayed International Airport and the Sheikh Zayed Medical College and Hospital, both at Rahim Yar Khan in Sindh, were both projects funded personally by Sheikh Zayed because the area is a favorite hunting destination of the UAE sheikhs. The Sheikh Zayed Medical Complex in Lahore, the Civil Hospital at Nagarparkar in Sindh, and the Sheikh Zayed International School in Islamabad, all commissioned in 1986, were also described as personally motivated charitable projects.[100]

The architectural monument of the Faisal Mosque, Pakistan's biggest mosque and briefly the largest mosque in the world, has drawn great attention the fact of Saudi support for Sunni practice in Pakistan's intolerant religious environment.[101] Its grounds house Zia ul Haq's mausoleum, and its image has been replicated on the Rs 5,000 note since 2006. Faisal Mosque has broadened Pakistan's definition of its architectural heritage, which includes Naulakha pavilion, the Badhshahi mosque, Mohenjodaro, and the tomb of Jahangir—all sites signifying a regional territorial heritage and a predominantly Persianate one. However, Faisal Mosque, built at the same time as Islamic world–funded large power projects, refineries, and factories, is intended to be symbolic of national economic development. As many commentators have pointed out, Faisal Mosque demonstrates the confluence of Pakistan's national religious self-representation and Saudi Arabia's interests in religious patronage.

Pakistan interacts most directly and regularly with Saudi Arabia on the question of the hajj because of the close intergovernmental collaboration required to make arrangements for pilgrims and the demands for transparency in the allocation of hajj permits on the part of Pakistanis. Between 1948 and 1974, the number of Pakistanis who performed hajj each year increased from 12,300 to 58,743.[102] By the end of the century, that number crossed 100,000, and the number of Pakistani hajis anticipated for 2012 was 190,000.[103] Since the 1960s, each country has been awarded a quota under which its citizens' participation in hajj is managed.[104] Robert Bianchi notes that Pakistani participation expanded dramatically and was managed under a new and highly efficient hajj administration during Zulfiqar Ali Bhutto's premiership, peaking at the time of the 1974 Islamic Summit.[105] The quota systems and the sheer size of Pakistan's annual hajj contingent has made the hajj a major point of issue in Pakistan–Saudi relations. Each year, Pakistan bargains for an increase in the quota, and any success is widely publicized.[106] Hajj training schemes, which discipline pilgrims and prepare them for the strenuous rites, have been in place since Bhutto's time. The Pakistani state, in supporting the Saudi state in its hajj management objectives, implicitly supports the view that Pakistanis as Muslims have no claim on Mecca except as worshippers.

Bianchi argues that Saudi Arabia's management of the hajj is deeply affected by a perceived threat from pilgrims expressing any political motivation. In 1979, the Saudi dissident Juhayman al-Otaibi, along with 400 supporters, occupied the Grand Mosque in Mecca right after the conclusion of the hajj. It was rumored that a prominent Pakistani Ahl-i Hadith member who was studying and teaching in Saudi Arabia participated in the events of 1979, and the Iranian government openly appealed to other Muslims to mobilize politically in Mecca.[107] In 1987, at least 400 Iranian pilgrims were killed when Saudi security forces began shooting at Iranian pilgrims who had staged a "demonstration" in Mecca.[108]

Saudi Arabia's position is clear: Mecca and Medina belong to the Saudi state, and worshippers enter at the regime's behest.[109] Pakistani pilgrims are closely scrutinized for links either to Iran or to dissident religious factions, and Pakistani migrant workers are subjected to close surveillance and state monitoring in Saudi Arabia and the United Arab Emirates. In June 2012, Saudi Arabia's arrest of the Indian Muslim militant and Lashkar-e-Taiba member Abu Jindal on passport violations and his extradition to India to stand trial and give evidence against Pakistan for the November 26 Mumbai attacks confirm Saudi Arabia's intolerance of religious activism on its own soil.[110]

There is as yet little evidence of direct Saudi support to religious extremist groups in Pakistan, a fact that should caution us against drawing too many inferences about Saudi Arabia's role in Pakistan. But Saudi Arabia's recent commitment to build "100 wells, 100 mosques and 2,000 eye surgeries" in Pakistan, its sponsorship of Koran recitation competitions, and its gift of a Rs 30 million carpet to the International Islamic University in Islamabad are the most recent of many "gifts" from Saudi Arabia in support of Sunni interpretations of Islam in Pakistan.[111]

At an official level, most relations between Pakistan, Saudi Arabia, and the United Arab Emirates have rationalized a Sunni Muslim politics managed by governments and institutions and are marked by attempts to check mobile and transnational Islamist politics, which are perceived to compromise the interests of government. The most obvious cultural spillover of the official Saudi–Pakistan relationship is the proliferation of private tourism companies that have sprung up across Pakistan, putting together not only hajj and Umrah packages for religious travel to Mecca but also packaging tours for tourists and airline tickets for migrant workers to Dubai, Jeddah, and Doha. The religious transference of ideas inspired by such travel alone is no more and no less significant than the abaya and sheila, the woman's cloak and veil, which is fashionable in Saudi Arabia and the Gulf and increasingly preferred by religiously observant Pakistani Muslim women over the burka.[112]

TRANSNATIONAL ISLAMISM

During the Afghan war, Arabs committed to the preservation of the umma found their way to Pakistan's northwest and from there into Afghanistan and did so with the complicity of Zia's government in Pakistan and presumably the knowledge and approval of the governments of their own countries—among these, Saudi Arabia, Egypt, and the United Arab Emirates. During the 1990s, participants supported the rise of the dogmatic Sunni Taliban movement. Afghanistan therefore became an incubator of a Sunni transnationalism, taking shape around theological ideas about state, governance, sharia, and in opposition to Iranian-sponsored Shiism. Pakistan received the product of both Afghanistan's militarized Sunni dogma and Iran's newly politicized Shia identity.

Through the same period, Iran remained committed to speaking for and defending the interests of the Shias of Afghanistan. It supported the Bonn agreement and invested in construction projects in Afghanistan, offered aid and loans, and urged all parties to participate in a broad-based representative government at Kabul.[113] Shortly after the revolution in Iran, a Shia political front was established in Punjab as the Tehrik-e Nizaf-e Fiqha Jafaria (Movement for the Protection of the Jafari Fiqh).

By the middle of the 1980s, many of the Sunni groups that had been involved in the Afghan war began to set up militant and anti-Shia organizations in Pakistan, the first of which was the Anjuman-i Sipah-e-Sahaba Pakistan (Society of the Soldiers of the Companions of the Prophet) established in 1985 in the Punjab. This group was implicated in attacks on Iranian interests in Pakistan from the 1989 to 2001. In 1990, the cultural attaché at the Irani consulate in Lahore was killed by Haq Nawaz Jhangvi of the Sipah-e-Sahaba. In 1997, Riaz Basra of the offshoot group Lashkar-e Jhangvi claimed responsibility for an attack that killed five Iranian cadets visiting Rawalpindi.[114] Sunni extremist groups claimed responsibility for attacks on the Iranian cultural center in Multan in 1997 and 1998, claiming that the center was advocating Shia militancy in Pakistan.[115]

Mariam Abou Zahab argues that the rising conflict between Sunnis and Shias in Pakistan during the 1980s and 1990s should be read as an extension of Saudi–Iran tensions in Pakistan because of the material support extended to Sunni extremist groups by Arab benefactors and selective targeting of the Ithna 'Asharia Shias of Pakistan over Bohris and Ismailis.[116] That the Pakistani establishment—particularly the military intelligence—showed itself willing to suffer the proliferation of Sunni militant groups in Pakistan and their targeting of Shias and Iranian interests in the country suggest its complicity in the regional competition. From all accounts, this forbearance was linked to the ability of religious extremists to penetrate the borders of Afghanistan and Kashmir rather than to particular ideological preferences.

A popular understanding of Islamic regionalism has been supported in Pakistan by both the Urdu- and regional-language press and by preachers. This trend emerged first in response to Pan-Arabism and was invigorated during the Soviet occupation of Afghanistan, the Israeli state, and prevailing Western interests in the oil-rich Middle East. Transnational Islamic discourses critique government action in pursuit of what are seen to be American-directed policy ends and often propose an empathy with Islamist movements. After September 11, 2001, the politics of religion in Pakistan became increasingly colored by sectarian rivalries. Pervez Musharraf's government banned several religious sectarian groups, among them Lashkar-e Taiba, Lashkar-e Jhangvi, Sipah-e Mohammad, Jaish-e Mohammad, and Sipah-e-Sahaba.[117] However, these groups continued to operate, often under new names, claiming responsibility for massive attacks on Shia communities across the country and inspiring, if not directly carrying out, isolated attacks on Shia professionals. Saudi and Gulf Arabs were implicated in providing funding for religious extremists through "cash couriers," suggesting Al Qaeda–inspired Islamist organization.[118]

Significant though these events have been, the war on terror, the occupation and subsequent fall of Iraq to the Islamic State of Iraq and the Levant (ISIS), and efforts to rebuild Afghanistan alongside an American withdrawal have had a tremendous impact on regional infrastructure, militarization and arms production, diplomacy, aid and development, and telecommunications, the consequences of which for Pakistan have yet to be fully explored. Theoretically, the study of Islamism in Western Asia since 2001 has yet to propose viable frameworks for understanding the evolution of political Islam, its possibilities, and its dangers. Asef Bayat's important volume exploring post-Islamism suggests attentiveness to movements and discourses that seek to reconcile Islamic piety and democratic practice,[119] but Shadi Hamid warns against the assumptions of post-Islamism, stating that Islamist movements moderated under conditions of repression and not those of political participation.[120] A continued attention to the sorts of relationships engendered by such movements is essential alongside study of state-centered politics of Western Asia.

PAKISTAN AND WEST ASIA SINCE 2008

In the period since 2008, we have also seen the completion of the full term by the PPP-led Parliament in 2013 and the inauguration of a Parliament led by the Pakistan Muslim League—Nawaz (PML-N). Rather than military leaders, political parties and parliamentary consensus directed Pakistan's relations with Saudi Arabia and Iran through this period, and it may be anticipated that they will continue to do so.

The needs of Pakistan's ailing power sector dominated policy concerns regarding relations with both fuel-rich countries during this period. From 2008 to 2013, the PPP championed the building of the Iran–Pakistan pipeline and was snubbed by the Saudi government, which had long professed a dislike of the PPP leadership. On the PML-N's assumption of power in 2013, the progress over the gas pipeline immediately slowed, and local news was dominated by Nawaz Sharif's immediate appeal to Saudi Arabia for aid, suggesting a repetition of his policies of the 1990s, which led to greater closeness to Saudi Arabia at the expense of economic ties and diplomatic ties to Iran. Nawaz Sharif's approach envisages aid primarily in the form of deferred payment for furnace oil imports. Other forms of financial support offered by Saudi Arabia, such as funding for the Neelum Jhelum Hydropower Project, are for small amounts.[121]

Pakistan's balance of payments has continued to be affected by worker remittances from Saudi Arabia and the United Arab Emirates, the most recent figures reporting that of $13.9 billion in worker remittances over the financial year July 2012–June 2013, $4.1 billion came from expat workers in Saudi Arabia and $2.7 billion from the United Arab Emirates.[122] The news that Saudi Arabia intends to regularize and reduce its expat workforce by fining and jailing guest workers violating the conditions of residency and work authorization in order to give a relative advantage to its own citizens was met with some concern in Pakistan, which estimates that thousands of low-wage Pakistani workers in Saudi Arabia will be affected by this.[123] The boost to the budget from remittances, however, does little to correct a growing deficit in its balance of payments with Saudi Arabia.[124] Weinbaum and Khurram describe a series of high-level meetings that cemented Nawaz Sharif's government's relationship with the Kingdom in early 2014 and began to tilt the balance of Pakistan's Western Asian relations in favor of Saudi Arabia.[125]

In addition to its economic concerns, Pakistan faces worsening sectarian tension in the country, which both of the country's main political parties seem unwilling or unable to confront. Despite the Shia background of the Bhutto-Zardari family and the secular professions of the party, attacks on the Shia Hazaras in Baluchistan[126] and on urban Shia communities in other parts of the country[127] suggested little in the way of government efforts to stem sectarian tensions from 2008 to 2013. The popularity of leaders campaigning for negotiation with the Taliban in the 2013 election and the fact that the PML-N has links with anti-Shia Sunni extremist individuals and organizations in the Punjab indicate a mainstreaming of a pro-Sunni political agenda in Pakistan.[128]

Tensions between Saudi Arabia and Iran have also escalated over the last decade. This tension has played out most directly in Bahrain, where Iran supports the local disadvantaged Shia population, while Saudi Arabia has lent men, arms, and money to defend the royal family and Sunni interests on this island.[129] Increasing international isolation of Iran and the political uncertainty in Egypt, Syria, and Libya have increased the determination and ability of the Saudi government to resist political challenge in its own country and in the region.

In Pakistan, the rise of the Sunni extremist group Jundallah in Baluchistan,[130] attacks on Iran's consular staff in Peshawar, and attacks on Shia pilgrims either traveling to or returning from visits to Iran[131] suggest that the Saudi–Irani competition continues to spill over. Although there is no identifiable single source of rising anti-Shia sentiment and militancy across the country, the impunity with which madrasahs and mosques across the country may preach anti-Shia sentiment and the links of Arab patrons to such institutions have indicated to many observers of the region that such institutions are the linchpins for Arab sponsorship of a sectarian agenda.

CONCLUSION

Pakistan's relations with Saudi Arabia and Iran were driven primarily by military and security concerns and management of relations with the United States until 1973, when the change in the price of oil alongside new ideas about economic regionalism made regional trade, capital flows, and economics the primary motivating factors behind these relationships. Curiously, during both these periods, an idea of Islamic transnationalism was employed in different ways—first to cement anti-Soviet and anti-Israeli cooperation and then to formulate an ethically derived system of economic cooperation.

Through both these periods, a Sunni- and Arab-centered Islamic vision prevailed, with some key differences. Until the 1970s, the Arab center of regional pan-Islamism was Egypt, a center of Salafi revivalism and transnational religious debate fostered at Al Azhar while cultural and intellectual relations with Iran were strongly supported for historic and linguistic reasons.[132] However, with the circulation of capital, the growth in hajj travel since the 1970s, urban development, and increase in economic migrations from Pakistan to the Gulf and Saudi Arabia, these countries have become the embodiment and center of an Arab world as seen from Pakistan.

Relations with Saudi Arabia, and to a lesser extent the United Arab Emirates, emerged through regional bilateral alliances and were closely controlled by governmental oversight on both sides. But the Arab economy and relations with Pakistan have incubated a Sunni, Arab-centered regionalism, which has implications outside the sphere of bilateral relations. The agents of this regionalism are the moneyed sheikhs and the oil industry of Saudi Arabia and the United Arab Emirates, which have acted as patrons of Pakistan's Sunni worshippers, students, ulama, military, politicians, and professionals. Largesse, distributed through personal and diplomatic gestures of "friendship," have simultaneously incubated a Sunni identity and oil dependency in Pakistan.

Military exigencies in the Middle East, Nawaz Sharif's political leanings, and Iran's continued refusal to give up nuclear technology will only increase the importance of Pakistan to Saudi Arabia as a source of arms, military training, and nuclear technologies. Yet it is important to note that while the political tensions created by Pakistani Baluch interest in Iran's Sistan-Baluchistan and Iran's interest in Afghanistan have not been resolved and the fate of the gas pipeline remains uncertain, tensions between the two countries have not escalated and Iran's own political, cultural, and religious ambassadors in Pakistan continue to exert a quiet influence. Pakistan's relations with Iran have survived dramatic political change in both countries, and there is little to suggest that Pakistan wants another hostile neighbor. Like many others in the region, it is most likely that Pakistan will wait to see how its two allies will confront ISIS and respond to American concerns and that it will continue to work with both of them militarily and diplomatically as they do so. Historically, such realpolitik has clearly marked Pakistan's foreign relations position in Western Asia, over religious interpretative considerations.

NOTES

1. Significantly, I do not cover the events of 1999–2008 and the transformation of Pakistan's relations with the Middle East during the war on terror and around the question of Afghanistan. This is a topic that has great bearing on Pakistan's relations in the Middle East and is deserving of serious scholarly inquiry on its own terms.

2. I base this assertion on the restrictions on travel through border controls and technologies of identification, which began from the late nineteenth century, and British monopolies on trade in the Persian Gulf and Indian Ocean from the late eighteenth century. Other sorts of relations between South Asia and the Gulf were fostered through the native agency system so compellingly described by James Onley in *Arabian Frontiers of the British Raj: Merchants, Rulers, and the British in the Nineteenth-Century Gulf* (Oxford: Oxford University Press, 2007).

3. Onley's *Arabian Frontiers of the British Raj* considers this relationship in light of the work of the agency system. He argues that the colonial administration on the Gulf coast molded this into an extended frontier of colonial India.

4. Christina Phelps Harris, "The Persian Gulf Telegraph of 1864," *Geographical Journal* 135, no. 2 (1969): 169–190.

5. J. F. Standish, "British Maritime Policy in the Persian Gulf," *Middle Eastern Studies* 3, no. 4 (1967): 324–354.

6. Priya Satia, *Spies in Arabia* (New York: Oxford University Press, 2008); and Barbara Metcalf, *Husain Ahmad Madani: The Jihad for Islam and India's Freedom* (Oxford: Oneworld, 2009).

7. Radhika Singha, "Passport, Ticket and Indian Rubber Stamp: 'The Problem of the Pauper-Pilgrim' in Colonial India, c. 1882–1925," in *The Limits of British Colonial Control in South Asia*, ed. Ashwini Tambe and Harald Fischer-Tine (London: Routledge, 2009), 49–83.

8. See the memoirs of Samiullah Koreishi, *Diplomats and Diplomacy: Story of an Era, 1947–1987* (Islamabad: Khorsheed Printers, 2004).

9. S. M. Burke, former foreign minister of Pakistan, elaborates these early relations in his detailed and convincing account, *Mainsprings of Indian and Pakistani Foreign Policies* (Minneapolis: University of Minnesota Press), 136–137.

10. Ibid., 134–135.

11. Zafrulla Khan, "Pakistan's Place in Asia," *International Journal* 6, no. 4 (1951), 265–274.

12. James W. Spain, "Military Assistance for Pakistan," *American Political Science Review* 48, no. 3 (1954): 750.

13. This will be discussed further in the section on military relations. See Muhammad Ayub Khan's discussion of these alliances in Ayub Khan, "The Pakistan-American Alliance," *Foreign Affairs*, January 1964, 195–209.

14. A. M. Ghayur Hyman and N. Kaushik, *Pakistan, Zia and After* (Delhi: Abhinav Publications, 1989), 22.

15. Shahid Amin, *Pakistan's Foreign Policy: A Reappraisal* (Karachi: Oxford University Press, 2010), 132. Also see also Burke's account of *Dawn*'s editorial writings on the subject, *Mainsprings of Indian and Pakistani Foreign Policies*, 154–155.

16. Zulfiqar Ali Bhutto, "Pakistan and the Muslim World," in *The Quest for Peace: Selected Speeches and Writings* (Karachi: Pakistan Institute for International Affairs), 90.

17. Yitzhak Oron, *Middle East Record*, vol. 1 (London: Israel Oriental Society, 1960), 219, 381.

18. L. W. Adamec, *Historical Dictionary of Afghanistan* (Lanham, Md.: Scarecrow Press, 2011).

19. The United Arab Republic, led by Nasser, supported the republican government and was critical of Pakistani support. Bhutto, "Pakistan and the Muslim World," 91.

20. "Agreement with Saudi Arabia," *Dawn*, August 9, 1967.

21. Malcolme W. Browne, "Pakistan Said to Have Got U.S.-Built Jets from Arabs," *New York Times*, March 29, 1972.

22. Mujtaba Razvi, *Frontiers of Pakistan* (Karachi: National Publishing House, 1971), 203–220.

23. "Chronology," *Middle East Journal* 13, no. 4 (1959): 429.

24. Nigar Sajjad Zaheer, "Pakistan-Iran Relations (1947–1979)," in *Pakistan-Iran Relations in Historical Perspective*, ed. Syed Minhaj ul Hassan and Sayyed Abdolhossain Raeisossadat (Peshawar: Culture Center of the Islamic Republic of Iran Peshawar, 2004), 159–168.

25. "Iran Gave Aid During War as a Duty: Shah's Speech at Peshawar Banquet," *Dawn*, March 12, 1967.

26. Bhutto, "Pakistan and the Muslim World," 82.

27. The fact that neither his party nor his politics represented East Pakistan but rather denied the Awami League and Mujibur Rahman the rightful authority to convene Parliament in 1970 is a matter that requires far greater consideration for its implications for Bhutto's brand of nationalism.

28. Browne, "Pakistan Said to Have Got U.S.-Built Jets from Arabs."

29. Zulfikar Ali Bhutto, "I Have Kept My Pledge with Man and God," Collection of President Bhutto's speeches (Karachi: National Forum, 1972), 77–83.

30. "Bilateral Air Service Agreement of 1972 Between Pakistan and Saudi Arabia," Policy Note, May 20, 2010, Competition Commission of Pakistan, Islamabad, Pakistan.

31. Qutubuddin Aziz, "Pakistan Woos Persian Gulf Emirates," *Christian Science Monitor*, December 27, 1973.

32. Saad S. Khan, *Reasserting International Islam* (Karachi: Oxford University Press, 2001), 69.

33. Nasser recognized Arafat as spokesman for the Palestinians in 1967.

34. It is widely believed that Zia ul Haq, who was a brigadier at the time, led the Jordanian troops in the action against the Palestinian refugee camps.

35. Koreishi, *Diplomats and Diplomacy*, 274.

36. Gordon Corera, *Shopping for Bombs* (New York: Oxford University Press, 2006), 10.

37. Ibid., 11–13.

38. "Pakistan's Withdrawal from CENTO," March 14, 1979, BBC Summary of World Broadcasts, Proquest.

39. Ibrahim Khan, "With Ports Periled by War, Iran Boosts Trade with Pakistan," *Washington Post*, December 8, 1983.

40. "Iran—Trade, Oil, Imports," June 8, 1988, BBC Summary of World Broadcasts, Proquest.
41. Kathy Evans, "Pakistan Doubles Its Forces in Saudi Arabia Despite Public Opposition," *Guardian*, January 8, 1991.
42. This is discussed further in the section on hajj below. See Barbara Crossette, "Confrontation in the Gulf," *New York Times*, August 14, 1990; Richard Weintraub, "Saudis to Send Pakistani Unit back Home," *Washington Post*, November 28, 1987.
43. Adel Darwesh, "King Fahd Seeks Muslim Favour by Backing Bhutto," *Independent* (London), April 17, 1990.
44. Evans, "Pakistan Doubles Its Forces."
45. Bahrain still hires Pakistanis for its security forces through annual road shows arranged in Pakistan with the assistance of the Pakistan military. See David Commins, *The Gulf States: A Modern History* (New York: I. B. Tauris, 2012), 212.
46. The governments jointly agreed to invite expressions of interest in building the pipeline from the private sector through an open bidding process. "Iran/Pakistan Trade: Now Bhutto Pushes Iran Option," *FT Energy Newsletters: International Gas Report*, June 21, 1996, 23.
47. Zahid Ashar and Ayesha Nazuk, "Iran-Pakistan-India Gas Pipeline—An Economic Analysis in a Game Theoretical Framework," *Pakistan Development Review* 46, no. 4, Part II (2007): 537–550.
48. David Sanger, "Pakistan Found to Aid Iran Nuclear Efforts," *New York Times*, September 2, 2004.
49. In 2004, Pakistan's top nuclear scientist, A. Q. Khan, confessed to having masterminded the transfer of nuclear secrets to Iran, Libya, and North Korea. He later retracted the confession, saying it was made under duress. See John Lancaster and Kamran Khan "Musharraf Named in Nuclear Probe," *Washington Post*, February 3, 2004.
50. "Iran Warns Taliban, Pakistan," *Washington Post*, September 15, 1998.
51. Amin, *Pakistan's Foreign Policy*, 143.
52. Jahangir Amuzegar, "Iran's Economy and the US Sanctions," *Middle East Journal* 51, no. 2 (1997): 185–199.
53. Sartaj Aziz, key economic advisor to the government, was quoted in this *Dawn* report, "Pakistan May Be Next in Line for an Economic Bailout," May 31, 2013.
54. Prices of Pakistani cotton and jute increased by 50–100 percent between 1950 and 1951. Pakistan Ministry of Finance, *Budget of the Government of Pakistan 1958* (Islamabad: Ministry of Finance, 1959), 4.
55. *Budget of the Government of Pakistan 1958; Economic Survey and Statistics* (Karachi: Government of Pakistan Press, 1958), 84.
56. S. A. Meenai, *The Islamic Development Bank: A Case Study of Islamic Cooperation* (London: Kegan Paul International, 1989), 2–8.
57. "Report of Mohammed Hasan Mohammed Al Tohami, Secretary-General of the Islamic Conference," in Ministry of Films and Broadcasting Government of Pakistan, *Report on Islamic Summit 1974 Pakistan* (Karachi: Ferozesons, 1974), 193.
58. Ibid., 207–208.
59. *Pakistan Economic Survey 1971–72* (Islamabad: Ministry of Finance, 1972), 88.

60. *Pakistan Economic Survey 1978–79* (Islamabad: Government of Pakistan Finance Division, 1979), 151–158.

61. Ibid., 161.

62. This loan was rescheduled in November 1979.

63. Summarized from the Pakistan Economic Surveys for 1971–1979.

64. A recent study quantifies remittances at an average of Rs 200,000 per annum. The impact is felt through improved access to education for children, an increase in family social status, increased decision-making power for women, increased economic security, and participation in local social organizations. See G. M. Arif, "Economic and Social Impact of Remittances on Households: The Case of Pakistani Migrants Working in Saudi Arabia," Pakistan Institute of Development Economics, December 2009, 4. These numbers do not include the remittances received through hundi (informal) channels, and those carried back in cash through a family member.

65. In addition to supplementing Pakistan's balance of payments, professionals and trained and unskilled Pakistani workers in the Middle East have had a social impact on Pakistan. Families of trained or semiskilled migrant workers boast an elevated status and have an increased influence on their communities. The impact of this in Saudi Arabia and the Gulf can be estimated from the fact that by 1985, 43.5 percent of employees in technical and professional roles in the Gulf states and Saudi Arabia were non-nationals. See Ismail Serageldin, James Socknat, J. Stace Birks, and Clive Sinclair, "Some Issues Related to Labour Migration in the Middle East and North Africa," *Middle East Journal* 38, no. 4 (1984): 615–642.

66. Munawar Iqbal and Philip Molyneux, *Thirty Years of Islamic Banking* (London: Palgrave Macmillan, 2005), 36–38.

67. Dubai Investment Bank set up operations in Pakistan in 2006. Financiers found not only employers but also investors. The Pakistani financier Agha Hassan Abedi, who had set up the Bank of Credit and Commerce International in Dubai in 1972, was backed by the government of Abu Dhabi. Cupola Group, which invested in commercial ventures in Pakistan, had investors from and was incorporated in the United Arab Emirates.

68. See Shuja Nawaz, *Crossed Swords: Pakistan, Its Army, and the Wars Within* (New York: Oxford University Press, 2008), 388–390, for a provocative account of the Bank of Credit and Commerce International's connections to the Zia regime.

69. Iqbal and Molyneux, *Thirty Years of Islamic Banking*, 39.

70. Yousuf Qasim, *San'at o Tijarat ki Zakat aur Saudi Arab mein us ka Nifaz* (Lahore: Darul Tabligh Rahmaniya, 1980).

71. Under the "Zakat and Ushr Ordinance of 1980," the State Bank of Pakistan came to exercise oversight over the payment of zakat assessed on bank balances. See Muhammad Akram Khan, "An Evaluation of Zakah Control Systems in Pakistan," *Islamic Studies* 32, no. 4 (1993): 413–431.

72. An example is the Citibank Islamic Investment Bank incorporated in Bahrain in 1996. See www.citibank.com/ciib/homepage/index.htm.

73. See State Bank Pakistan, "Islamic Banking Review 2003–2007" and "Guidelines for Islamic Modes of Finance," April 15, 2005, www.sbp.org.pk/press/essentials/Essentials-Mod-Agreement.htm (accessed June 6, 2012).

74. Zakat receipts started at Rs 844 in 1981 and rose to Rs 6.5 billion by 1999. Total philanthropic giving in Pakistan is estimated at 5 percent of gross domestic product (GDP) by Anatol Lieven in *Pakistan: A Hard Country* (London: Allen Lane, 2011), 361. This would have been approximately Rs 7.5 billion in 1981 and Rs 272 billion in 1999. Compare to the collection of direct taxes of Rs 7.1 billion in 1981 and Rs 110 billion in 1999: "3.6: Zakat Receipts," *Handbook of Statistics on Pakistan Economy 2010*, www.sbp.org.pk/departments/stats/PakEconomy_HandBook/index.htm. Total tax collection in Pakistan is estimated at between 9 and 20 percent of GDP.

75. Zahid Ali Khan, "Balochistan Factor in Pak-Iran Relations: Opportunities and Constraints," *South Asian Studies* 27, no. 1 (2012). This is also noted in Fouzeiyha Towghi, *Scales of Marginalities: Transformations in Women's Bodies, Medicines, and Land in Postcolonial Balochistan, Pakistan* (San Francisco: University of California, San Francisco, with the University of California, Berkeley, 2008), 64.

76. Sadeqh Haqiqat, "National Interests and Trans-National Responsibilities in Pakistan–Iran Relations," in *Pakistan–Iran Relations in Historical Perspective*, ed. Syed Minhaj ul Hassan and Sayyed Abdolhossain Raeisossadat (Peshawar: Culture Center of the Islamic Republic of Iran Peshawar, 2004), 124–136.

77. Asma Shakir Khawaja, "Pak-Iran Trade Relation and Its Future Prospects," in *Pakistan–Iran Relations in Historical Perspective*, ed. Syed Minhaj ul Hassan and Sayyed Abdolhossain Raeisossadat (Peshawar: Culture Center of the Islamic Republic of Iran Peshawar, 2004), 181–202.

78. Gal Luft, "Heavy Fuel," *Journal of International Security Affairs* 20 (2011): 67.

79. Zafar Bhutta, "'Brotherly' Countries Turn down Pakistan's Request," *Express Tribune*, January 9, 2012, http://tribune.com.pk/story/318703/oil-on-deferred-payment-brotherly-countries-turn-down-pakistans-request/.

80. See Barbara Metcalf on Husain Ahmad Madani and Seema Alavi on Siddiq Hasan Khan on some of the implications of this sort of travel in colonial India. Seema Alavi, "Siddiq Hasan Khan (1832–90) and the Creation of a Muslim Cosmopolitanism in the 19th Century," *Journal of the Economic and Social History of the Orient* 54 (2011): 1–38; Metcalf, *Husain Ahmad Madani*.

81. Justin Jones, *Shia Islam in Colonial India* (Cambridge: Cambridge University Press, 2012), 16–17 and 33.

82. Yoginder Sikand mentions one such person, Sayyed Talib ur-Rahman, an Ahl-i Hadith scholar who remained in Saudi working for an official Islamic organization. See "Stoking the Flames: Intra-Muslim Rivalries in India and the Saudi Connection," *Comparative Studies of South Asia, Africa and the Middle East* 27, no. 1 (2007): 95–108. This is a topic that needs to be explored in detail. My knowledge of such knowledge transfers comes from oral accounts of the lives of people such as the Ahl-i Hadith scholar Badiuddin Rashidi from Peer Jhando in Sindh, Maulaan Makki al-Hijazi, a scholar originally from Pakistan who lives and teaches in Mecca (although he circulates audiocassettes of lessons in Urdu).

83. See Laurence Louer's account of the Saudi Shia Hasan al-Saffar's education in *Transnational Shia Politics: Religious and Political Networks in the Gulf* (New York: Columbia University Press, 2008), 145–146. Louer's account also discusses

the teaching circles that grew up in Kuwait and the growth of religious teaching in Qom.

84. Iran also pledged funds to set up a petroleum research laboratory in Pakistan in 1966. "Iranians Interested in Petro-Chemicals, Engineering Sector for Joint Ventures," *Morning News* (Karachi), April 14, 1966.

85. Web site of the Islamic Culture and Relations Organization, the Cultural Consul of the Islamic Republic of Iran in Islamabad: http://islamabad.icro.ir/index.aspx ?siteid=171&pageid=5240.

86. Nosheen Fatima Warraich, "Manuscript Collection in the Punjab University Library: Assessing Management Issues," Punjab University, http://www.iclc.us/cliej /cl29NM.pdf (accessed May 30, 2012).

87. Cultural Consul of the Islamic Republic of Iran in Islamabad, http://islamabad .icro.ir/.

88. "Pakistan–Iran Cultural Agreement," *Dawn*, March 9, 1956. In the 1960s, Saudi Arabia also sent delegates to survey Pakistani universities in an effort to open up educational exchange programs, but there is no evidence that these programs were popular.

89. See S. Vali Nasr, *The Shia Revival: How Conflicts Within Islam Will Shape the Future* (New York: W. W. Norton, 2007).

90. Saqib Akbar, *Chalo Phir Iran Ko Chalte Hain* (Islamabad: Al-Basirah, 2009).

91. See Alex Vatanka's appraisal of this relationship. Vatanka takes particular note of Iranian statements about the Shias in Pakistan's northwestern Parachinar region in recent years. Alex Vatanka. "The Guardian of Pakistan's Shia," *Current Trends in Islamist Ideology* 13 (2012): 5–17.

92. Mariam Abou Zahab, "Regional Dimensions of Sectarian Conflicts in Pakistan," ed., Christophe Jaffrelot *Pakistan: Nationalism Without a Nation* (New Delhi: Manohar Publications, 2004), 115–129.

93. Muhammad Qasim Zaman, *Modern Islamic Thought in a Radical Age: Religious Authority and Internal Criticism* (New York: Cambridge University Press, 2012), 93.

94. Muhammad K. al-Atawneh, *Wahhabi Islam Facing the Challenges of Modernity: The Dar al-Ifta in the Modern Saudi State* (Boston: Brill, 2010), 7.

95. "Analysis: Saudi Arabia Helps Pakistan with Red Mosque Crisis," *BBC Monitoring Media*, June 14, 2007.

96. See "Saudi Ambassador to Pakistan Receives the Chairman of Jamiatul Ulema-e-Islam and Chairman of National Assembly Kashmir Committee," Saudi Arabia Ministry of Foreign Affairs, July 26, 2011, hwww.mofa.gov.sa/sites/mofaen /servicesandinformation/news/ministrynews/pages/articleid201172712181967 .aspx.

97. See Sheikh Zayed Islamic Centre, www.szic.pk/.

98. *Pakistan Economic Survey 1978–79*, 155.

99. The International Islamic University has recently moved from Faisal Mosque to a purpose-built campus in another part of Islamabad.

100. Ibrahim Al-Abed and Paula Casey-Vine, *Chronicle of Progress* (London: Trident Press Ltd, 1996), 255.

101. See Declan Walsh, "Saudi Arabian Charity in Pakistan Offers Education—or Is It Extremism?" *Guardian*, June 29, 2011.

102. Central Haj Organization, *Haj Statistics December 1974* (Islamabad: Ministry of Religious Affairs, 1975), 1.

103. Ministry of Hajj, Kingdom of Saudi Arabia, www.hajinformation.com/index .htm.

104. Robert Bianchi, *Guests of God: Pilgrimage and Politics in the Islamic World* (New York Oxford University Press, 2004), 5.

105. Ibid., 78–85. Bianchi argues that since Z. A. Bhutto's death, the PPP has maintained a hajj policy aimed at equalizing hajj participation between urban and remote locales.

106. The 2006 quota was 150,000; amid great media interest, this was increased to 160,000 after the minister for religious affairs, Ijazul Haq, met with his Saudi counterpart. "Pakistan's Haj quota will increase to 160,000 in 2007," *Daily Times,* August 11, 2006, http://archives.dailytimes.com.pk/national/11-Aug-2006/pakistan -s-haj-quota-will-increase-to-160-000-in-2007.

107. Warren Richey, "Iran Urges Other Muslims to Join Rallies at Pilgrimage," *Christian Science Monitor,* April 14, 1988.

108. Jim Paul, "Insurrection at Mecca," *Merip Reports* 91 (1980): 3–4; John Kifner, "400 Die as Iranian Demonstrators Battle Saudi Police in Mecca; Embassies Smashed in Teheran," *New York Times,* August 2, 1987.

109. Subsequent to the events at Hajj 1987, Saudi Arabia cut the Iranian hajj quota. Iran responded by boycotting the hajj for three years.

110. "The Arrest of Abu Jindal: What Happens Next?" *Rediff News,* June 25, 2012.

111. "Saudi Arabia's Gift to Pakistan," *Pakistan Today,* June 8, 2013.

112. Some of Pakistan's top designers are producing abayas to supplement their usual evening and party-wear lines. See http://cdn.fashioninstep.com/wp-content /uploads/2012/04/Tapu-Javeri-Handbags-Abayas-at-Fashion-Pakistan-Week -2012-n.jpg (accessed June 6, 2012).

113. Harsh Pant, "Pakistan and Iran's Dysfunctional Relationship," *Middle East Quarterly* 16, no. 2 (2009): 43–50.

114. "Iran Terms Murder of Cadets Plot," Iran-News ListServ, September 18, 1997.

115. "Iranian Radio Reports Attack on Center in Pakistan," BBC Monitoring Newsfile, October 9, 1998.

116. Zahab, "Regional Dimensions of Sectarian Conflicts in Pakistan," 119.

117. Pervez Musharraf's speech of January 12, 2002, "The Kashmir Dispute: Past, Present and Future," in *Handbook of Asian Security Studies,* ed. Sumit Ganguly and Andrew Scobell (New York: Routledge, 2010), 114 fn 43.

118. Qasim Moini, "U.S. Wanted Closer Scrutiny of 'Cash Couriers' Providing Terror Financing," *Dawn,* June 16, 2011.

119. Asef Bayat, ed., *Post Islamism: The Changing Faces of Political Islam* (New York: Oxford University Press, 2013).

120. Shadi Hamid, *Temptations of Power: Islamists and Illiberal Democracy in New Middle East* (New York: Oxford University Press, 2014), 39.

121. See the project description at www.wapda.gov.pk/vision2025/htmls_vision2025 /njhp.html. Saudi funding was released for the project shortly after the PML-N government came to power. "Neelum Jhelum Project: Saudi Arabia Clears Way for $100 Million Loan," *Express Tribune,* July 4, 2013.

122. "State Bank of Pakistan, Statistics and DWH Department, Country-Wise Workers' Remittances FY 13," http://sbp.org.pk/ecodata/Homeremit.pdf.

123. Diplomatic intervention resulted in an extension of the "grace period" for Pakistanis in Saudi Arabia to regularize their status, indicating the bearing of this issue on relations between the countries. Press release by Pakistan Ministry of Foreign Affairs, July 4, 2013, www.mofa.gov.pk/pr-details.php?prID=1299.

124. Marvin Weinbaum and Abdullah B. Khurram, "Pakistan and Saudi Arabia: Deference, Dependence, and Deterrence," *Middle East Journal* 68, no. 2 (2013): 211–228.

125. Ibid., 227.

126. Saleem Javed, "Hope Fades Away for Hazaras of Pakistan," *Dawn*, June 20, 2012.

127. At least forty-five people were killed in an attack on a Shia neighborhood, Abbas Town, in Karachi in March 2013. "Blast Ravages Shi'a Neighbourhood," *Dawn*, March 3, 2013. At least twenty-five people were killed in attacks on Muharram processions in Karachi and Rawalpindi in 2012. "Pakistan: Shi'a Killings a Failure of Government Protection," Amnesty International Media Center Press Release Index Number PRE01/578/2012.

128. Party tickets were given to Abid Raza of Lashkar-i Jhangvi and Ebaad Dogar of Sipah-e-Sahaba. Amir Mir, "SSP Leader Who Fixed Bounty on Taseer Given PML-N Ticket," *The News*, May 7, 2013.

129. Mehran Kamrava, "The Arab Spring and the Saudi-Led Counterrevolution," *Orbis* 56, no. 1 (2012): 96–104.

130. Abubakar Siddique, "Jundallah: Profile of a Sunni Extremist Group," Radio Free Europe/Radio Liberty, October 9, 2009.

131. Two recent attacks suggest that this sort of violence is rising. In September 2011, twenty-six Shia pilgrims on their way to Iran were pulled off a bus and executed in Baluchistan. In February 2012, eight Shia pilgrims returning from Iran were killed in Khyber Pakhtunkhwa. "Gunmen Kill 29 Shia Pilgrims in Two Attacks," *Dawn*, September 20, 2011; and "Sectarian Violence: Jundallah Claims Responsibility for Kohistan Bus Attack," *Express Tribune*, February 28, 2012.

132. The president of the Islamic University Islamabad from 1979 to 1999 was Hussain Hamid Hassan, a sharia scholar trained at Al Azhar in Cairo. See State Bank of Pakistan, Islamic Banking Bulletin, October 2008, 11.

CONTRIBUTORS

DR. HASSAN ABBAS is professor and department head of regional and analytical studies at the National Defense University's College of International Security Affairs in Washington, D.C. He is also a senior advisor at the Asia Society. His research interests are nuclear proliferation, religious extremism in South and Central Asia, and relations between Muslims and the West. Hassan is a former Pakistani government official who served in the administrations of Prime Minister Benazir Bhutto (1995–1996) and President Pervez Musharraf (1999–2000). His most recent book is *The Taliban Revival: Violence and Extremism on the Pakistan–Afghanistan Frontier* (2014).

SHAHID JAVED BURKI, former finance minister of Pakistan and vice president of the World Bank, is currently chairman of the Institute of Public Policy, Lahore. He served at the World Bank for twenty-five years (1974–1999), as division chief and senior economist, Policy Planning and Program Review Department; senior economist and policy adviser, Office of the Vice President of External Relations; director, International Relations Department of the Office of the Vice President of External Relations; director of China and Mongolia; and vice president of the Latin American and Caribbean region. He is coauthor of *Sustaining Reform with a U.S.–Pakistan Free Trade Agreement* (2006).

SERGE GRANGER is associate professor at Sherbrooke University (Canada) and teaches international relations. He is particularly interested in India–China relations and the impact of the emergence of these two countries on Quebec. Visiting professor at the Jawaharlal Nehru University and visiting researcher at the University of Baroda and the University of Pune, he is the author of the book *Le lys et le lotus: Les relations du Québec avec la Chine de 1650 à 1950* (2005) and is preparing a second book on Quebec–India relations.

SANA HAROON is assistant professor of history and Asian studies at the University of Massachusetts Boston. She authored a study of the history of religious mobilization in the Pakhtun northwest entitled *Frontier of Faith: Islam in the Indo-Afghan Borderland* (2007) and has studied the rise of Deobandi Islam in the North

West Frontier Province of colonial India. She is currently working on a study of Muslim cultural history in North India since 1747.

CHRISTOPHE JAFFRELOT is research director at the Centre National de la Recherche Scientifique. He teaches South Asian politics and history at Sciences Po (Paris) and at the King's India Institute (London). He was director of the Centre d'Études et de Recherches Internationales at Sciences Po between 2000 and 2008. His research interests include theories of nationalism and democracy; mobilization of the lower castes and Dalits in India; the Hindu nationalist movement; and ethnic conflicts in Pakistan. He has recently published *The Pakistan Paradox: Instability and Resilience* (2015).

FARAH JAN is a teaching associate and a Ph.D. candidate in the Department of Political Science, Rutgers University–New Brunswick. Her research focuses on interstate rivalries; South Asian security, nuclear proliferation and national security strategies. Her dissertation examines the variation in the interaction between nuclear rivals.

ADNAN NASEEMULLAH is lecturer in South Asia and international relations at King's College London. His research interests include the political economy of industrial development, state building, and political order, in relation to the Indian subcontinent. His current book manuscript explores the strategies of manufacturing firms in the postreform Indian and Pakistani economies. Dr. Naseemullah holds a Ph.D. in political science from the University of California, Berkeley, and has previously taught at Johns Hopkins University and the London School of Economics.

PHILIP OLDENBURG is a political scientist specializing in South Asia, who has taught as a regular member of the faculty and then as an adjunct at Columbia University since 1977 and has served there as director and associate director of the Southern Asian Institute. He has published scholarly work mainly on local government and politics of India (a book on Delhi municipal government and articles on land consolidation in the state of Uttar Pradesh) and on elections in India. He was editor or coeditor of ten volumes in the Asia Society's India Briefing series. His most recent publication is *India, Pakistan, and Democracy: Solving the Puzzle of Divergent Paths* (2010).

AVINASH PALIWAL is the Defence Academy Postdoctoral Fellow at the King's College London. His current research concerns South Asian strategic affairs, Indian foreign policy, foreign policy analysis, and Afghanistan. Dr. Paliwal is currently writing a book on India in Afghanistan after the Cold War, and was the chairperson of the Afghanistan Studies Group at King's College London. He was previously a visiting fellow at the Observer Research Foundation, New Delhi, and at the Paul H. Nitze School of Advanced International Studies at the Johns Hopkins University.

AQIL SHAH is the Wick Cary Assistant Professor of South Asian Politics in the Department of International and Area Studies at the University of Oklahoma, Norman. His research interests include democratization, civil–military relations, and South Asian security. He earned his Ph.D. in political science from Columbia University and an M.Phil. in International Development from Oxford University, where he read as a Rhodes Scholar. Dr. Shah has been a postdoctoral fellow at Harvard University and has taught at Princeton and Dartmouth. He is the author of *The Army and Democracy: Military Politics in Pakistan* (2014).

MOHAMMAD WASEEM is a professor of political science at the Department of Social Sciences, Lahore University of Management Sciences. He was chairman of the International Relations Department, Quaid-e-Azam University, Islamabad. He has written on ethnic, Islamic, constitutional, electoral, and sectarian politics of Pakistan. His books include *Politics and the State in Pakistan* (1989), *The 1993 Elections in Pakistan* (1994), and *Strengthening of Democracy in Pakistan* (coauthored with S. J. Burki, 2002). He also edited the book *Electoral Reform in Pakistan* (2002).

MARIAM ABOU ZAHAB is a researcher affiliated with Sciences Po in Paris and has also worked at Centre d'Études et de Recherches Internationales and has lectured at Institut d'Etudes Politiques de Paris and Institut National des Langues et Civilisations Orientales. She is an expert in the area of Pakistan and Afghanistan, Shiism, sectarianism, jihadi groups, Pashtun society, and the Tribal Areas of Pakistan. She coauthored *Islamist Networks: The Afghan–Pakistan Connection* (2004) with Olivier Roy.

INDEX

Faridi, Sharaf, 105
Fazlullah, Mullah, 191
Federal Investigation Agency (FIA), 48,
    140, 142, 147, 153–154
Feldman, Dan, 261
Feldman, Daniel, 264
Frontier Constabulary, 140
Frontier Corps (FC), 48, 140–141, 143,
    147, 229, 240, 287

Gandhi, M. K., 174, 194
Garver, John, 280, 285
Gates, Robert, 238
Geo TV, 45
Ghailani, Ahmed Khalfan, 227
Ghani, Ashraf, 191–192, 197, 207–210,
    213–214, 261
Ghani, Awais, 132
Ghayur, Safwat, 160
Ghazi, Abdul Rashid, 318
Ghias, Shoaib A., 93–94
Gilani, Yousaf Raza, 16, 37, 47, 66, 74, 92,
    98, 109, 178, 259, 290
Granger, Serge, 6, 279
Grare, Frederic, 156, 266
Grossman, Marc, 256

Hagel, Chuck, 258
Haider, Eijaz, 107
Haider, Moeen-ud-din, 159
Haig, Alexander, 226
Hamid, Shadi, 322
Haq, Mahbubul, 176
Haq, Sirajul, 81
Haq Prast Lashkar, 78
Haqqani, Hussain, 46, 231, 237, 242, 248,
    287
Haqqani, Jalaluddin, 192, 208, 214
Haqqani, Sirajuddin, 209
Haqqani Network, 43, 191–192, 196–199,
    206–207, 212, 239, 253–256, 258, 260
Harkat-ul-Mujahideen, 197
Haroon, Sana, 8, 301
Hasan, Ali Dayan, 95
Hasan, Amir Munawwar, 81
Hashmi, Javed, 85

Helmke, Gretchen, 106
Hikmatyar, Gulbuddin, 2, 80, 196–198
Hizb-e-Islami, 198
Hizb ut-Tahrir, 81
Holbrooke, Richard, 233, 238–239, 256
Hoodboy, Pervez, 219
Human Rights Watch, 146
Huntington, Samuel, 28
Hussain, Altaf, 38, 63, 77–78, 85–86
Hussain, Chaudry Shujaat, 14, 74
Hussain, King, 306
Hussain, Mamnoon, 38, 102, 181
Hussain, Mushahid, 14
Hussain, Zahid, 7, 260

Ijaz, Mansoor, 46
Ijaz, Saroop, 104
Ijaz-ul-Haq, 15
Ilahi, Choudhry Zahoor, 70
Illahi, Pervez, 74
Indian National Congress (INC), 3, 10,
    25, 194
Indo-Tibetan Border Police, 206
Insaf Students Federation, 75
Intelligence Bureau (IB), 140, 153
International Islamic University, 318, 320
International Monetary Fund (IMF), 82,
    165–166, 176–177, 182, 185, 258
Interpol, 73
Inter-Services Intelligence (ISI), 14, 32,
    39, 40, 42–44, 49, 50, 67, 69, 72, 74, 76,
    80, 93, 101, 140, 144, 153–154, 237, 250;
    and Afghanistan, 43, 191, 197–199,
    202, 207, 209, 211, 224, 239; and India,
    43, 211; and judiciary, 16, 47–48, 50,
    102; and PML–Q, 30, 35; support to
    militants, 43, 45–46, 80, 197, 254; and
    the United States, 29, 43, 45, 224, 228,
    247–248, 252–253
Inter-Services Public Relations (ISPR),
    42, 44, 259
Iqbal, Ahsan, 12
Iran-Pakistan Language Authority, 317
Iran-Pakistan Persian Research Center,
    317
Ishaq, Malik, 155

Lau, Martin, 100
Leghari, Farooq, 172
Lieven, Anatol, 172, 186
Lodhi, Maleeha, 12
Lombardi, Clark B., 100
Lugar, Dick, 45–46, 232–236, 243, 249, 254, 257

Mahmud, Tayyab, 90, 109
Mai, Mukhtaran, 96, 105
Majlis Wahdatul Muslimeen, 80
Malik, Muneer, 103, 105
Mansour, Mullah Akhtar, 207–210
Markey, Daniel, 236, 243
Massoud, Ahmad Shah, 80, 196
Massoud, Ahmad Wali, 205
Maududi, Maulana, 303
McChrystal, Stanley, 239, 251
Médard, Jean-François, 219
Mehsud, Baitullah, 43, 125, 231, 246
Mehsud, Hakimullah, 128–129, 259
Menon, Shivshankar, 203
Military Intelligence (MI), 48–49, 102
Military Staff College, 306
Minhajul Quran, 85
Mir, Hamid, 45
Mirza, Zulfikar, 63, 78
Modi, Narendra, 183, 206, 213
Mohammed, Khalid Shaikh, 227
Mohaqiq, Haji Mohammad, 205
Mountbatten, Lord, 174
Movement for the Restoration of Democracy (MRD), 13, 29
Muawiya, Asmatullah, 129
Muhammad, Ghulam, 90, 303
Muhammad, Nek, 231
Mukhopadhaya, Gautam, 203–204
Mukhtar, Ahmed, 74
Mullen, Michael, 238, 247, 253–255, 257
Musharraf, Pervez, 13–15, 32–33, 35, 37, 49, 63, 67, 73–78, 80, 82, 86, 91–92, 103, 125, 145–146, 153, 159, 178, 226–227, 237, 259, 322; coup d'état, 15, 28, 30, 32, 172, 177, 224, 226; fall of, 46, 51, 72; foreign relations of, 13, 29, 32–33, 72, 177, 199, 225, 227–228, 231–232, 244,

263, 309; and judiciary, 16, 31–32, 48, 50, 51, 71, 91–94, 102, 104–105, 159; military government of, 12, 23–24, 33–34, 44, 177, 198
Muttahida Majlis-e-Amal (MMA) (United Action Front), 30, 80–82, 125
Muttahida Qaumi Movement (MQM), 38, 62–63, 65, 68, 70, 77–81, 83–84, 86, 128, 178, 180
Muttahida Qaumi Movement-Hakiki (MQM-Hakiki), 77

Nabil, Rahmatullah, 192, 197, 213
Nadiri, Khalid, 195
Najibullah, Mohammad, 196–197
Naqvi, Feisal, 106
Naseemullah, Adnan, 9, 165
National Accountability Bureau (NAB), 49, 73
National Assembly's Public Accounts Committee (PAC), 49
National Awami Party (NAP), 79, 122
National Counter-Terrorism Authority (NACTA), 140, 143, 153, 157–158
National Police Bureau (NPB), 140, 143
National Reconstruction Bureau (NRB), 145
National Security Council (NSC), 30, 35, 50, 283
Naval Special Warfare Development Group, 247
Naveed, Malik, 153
Nazimuddin, Khwaja, 309
Nehru, Jawaharlal, 5, 194, 220, 222, 280–281, 284, 304
New America Foundation, 133, 245–246
Nichols, Robert, 122, 133
Nisar Ali Khan, Chaudhry, 15
Nixon, Richard, 5, 222–223, 286
Noorani, Shah Ahmad, 80
North Atlantic Treaty Organization (NATO), 125, 193, 195, 197, 199, 228, 231, 241, 248, 253, 256, 260, 266; supplies to, 40, 66, 201, 227, 242, 249, 255, 259; withdrawal of, 133, 192, 202, 239

Northern Alliance, 124
Nuland, Victoria, 253

Obama, Barack, 4, 9, 44, 46, 219–221, 223, 225, 227, 231–259, 261–265
Oldenburg, Philip, 16, 89
Omar, Mullah, 192, 198, 207–210, 214, 239, 254
Organization of Petroleum Exporting Countries (OPEC), 1, 4, 306, 310–311
Organization of the Islamic Conference (OIC), 306, 308, 310, 312
al Otaibi, Juhayman, 319

Pak-Arab Refinery Limited, 311
Pakhtunkhwa Milli Awami Party (PKMAP), 82
Pakistan Awami Tehreek, 183
Pakistan Institute of Legislative Development and Transparency (PILDAT), 12
Pakistan Media Regulatory Authority (PEMRA), 45
Pakistan Muslim League (Nawaz) (PML-N), 14–15, 33, 35–36, 38, 47, 50–51, 63, 65, 68, 71–73, 76, 83–84, 92, 94, 165, 178, 180, 185, 323
Pakistan Muslim League (Quaid e Azam) (PML-Q), 14–15, 30, 65, 70, 73–74, 84
Pakistan Muslim League-Functional (PML-F), 70
Pakistan National Alliance (PNA), 15
Pakistan Peoples Party (PPP), 11–12, 14–15, 23, 29–30, 32–33, 35–38, 41, 45–46, 51, 62–63, 65–74, 76–79, 82–86, 92, 94, 97–98, 170–172, 175–176, 178–180, 185, 257, 305, 309, 313, 316, 323
Pakistan Rangers, 140–141
Pakistan Refinery, 311
Pakistan Steel Mills Corporation, 93
Pakistan Tehreek-e-Insaaf (PTI) (Pakistan Movement for Justice), 36, 38, 52, 62–63, 66, 68, 71, 74–76, 81–86, 180, 183, 185, 257, 259
Palestinian Liberation Organization, 306

Paliwal, Avinash, 18, 191
Panetta, Leon, 248
Panikkar, K. M., 280
Paris Club, 182
Pasban and Shabaab Milli, 81
Pasha, Shuja, 39–40, 49, 69
Patel, Dorab, 98
Patterson, Anne, 240, 254
Pervez, Tariq, 158
Peshawar Group, 198
Peshawar University, 132, 318
Pew Research Center, 71, 237, 249–250, 264, 289–290
Pinochet, Augusto, 24
Pirzada, Syed Sharifuddin, 15
PPP Youth Organization, 69
Punjab University, 317–318

Qaddafi, Muammar Al, 305–306
Qadri, Tahirul, 50, 85, 180–181, 183
Quetta Shura, 192, 204, 254, 258

Rabbani, Burhanuddin, 196, 204
Rabbani, Raza, 66
Rahman, Abdur, 15, 193–194
Rahman, Akhtar Abdur, 15
Rahman, Mujibur, 10, 170, 305
Raja Mohan, C., 211
RAND Corporation, 137
Raphel, Robin, 243
Reagan, Ronald, 223
Rehman, Fazl ur, 82, 85
Rice, Susan, 260
Riedel, Bruce, 232, 235
Rizvi, Hasan Askari, 302
Robinson, Nick, 99
Rome Group, 198
Rosenbluth, Frances, 106

Saad, Malik, 160
Saeed, Hafiz Muhammad, 263
Said (alias Sajna), Khan, 129
Sajna, 129
Saleem, Sheikh Ahmed, 227
Sanger, David E., 265
Sattar, Abdul, 198

WikiLeaks, 73, 239, 245
Woodward, Bob, 236
Work, Bob, 260
World Bank, 82, 123, 176–177

Xe, 246
Xiaoping, Deng, 292–293, 296

Yacoob, Mullah, 208–209

Zaidi, Akbar, 221, 266
Zakir, Mullah Abdul Qayum, 207–209
Zaman, Gul, 210
Zaman, Muhammad Qasim, 318
Zardari, Asif Ali, 12, 69, 71, 79, 98, 131,
180–181, 247–248, 309; action against

terrorism, 44; foreign relations, 46,
232, 234, 237, 250; and judiciary, 16,
69, 71, 74, 83, 92, 94, 102; party-
politics, 32–33, 36, 38, 68, 70, 73–76,
85, 94, 172, 178
Zayed, Sheikh, 306, 318–319
Zedong, Mao, 287, 292
Zia, Ahmad, 205
Zia-ul-Haq, 14–15, 70, 77, 98–100, 172,
176, 181, 223, 319; coup d'état, 28–29;
foreign relations, 2, 7, 181, 196, 223,
226, 263–264, 266, 287, 307–308, 312,
321; Islamization policy of, 8, 13, 17,
72, 123; military government of, 34,
96, 171, 301
Zubeida, Abu, 227

Mormonism and American Politics, edited by
Randall Balmer and Jana Riess

Religion, Secularism, and Constitutional Democracy, edited by
Jean L. Cohen and Cécile Laborde